WOMEN

THE DIRECTORY OF SOCIAL CHANGE

by Wendy Collins, Ellen Friedman
and Agnes Pivot

WILDWOOD HOUSE LONDON

WOMEN

The Third volume published in THE DIRECTORY OF SOCIAL CHANGE

written and compiled by Wendy Collins, Ellen Friedman, Agnes Pivot
series editor Michael Norton
designed by Helen Brown
illustrated by Liz Mackie

The Directory of Social Change is a registered educational charity.

This volume was first published in 1978.

Wildwood House Ltd., 1 Prince of Wales Passage, 117 Hampstead Road, London NW1 3EE

ISBN hardback   0 7045 0335 2
     paperback   0 7045 0336 0

IBM typeset by Supreme Litho Typesetting, Ilford, Essex.
Printed and bound in Great Britain by
Biddles Ltd, Guildford and Redwood Burn Ltd, Esher.

INTRODUCTION

This book is part of a series on social change. The series, including this volume, should be considered as a whole. No social change can occur in one area of our lives without affecting every other area. This is especially true when talking about women. Any social change that does not include a change in the position of women is futile and is ultimately bound to fail; there can be no genuine progress that leaves behind half the human race.

Although this book is divided into chapters based around specific themes, all the topics we have dealt with are inextricably linked. It may not appear at first glance that contraception and women's history have anything to do with each other, nor that equal job opportunities are in any way connected with the lack of positive images of women in the media. In fact, these issues are all related, and we see the negative treatment of women in such different fields as health and history as part of a whole way of life that has, up until now, been oppressive to women. We have tried to bring out these links in the introductions to each chapter; we also feel that it is important to re-emphasize that as long as one freedom is denied to women, all the others are invalidated.

Those who benefit from the present condition of women are not, out of choice, going to give up their privileged position. So women must fight back for themselves. And this we are doing. We are challenging the status quo which conditions every aspect of our lives: we are developing new ways of working together, and are creating new goals and models for ourselves.

We are discovering the importance of the links between our personal experiences and the economic and social systems that direct our lives; we are trying to understand how our individual feelings of inadequacy and weakness have been formed by external forces and have been used to keep us in our place. We are trying to put into practice the crucial realization that social change means *changing ourselves* as well as changing the institutions that surround us. This is why we feel that it is important to record the personal experiences of people's struggles, and so we have put this book together using interviews, talking to the women who are actively involved in various aspects of the women's movement. They know about their work better than anyone else, and are able to give a much more thorough idea of what they are doing and what they are trying to achieve than anyone else.

Women are divided about the sort of social change they want and the means that should be used to achieve it. We have tried to reflect these differences and have given each person or group interviewed the ultimate veto on what is included about them and their work, so that what is said represents *their view and is not necessarily ours.* We have, of course, been selective in the groups we have included; for example, we have deliberately chosen to exclude groups that we feel directly hinder and obstruct social change, such as the anti-abortion groups.

Change is by definition fluid, and new ideas are continually being generated to replace old ones; new groups form and existing groups break up. For this reason we have not included the addresses of a large number of local groups; instead, we have included information on the more stable groups and those organizations that can provide more detailed information. We hope this book will encourage women to consider new ideas and will give them some way to go about putting their ideas into practice. We hope it will facilitate change at the same time as describing it.

Wendy Collins, Ellen Friedman, Agnes Pivot
Leeds, June 1978

CONTENTS

HEALTH AND CHILDBIRTH

WOMEN AND THERAPY

CHILDCARE

CRIMES AGAINST WOMEN

UP AGAINST THE STATE

POWER TO THE SISTERS

INDEX

HOW TO USE THIS BOOK

This book is not meant to be read through from beginning to end. It covers all sorts of different ideas and activities. Some may be of particular interest to you, and others totally irrelevant.

It is divided into eleven main sections: Learning about Women; Women at Work; Relationships and Life-styles; Women's Art; Women and the Media; Health and Childbirth; Women's Therapy; Childcare; Crimes against Women; Up against the State; and Power to the Sisters. And each of these sections covers many different topics which are listed in the table of contents. We have tried to discuss something of the issues involved, what people are doing to fight for their rights or create working alternatives and where to go or what to read to get more information. The book is in no way meant to be a comprehensive directory, but a starting point for finding out more and getting new ideas. There is also an index of subjects and an index of groups to help you find your way around the book.

There was not room to provide a listing of all local groups in each particular field and this would have made the book into an unreadable sort of telephone directory anyway. Instead, there are usually umbrella organizations you can contact if you want to find out about what is happening in a particular area, and these are listed where possible. Many of the organizations mentioned in this book operate on a shoe-string budget, so don't necessarily expect a reply by return of post. And it would be helpful if you enclosed a stamped addressed envelope with your enquiry. Such is the pace of change that some of the groups will have changed their address (or even ceased to exist) by the time you get round to contacting them. Your letter should be forwarded when this happens. If you have any difficulty, try contacting the Women's Information Referral and Enquiry Service (WIRES), 32a Parliament Street, York, or Spare Rib, 27 Clerkenwell Close, London EC1, who should be able to help.

Prices have been listed for most of the publications mentioned. But in these inflationary times, many may have gone up by the time the book is published. The prices are meant as a guide only; to tell you whether something costs a few pence or several pounds. Books can be bought through a bookshop, or ordered direct from the publishers. When ordering a pamphlet from a group, please allow for postage adding around 15 per cent to the listed cost.

Many of the books and pamphlets we have mentioned will not be easily obtainable at your local bookshop. Where you do have difficulty, we suggest that you contact one of the four listed below, which will usually be able to get most of the books you want, and are all willing to supply orders through the post: *Feminist Books*, P. Box HP5, Leeds 6; *Grass Roots Community Bookshop*, 109 Oxford Street, Manchester; *Compendium Books*, 240 Campden High Street, London NW1; and *Corner Bookshop*, 162 Woodhouse Lane, Leeds 2.

1. LEARNING about WOMEN

SCHOOL

15-year-old boy: 'You can't expect women to go out to work for about ten years after they've had a child. Their responsibility really lies at home, doesn't it, for the wife. You can't go out to work when you've got young kids around the house, can you?'
Me: *'Can men go out to work when they've got young kids?'*
Boy: 'Oh yes, they can.'

15-year-old girl: 'I'd like to be an engineer. But I'm going to be a secretary. I wouldn't dare go in for engineering because it would be all boys. I think I'd be just as good at it though.'

It is often said that women choose to occupy a lowly position in the world; that no one forces us into low-status, badly-paid jobs; that none of us have to become wives and mothers if we don't want to. Even with the Sex Discrimination Act, which in theory opens all careers to women, there are no queues of women asking to be engineers or stockbrokers or miners. Some people would argue that this proves that it is 'natural' for women to do some jobs while men do others. But this ignores the massive forces that women have to fight to win equality.

There is obviously still enormous prejudice against women in the world of work. But long before we reach the age of choosing what we *want* to do with our lives, social pressures have been at work teaching us what we *ought* to do. From birth onwards, girl and boy children are treated differently; they are given different toys, different clothes and expected to behave in different ways. Because we all want to be loved and approved of, we tend to do what is expected of us, rather than risk rejection from our families and friends.

By the time a child goes to school, she has a fairly clear idea of what men and women should be like, how each should behave, and what adult men and women do. Far from encouraging all children to develop their full potential and talents regardless of sex, school reinforces the sex roles that the child has already begun to learn. School has two roles: it passes on a body of knowledge, and it teaches a set of values and beliefs about the world. The two are closely connected in the sense that what is taught as fact (and what is left out of our learning) is strongly influenced by accepted opinion. (For instance, children often learn about Jesus as if Christian doctrine were an incontrovertible fact rather than one belief among many.)

In both areas, that of 'knowledge' and that of belief, girls and boys learn a very traditional view of how a 'good' woman should behave. The books children learn from show women in passive roles, working in the home or doing acceptably feminine jobs like nursing. They learn that men have made all the important scientific discoveries, men have produced all the great works of music and art, men have made civilization as we know it. Even maths problems are centred around men digging holes! The attitudes that school conveys rarely contradict those prevailing in the outside world; girls are expected to be concerned about their appearance, to be unaggressive, to be neater and more tidy than boys. In mixed schools sex is often used as a basis for dividing students into groups ('boys one side, girls the other') and boys are given tasks like moving desks or carrying heavy things, while girls are asked to tidy the classroom or clear out the cupboards.

The Sex Discrimination Act makes it illegal for a school to offer facilities to one sex that are denied to another. But it makes no suggestions about giving positive encouragement to girls or boys to take up skills or subjects that are usually thought of as more appropriate to the opposite sex. For instance, girls must now be offered the choice of doing woodwork if the boys are offered this subject; but by the age of ten or eleven when they are offered this choice, girls have already learnt that this is a boys' subject, and they have missed out on years of playing with Meccano, helping their fathers to do repairs around the house, and doing all the things that prepare you for learning woodwork. Simply offering girls a choice is not enough; they are already at a disadvantage, and need positive help to overcome this.

Many teachers are working to change attitudes to women within the school system; but in education, as in most fields, those in positions of power tend to be older and more fixed in their ideas. Other groups are working around the question of children's books, trying to discourage schools and parents from using books that show women only in limited, traditional roles, and to provide literature that shows more positive images of women and girls.

Next Stop O-Level feminism?

Many women teachers are aware of the ideas of women's liberation, and try to introduce the question of women's position to their students whenever they have the opportunity. But so far there has been very little formal teaching of women's studies in schools; teachers can slot 'Women's Rights' into a Social Studies course, or 'Woman in Literature' into an English course, but at the moment (1977) there seems to be only one Women's Studies course at a school.

This is at a girls' comprehensive school in Croydon. It is a one-year CSE Mode III course, which ran for the first time in 1976/7. The aims of the course are:

1. to help the students to have a greater awareness of themselves as people, of their own roles present and possible in the future, and of other people's roles;
2. to give an historical outline of the changes in women's legal and social position in the period 1800 to the present day;
3. to improve students' knowledge of contemporary legislation and customs as these affect women in particular;
4. since many pupils read and see material in which their sex is presented on a trivial level, to give some consideration to the ways women are shown in literature and film/TV, and the parameters behind these presentations.

The syllabus is built around five themes, one theme per half term. It begins with a general introduction to the purposes of the course and background ideas, including women in mythology and pre-history and ideas from psychoanalysis. The second theme is an historical survey of women's position in the UK from 1800 to the present day, the effects of industrialization, and comparisons with women in other countries (which countries depends on what nationalities are in the class). 'Women's Roles in Society' looks at roles in the home as housewife, mother, wife, working mother, and roles outside the home at work, in trade unions, etc. 'Women's Biological State' examines the conditioning that derives from women's biology and other factors, and the way in which biology affects women's social functioning. The final theme looks at 'Women in Print and on Film and TV'.

The course includes visits to places like a factory employing women, a day nursery, or a large department store, and speakers are invited from trade unions, women's groups and so on. It is examined by a multiple-choice paper, a written paper, course work and an oral exam. The papers are set and marked by the woman who organized the course.

This year, twenty-eight girls at the school have taken the course, and about ten students in a mixed class at a further education college. There has been almost no money available to buy books or course material; and there is no separate department, so that Women's Studies comes under Sociology for some purposes and Creative Studies for others. This has caused some problems; one class is set against Physical Education and Music on the timetable, and the numbers and composition of the group have varied from week to week. Nevertheless, many of the students have enjoyed the course, and some of the staff have borrowed the books and turned up to hear speakers!

There is also a proposal to set up a GCE O-Level in Women's Studies. This is at present being considered by the Associated Examining Board, and it will probably be some time before it is cleared. The proposed course is designed to 'offer students a general perspective, both historical and contemporary, on the sexual structure of our society'. The course should be of interest both to adults and to students in their last years at school, and is intended for people of both sexes. Its aims are:

1. to enable students to question and assess the sexual role traditionally assigned to them in contemporary society, with particular reference to the relevance of these roles to their lives and expectations;
2. to give an hisjtorical outline of the changes in women's legal and social position;
3. to give students the possibility of using practical information e.g. knowledge of Equal Rights legislation, laws relating to marriage and divorce, etc.);
4. to inform students of the culture and history of women, which has traditionally been obscured or denied (e.g. women and literature, women and medicine, women and science, women and music);
5. to give students a general perspective on the women's movement at home and abroad.

The proposed syllabus looks really interesting, and covers such areas as sexuality, women from other cultures, and present day women's movements. It sounds almost worth going back to school for!

For further information send a stamped addressed envelope to Ms Brenda Able, 1 Annandale Road, Addiscombe, Croydon, Surrey.

WOMEN'S STUDIES

Women want to know more about ourselves: about our past, our present, our bodies, our rights. A whole range of groups, books, and courses is emerging to help us do this. Some women are setting up Women's Studies courses in universities, colleges, evening classes and other forms of higher education. Other women are forming groups to study particular subjects and work out a feminist perspective on science, history, religion or economics.

As yet, this new knowledge has hardly filtered into schools; until it does, we shall have to unlearn most of what our 'education' taught us, and relearn the truth for ourselves.

Two very different examples of Women's Studies courses are the 'Women in Society' course at Cambridge University and the Workers Educational Association Women's Studies Branch in Aberdeen.

Women in Society Course

'The course got started in 1973 because a number of feminists, including staff, students and non-university people, thought that we should start an inter-disciplinary course on women in the Social and Political Sciences (SPS) Tripos. Lots of new courses were getting set up then, and it seemed an obvious thing to do. We worked out the outline for a course, and after a lot of hassling it was accepted.

'The course is open to male and female SPS students, as one of the papers in a one-year or two-year course; it is not a compulsory paper. In fact anyone can attend, whether they are inside the University or not, though we try and design the course with the SPS students in mind. It is run by a women's collective consisting of past and present students of the paper and other interested women. These are usually graduate students, research fellows or teaching staff, but we have had people in the collective who have had no formal connection with the University.

'In accordance with the University's requirements, there is an official co-ordinator for the paper, who is formally responsible for the course; but in practice the collective takes joint responsibility, subject to minimal practical constraints (it cannot, for example, control the examination process). The collective meets regularly throughout the year and its main work is the development and organization of each year's course, deciding on the syllabus, organizing the timetable, arranging the speakers, etc. In addition, the collective is committed to working democratically and to developing a feminist practice. All women taking the course to exam level can join the collective and we really welcome new members. Anyone who is not taking the exam but who intends to follow the course throughout the year can also be invited to join the collective. The course is examined either by dissertation or by a three-hour paper set and marked by two examiners.

'Much of the Women's course is critical of the theoretical approaches taken by traditional academic disciplines, and increasingly it has come to be a forum for exploring recent developments in feminist theory, rather than being an introduction to basic feminism, which is more as it used to be. This reflects both the changing composition of students taking the paper (we can now assume some knowledge of or commitment to feminism) and the developing needs and interests of the collective.

'The collective tries to make use of the insights gained from our experience of the course, and not simply reproduce what we have offered in the past. In fact, the collective has never simply served up last year's course for a second time. We have always made an effort to learn from our own work and use our own history; we have always built up each year's course through criticism and debate about the old courses.

'We are interested in sharing the ideas and experiences of our course, so we've started making contact with a few other Women's Studies courses, to try and work out what issues need to be talked out.'

At the beginning of the 1976—77 academic year the collective produced a discussion paper dealing with some of the problems encountered with the course. They felt that they were to some extent trapped within the traditional academic disciplines, without fully knowing how to adapt them in order to include a feminist perspective; that they had been mentally separating 'the political' from 'the academic' and slotting the political issues into a separate category or session, if at all. They are now trying to develop a new structure which avoids the standard approach of looking at women through the various disciplines that already exist. They want to create a course that is feminist in conception, instead of leaving loopholes for intermittent insertions of feminism. The problems faced by the Cambridge women are common to many women trying to develop women's studies within the limits of traditional academic institutions; trying to change the hierarchical structure and the accepted ideas of what is academic.

WEA Women's Studies Branch

The Workers' Educational Association has held local classes on topics concerning women in many areas. The courses vary in length and subject matter ('Women in Literature', 'Women's Rights', 'Women and Society') and are not directed towards any qualification.

In July 1976 the district council of the North of Scotland WEA approved the formation of a new branch, the North East (Women's Studies) Branch, with the aim of interesting more women in education, and to promote women's studies generally in the North East of Scotland. The history of how this branch came about is an interesting example of the development of women's studies in one area.

The Aberdeen Women's Group persuaded the extra-mural department of Aberdeen University to hold a series of ten talks called 'Women in Society', which ran in the session 1974—75 and attracted quite a lot of women who had never been to women's movement events before. Students on this course set up a twenty-week course themselves the following year, again under the auspices of the extra-mural department, but because of cuts in the extra-mural budget they were unable to do so in 1976—77. At the same time a woman who was working for the WEA in Aberdeen set up a Women's Rights course. This was held on a Thursday evening (the same evening as late-night shopping in Aberdeen), and attracted working-class women as well as those already involved in women's activities.

In the following year, 1975—76, the WEA set up two courses, one on 'Women's Rights' and one on 'Women in History'. Only the 'Women in History' course eventually got off the ground, as the 'Women's Rights' course failed to attract enough students. At the end of the 'Women in History' course the group of fifteen or sixteen women who had been attending decided that they didn't want to give up meeting and formed themselves into the Women's Studies Group, continuing with fairly formal study discussions most weeks, although some weeks were given over to business and women's campaign activities. Group members take it in turns to lead discussions, and collectively arrange ways of reaching and involving other women.

The Studies Group began to negotiate with the WEA about becoming a branch. There were two reasons for this. Firstly, that as a branch they would have greater access to resources available to the WEA, such as video equipment and library facilities, and would be able to have some influence over policy decisions within the WEA. And secondly, that they could support any initiatives in the field of women's studies taken by the full-time staff of the WEA, or could make those initiatives themselves. They all agreed that current Women's Studies courses were appealing mostly to a small educated minority, and that they must find ways of getting and holding the attention of working-class women.

As well as continuing as a study group, looking at different subjects in their relation to women, the group has organized several events for women from outside the group, including three Women and Health Days, well attended by local women, with a creche provided free. There were films and discussions on childbirth, mental health, the menopause, the drugs industry, self-help and many other aspects of women's health, trying to relate individual women's experiences to the position of women in society, and popular attitudes to the 'healthy woman'. The group has also co-operated with Playtime, an umbrella organization involved in promoting political theatre, and several women have attended a variety of workshops on theatre and collective writing. Women's classes have continued using many of the people from the Women's Studies Group as teachers and course planners. 1976—77 courses have included 'Women and Psychology', 'Women and History', and 'Women, Work and the Trade Unions'. There has also been a course for single parents at Ellon, a small town north of Aberdeen, on 'The Child and the Family', which looked critically at things like maternal and paternal deprivation.

Over the last eighteen months the group has been working spasmodically on a Women's

Rights Pack, for people outside Aberdeen to use in starting new discussion groups. They want to make the material particularly relevant to Scotland as most of the material already available refers only to English law. Some of the other ideas they would like to implement are giving 'careers talks' with a feminist perspective to girls at school, setting up discussion groups for mothers of young children through the Pre-School Playgroups Association, and arranging seminars and discussions through the trade unions.

Much of the funding necessary to organize all these activities has come from the WEA, but as cuts in local government finance take effect the group may have to look for other sources of funds such as grant-giving trusts, or try to make the work they do pay for itself in some way.

The experiences of the Aberdeen group illustrate in many ways how women's studies often differs in method as well as in content from conventional educational courses. There are no strictly fixed distinctions between 'teachers' and 'students'; women who take part in a class one year may well go on to help plan and teach the course the following year. 'Education' is interpreted in the widest possible sense, with women learning from each other and from their own experience. 'Learning' is not confined to the classroom — the group deliberately goes out to reach women rather than waiting for women to come to them, and is constantly on the lookout for ways of involving women who would not normally take part in adult education. And the effect of what women's studies teaches often carries over into women's lives; they may form women's groups or get involved in campaigns and activities. Once we understand the position of women, the obvious next step is to try to change it!

WOMEN'S STUDIES IN THE UK
published by London Seminars (Dr M. Rendel), 71 Clifton Hill, London NW8
A comprehensive list of Women's Studies courses at universities, polytechnics and colleges. Gives a brief summary of each course. It was published in 1976 but it is hoped to bring out up-to-date editions regularly.

WOMEN'S RESEARCH AND RESOURCES CENTRE
27 Clerkenwell Close, London EC1
They are compiling information about women's studies courses. If you want to know about courses in your area, or which colleges do courses, or if you are involved in a course which they don't already know about, they will be pleased to hear from you.

WOMEN AND EDUCATION GROUP
4 Cliffdale Drive, Crumpsall, Manchester 8
The Group holds occasional meetings on subjects ranging from pre-school to women's studies, and has arranged Non-Sexist Teaching Days, to consider practical approaches. They also produce the *Women and Education Newsletter*.

SEXISM IN CHILDREN'S BOOKS

Most parents choose children's books if the story looks interesting and the writing is lively, imaginative, positive and colourful. But the content is equally important. Books which portray white middle-class children but no black children, active boys but passive girls, working fathers but house-bound mothers reinforce these stereotyped images of our society. Stereotyping is particularly harmful, because it means we stop valuing people as individuals, and form over-simplified generalizations about a group, race or sex, very often with derogatory implications such as lack of intelligence, peculiar habits or passivity. Children's behaviour is very much influenced by the images they are presented with, and books play a large part in shaping children's ideas and attitudes by opening new areas for exploration, consideration, imagination.

Over the past few years, overwhelming evidence has been gathered that the books our children learn from present men and women in very strict and limited roles. In many cases, the behaviour of men and women in books for young children is even more traditional and conventional than what goes on in the real world.

What effect does this have on children? No doubt it is great for the ego of white middle-class boys, but what about the other 90 per cent of British children? Who are they to identify with? Where are their heroines, heroes, and life-styles represented? An awareness of the dearth of heroines was shown by one seven-year-old girl who refused to read from the Pirates reading scheme because, she said, 'There's no girls in them books, Miss.'

Several books and pamphlets have appeared outlining the way in which children are taught how the sexes 'should' behave, and there are groups campaigning to change this or to publish and publicize books which do not perpetuate traditional sex roles.

Recognising Sexist Literature

Sexist children's books are those which do not take account of the full range of activities open to children of both sexes. Girls are shown as passive, caring, helping mother, cooking, adapting to suit others, dependent, home-making, soft and helpless or are omitted completely. Boys are shown as brave, adventurous, imaginative, humorous, mechanically dexterous, independent, striving to reach their potential. Both sexes can suffer from pressure to conform to these roles, but a glance at the list is sufficient to show who comes off second best. Sometimes illustrations convey these images more forcefully than the text:

Text:	*'Peter is in the tree, Jane is in the tree.'*
Illustration:	Peter sitting gaily on the top branch, Jane gingerly clinging to the lowest!
Text:	*'We dress up as doctors and nurses.'*
Illustration:	Girls dressing up as nurses.

Sexism extends to the language we use. English language uses 'he', 'him', 'man' and other masculine pronouns and nouns on the assumption that these include the feminine. However technically correct this may be, the words do not convey the feminine and the effect is subtly alienating for girls.

The aim of non-sexist books is not to illustrate a complete reversal of roles, but to allow both sexes a variety of activities, with tough girls and tender boys, and with both sexes initiating activities, learning skills, being resourceful and independent; and both sexes showing tenderness, fear, worry, helpfulness and occasionally crying.

CAMPAIGN TO IMPEDE SEX-STEREOTYPING IN THE YOUNG
c/o Pam Isherwood, Village Books, Shrubbery Road, London SW16
CISSY is currently preparing a bibliography of useful books, including children's picture books, and are interested in hearing from other groups working on children's books. *CISSY Talks to Publishers: Sexism in Children's Books* is a duplicated record of discussions with publishers and is well worth reading.

WOMEN IN THE PUBLISHING INDUSTRY
c/o 19 Novello Street, London SW6
They produce a *Non-Sexist Code of Practice for Book Publishing,* 10p.

CHILDREN'S RIGHTS WORKSHOP (Book Project)
c/o 73 Balfour Street, London SE17
The Workshop has probably contributed more than any other organization in Britain to increasing awareness of racism and sexism in children's books. The project campaigns, reviews books, writes and edits pamphlets (published by Writers and Readers), lectures, and keeps up-to-date information. All this work is done on very limited funds. The Workshop produces a magazine on racism and sexism in children's books, published and distributed by Writers and Readers, three times a year, which is available through bookshops. The Workshop was also instrumental in establishing 'The Other Award'. This is an alternative children's book award for non-biased books of literary merit which was made for the first time in 1975, and has become an annual event. The Book Project of the Workshop has four main aims: to campaign against bad children's books; to help develop a critical approach to children's books; to campaign for more good children's books; and to see developed a more grass-roots distribution of good children's literature.

WRITERS AND READERS PUBLISHING CO-OPERATIVE
9, Rupert Street, London W1
> *'We are a new publishing group which works on a non-profit basis: all income above production costs and overheads is re-invested in projects which the group supports. Our objectives are: to produce books and pamphlets cheaply; to distribute our publications so that parts of the public not generally reached become our readers . . . to act as a co-operative distribution centre for other non-profit based publishing groups.'*

They have produced a number of pamphlets on sexism in children's literature, and have published some non-sexist children's books.

Books

CHILDREN'S BOOKS: A Statement and Lists from the Children's Rights Workshop
Writers and Readers Publishing Co-operative, 10p
This is indispensable for anyone concerned with the content of children's books. Contents include: a list of principal references on sexism, racism and class bias in children's books; a list of useful children's picture books; and a statement by the Children's Rights Workshop itself.

RACIST AND SEXIST IMAGES IN CHILDREN'S BOOKS
Writers and Readers Publishing Co-operative, 45p
First published in the USA this collection of ten papers is extremely relevant in Britain too for anybody concerned about stereotyped attitudes children receive through their reading material (from *Women's Report*).

JUST LIKE A GIRL: How Girls Learn To Be Women
by Sue Sharpe, Pelican, 95p
Based on the results of a survey at four Ealing schools this book describes and analyses how society teaches women what their role should be, through school, the media, etc. Contains plenty of quotes from the girls themselves, which makes it both more enjoyable and easier to read than a more 'scientific' use of the material.

SEXISM IN CHILDREN'S BOOKS: Facts, Figures and Guidelines
Writers and Readers Publishing Co-operative, 60p
A fascinating collection of papers that look at children's books in some detail and show exactly what image of women they are putting across.

THE GENDER TRAP
by Carol Adams and Rae Laurikietis, Virago
A three-volume series for use in schools, designed to get young people thinking and talking about sex roles. Very useful for teachers, especially as there is so little material available on this subject in a form which is ready for use with a class. The three Titles are: Book 1, *Education and Work*; Book 2, *Sex and Marriage*; and Book 3, *Messages and Images.* They cost £1.25 each.

LITTLE GIRLS
by Ilena Gianini Belotti, Writers and Readers Publishing Co-operative, 95p
Ms Belotti examines how infant females are pressed into their 'proper' submissive role from birth. She looks at how parents react to boys and girls, and how educational institutions continue the process. There is a section on games, toys and literature.

WOMEN'S RESEARCH

Meanwhile, at the other end of the academic spectrum, women are working in universities and colleges to right the balance between the sexes. In the academic world, in what we actually learn at college or university, women are excluded. Our history is largely ignored — one woman who studies nineteenth-century history at university said that women would never have been mentioned if she hadn't been particularly interested in the subject. In psychiatry and medicine, women are regarded as exceptions; many psychiatrists have two sets of criteria for what constitutes mental health — if you say a person's very submissive, if it's a man it means he's sick, but for a woman it's normal! Again, in psychology it's been shown that in experiments where all the subjects are men, the experimenters will generalize from this and say, 'This proves that *women* are . . . '. To the specialists and experts in many fields, men are the human race and women are a deviation.

Women researchers are beginning to look at academic disciplines to find out how women have been excluded, and what this means for us. Besides looking at the implications for women of being left out of whole bodies of knowledge, we need to correct things that are simply untrue, but are put forward as facts. There is still a lot of hostility to this in conventional academic circles. Many women have found their tutors extremely unhelpful at suggesting reading material, or have had to deal with supervisors who, on their own admission, knew nothing at all about the subject. But it can be exciting work, because it sometimes involves finding out entirely new things.

The Women's Research and Resources Centre was set up by a small group of women, most of whom were working on women's studies, who felt there was a need for a register of the research being carried out in this area. They had already found themselves meeting this need informally, putting people in touch with others doing similar research, and thought it would be a good idea to bring all this information together, and to add to this feminist publications and other information. The Richardson Institute for Peace and Conflict Research let them have a room, and they advertised for a worker. Zoe Fairbairns got the job:

'I started working here in July 1975. All we had was this room, two desks, a small pile of books and a rubber stamp saying 'Women's Research and Resources Centre'! Someone had donated £50, and we had a list of about 100 people who we knew were interested, so we wrote to them saying we couldn't start without any money, could they send £5. And enough people sent £5 for us to produce a newsletter. From then until now enough subscriptions have come in every week, somehow or other, to cover the costs. The Richardson Institute have been very good to us; we didn't pay any rent at first, and later only a few pounds a week. We have recently moved to a "Working Community" in Clerkenwell.

'The subscription covers the running of the centre and the cost of the newsletter, which comes out bi-monthly. It has news of publications, some reviews, details of our own meetings, and any relevant information such as reports of conferences. There's also a section called "Contacts" for people doing research who want to find others doing similar work, or who are trying to get hold of a particular piece of information. At the Centre we have a small but growing library of feminist and related books, most of which have been donated by publishers; files of periodicals relevant to women and to feminism; files for things produced by different organizations, and from different countries; and a collection of pamphlets. Anyone can come in and use the material, but only subscribers can borrow publications.

'We also have a research index: if someone's doing research on sex roles, for example, she could look under that topic in the research index and see who else is working on it. Some would just be names and addresses, others would refer to a questionnaire that the researcher has filled in giving details of her research.

'*The collective meets every two months to make decisions and to organize seminars; we usually invite someone we know who's doing an interesting piece of research, or occasionally someone writes in and offers. I think ideally a seminar should be of as much use to the person who's doing the work as to those who attend. What often happens is that people who are doing research on a feminist topic find they're not taken seriously, so they can't get proper feedback from the people they work with. Either they've got conventional, or even anti-feminist, academic supervisors who don't treat them seriously, or they've perhaps got politically committed people around them to whom everything is right so long as it's feminist. So we try to provide a balance, maintain a sympathetic feminist environment and "academic rigour" (though I hate that phrase), basically trying not to let things go by unquestioned just because they're feminist.*

'*We get a lot of letters, from school students wanting information, university students, lecturers who are preparing courses and want us to recommend books. Either we answer them ourselves, or forward it to the appropriate group, or if they're in London suggest they look in. Although I only know of one Women's Studies course being held in a school, from the number of school students who write in I think there must be a lot going on that isn't called women's studies. I find it really encouraging when a school student has the initiative and sufficient interest to write to us, or come in and use the material, some of which isn't all that readable.*

'*I'm the only regular paid worker; another woman comes in two days a week unpaid at the moment, and there's a group of about a dozen women who are involved in the collective who help with the newsletter and so on. And occasionally women you've never seen before just come in and do an afternoon's work.*

'*Our future depends very largely on money. We're bursting at the seams, we get new enquiries, new material, new people interested every day. If we had the resources, like more space and enough money to have a paid worker here every day, we could do a lot more.*

'*So far we've been unable to get charitable status. The usual reason that feminist organizations are refused is because they're accused of being political, but they've told us we're not charitable because we're not educational! The Charity Commission says we're concerned with the dissemination of information rather than education — apparently they think there's a difference. What we're involved with is "the increase of knowledge rather than the advancement of education", according to their letter. We're going to challenge their ruling, but while we haven't got charitable status it's very difficult to get big grants. We have recently received a small grant from the Equal Opportunities Commission.*

'*It would be very nice to have more money, but at the same time it's exhilarating to know that you're surviving solely on the support of the people you're there to serve, to know that you're meeting a need. Whereas if you get a large grant it is possible to take off and completely lose touch — then when your grant disappears you fall down to earth again. Our base here is very solid.*'

WOMEN'S RESEARCH AND RESOURCES CENTRE 27 *Clerkenwell Close, London EC1*
A subscription is £5 a year, or what you can afford.

Two other groups concerned with women's research are:

FEMINIST HISTORY GROUP
c/o Women's Research and Resources Centre
The feminist history group is an informal seminar which meets at the Women's Research and Resources Centre in London. The group is intended to provide a focus of support and encouragement for women engaged in historical research on women, and a forum in which they may discuss their work with other feminists. The group's meetings are open to all women, and only to women; we try to involve non-historians as much as possible since we see our purpose as the development of a historical approach to the issues facing the women's movement today. Papers are presented at the group, then, are usually informal, often 'work in progress' rather than completed projects.

LIBRARIANS FOR SOCIAL CHANGE
c/o John Noyce, PO Box 450, Brighton, Sussex
This group seeks to provide a forum for the re-appraisal of methods of getting information to the people. It is an umbrella group which includes a lot of library workers who want to have more say in the running of their libraries; to challenge conventional library theory and practice; to establish alternative libraries and information services; to index the radical and alternative press; to fight capitalism, fascism, racism, sexism and other oppressive ideologies. There is a feminist group within Librarians for Social Change.

Her-Story in History

The history we learn at school is the story of what men have done (soldiers, politicians, inventors, heroes of one sort of another) and 99 per cent of the famous characters we all know about are male. The message to little boys is clear: 'You can be brave, you can do important things, you can change the world as other men have done before you.' To little girls it's: 'It's somewhat bewildering; women in history are virtually non-existent, unimportant, invisible. Not only are you as a woman not expected to do anything important — it's made obvious to you that no woman ever has, and who are you to fight against the tide of history?'

The few women who do appear are obviously exceptions, and what's more are generally confined to 'feminine', caring occupations like Florence Nightingale or Elizabeth Fry; and we're given very little indication of how hard they had to fight, in the most unfeminine conditions, to achieve their fame. We have a hard time finding brave, adventurous women to identify with . . . about the nearest we get is Joan of Arc, and look what happened to her!

When we look at the way women are portrayed in the media now, we can see the process whereby women's contribution to the world is made as little of as possible. Women are described in terms of their family status or their physical appearance rather than their achievements.

Because we question our 'natural' position as inferior, unimportant beings, we need to take a new look at history to find out what women have achieved. And if we haven't been at the forefront of the world stage, we need to find out why not. Much of what women have accomplished has been in opposition to men: fighting for education, fighting for the vote, fighting for the right to own our own property — and many seem less heroic than the male military exploits we all learn about. But when we examine the weight of oppression, ignorance and prejudice that women had to fight, the smallest act of defiance seems extremely courageous.

Because it has been men who have written history, much of the guesswork involved in reconstructing past events has been guessed from a male point of view. This has been especially true of the study of the earliest history of our species, where lack of firm evidence has left the most room for imagination. Archaeological evidence, ancient customs and so on have all been interpreted from a position which assumed that hunting was a high-status occupation. Logically, it's not necessarily so. The study of the earliest history as *man's* development has ignored many possible and probable explanations because they were unthinkable and unpalatable to men.

Her-Story Books

SHOULDER TO SHOULDER
by Midge Mackenzie, Penguin, £3.50
The story of the Suffragette movement in the form of contemporary letters, diaries, newspaper articles and other documents. There are lots of photographs. It is a very interesting, and easy to read book if you know nothing about the subject.

FEMINISM: The Essential Historical Writings
edited by Miriam Schneir, Vintage, £1.25
A collection of writings by or about women, from the eighteenth to the early twentieth century. It includes extracts from Mary Wollstonecraft, Emma Goldman, Virginia Woolf and many others.

HIDDEN FROM HISTORY
by Sheila Rowbotham, Pluto Press, 75p
A study of the changing position of women in England from the puritan revolution to the 1930s. It contains a lot of information on different views of female sexuality at various times, birth control, and the relationship between other left-wing movements and the struggle against women's oppression.

THE HARD WAY UP: The Autobiography of Hannah Mitchell, Suffragette and Rebel
edited by Godfrey Mitchell, Virago, £2.25
An autobiographical account of the Suffragette movement, written by a working-class woman who became a leading member of the Suffragette and Labour movements.

THE DESCENT OF WOMAN
by Elaine Morgan, Corgi, 50p
A history of human evolution that takes woman as its starting-point, and concentrates on how her needs could have shaped development rather than man's needs. Some interesting theories about womankind emerging from the sea, our sexual development and many other herstorical interpretations, although Elaine Morgan's flippant, 'feminine' style detracts from the seriousness of her work.

WOMAN'S EVOLUTION
by Evelyn Reed, Pathfinder Press, £2.05
A feminist look at anthropology. Includes topics such as: the incest taboo; the 'dominant' male, fact and fiction; the productive record of the primitive woman. Really fascinating and very morale-boosting to learn about women developing crafts and skills, and matriarchal civilizations. A long book, but it makes you feel good!

WOMEN, RESISTANCE AND REVOLUTION
by Sheila Rowbotham, Pelican, 60p
A survey of women struggling to achieve liberation, from the seventeenth century to the present day.

LIFE AS WE HAVE KNOWN IT
by Co-operative Working Women, Virago, £1.50
Accounts of their lives by members of the Co-operative Women's Guild. It is rare to find 'ordinary' women telling their history; this book is very interesting for its detail of homes, work and the fight against poverty. The sense of increased self-confidence and support that these women gained from getting together with other women in the guilds comes across very clearly.

Her Religion

Silver star of the waters
that have laughed all the world into being;
beyond all knowing is the splendour of Your light.
Enfold my spirit in Your mighty hand
that the pure stream of Your force may flow within me in this world
and in all the worlds to come.

Much the same process as with history has occurred with religion. The image of God as a man is very deeply entrenched, even in people who have rejected the idea of God: the God we no longer believe in is still envisaged as male. It's hardly surprising, and very convenient, for a world ruled by men to see its creator as a man. Where power is equated with masculinity, the most powerful figure of all must be masculine.

Nor is it mere coincidence that he's God the *Father*. The spiritual head of the universe endorses the position of the earthly head of the family; male religious authority reinforces male secular authority, and gives it a mystical, unquestionable basis. Not only is woman's situation 'natural', it's 'God-given' too. Fight it, and you risk trouble not only in this life but also in the life to come!

There is mounting evidence that for thousands of years before the rise of Judaism and Christianity, and all the other male religions, the world worshipped the Goddess in one form or another. Goddess worship has been dismissed as an unimportant 'fertility cult' by men writers; in fact She was worshipped as the Creator of the Universe and giver of life.

At the root of the growing interest in the spiritual dimension of feminism is the conviction that to bring about change we must free ourselves from man's *values* as well as man's laws, and rediscover the woman-values that have been suppressed for the past four thousand years. Many women find spiritual satisfaction and joy from the women's liberation movement and gain strength from the knowledge that the life-force of the universe was worshipped as a woman for countless millennia before man took control; nevertheless they reject the specifically religious aspects of Goddess worship. But for some women a renewal of their religious life is central to their liberation as women.

Lux Madriana is a group of women who are reviving the Madrian faith, the worship of the supreme Goddess. The religion of the Goddess, they feel, is a revolution: 'It is the creation of a new life centred upon the adoration and celebration of the beautiful and vibrant female creative force of the universe.'

The Madrian movement in this country began a little before the recent wave of publications on women's religion, and grew out of the common need and experience of a group of women who were together at that time; an experience they describe as an encounter with the Goddess:

'We have since realized that this experience is one shared by a surprisingly large number of women, and some men too . . . It is an experience which can happen at any time of life, but very often first occurs in the early teens. For many people the experience is quite overwhelming and they go through a period of intense anguish and isolation, being cut off from any personal support or spiritual nourishment. In several cases this has led to breakdown or near breakdown . . . In a sense, then, we may be regarded as a healing community.

'We have our own calendar based on the thirteen lunar months of the year, and celebrate rites four times in each lunar phase at full moon, new moon and two other days in between. There are also ten major festivals in the year and some minor ones. The rites are of two main kinds, Communion, which can only be celebrated by a priestess, and Sacrifice (which involves the offering of a small honey-cake) which can be celebrated by any woman with any group of people. Both of these go back at least as far as recorded history and almost certainly much further. The Rite of Sacrifice is roundly condemned by Jeremiah in the name of his male god in the Old Testament (Jeremiah 34, 15–30).

'At the moment we are working to set up groups in as many areas as possible in this country and in America. We are also publishing the basic texts of our religion in a series of small booklets, and are bringing out a quarterly magazine entitled The Coming Age.'

Lux Madriana recognizes the prevailing anti-religious feeling and the problems that it brings:

'Of course it will be difficult. For many of us, brought up in the last decadence of patriarchal culture, there are genuine intellectual difficulties in accepting any kind of religion. We may also face ridicule, the ridicule of the ignorant and of the "clever". We will need courage, a courage in its way as great as that of our sisters down the ages: the matriarchal resistance-fighters, the Amazons, the so-called witches, who suffered and died for their spiritual vision. These have carried our Lady's torch across the centuries, waiting for a generation that should have the freedom to kindle it into a fire. We have that freedom now. We must not let the opportunity pass.'

Lux Madriana produces a number of books, prayers and pamphlets, as well as a course of personal instruction, all as cheaply as possible — they make no profit on anything.

LUX MADRIANA *c/o M. Evans, 37 Heywood Road, Great Sutton, Wirral, Cheshire*

THE GODDESS AND RELIGION: Some Books

THE PARADISE PAPERS: The Suppression of Women's Rites
by Merlin Stone, Virago, £2.50
Examines the evidence of Goddess-worshipping civilizations in the pre-Hebrew eras, the link between male gods and male dominance, and how the god-worshippers imposed sexual repression on women in the interests of male property ownership. Explains many Old Testament stories, especially the Adam and Eve myth, in terms of the suppression of Goddess-worship. It is a bit difficult and confusing to read, but the central points are important.

GODDESS SHREW
c/o A Woman's Place, See Stop Press, 30p
The Spring 1977 issue of *Shrew* contains a number of very good articles about the Goddess and matriarchal cultures.

THE ANCIENT RELIGION OF THE GREAT COSMIC MOTHER OF ALL
by Monica Sjöö, from 18 Beaufort Road, Bristol 8, 55p
Monica Sjöö's account of the ancient (and not-so-ancient) Goddess religions, and the meaning the Goddess has for her. An inspiring and thought-provoking document.

THE COMING AGE
from Lux Madriana, 30p
A quarterly magazine about the Madrian religion and other related subjects like the origin of patriarchal myth, how religion was adapted to suit the emergence of male dominated society.

JUDAISM AND WOMEN
JUDAISM AND THE NEW WOMAN
both by Rabbi Sally Priesand, from Behrman House, 1261 Broadway, New York, NY 10001, USA, £1.95
Sally Priesand is the first ordained woman rabbi in America. She put together this book to show that although Jewish law has been oppressive to women, it is flexible enough to change and to grant women total equality. If this does not happen, she feels, it will be an 'insult to the dignity of women'.

Rabbi Priesand discusses Biblical concepts of womanhood, rabbinic attitudes towards women (including laws on marriage, divorce and womanly duties), the reform movement in Judaism that has feebly called for women's equality, the creation of Israel and the role that women played in this, changes needed in Israeli law, the position of women in Israel today. She puts forward the image that the modern world has of Jewish women as opposed to the reality and explores four 'great Jewish women' in depth. The section, 'Creating Tomorrow's Jewish Women', calls for more than token equality: a total rewriting of the laws of marriage and divorce, rewriting of textbooks used in schools, granting women equal roles in customs and ceremonies and positions of leadership.

Rabbi Priesand has been involved in the women's movement in America and feels that a type of consciousness raising is necessary to change people's ideas about Jewish women. She emphasizes the need to change laws as well as attitudes.

Women and Science

'When I tell men I'm a scientist they say "You don't look like one," and think that's the biggest compliment they can give me.' This comment from a woman scientist expresses the popular notion that a woman who studies or works in science is some kind of unfeminine freak. In schools, the general prejudice against women displaying *any* intellectual ability is intensified in the sciences; it's just about OK to be good at English, or languages, so long as you're not better than the boys. But to compete with them on what they consider to be their own territory is going too far. When at school, the few girls determined enough to follow science courses were considered completely beyond the pale, by boys and by girls alike. We judged each other by our ability to attract men, and what boy would go out with a girl who knew more about physics than he did?

From the day our brothers got their first chemistry set, and we're fobbed off with a Little Mother Cooking Kit, we learn that science is something mysterious and complicated done by men. We're not only discouraged from becoming scientists, we also believe that we can't understand anything scientific. More than any other part of our lives, science suffers from the 'expert' syndrome (we're told we have to accept the opinions of 'experts' about a whole range of issues, because we wouldn't understand if they tried to explain it to us). So important decisions, from whether to take the Pill to whether to accept fluoride in our drinking water, are taken on the basis of no real information at all except what the 'experts' tell us, what *they* think we'll understand. *We* don't need to worry about nuclear energy, or the effects of pollution, or exactly what food additives do to our bodies, because the nice men in white coats are taking care of everything for us.

Along with other radical groups, women are questioning this attitude, and trying to find things out for themselves.

At the moment there are very few Women and Science groups in this country, but the idea is spreading. The first group, predictably, began in London. Some women in Brighton heard about this and decided to set up their own group:

'The London collective were working on the basis of reviewing areas of scientific literature and trying to draw together some kind of critique of this, showing how it was

oppressive to women; science as an ideology can be seen as oppressive to many sectors of society, but obviously we're concentrating on how it affects women.

'We've tried to pick on areas the London group hasn't covered; they've been mainly interested in sex differences, oral contraception and things like that, so we've been talking about mental health, anorexia, sexuality and so on. We've had fantasies of doing some kind of survey of female sexuality, but haven't worked out how to go about it yet. Not all the women who've come along to the group are involved in anything within the context of what is normally thought of as science, so we didn't want to limit ourselves to discussing things only scientists could understand, nor to the context of women working in science, because only women who are actually involved with science would be very interested in that. So we've concentrated on examining science as an oppressive ideology, what the "technocratic society" does to women.

'At the moment we're working on getting a collection of slides together into an audio-visual kit, so that we can approach schools and talk to girls who might be thinking of a career in science; we're trying to get a grant from the Education Department. But there are an awful lot of obstacles in the way of doing anything about feminism in schools, let alone something like women and science. It's the kind of thing head teachers will shy away from — we could be dishonest about what we're intending to do, but that raises whole new questions.

'In single-sex schools you probably find a higher proportion of girls encouraged to take up science in one form or another; not necessarily working towards a science degree, but being technicians and so on. Whereas in mixed schools it's all geared towards the boys. We're trying to get the facts together about the provision of science facilities for girls, so if the group does get into schools we'll be learning as much from it as they will.

'We're also organizing a Women and Science conference at the moment, the first in this country. We want to present something on advertising for the conference, as a collective effort. That can be fairly forcefully presented visually, and a lot of women in the group don't feel confident enough, or don't feel they have enough access to the knowledge, to present a formal paper. We want to show the dichotomy between how women are seen in the media and how science is seen in the media, and to show how totally disparate the two things are. And also show how science uses women in the media — for instance, if they want to show that a piece of machinery is easy to operate, they show a woman using it. Advertising is full of the mystification of science, "magic ingredients" in washing powder and toothpaste; and doctors and scientists portrayed as men in white coats.

'Our links with the women's health movement could be extended to bring in some of the information about women's health that is hidden away in the scientific textbooks, so that there's a more theoretical basis for it as well as a practical one. The London group, for instance, has made a lot of information available about the research into the contraceptive pill, when you need to start worrying about thrombosis or infertility, what's being done about a male pill and so on. And women who work in science laboratories could get hold of equipment like microscopes so that other women could learn about things like the changes in cervical cells. Health groups still tend to stop at a certain theoretical level, and have a block about going any further. They're still mystified by medical technology too.

'The women's movement up till now doesn't seem to have done anything to help women over these hurdles, because the movement itself still mystifies science and perpetuates the alienation. Like most radical movements it has this attitude that science is a nasty skeleton in the cupboard, and still sees science as "male" and scientists as awful people. Being a feminist and a scientist is dreadful because it means that either way you get bitten by the people you're supposed to be working with — by women for being a scientist, and by scientists for being a woman. It's something the movement needs to discuss.'

WOMEN AND SCIENCE GROUP c/o 15 Camelford Street, Kemp Town, Brighton, Sussex

Women's Study Groups

Like any other political movement, feminism has a theoretical aspect as well as a practical side. Many discussion groups and study groups are formed to look at particular aspects of feminist theory, and its relationship to other political theories and movements. These groups are often informal and have no 'teachers', but are just women learning together.

'I'd been involved in a local women's group in Manchester, and when I moved to Brighton I still felt the need for a group like that — reading, learning and doing things together. So I asked women who were interested in socialism and feminism and got enough people together to start a group.

'We really didn't know where to start. There were eight of us to begin with; some were already involved in the women's movement, some had never been involved at all. We needed to get to know each other, to define our terms and work out what we wanted to aim towards. None of us knew all that much about Marxism, so we thought it would be useful to start with some of the basic concepts. We wanted to find a way of understanding some of the debates that are going on, about housework for instance.

'We started on a small volume about "Capital" by Engels, which explains surplus value and so on. Once we'd decided what to read, we read out loud in the group. It was the first time most of us had done that, and a whole lot of interesting things came out as we began to realize the hang-ups we had about words and books. We didn't want to structure the group too much, but we didn't want it to be totally structureless either. We read through things quite slowly, skipping the bits that seemed boring or obvious, and discussing it as we went along. Sometimes someone would suggest that it might be helpful to read something else in connection with a particular section, and then come back to it.

'Occasionally we tried having one or two people summarizing things instead of reading them in the group, but most of us haven't got time to prepare things. There's been a real commitment to the group, everybody comes nearly every week, because there's no pressure, the work is done in the group, it's a place to relax.

'Different people approached the reading in different ways, and brought in other things that they were doing — a couple of women were doing anthropology and another woman had read Capital in another group. When concepts needed to be explained, we brought our own experiences to it.

'The big problem is always deciding what material we're going to look at. After Capital we looked at the "Women and Socialism Conference" papers, and then The Dialectic of Sex. We felt differently about things that had come out of the women's movement, because we were bringing our own experiences directly into it, and the books themselves were acting as a catalyst. Especially with The Dialectic of Sex, we had some really good discussions when people were opening up about themselves much more. There were so many things to debate in it: racism, the connection between race, sex and class, treating women as a class and so on. But it's difficult to find material like that.

'It took quite a long time to break down the nervousness we felt at first. But by the summer we were having much longer meetings, eating together and taking it in turns to cook. Sometimes we'd go out into the country and sit reading Engels' Origins of the Family with a great big picnic; it was really nice, learning and reading and doing things that are supposed to be academic in a situation like that.

'We spent a whole weekend in the country and tried to review what we'd been doing. We'd been accused of being a small elitist group, and other people in the women's movement were curious about what we were doing, so we tried to write something about it collectively. We actually physically passed the book round and wrote things ourselves,

and that again brought out a whole lot of problems we had about writing and expressing ourselves, and the different ways we did it. Doing it like that, you've got a critical
process at work, you've got confidence to do the thing and finish it, which you might
not have on your own, and you try to do it in the best possible way. We wrote it
specifically for our local newsletter, to encourage other people to set up study groups
and explain why we thought it was a good idea.

'I think the social aspects of the group were essential to gaining the kind of trust
where we could work together. But now it's come round in a full circle and we meet
much more rigorously for two hours a week, then go to the pub together afterwards.

'I think the study group has helped me in a very selfish sense in that I wanted to get
to know a small group of women; I find it important to have people you're committed
to seeing once a week, not necessarily in a purely social way. I find that unless I express
what I'm thinking at a particular moment, or write it down, the idea just disappears
somewhere. But doing things collectively means that there's a whole lot of creativity
going on, ideas bounce off each other and your thoughts don't fly off everywhere.

'We're finding a way of learning apart from the way that's put forward by the academic system, and that's really worthwhile. At the same time it's been fantastic for giving
me confidence academically, taking this sort of learning back into the seminar room and
the sterile academic area, and having the confidence to try and change that area.

'I've now gone into a mixed study group as well, but it would have been very difficult
doing it with men right from the start. I think it's dangerous to say that only women
have certain kinds of learning problems, you can get carried away with that kind of
argument, but nevertheless there's some truth in it. Women are more relaxed together
and a whole lot of things. What is interesting about learning with a group of women is
bringing together the personal and the political; constantly, inevitably striving to do that
(even when you're reading some highly theoretical Marxist work), wanting to really
understand it yourself and to see how it's relevant to your own life, to see how the
structures fit together, how you are influenced and influence other things.

'Two other study groups have been set up in Brighton; it certainly seems to fill a gap.
Consciousness-raising can be rather artificial — you go to a group to talk about problems
you haven't actually experienced with the people in the group. Studying collectively
means that you're experiencing reading something together, rather than coming to the
group and describing how you felt when you read it. It's a practical activity like chopp-
ing wood. It's like going for a walk together or climbing a hill. Definitely like climbing
a hill!'

2 WOMEN AT WORK

WOMEN AND WORK

Women have always worked, either outside or inside the home or both. We were craftworkers, peasants and . . . mothers. We were both breadwinners and breadmakers. Our work was seen as part of the productive effort of society.

With the growth of capitalism a new phenomenon occurred. Industrialized society became centred on wage earning, which was only offered to those who worked in the new productive centres (factories, shops and now offices . . .). The contribution women make to the production process by staying at home, raising future workers, and allowing husbands and fathers to go to work is seen as 'natural women's work'. No price is attached to this work, and its value to society is obscured.

Many women still work outside the home, not for pin money, but for sound financial reasons; very often one pay packet is not enough to make ends meet in a family. In 1974 women made up nearly 40.1 per cent of the labour force.

Most women are unskilled and untrained, therefore we end up doing 'women's work'; half of women's jobs are concentrated in three major service industries: the distributive trades (17.7 per cent); professional and scientific services (23.1 per cent); and miscellaneous services (11.7 per cent). These jobs correspond to 'feminine values'. They require an endless supply of sympathy, understanding, tolerance and fortitude: the teacher who is involved with children; the nurse who cares for the sick; the office cleaner who tidies up; the shop assistant who is pleasant and smiling . . .

This confinement to special jobs is not accidental. 'Feminine qualities are taught to girls both at home and at school. Sexual discrimination is reinforced in training, to which women do not have equal access. In 1970 only *110 women* were in apprenticeships to skilled craft occupations as against *112,000 men*.

Despite the risk of over-generalization, we shall try to give a few characteristics of the female labour market. There are three readily distinguishable features: firstly, the *use of part-timers*; secondly, the *double shift of a 'worker-housewife'*; and thirdly, the *lack of participation in trade unions.*

Since the war, there has been a massive increase in the number of part-time workers, the majority of whom are women: one in three women (compared with one in twenty men) works part-time. A large proportion of women take part-time jobs which enable us both to earn money *and* carry out our other jobs as wives, mothers and housewives. This makes us particularly vulnerable to exploitation. We usually have tedious jobs with little expectation of promotion, and we are very often paid less per hour than full-time workers. The average hourly earnings for part-time female manual workers in all manufacturing industries was 85.89p in 1973, compared to 93.02p for full-timers.

Women part-timers are a conveniently manipulated sector of the workforce because of the two jobs we have to do as workers and housewives. When we go home, we women do a second shift: we do housework, for which we are not paid. This issue will be discussed later (see: Wages for Housework).

To understand our lack of participation in the labour movement, it is useful to bear in mind that women do two jobs. This has often been attributed to 'women's nature' (women are not interested, they are not aggressive, etc.), but how can you go to a meeting at 8pm when you have to feed husbands, get the children to bed, wash up, tidy up and babysit? (See: Trade Unions)

Women are doubly exploited, as workers and as females. The social service cuts of 1977 affected us in two ways: on the one hand the sectors that bore the brunt of the cuts were those employing large numbers of women, for example welfare services and primary school teaching, so on the one hand we lost our jobs; on the other hand, as housewives we were forced to stay at home for lack of nurseries, hospital facilities and other services affected by the cuts.

The struggle has therefore to be fought on two inter-dependent levels. Firstly, we need to secure equal pay and the right to work outside the home (although this will not in itself solve the problem of sexual discrimination). And secondly, the roles of housework and child-rearing need to be re-evalued, and to be restructured so that they can (where desired) be equally shared between men and women. Only when these 'women's jobs' both at work and at home are no longer considered as inferior and reserved solely for women, will women achieve a meaningful level of equality in their working lives.

OUR PRESENT RIGHTS

In law, women have special rights. They are changing and women ought to know them and to be able to use them to the best advantage.

The Equal Pay Act

This is an Act of Parliament, passed in 1970, which came into effect in 1975; its aim is to 'prevent discrimination as regard terms and conditions of employment between men and women'. It covers not only basic wage rates and salaries, but also overtime pay, bonuses, and other conditions of employment such as holidays, hours of work and terms of notice. Nevertheless, it does not deal with areas of family responsibility such as maternity leave (a man cannot get paid maternity leave), nor retirement ages (although this will change in April 1978 when employers will not be allowed to place different conditions to membership of company pension schemes for women and men). But victory is elusive: the longer life expectancy of women often means that their pensions are lower than men's!

The Act requires employers to give equal pay for the *same work* and also equal pay for *work of equivalent value*. This is very important because it explains why the Act has failed to implement equal pay. Women's jobs are evaluated to assess whether they are of equal value to men's, but they are frequently graded lower. Jobs requiring manual dexterity (and monotonous working) are traditionally filled by women, but these factors receive low 'weightings' compared to physical effort and the predominant factors in 'equivalent' traditionally-male jobs.

There is a wide assumption that certain jobs are 'female' and others 'male'. Jean Coussins in *The Equality Report* cites the case of a firm which thought that the difference in pay between its male and female toilet attendants was justified because 'a male toilet attendant had to approach the job from the labouring point of view and a female from a housekeeping point of view'!

Women are fighting for equal pay, either individually or in groups. Perhaps the best known example is the TRICO Women's Strike at the American-owned windscreen-wiper factory in Brentford. The dispute centred on five men transferred from nightwork to a day shift. They brought with them a £6.50 pay differential with the women who performed identical work on the assembly line they joined. The men got £52.50 a week, the women £46.00.

After a year's fruitless negotiation for equal pay, nearly 400 women came out on strike in 1976.

The employers took the strikers to an Industrial Tribunal in order to settle the case; the strikers boycotted the Tribunal. The Tribunal ruled that the men had displayed 'flexibility' by moving to the day shift. This ignored the fact that workers on the twilight shift (all men) were paid the same basic rate as the men on the day shift, plus a premium for unsocial hours. After twenty-one weeks of the strike, equal pay was eventually conceded by TRICO, though Sally Groves, an assembly worker at the factory said: 'We didn't get it through the Equal Pay Act. You could say we got it *despite* the Equal Pay Act.'

The interesting point here is the gap between the Tribunal and the women. On one hand, the Tribunal concentrated on trying to establish why unequal pay in its eyes was legal. On the other hand, the women were concerned with the *principle* of equal pay. The fight was not about 'which clause, which paragraph, what interpretation can, or should, be placed upon the complex mystifying language of the Equal Pay Act. It was about the principle behind the Act, the concept that women have the right to the same rate for the job as men, and that people should be paid for *what they do*, not *who they are*.' (*Shrew*, Autumn 1976)

Action Points

If you want to fight for equal pay, here are a few tips:

1. Decide exactly what your complaint is. In order to do this you must understand the language of bureaucracy. Are you being victimized or discriminated against, or is it just a question of applying for equal pay? The Equal Opportunities Commission has published several pamphlets to help you decide this.

2. Go to your nearest Employment Exchange to discuss your situation with someone. You will then be required to fill in a form (IT1) stating your case.

3. This form is passed on to a Conciliation Officer, and a copy is also sent to your employer who is free to dispute it. The Conciliation Officer acts as a go-between between you and your employer to try to reach some agreement before taking the matter to a tribunal. The employer can agree to give equal pay before it reaches a tribunal, or you can be advised to drop your complaint if the officer thinks that there is not enough ground for a tribunal case.

4. If you are told to drop your complaint, but still feel you have a good case, then you have to take up the matter privately through a solicitor. If your case reaches the tribunal, it is up to you to prove your case against your employer. Two laypersons and a judge then reach a decision. A ruling to back-date pay is very rare, and even when this happens, it can only go back to 29 December 1975.

5. At an early stage, go to your local Community Law Centre, or to a women's group or sex discrimination group; they may be able to help and support you through the proceedings.

Details of cases notified to the Equal Opportunities Commission for the period 29 December 1975 to 13 October 1976 are as follows:

Successful	Dismissed	Total
62	162	224

The Central Office of Industrial Tribunals produces a monthly publication available through HMSO bookshops showing details of important cases and cases which set precedents. Decisions made by the tribunals are on view at the Central Office of Industrial Tribunals at 93 Ebury Bridge Road, London SE2, and also at the Regional Offices of the Industrial Tribunals.

For more information read:
EQUAL PAY AND HOW TO GET IT
by Ruth Lister and M. Lower, 20p
THE EQUALITY REPORT
by J. Coussins, £1
Two reports produced by the National Council for Civil Liberties and available from NCCL, 186 Kings Cross Road, London WC1. NCCL has a Women's Rights Officer, who can be contacted for information; or if you support NCCL's work, you can become a member.

Or you can contact:
EQUAL OPPORTUNITIES COMMISSION
Overseas House, Quay Street, Manchester 3

RIGHTS OF WOMEN
2 St Pauls Road, London N1
A small group consisting mainly of women lawyers formed to press for more effective working of the equal pay and sex discrimination legislation.

Maternity and Paternity Leave

WHAT YOU CAN GET FROM THE STATE

Women in many Western countries receive some or all of their wages from the state for a limited period before and after childbirth. The National Council for One Parent Families says in its Spring 1977 Journal that France is the top country for aid to the unmarried mother. It calculates that over the six months of pregnancy and the three years after birth, an unmarried mother whose average weekly income is £35.56 would receive £5,472.60 in benefits (*Guardian*, 2 May 1977).

So far Great Britain has lagged behind in implementing state maternity schemes and in placing legal obligations on employers to keep jobs open for people who are temporarily caring for a child.

Under the Employment Protection Act 1975 women are entitled to three basic rights:

1. Dismissal from your job purely or mainly on grounds of pregnancy is now classed as unfair dismissal.
   If you have been working for the same firm for six months, your employer cannot sack you just because you are pregnant (for example, if you come in late several times because of morning sickness and are sacked, you can make a complaint to an Industrial Tribunal).
   If you think you have been unfairly dismissed you can now claim up to £11,720 compensation though in practice you are more likely to get about two or three hundred pounds.
2. A woman has the right to be reinstated in her job for up to twenty-nine weeks after the birth of her baby.
   You only have the right to retain your job until the baby is born if you have been working for the same firm for two years (at a date eleven weeks before the baby is due) and are employed full time (that is at least sixteen hours a week, or if you have worked for five years with the same firm at least eight hours a week).
   Your employer is only required to give you the same job defined according to your contract of employment. This can be vaguely defined (sales assistant, teacher, etc.), so you have no legally enforceable right to return to *exactly* the same job as you had before.
3. A woman has the right to six weeks' maternity pay.
   There is a two-year service rule to fulfil. This means that you have to work at least two years full-time or five years part-time with the same employer to get maternity pay. It will be paid at a rate of 90 per cent of the basic pay you were paid by your employer.

The conditions above eliminate a great many women, for example women under sixteen, or women who have just changed their job.

In *addition* to these new rights there are still the old state maternity benefits under the National Insurance Scheme:

1. A maternity grant of £25 to help you with the immediate cost of having a baby. This has not gone up since 1969 (compare it with a grant of £396.60 available in ante-natal and post-natal allowances to all mothers in France!)
2. A maternity allowance. You can get a weekly allowance for at least eighteen weeks before the expected birth. You can only claim it on your own full-rate or self-employed rate National contributions.

WHAT YOU CAN GET FROM YOUR UNION

Maternity agreements negotiated through your union will usually give you a better deal than the state scheme. Women employed by the Civil Service, for example, get twenty-six weeks' leave (thirteen on full pay, thirteen on half pay). Penguin Books give twenty-four weeks' leave.

The TUC Women's Advisory Committee has drawn up a list combining the best practices achieved in the public sector (at least to their mind!):

1. All women should be entitled to paid maternity leave, whether married or unmarried, and whether they are working full-time or part-time.
2. Women should be eligible for maternity leave after working for a company for one year. A period of up to three months off work should not count as a break in service.
3. The best employers in the public sector give eighteen weeks' leave, including four weeks on full pay.
4. Most employers withhold a part of the maternity benefit until the woman returns to work. The minimum penalty the TUC found was four weeks' pay.

However some unions go further than the TUC advise and are pressing for *paternity leave*. The Association of Scientific, Technical and Managerial Staffs (ASTMS), the Association of Cinematograph, TV and Allied Technicians (ACTT), the National Union of Journalists (NUJ), the National Association of Local Government Officers (NALGO) are all at least in theory committed to paternity leave. Congratulations to *Time Out* magazine; they allow eighteen weeks' maternity leave on full pay for their women employees, *and paternity leave of six weeks with full pay.*

For more information read:
MATERNITY RIGHTS FOR WORKING WOMEN   **SPARE RIB GUIDE TO MATERNITY RIGHTS**
by J. Coussins, National Council for Civil Liberties,   *by Rose Ades, in Spare Rib No. 56*
186 Kings Cross Road, London WC1, 30p

Protective Laws

These laws are embodied in the *Employment of Women, Children, and Young Persons Act 1920*, the *Hours of Employment (Conventions) Act 1936* and the *Factories Act 1961*.

The main effect of these laws is to prevent women and young people doing shift work and excessive overtime. These regulations apply only to factories; exemption can be obtained if the employer applies to the Secretary of State. About two million women work in factories. Nearly 200,000 are covered by exemption orders.

Under these laws it is illegal for women:

1. to work for more than nine hours a day or forty-eight hours a week;
2. to start work before 7.00am or go on working after 8.00pm (1.00pm on Saturdays);
3. to work more than six hours overtime per week and 100 hours a year;
4. to work on Sundays, Bank Holidays, Christmas or Good Friday without a day off in lieu;
5. to clean machines if this would expose them to risk of injury;
6. to work with certain toxic substances.

These laws were introduced in the mid-nineteenth century after the recognition of the sordid conditions in which women and children had to work. An assortment of groups, parties and organizations including Mr Heath's Conservative Government, the Confederation of British Industry and a few women have argued that such conditions no longer exist and the Protective Laws are only a restriction on the right of women to work. They argue that women cannot attain equality if special laws exist which treat women unequally. Therefore the Protective Laws should be repealed.

Anna Coote in her pamphlet *Women in Factories* refutes these arguments. Working women already have two jobs (see: Wages for Housework), and are often exploited as paid workers through low pay or poor conditions (for example, night cleaners, nurses). In fact, as shift work is unhealthy and socially disruptive, far from being repealed, a good case can be made for the Protective Laws to apply to all workers; and special conditions such as shorter hours or longer holidays should apply when night work is unavoidable.

For more information read:
WOMEN IN FACTORIES
by Anna Coote, 20p
PROTECTIVE LAWS: Evidence to the Equal Opportunities Commission
by Tess Gill, 30p
Two pamphlets produced by the National Council for Civil Liberties, 186 Kings Cross Road, London WC1

And contact your local Labour Exchange or the Factory Inspectorate, or send for the Department of Employment pamphlet on the Factory Acts from HMSO, 49 High Holborn, London WC1.

Income Tax

'. . . a woman's income chargeable to income tax shall . . . be deemed for income tax purposes to be his income and not to be her income.'
(Section 37, Income and Corporation Taxes Act, 1970)

Our present tax system evolved over a period when paid work outside the home was the exception rather than the norm for married women. It also reflects the then pervasive social assumption that women, married or single, were essentially dependents, and if they were not, were likely to become so. And there is a growing consensus for the need for reform to promote greater equality between men and women in terms of treatment, benefits and allowances.

The most usual complaint is that the Inland Revenue appears to assume that married women simply do not exist. The Tax Return form contains the phrase, 'If you are a married woman, living with your husband, will you please ask him to complete this form as if it were addressed to him.' And occasionally women find that on writing to the Revenue, the replies are addressed to their husband; for example: 'I refer to *your wife's* letter, and apologize to *her* for not replying to *her* letter. If *your wife* wishes to claim expenses, let me have full details of expenses *you* wish to claim . . . '

Then there are problems of privacy. Where there is no 'separate assessment' or 'earned income election', and in all cases for a married woman's unearned income, the husband is liable for tax on the joint income. The woman is asked to give full details of her income. The reverse does not apply; there is no legal obligation for the husband to give his wife details of his income, and many women do not in fact know what their husbands actually receive. A more hopeful note: where the husband is liable for tax, he is legally responsible for giving details of his wife's income, but there is no legal compulsion for the woman to inform him of her sources of income.

With regard to allowances, there are many anomalies. Since for tax purposes, the man owns the joint income, he also is deemed to own the allowances. In the case of mortgage interest relief, he will receive the allowance for this whether the house is in his name, joint names or his wife's sole name, and indeed even if his wife is making the repayments. Where the husband is employed and the woman is not, he is entitled to the married man's allowance, but since the woman has no income, she cannot receive an earned income allowance. In the reverse case, where the woman is working and her husband is not, she can set against her income, not only the married man's allowance, but, also her earned income allowance. The effect is that the Inland Revenue is recompensing the husband for not working, but not the wife.

These are just a few of the ways that the system of personal taxation discriminates against women. The Equal Opportunities Commission receives many complaints and has now published the excellent and clearly written pamphlet *Income Tax and Sex Discrimination* which sets out the problem together with putting forward some options for change. It is meant as a discussion document, as a starting point to bring greater pressure to bear on a system which is so clearly discriminatory both in attitude and in actual fact. The pamphlet is available from the EOC, Overseas House, Quay Street, Manchester 3. (See also: Up Against the State, The Demand for Independence)

THREE CAMPAIGNS

Interest in the discriminatory nature of the tax system has heightened since the beginning of 1978. The Women's Liberation Movement has started a campaign under the slogan *YBA Wife*. They recommend the following reforms: the abolition of the married man's tax allowance; allowing married women to be responsible for filling in their own tax returns; allowing wives to claim tax rebates against their own income on mortgage interest payments; allowing wives to claim investment tax relief; the abolition of the earned income allowance for wives in favour of one basic personal tax allowance for all adults; allowing tax relief for sons (as well as for daughters) who stay at home to care for aged or infirm parents.

Following various conferences, publications and campaigning which have all helped expose the discriminatory nature of the tax system, the media have taken upon themselves the task of bringing the extent of the problem to the notice of the authorities. Deidre Sanders invited readers of *Woman's Own* to contact her if they disapproved of the present (sexist) nature of the tax regulations, and she received over 5,000 replies which she plans to pass on to the Treasury. The *Sunday Times* has started a Tax Campaign (address: 12 Coley Street, London WC1) to solicit signatures from the public for the statement that 'the system of taxation in this country should be reformed to eliminate discrimination against married women', and like *Woman's Own* they plan to bring pressure to bear on the Treasury and the Government.

Training and Retraining

Opportunities for training are important. Training greatly improves our job prospects (see: Women in Traditionally Male Jobs, 'Being a Carpenter'). With training, women can reach higher levels of achievement, or switch into completely different kinds of jobs.

Many women would like to resume work in their late thirties. Either we have given up our jobs to bring up our children or we never worked at all. In both cases, we find ourselves in a cul-de-sac when we are looking for a job. Because we are unqualified or our qualifications are out-of-date, the only jobs available to most of us are low-grade ones.

It is now possible to acquire new skills, even if you are older, and *to get paid for this*. The government has organized a Training Opportunities Scheme (TOPS) which they claim is available to anybody. 'With TOPS, you are not too old in your fifties. Nor does it matter if you have not worked for a long time; more and more housewives turn to TOPS trainings when their families have grown up.' (TOPS blurb.)

The TOPS scheme covers over 500 occupations (under the following headings: craft and technical skills, factory operators, secretarial and clerical work, business management and administration).

Training is given in the Training Services Agencies' own Skillcentres, in colleges of further education, employers' establishments and residential colleges for the disabled. Courses are free and vary in length depending on the kind of training chosen. Trainees are paid tax-free allowances. There are also special facilities for redundant apprentices and unemployed young people.

Unfortunately it is quite difficult to get enrolled on a TOPS course (waiting lists can often be two to three years). For the craft skills a bit of experience is sometimes required, which means that women are in effect excluded, but unless we keep trying nothing will be done to change this.

For further details of TOPS, contact:
TRAINING SERVICES AGENCY *162—8 Regent Street, London W1*
This is the head office; your local TSA will be in the phone book. Or contact your local employment office or Employment Service Agency.

A conventional but useful book to read would be *Equal Opportunities: A Careers Guide for Women* by Ruth Miller, Penguin, £1.95. This is a detailed guide to over 300 careers from accountancy to window display. It states in each case whether or not part-time work is available. It is an updated edition which was previously (before the Sex Discrimination Act) called *Careers for Girls*.

FIGHTING FOR EQUALITY

Trade Unions

Trade unions were formed by workers to maintain and improve the working conditions of their members. It seems that this formula applies to male members more than to female members although 24 per cent of the total membership is made up of women.

Here again we have the dilemma that if women don't raise 'women's issues' these issues are not raised at all. But if only women raise them, this reinforces the idea that they are 'women's issues' and men don't feel concerned about them. Nevertheless trade unions are powerful bodies which cannot be ignored by women. We should get into them, change them and use them for our own ends.

Many criticisms have been made of the attitudes of trade unions to women's issues. Very few unions fight for creches, for maternity or paternity leave, or for branch meetings to be held at lunchtime or during working hours. And hardly any unions put much pressure for equal pay into their negotiations.

This under-representation of women is emphasized when one looks at the number of women full-time officials in several unions:

Union	Total Membership	Women as Percentage	Full Time Officials		Women as Percentage
			Men	Women	
GMWU	848,481	30.8	145	5	3.4
TGWU	1,746,554	14.1	600	2	0.3
AUEW	1,145,826	11.7	190	0	0
CPSA	208,099	65.0	15	2	13.3
USDAW	443,354	54.1	147	5	3.3

(Source: *Trade Union Studies*, BBC publications, PO Box 234, London SE1)

This problem of under-representation is only part of a larger one; it is also a reflection of the oppression of women at home by men. The misogyny of the worker mirrors his misogyny at home.

Trade unionists complain that women are not motivated, that women work for pin money, that women are dependent, that women don't go to meetings. But women are trapped in a vicious circle. On the one hand we have our duties at home, on the other hand, we have our 'outside work'. This is well illustrated by the following extract:

Helen: The women have got the steward to call a mass meeting.
Dave: Good! I remember the time when you used to argue with me about even being in the union.
Helen: The meeting's on Saturday.
Dave: You going, then?
Helen: I'm Chairing it.
Dave: Who's going to look after the kids then?
Helen: We've organized a playgroup, so more of the women can get involved.
Dave: Now that's a really good idea, love. You can go to your meeting, and I can go to the football.
Helen: Actually, love, I've put you down for the playgroup.
Dave: You did WHAT? ... I don't mind looking after me own two once in a while, but I really do draw the line at other people's kids. Why can't the other women's husbands look after them?
Helen: Some of them haven't got husbands. And some of the husbands work on Saturdays. And not all of them are as good with kids as you are.
Dave: Bloody Hell!

(Red Ladder Theatre Group: *A Woman's Work Is Never Done*)

The TUC has drawn up a Charter of fourteen aims for women at work. We had tremendous difficulty in obtaining a copy; we wrote twice, rang three times and in desperation actually went to Congress House in London. Each time we got the same answer: 'Leave us your address; we'll write to you.' Eventually a journalist friend of ours (a man!) rang the TUC press office and miraculously obtained the desired information. (If this is the way that unions stand up for women's rights, it is hardly surprising that they are accused of not bothering very much.)

The Charter is meant to cover a large area but is mostly extremely vague and generalized:

1. *Education*   Unions want real equality of opportunity for girls with boys right through the educational system.

2. *Starting Work*   Unions want complete equality of job opportunity for women with men; apprenticeships for girls on the same terms as they are available to boys; and day release for further education for all young workers, girls as well as boys.

3. *Marital Status*   Unions say there must be no discrimination whatsoever against any woman worker on grounds of her marital status.

4. *Pay*   Unions call for the proper rate for the job for all workers, male and female, and an end to all pay discrimination against women workers.

5. *Promotion*   Unions want women to have equal promotion opportunities with men.

6. *Occupational Pensions*   Unions say that the coverage of occupational pension schemes should be the same for men and women and that they should contribute on the same basis with equal pension rights.

7. *Sick Pay*   Unions want sick pay to cover all workers, and will not accept any discrimination against women.

8. *Health and Safety at Work*   Unions oppose any moves to allow women to work on jobs which might endanger their health or that of an unborn baby.

9. *Family Planning and Abortion*   Unions support the extension of these services, and oppose any moves to restrict women's access to any family planning or abortion services.

10. *Maternity*   Unions want improved maternity provisions.

11. *Returning to Work*   Unions want advice centres in local employment offices and job centres to assist women to return to work, refresher courses for women who want to take up the same kind of job again, and training for women who want to learn new skills and enter new fields of employment.

12. *Part-Time Work*   Unions say that part-time workers should receive pay and conditions at least pro rata to the full-time workers with whom they work.

13. *Care of Children*   Unions say local authorities should be obliged to provide day nurseries open throughout the day (and throughout the year) to assist working mothers, nursery school education for children below school age, and interesting activities for school children after school and during holidays.

14. *Members of the Community*   Unions say women are equal members of the community with men and all discrimination against them must be abolished. Men and women should organize and work actively within the trade union movement to achieve this and all the aims within the Charter.

As we have seen trade unions have been very slow in tackling women's rights. Nevertheless, they are a very powerful institution, and can be an important weapon in the hands of women. They provide a structure within which women can get together to fight for our rights at work and against male prejudices. More specifically, the TUC advises women to fight for:

1. branch meetings to be held in worktime or lunchtime;
2. the election of women as shop stewards and branch officials;
3. the appointment of a women's officer as one of the branch officials with responsibility for the work, pay and conditions of female members;
4. meetings of female members which plan campaigns on women's issues such as equal pay, the provision of creches, etc.

And we would add:

5. the adoption of the Working Women's Charter by the TUC (see: section on the Working Women's Charter Campaign);
6. the provision of childcare, which should no longer be seen as a 'women's issue' but as a matter of concern to all people, men and women, parents and non-parents.

HOW TO JOIN A UNION

You can write to the Trades Union Congress, Great Russell Street, London WC2; or if you know already which union you want or need to join, you will find a list of local trade unions under 'T' in the Telephone Directory Yellow Pages. If you meet opposition contact the National Office of the union involved.

And don't forget, the more women in the unions, the better!

The Working Women's Charter Campaign

More and more women go out to work both because we have to and because we want to, but we are still seen primarily as wives, mothers and homemakers. Women will not win equal pay without equal job opportunity, adequate nurseries, satisfactory abortion and contraception facilities, and the right to organize within trade unions. All these issues have been tackled by the Working Women's Charter Campaign.

The Working Women's Charter, drawn up by the Women's Sub-Committee of the London Trades Council in March 1974, is not a blueprint for equality, but a series of interlinked demands around which women can organize together. Groups all around the country are promoting its aims and it has been officially adopted by several national unions including AUEW, TASS, NALGO, CPSA, SCS, Equity, the Musician's Union, ACTT and NUPE.

In brief, the Working Women's Charter gives women the right to full equality of treatment with men with regard to pay, entry to occupations, education, working conditions and all matters to do with tenancies, taxation, social security payments. It seeks improved provision of local authority nurseries, paid maternity leave, free abortion and contraception and campaigns for women to take an active part in political and trade unions. The demands of the Working Women's Charter are as follows:

We pledge ourselves to agitate and organize to achieve the following aims:

1. The rate for the job, regardless of sex, all rates negotiated by the trade unions, with a national minimum wage below which no wages should fall.
2. Equal opportunity of entry into occupations and in promotion, regardless of sex and marital status.
3. Equal education and training for all occupations and compulsory day-release for all 16—19 year olds in employment.
4. Working conditions to be, without deterioration of previous conditions, the same for women as for men.
5. The removal of all legal and bureaucratic impediments to equality e.g. with regard to tenancies, mortgages, pension schemes, taxation, passports, control over children, social security payments, hire-purchase agreements.
6. Improved provisions of local authority day nurseries, free of charge, with extended hours to suit working mothers. Provision of nursery classes in day nurseries. More nursery schools.
7. Eighteen weeks maternity leave with full net pay spread before and after the birth of a live child; seven weeks after birth if the child is stillborn. No dismissal during pregnancy or maternity leave. No loss of security, pension or promotion prospects.
8. Family planning clinics supplying free contraception to be extended to cover every locality. Free abortion to be readily available.
9. Family allowances to be increased to £2.50 per child, including the first child.
10. To campaign amongst women to take an active part in the trade unions and in political life so that they may exercise influence commensurate with their numbers and to campaign amongst men trade unionists that they may work to achieve this aim.

Here is the amended charter which was adopted in 1977. It is interesting in that it shows the changes that have taken place in the fight for women's rights. Since the first charter, the passing of Equal Pay, Sex Discrimination and Employment Protection Acts, together with the fight for free abortion on request in the NHS, have made it necessary to update the charter so that it takes a stand on these later developments.

This charter takes up a woman's right to work (though it fails to mention that all women work *inside* the home), sliding scales of wages, paternity leave, amongst other issues.

The revised charter demands:

1. The right of women to work. Security of employment for part-time and casual workers. The full integration of all women workers into a fight against unemployment.
2. The rate for the job, regardless of sex or race. A national minimum wage. For this national minimum wage, and all benefits and wages, to be fully protected against inflation by automatic increases based on a working-class cost of living index.
3. Equal opportunity of entry into occupations, in promotion, and equal rights in defence of jobs, regardless of sex, age, race, marital status, sexual orientation and hours worked.
4. Equal education and training for all occupations, regardless of sex, age, race, marital status, sexual orientation, and compulsory provision of day release for 16–19 year olds in employment. Equal access to apprenticeships and positive discrimination in training for jobs where few women are presently employed. Increased training and re-training provisions and grants for women returning to work. Occupational training to be a right for all unemployed persons.
5. Equality for women in working conditions and conditions of employment, without deterioration of previous conditions. Protective legislation to be extended where appropriate to cover men, and not to be used as grounds for discrimination against women. Part-time workers to receive the same benefits and protections as full-time workers. Improved health and safety at work. Opposition to any move to allow women to work on jobs or with materials which might endanger their health.
6. The removal of all legal and bureaucratic barriers to equality, regardless of sex, marital status, and sexual orientation, with regard to tenancies, mortgages, pension schemes, taxation, passports, care, control and custody over children, social security payments, insurance and supplementary benefits, and hire-purchase agreements.
7. Free state-financed, community-controlled childcare facilities with flexible hours to suit all parents, to be available for all under-fives. The integration of daycare and educational facilities. The provision of play facilities after school and during the school holidays for all children.
8. A minimum of eighteen weeks paid pregnancy leave. Adequate paternity leave. The right for either parent to take a year's childcare leave after birth, half of which to be paid. No dismissal during pregnancy, paternity or childcare leave. No loss of security, pension or promotion prospects. Paid leave to care for sick children or deal with other family responsibilities to be given to men and women alike.
9. Birth control clinics to be extended to cover every locality. Free and safe abortion, contraception, vasectomy, and sterilization on demand on the NHS.
10. Child benefits to be increased to £5 for each child now. Benefits to be protected against inflation and to be tax-free, and non-deductible from social security, supplementary and insurance benefits.
11. To campaign amongst women to take an active part in trade unions and political life, and to push for any structural and organizational changes needed to achieve this. To campaign amongst trade union men so that they too work to achieve these aims.
    (a) Free membership and the right to participate in all union affairs for all unemployed and those absent from work due to family responsibilities.
    (b) Trade union meetings to be in work time to enable women with family responsibilities to attend. Where this is not possible creche facilities to be provided.
    (c) A campaign in the trade unions to organize women workers.
    (d) The right of women in unions and workplaces to meet together to discuss their problems and needs as women workers and as members of a trade union and to win support for their struggles and demands. This right to be extended to all oppressed groups.
    (e) The adoption of policies of positive discrimination to enable women to participate fully on leading bodies in the trade unions.

In April 1976 it was decided to reorganize the Working Women's Charter Campaign. The new structure consists of a National Secretariat, which is elected by the National Conference, and regional groups. The Secretariat has sub-committees looking at finances, solidarity, publicity and legislation; these meet once a month and report monthly back to the Secretariat. This allows for a great deal of co-operation in co-ordinating campaigns. For example, when the TRICO women were striking (a long and eventually successful strike for equal pay in 1976), the strikers called for demonstrations, and got Charter groups to support them in their struggle.

Money comes from affiliation fees from unions and individuals. National communication is through an internal newsletter produced by the Secretariat. This includes minutes of meetings and directions for action. There is also a bi-monthly paper to spread ideas into different places, which is sold at meetings, factories, and in the streets.

At a local level there are local Charter Groups. There are twenty-five of these at the moment. They take up the demands of the Charter that are applicable to their particular area; and they co-ordinate regional activities such as conferences, rallies, demonstrations.

For information on the national campaign and local charter groups contact:
WORKING WOMEN'S CHARTER CAMPAIGN *1a Camberwell Grove, London SE5*

An Equal Pay and Opportunity Campaign

If you wish to fight for your rights within the unions, you might join a group like EPOC:

EPOC (the Equal Pay and Opportunity Campaign) is a pressure group which includes both men and women who are campaigning for women's rights in employment and within the trade union movement. Four broad aims seem to cover most of their particular areas of concern:

1. to end discrimination *within* the trade union movement: (a) by encouraging rank and file women to join trade unions, to participate more fully in trade union activities, and to take office; and (b) by putting pressure on union officials to encourage women to join and take an active part in their unions;
2. to end discrimination in employment by getting trade unions to put pressure on: (a) employers, by means of negotiation and other traditional methods of influence; and (b) government, through whatever channels unions normally use to communicate their desires and demands to the government;
3. to end discrimination in employment by putting direct pressure on employers to give equal training, equal job opportunities, and equal terms and conditions of employment; and
4. to end discrimination by both employers and trade unions by providing women with practical information, particularly about how to deal with their grievances under the equal pay and sex discrimination legislation.

EQUAL PAY AND OPPORTUNITY CAMPAIGN *20 Canonbury Square, London N1*

Equal Opportunity and Sexuality

Those who do not happen to have the 'right' sexuality are strongly discriminated against, especially at work where they often do not dare unveil their homosexuality. Most of the time they are well justified, as proved by the recent case of Louise Boychuk, a clerk who was found wearing a lesbian badge, and was dismissed for refusing to take it off.

There are a few groups involved in the crucial issue of homosexuality and work, including Gay Liberation Front and the Campaign for Homosexual Equality. There is no specifically *lesbian* national group; but NALGAY provides a good example of what could be done within trade unions.

NALGAY is organized through the National Association of Local Government Officers (NALGO) and is working both to change the position of their union and, in conjunction with other Union Gay Groups, to change the position of the Trade Unions Congress towards sexuality.

It was set up to provide support and welfare to homosexual, bisexual, transvestite and trans-sexual people in NALGO. 'It opposes discrimination against those who do not happen to be heterosexual, and seeks to show both employers and fellow workers that heterosexuality is not the sole natural sexuality as it is so often made out to be.'

Recognized by NALGO as a members' special interest group, NALGAY wants to ensure a full-scale debate on the subject of gay rights, hopefully leading to concrete measures for the future. The union has further stated that it will support any member victimized because of their sexual orientation. The group has its own publication *NALGAY NEWS*.

Though they do not have many women involved at the moment, they would like to appeal more to NALGO women as they see the oppression of gays, on the grounds of their sexuality (both men and women) and the oppression of women, on the grounds of their sex, as part of the general spectrum of sexism.

NALGAY *c/o Howard Hyman, Flat 2, 108 Foxhall Road, Forest Fields, Nottingham*

Racial Discrimination and Women

There is no group (that we know of) of immigrant working women, or that is involved in working specifically with immigrant working women (apart from English language teaching groups). But we want to include something on the subject of immigrant working women because of their increasing number amongst the female labour market and their growing militancy. Like sexism, racism is an issue which trade unions as a whole have failed to tackle.

Immigrant women, particularly those from non-English-speaking countries, are isolated by their colour, their language, their culture and their sex. Because they feel grateful for any kind of work which will bring home badly needed extra cash, because of their lesser ability to find their way around the labour market, and because for some of them conditions in a British factory are so unfamiliar, they are often subject to great exploitation. A Counter Information Services report on Racism gives the example of an Asian woman who works as a cleaner in the foyer of one of the terminals at Heathrow Airport. She works a forty-eight-hour week, much of it shift work, for which she is paid just £29. Although work begins at 6am, her days begins at 4am when the company bus picks her up in Southall. And she pays around £2 a week for this service! And many immigrant people, besides supporting their families, send money home and are very dependent on their jobs.

An immigrant woman is exploited as a worker, as a woman and as a coloured person. Namida Kazi, an Indian community worker, explained it to Amrit Wilson in *Spare Rib*:

> 'Often employers create a situation where they can dismiss people and cheat them out of redundancy pay as well. When a woman who's ill sends a sick note, she may be given warning when she returns. If it happens again, she could be given a written warning or even dismissed. If these cases go to an industrial tribunal, the employers always win. They have better legal representation, and the personnel officer can produce evidence that the woman was warned. Even if she wants to produce witnesses, those witnesses can be intimidated.
>
> 'When the job situation is so bad, it's enough for them to be told "just you watch it". As for the unions, in the case of Asian workers, they are usually on the management side; in racialism there is no sex discrimination!'

Immigrant working women have to face racism at work and a very repressive culture at home. Asian women often cannot go out at night, so cannot attend union or other meetings. To work is often a first step towards independence.

But more and more immigrant women are recognizing their exploitation at work and are fighting it. More and more are going on strike: at Imperial Typewriter, at Decca, at Grunwick . . . Change is slowly happening. A personnel officer in Bradford states it thus: 'Asian ladies are so well behaved, they never complained . . . But just lately I am a bit concerned about some of them . . . *They can be rude.* It is not like Asian ladies to answer back or just walk away.'

For anyone wanting more information on immigrant women at work, the following organizations are worth contacting (in addition to the Equal Opportunities Commission and the Commission for Racial Equality):

RUNNYMEDE TRUST
62 Chandos Place, London WC2
An information agency on race relations which has an industrial unit concerned with action-research on employment issues.

INSTITUTE OF RACE RELATIONS
249 Pentonville Road, London N1
The Institute has a large library and publishes the monthly *Race*.

NATIONAL ORGANIZATION OF AFRICAN, ASIAN AND CARIBBEAN PEOPLES
2nd Floor, 175 Piccadilly, London W1
A central group in touch with many minority organizations.

One of the main needs of immigrant women from non-English-speaking backgrounds is for tuition in basic English. Courses are run at work with the co-operation of employers, and people interested in teaching English can undergo some basic training, and either participate through one of the on-going programmes, or help start something in their area. Anyone interested should contact their local Community Relations Council or the following groups which have developed work-based English tuition programmes:

NATIONAL CENTRE FOR INDUSTRIAL LANGUAGE TRAINING
Pathway Centre, Recreation Ground, Southall, Middlesex
The National Centre has information on industrial language courses being run throughout the country. They publish a range of explanatory leaflets and a collection of unpublished materials devised for these courses.

NEIGHBOURHOOD ENGLISH CLASSES
185 Highgate Road, London NW5
Not a feminist group, but NEC was formed explicitly to deal with the problems of isolation and the need to speak English for immigrant women. Started by a woman, and run by women, it has now grown fairly large and runs language classes for men too.

PROSTITUTION

'If I didn't do it my little boy wouldn't have had the things he wanted and he'd suffer. What other opportunities would I have? Stacking tins of beans on a supermarket shelf for a pittance.'
(A member of PROS)

Prostitution is the 'oldest profession'. Economic circumstances rather than straight greed helps to get women onto the streets in the first place, and keeps them there. Whatever your moral view on prostitution it should be recognized that prostitutes mostly work in very bad conditions. They are also disapproved of socially, harassed by the police and at risk of physical danger. Recently groups of prostitutes have formed to say what *they* think about their work.

Prostitution Laws are Nonsense

PLAN (Prostitution Laws Are Nonsense) is replacing PUSSI (Prostitutes United for Sexual and Social Integration) which Helen Buckingham launched in 1975.

'We feel that PUSSI has served its purpose as a name which got the prostitution issue noticed by the press, but that now we are noticed we would like to be noticed as women of action and not as passive sex objects.

'Prostitutes and other people alike found it difficult to bring themselves to say PUSSI because of its sexual connotations (which were at that time deliberate). The word was chosen because it was the only term of endearment that appears to exist concerning women and sex. All other terms are medical or derogatory.

'We hope that people will find the new name acceptable. PLAN hopes to make or participate in the making of films about prostitution in order to bring the general public

closer to the realities of it, as opposed to the sensationalism which usually surrounds any mention of it. PLAN aims to work for the following reforms:

1. the total abolition of all laws concerning prostitution;
2. that people experiencing persistent nuisance in public places should have recourse to law but should be required to give evidence in court;
3. that the Hotel Act giving managers the right to evict without having to commit themselves to a reason should be repealed;
4. that appropriate publications and agencies should be allowed to advertise sexual services and accept a fee for doing so;
5. that people who sell sexual services should have recourse to the same protective laws which cover other people;
6. that greater effort should be made to provide real alternatives to prostitution rather than the futile attempts to deter or reform women into low-paid jobs.

'The Home Office believes that prostitution should be harassed so that the people of this country can fool themselves that something is being done to stop prostitution.

'As prostitutes we know that certain people in this country do not want to stop prostitution. They want to exploit it. Since 1959, the law has driven us off the streets where we could choose our clients and state our prices, and forced many of us into places which call themselves everything but the brothels they are, so that much more of our earnings go to bosses and less and less come to us.

'Little by little prostitution is being organized, but not by us, the prostitutes. It is being bent so that the maximum profits can be squeezed out of it. Harassing those of us who will walk the streets or cruise the hotels is a good way to make sure that we don't earn any money that can't be taken away from us.

'If you think about it, things have tightened up for us in this so-called permissive society where women are supposed to be free to do their own thing. It's obvious why. We make money out of sex and this could make us economically independent from men. No man likes that. Whether it is the pimps and ponces who push us around as slags, or the police who chase us about as criminals.

'Lawyers tell us we should work from flats, and that as long as we don't advertise nothing will happen to us. Of course it won't, because we won't be doing any business if we don't advertise. If we do, the police are likely to "run in" the magazines concerned or order all the cards out of the windows from time to time.

'There is only one way at the moment by which we can be legally advertised and that is the one way none of us want. Without our permission investigative magazines publish our photographs, names and addresses at the end of articles which describe us as filthy sluts who should be chased off the face of the earth. We all know what kind of woman hater that sort of thing brings running to our doors, to rape us, sneer at us and generally gratify his nasty fantasies at our expense. The Home Office says nothing about this.

'Some of us have turned to the women's liberation movement for sympathy and support, but they do not come out in support. They say that prositution exists for the benefit of men and that they do not want to aid and abet anything which helps men. They are right of course. Men have categorized us for their own convenience and played us off against their wives whilst benefiting from alliances with both us and their wives. We are a class of women who have been deliberately set apart so that we can be quietly and unprotestingly exploited.

'Are we going to wait until some commercially-minded local authority decides to tidy us away into state brothels where they can make us work for them? It is the next logical step. A lot of well-meaning people think it would be very good for us too. Do you?

'Do you know how state brothels are run in, say, places like Nevada? The girls must work fourteen hours a day whether they like it or not, and sign on with the sheriff for *not less than three weeks. How do you fancy having that on your record for life?*

'One day the women's movement will recognize us, but first we have to convince them that we are not campaigning to make prostitution better for men. We are campaigning to get rid of prostitution altogether by decriminalizing *it so that no one can point a finger at any woman who chooses to sell sex rather than work for the usual pittance handed out to women in jobs which women mostly do. One day the laws concerning prostitution will go, but if we are not careful they will be replaced by something much worse.'*

PLAN: Prostitution Laws Are Nonsense *Josephine Butler Clearing House, c/o Chief Librarian, City of London Polytechnic, Calcutta House, Old Castle Street, London E1*

Programme for the Reform of the Law on Soliciting

PROS (Programme for Reform Of the law on Soliciting) is a group of prostitutes, lawyers and social workers campaigning for reform of the law on soliciting. They started working together in the summer of 1976 in Birmingham, convinced that street prostitutes faced daily injustice through the operation of harsh and oppressive laws. PROS aims to work for the following reforms:

1. Abolition of the term 'common prostitute' in legal proceedings
'In England and Wales the act of prostitution, which is taking money for sexual services, is legal. But certain other activities, including loitering for the purposes of prostitution, soliciting, brothel keeping, and living off the earnings of prostitution are all offences. In relation to soliciting and loitering which concern us here, the bare bones of the law is as follows: A woman receives two cautions. Then when she is apprehended by the police for the third time she is charged and brought to court. There the charge is read out in these terms, "I know this woman to be a common prostitute." Penalties are a maxi-mum £50 fine for the first offence, £200 for the second offence, £200 or three months imprisonment for the third offence.

'Starting with the term common prostitute. *We object to this because the use of the word "common" is degrading but also because the use of the phrase has serious legal consequences. When a woman appears in court she is at a disadvantage virtually unknown in any other legal proceedings. She appears before the magistrates with everyone concerned with the working of the court knowing that she is either a convicted prostitute or at least has two cautions for soliciting. In this way she is almost convicted before the hearing begins. This seems to run*

completely counter to the idea of being innocent until proven guilty, which is supposed to underpin English law.'

2. Abolition of the offences of loitering or soliciting for the purpose of prostitution
'The offence of soliciting means that a woman can be charged if it can be shown that she has approached a man and suggested that they "do business". The customer meanwhile can go quietly on his way with no fear of legal proceedings. In the case of loitering all that has to be proved in practice is that a woman is in the street in an area known for prostitution and that she has previous convictions or cautions for soliciting. It is then up to her to prove her innocence and she would need to put forward a very good story indeed to do so. Some idea of the infringement of individual liberties involved can be gained from the comment of one of the members of our group: "Even if you're not doing anything you can still be charged with it once you have set foot outside the house. If you happen to live in a red light area you can be charged if you just walk down the street".'

3. In the short term, abolition of imprisonment
'It seems very excessive and illogical to use imprisonment, the heaviest penalty our society has, as a punishment for soliciting which itself leads to an act which is perfectly legal. There is no proof whatsoever that imprisonment has any deterrent effect either even if you are convinced that there is a need to deter. In the group we are also certain that in most cases there is little or no nuisance value caused by the act of soliciting anyway. However, in human terms imprisonment can result in considerable anguish. Another member of our group takes up this point: "The most horrible thing about prison is that you miss your kids. They have to go into care usually as they won't let your relatives mind them. They think that because you're a prostitute you're not fit to be a mother." Compare this with a comment from a magistrate on a BBC local radio programme on prostitution: "I still believe in longer prison sentences. And their children, if they are proved prostitutes, should be taken off them." Even if you have no children the outcome can be
bleak when you come out of prison. You may have lost your lodgings, your clothes may have gone, and with nothing to start with you have to go straight out on the streets again.'

4. If any form of control of soliciting is required the following measures could be considered
'People experiencing any persistent nuisance in the street would have recourse to the law but be required to make a complaint to the police. A system of graduated fines or other non-custodial measures would be appropriate if such an offence is proved.

'The treatment of any activities resulting in serious nuisance or embarrassment in the street should be the same and we do not think that separate offences are necessary, simply because of the sexual element involved. We also think that the scale of penalties we suggest is ample for such offences. Any person so bothered should be required to be sufficiently moved to make a complaint to the police, rather than have charges rest on police observation and evidence alone as is so often the case with soliciting at present.'

5. Certain streets could be recognized as legitimate red light areas
'Having recognized areas would make the whole proceeding more civilized rather than relegating it to the status of a criminal activity. People who don't want contact with prostitutes or their customers needn't frequent such areas. Street girls would also prefer to retain some independence in how they operate, rather than become caught up in a sex factory which is what legalized brothels could become.'

6. The question of immoral earnings
'We have no specific proposals relating to living off immoral earnings. Two things have to be balanced which could not be contained in a simple proposal. Some women do need protection against violent exploitation by a ponce. Others are in a position of having reasonable relationships with the men they live with. These men face the threat of long prison sentences simply because to a greater or lesser extent they share in what their cohabitee earns from prostitution.'

HOW PROS WORKS

'We meet regularly as a collective. At the start we concentrated on working out a programme that would gain endorsement from other prostitutes in the locality and meanwhile encourage them to think that something could be done to change the law. While making contact with other pros we have produced the first issue of a regular bulletin to spread information about the campaign and its aims and to attract attention to it. The bulletin is being distributed around the networks of pros and supporters we have already acquired.

'PROS 2, our second collective, has started to develop in the Leamington/Coventry area as part of our plan to develop a nationwide network of prostitutes and supporters in the campaign. We are meanwhile following up other contacts which we hope will lead to other branches of PROS forming.

'Prostitutes organizing for themselves is the essential basis of our efforts. But just as individual PROS collectives are formed of prostitutes and other supporters, so PROS as a whole needs to form alliances among other groups who might be in sympathy or be able to offer useful support. In this way we have made contact with local and national politicians, various groups among social workers and among the women's movement.

'It is also crucial that we make an impact generally on people's consciousness of the problems prostitutes face and what PROS's programme offers. So we have gradually increased our involvement with the media and have taken part in interviews with the press and broadcasting.

'Our experience has justified our view that streetgirls are suffering from the stigma that a corrupt and hypocritical society can produce. It took us months to find a permanent address for correspondence and a telephone number. This was because of the risks of recriminations and unpleasant interference to individuals if we used a private address. We found that several "respectable" or philanthropic organizations dared not run the risk of being associated with our enterprise. Eventually the Peace Centre in Birmingham accepted us. Meanwhile our members who are pros continued to run personal risks of extra harassment by the law if their identity is revealed in activities for PROS. People associated with them in their work also run increased risks. Alternatively, trial by rumour or gossip can threaten their families or relatives.

'Some of the people best informed about the plight of prostitutes working on the streets have not been well placed to be allies. Some magistrates, sick of trying to avoid sending women to prison for this offence, have made sympathetic noises. The probation service has yet to make any systematic attempt to take action on a national scale. This is doubtless because of its unusual position in relation to the courts. Nevertheless, we are getting support from individual probation officers.

'Prostitutes are organizing in several countries and we have recently endorsed a campaign against police harassment mounted by "Coyote", the San Francisco movement. A quote from one of the early numbers of their paper, Coyote Growls, sums up the way they see the situation very succinctly: "Incarceration of the prostitute is an object lesson for all women; a woman is put in jail if she capitalizes on the sex system." But let the last word about what this means in personal terms come from one of our members: "You're mainly looked down on by everybody. If people don't know I'm a prostitute I'm perfectly accepted as a friend and as an equal. Once they find out, they'll say 'you knew she was no good from the start'. That is the situation we want to change." '

PROS: **Programme for the Reform Of the law on Soliciting** c/o The Birmingham Peace Centre, 18 Moor Street, Ringway, Birmingham 4

WOMEN IN TRADITIONALLY MALE JOBS

The number of women in traditionally-male jobs is increasing. It is a move which will get more common as a result of the Sex Discrimination Act.

For example, the National Graphical Association would not let women join the union before the Act, so women were unable to get apprenticeships and could not become printers. Now it is illegal to refuse a person for any training scheme or apprenticeship on the grounds of sex, and so there is no reason why a woman shouldn't become a printer and then join the union.

In this section we will see how women are fighting to hold down and be accepted in traditionally-male jobs, and how difficult it is. As one of the women interviewed said: 'In my apprenticeship, I had twenty odd years against me. I was like a new born kid — had I been given a compass instead of a needle at school it would have been easier now. But the struggle is on.'

Carpenter

Ginny is a carpenter; she trained in 1976 and is currently working in a small private firm as the partner of a joiner.

'I decided to be a carpenter when I was working in France, doing general building. I really enjoyed that and decided to take up a specific trade; carpentry was the one I liked most.

'I knew there were some government training schemes in England (TOPS courses) and I applied. It was thirty days before the Sex Discrimination Act came into operation and when I said I wanted to be a carpenter, I was told I could not because I was a "wom . . . wo . . well, if you apply in a month's time it might be different".

'Two months later, when I went for an interview, it was obvious that they had decided beforehand that I was going to be accepted. They weren't going to tangle with the Sex Discrimination Act! I have been lucky; I know of other women who have had a rough time, with interviewers asking tricky questions or just laughing at them.

'The course itself was pretty good in terms of what I learned. The learning situation really stimulated me. When I started there was only one other woman, out of 200 people in the centre, who left after three weeks. The worst thing was the isolation I experienced as a woman. It was not only a numerical isolation. All the men have been conditioned since they were kids to cope with mechanical things — the way bits and pieces fit together. As women we always had soft toys and non-creative games; so I found it much more difficult to get to grips with the basic geometry that the work needed. I always wanted to know everything before I started whereas men would just go on and have the confidence to work out a solution. I suffered very badly from lack of confidence.

'This was made worse because everybody expected me, as a female worker in a male job, to do better. I cannot and I don't think most women can. We can do as well as men but shouldn't be expected to do better.

'The first thing the other trainees say is "poor feeble woman, how are you going to manage heavy weights?" But the point is that when something is too heavy for one person, then two people carry it. Even men don't have to lift such heavy things. One of my friends applied for a course in heavy vehicle repairs. She was accepted only for motor vehicle maintenance because she would not be strong enough for the first course. They all recognized afterwards that she could have done it because there is hydraulic tackle for handling everything.

'Certainly on average woman cannot carry as much as the strongest man, but an average woman can manage as well as an average man — probably better because she will be determined not to give in and he may not be so bothered.

'My six months training was characterized by interminable discussion about women's

roles and housework. They all read the Sun *which has a pin-up on page three. Almost every week, there would be one man asking me: "Don't you think there ought to be men on page 3?" Then I started the eternal argument about women and men not being seen as sex objects.*

'Somehow it is difficult to see how feminist issues came across to them. They were such new ideas, and the men didn't feel threatened anyway. They think that women in their trades will never be numerous, and the ones who want to do it are rather special, freaks in some ways.

'After a while, they decided that I was OK. There was a strong atmosphere, at least in my training centre, of all the trainees getting together against the hierarchy: employees versus bosses.

'Don't get me wrong! The last thing I'd say is that it is easy for women to do this training. Although I didn't get too much sexism from the fellow workers at my workshop, it was not the same story with the men in the other sections. They would whistle at me and make abusive remarks.

'It is difficult to summarize my feelings because on the whole I really enjoyed my training, but there were times when I hated it. I was very conscious of my isolation, and when somebody teased me, I always took it as a specific attack on me as a woman. On the other hand, I was not interested in being one of them, I am not in any way trying to be a man.

'Unemployment in the building industry is very high and the competition stiff. As a female carpenter when I am looking for a job, I am always open to insults; but as a woman doing their jobs, I am doubly open to gross insults and many difficulties. Though I am working at the moment, I would want to find another job with better training facilities. Yesterday I went to an interview with the local council. When I rang up, the man thought I was making enquiries for somebody else, so he said: "give me his name and phone number." When I replied: "It's for me", there was a crushing silence. I could hear the man's brain going round and round thinking "what shall I do? I can't refuse because of the Sex Discrimination Act".

'The interview itself was a nightmare. I knew from the start that my fate was pre-arranged; they did not want any woman. I had this kind of dialogue with the interviewer:

Him: Do you realize that in repair and maintenance, we spend a lot of time repairing men's urinals; that would be a difficult situation, wouldn't it?
Me: *What do you do when you're repairing the women's loos?*
Him: We hang a sign on the door saying 'men working'.
Me: *Don't you think you can put up a sign saying 'women working'?*
Him: Oh!

And later:

Him: You'll have to carry heavy weights and it's not easy.
Me: *I know it's hard, but I know it doesn't happen very often. Besides I want the job and I am a carpenter and know what it entails.*
Him: Listen dear, I'm not trying to put you off, but you will have to carry your tools around . . . !

'Not only local authorities react this way, private firms do too. When you go along for a job, they just laugh and say: "We can't afford to pay for a bit of ornamentation."

'The union is pretty good with me. The branch secretary is quite concerned about my getting a job, and I know the branch would back me up if I was turned down for a job in a discriminatory way. However I know that if I wanted to be a shop steward they'd be scared, they would wonder why men are getting so soft to let women do this job for them. I think joining building unions is a necessary step to improve this situation. It is an important way to get more power.

'More and more women must get into traditionally-male jobs. Eventually they'll have to accept us; at the moment with a high unemployed male workforce, the last person they will take on is a woman.'

Building Worker

During most of 1975, a group of women in London were meeting from time to time to discuss the problems women find in acquiring the skills associated with, and working in, traditional-male jobs.

At the National Women's Conference in April 1976, they held a workshop on the subject. Since then, a number of women who are working or training in one building industry or similar trades have been meeting every fortnight in London.

'We tend to be a support group. We talk a lot about what is happening to us at work. Everybody has got so many stories about all the atrocities during the week. Janet has been sacked for "arguing on site". She is taking the firm to court; "no man would be sacked for arguing; but perhaps what hit me hardest was what the foreman said after he had physically thrown me off the site: 'Right, that proves it, I've learnt my lesson, women are just troublemakers. I'll never employ another woman. You weren't my type anyway!'* "*

'We are trying to discuss what we are doing and why. One thing we feel very strongly about is never to take a lesser wage than a man for the same job. It would be really bad if our behaviour made employers think that they could get a better deal out of us, thinking "here is this woman working really hard, not giving us any trouble about the wages or anything."

'It is women who have to live and work in houses planned by men for men. There's no landscape that any woman can look at that has any woman's hand in it; it goes even down to a park, to the flower beds. We want to work with other women and teach women what we've learned, share skills with a view to gaining more power. *The whole thing of women having more power means that we have to have practical skills as well, to be able to build for example. Women don't have any say in our whole environment from the house we live in, to the bed we sleep in, or the life-style we lead. In fact it seems that no one has any say except the planners (all men)!*

'We are developing practical ideas as to how our experience can be useful to women's liberation. We want to spend quite a lot of time going round to schools, trying to break down sexism, to show how women can be something other than hairdressers. There is nothing wrong with being a hairdresser, but if a girl wants to do something else, she has to know that she can. We have information about what to do if they want to get an apprenticeship, although we don't want to turn into careers officers.'

For more information on Construction Industry Training Board Courses, government courses and the whole subject of women in building, contact the group, which is also keen to talk in schools.

WOMEN IN BUILDING GROUP *c/o A Woman's Place, 42 Earlham Street, London WC2*

Printing Worker

Moss Side Community Press is a small press which provides a vital service to Manchester alternative groups, cheap printing handled by sympathetic people. It is in fact the only alternative press in Manchester. Started seven years ago when there was a sudden burst of alternative activity, it is now used by community papers, claimants unions, tenants groups, and by the women's movement.

In September 1976, Angela, Luchia and Sheila took over the Moss Side Community Press making it one of the few presses run by women in England. They have been friends for years and all three have the same outlook. The Press is run on a non-hierarchical basis and there is a notice on the wall saying: 'The press is a co-op run by women, so please don't ask to see the boss, the supervisor or the manager.' So far only Luchia knows how to operate the fifteen-year-old offset litho A3 press; she had worked there for three years on a voluntary basis learning how to work the machinery from the men who had previously owned it. Now she works full-time and earns a living from the press; the other two are training on a voluntary basis.

We asked them whether they encounter any difficulties as women printers and how they fight against them.

'When the last bloke who worked here left, it was up to Luchia to shape the future. She decided to make it a women's press. She knew a few women who wanted to learn how to print, and it seemed an ideal opportunity to get the idea off the ground.

'As far as the business is concerned, we haven't lost a lot of customers because we are women. People still bring in work with the odd sexist cartoon or comment on it. So far we've been able to sort this out by explaining our position, and we haven't had the same thing happen with the particular group again. We have a constant battle to make people aware of sexism.

'Our biggest difficulty is not to be seen as a cheap option. People just walk in and exploit us without thinking that they do. The consciousness of the Left can be a bit limited as far as we are concerned. They expect us to work ourselves to death for them. We don't want to be merely a cheap service to the Alternative, but as an essential part and expression of it.

'In the future, what we would like to do is to print more women's stuff, political writings and posters; to explain the printing process to other women. We have three Norwegian women coming to see the place because they want to start a women's press there. Since September we have concentrated on making ourselves known to the women's movement. Many women have sent work in and this has meant we've been able to survive, and for the first time we can think about expanding some time in the future.'

MOSS SIDE COMMUNITY PRESS *21a Princess Road, Manchester 14*

Two other women's presses are:
WOMEN IN PRINT *16a Iliffe Yard, London SE17*
THE WOMEN'S PRESS *12 Ellesmere Road, London N1*

Priest

Of all the jobs that women have been barred from, perhaps the most exclusively male occupation is the priesthood. The church may seem to some an unlikely area in which to carry on the struggle for women's rights, but in fact several groups are campaigning for the ordination of women. Pope Paul's ruling early in 1977 that women definitely cannot be ordained priests in the Roman Catholic Church has renewed controversy over this issue. But it is not just another new question thrown up by the current awareness of women's position; women and men within the Christian Churches have been working for the ministry of women for a great many years.

The Anglican Group for the Ordination of Women to the Historic Ministry of the Church is a Church of England group which came into being in 1930; it arose out of an approach made to the Anglican bishops at their annual conference for an enquiry into the alleged reasons against the ordination of women to the ministry.

Women are full members of the church: we are baptized and confirmed just as men are. But men can be ordained as deacon, priest or bishop, that is, they are able to be authorized to fill particular, recognized offices in the church. A woman can be appointed as a lay-worker, deaconess or reader, but we cannot become a deacon, priest or bishop. The Group for the Ordination of Women feel that this should change; they argue that the church needs *all* its resources in these difficult times, including the personal gifts and capabilities of its women members. They also question whether the ordained ministry can be truly representative of the whole church if it does not contain both sexes.

In a pamphlet, *Women and Holy Orders*, the group discusses the changing position of women and how the church has failed to respond to this:

> Throughout history, in many though not all societies, men have played the dominant role. There are many and diverse reasons for this. In such societies thinkers have held the view that women are inferior to men . . . Increasingly today, as more is learned about sex, men and women will be able to decide how much they will conform to traditional social behaviour and how far they will, severally and together, seek to use all their powers to live well together in partnership in families and in society. They could also do this, if they would, in the life of the church.
>
> Science and technology today are changing all societies in different ways and at different rates. Many of these changes are welcomed by thoughtful people as being of permanent value for human life; among such changes is the developing role of women . . . women are challenged to play a more significant role in public life, in work and in society. Meanwhile many men are enjoying more significant roles as husbands and fathers. This makes heavy demands on both sexes, there are many emotional and other strains. There are gains and losses. But we cannot put the clock back. To refuse to face the facts creates strains and stresses too. These changes which are coming gradually are related to a new recognition of women as persons. Many people believe that the Christian faith in God and man has been influential in bringing about these changes. They look to the church for leadership in the situation but – alas – they find that it has not accepted the new knowledge nor the social changes. The Church lags behind and hopes vainly that it can withstand the trends, or that they will be only temporary. So the Church continues to refuse to allow women to share the responsibilities with men in the lay and the ordained ministries.

Gradually, the church's position on this question has been changing; women's work in the church has been the subject of recurrent debate, and successive Archbishops have set up Commissions to consider the theological implications. Meanwhile, other churches have made their decisions. In 1968, two women were ordained to the priesthood of the Church of Sweden. In 1971, two women were ordained by the Bishop of Hong Kong. And theological colleges have opened their doors to women.

On 3 July 1975, the General Synod (the governing body of the Church of England) agreed that: 'There are no fundamental objections to the ordination of women to the priesthood.' The Bishop of Winchester, one of the speakers in the debate, asserted that: 'The responsibility for the life of this world cannot safely be left in purely male hands, for they are too authoritarian, too manipulative and too ready to turn our God-given dominion into raw domination.' However, no women have yet been ordained in this country, and the Anglican Group for the Ordination of Women carries on its work, seeking to build up an informed public opinion on the question, and to bring together and support those women who believe themselves to be called to Holy Orders.

Membership of the group is open to any man or woman who, being a communicant member of the Church of England, believes it reasonable and desirable that women should be ordained, and is prepared to give active support to the aims and methods of the group. *Further information and list of publications from:*

ANGLICAN GROUP FOR THE ORDINATION OF WOMEN *Hon. Secretary, Guillard's Oak House, Midhurst, Sussex*

SOCIETY FOR THE MINISTRY OF WOMEN IN THE CHURCH *Hon. Secretary, The Little House, Brownshill, Near Stroud, Glos.*
This is an interdenominational group working for the ordination of women. It was founded in 1929 and continues the work of an earlier body which has been advocating the ordination of women since 1918.

Maintenance Engineer

One Friday night it happened, some years after we were wed
When my old man came home from work, as usual I said:
'Your tea is on the table, clean clothes are on the rack
Your bath'll soon be ready, I'll come up and scrub your back.'
He kissed me very tenderly and said 'I'll tell you flat —
The service I give my machine ain't half as good as that' . . .

Chorus
**I said 'I'm not your little woman, your sweetheart or your dear
I'm a wage slave without wages, I'm a maintenance engineer.'**

Well then we got to talking, I told him how I felt
How I keep him running just as smooth as some conveyor belt.
For after all, it's I'm the one provides the power supply
(He goes just like the clappers on my steak and kidney pie)
His fittings are all shining cos I keep 'em nice and clean
And he tells me his machine tool is the best I've ever seen . . .

The terms of my employment would make your hair turn grey
I have to be on call you see for twenty-four hours a day.
I quite enjoy the perks though when I'm working through the night
For we get satisfaction — well, he will and then I might.
If I keep up full production I shall have a kid or two
So some future boss can have a brand new labour force to screw . . .

The truth began to dawn then how I keep him fit and trim
So the boss can make a nice fat profit out of me and him.
And as a solid union man he got in quite a rage
To think that we're both working hard and getting one man's wage
I said 'And what about the part-time packing job I do?
That's three men that I work for love, my boss, your boss and YOU . . .

He looked a little sheepish and he said 'As from today
The lads and me will see what we can do on equal pay.
Would you like a housewives union, do you think you should be paid
As a cook and as a cleaner, as a nurse and as a maid?'
I said 'Don't jump the gun, love, if you did your share at home
Perhaps I'd have the time to fight some battles of my own' . . .

I've often heard you tell me how you'll pull the bosses down
You'll never do it brother while you're bossing ME around.
Till women join the struggle, married, single, white or black
You're fighting with a blindfold and one arm behind your back.
The message has got over, he has realized at last
That power to the sisters must mean power to the class . . .

(by Sandra Kerr)

WOMEN WORKING AT HOME

Homeworking

Homeworkers are generally women who cannot work away from their homes either because they have sole responsibility for the care of young children or aged relatives or because they are disabled.

The work, which ranges from dressmaking, knitting and crocheting to packing contraceptives, finishing and assembling fishing rods and painting small toys, almost invariably involves sacrificing a good deal of family living space for storage and work.

The Victorians called homework 'sweated labour'. Since early this century, numerous attempts have been made to bring attention to the homeworkers' plight, the most famous being the *Daily Mail* 'Sweated Trades' exhibition in London in 1906. A Royal Commission was even set up and the Women's Trade Union League was active in publicizing the abuses. But in the boom years of the 1950s and 1960s the matter lapsed. Yet homeworking still persists and has changed little in essence since the days of the Victorians. In England today, homeworkers have been estimated to earn as little as an average £5 for a working week of up to sixty hours.

Despite the low rates of pay, there is competition for such work, largely because homeworkers form a captive labour force with no other possibility for employment open to them.

Very few are members of a trade union and they constitute an easy prey for the industrial market. They are often afraid to publicize their bad conditions because they have not declared their earnings to Social Security. Homeworkers have always had the dubious privilege of being self-employed, and so carrying the cost of heating, lighting and maintenance during the slack seasons. This status relieves employers of the responsibility for providing sick pay, pensions and payment of National Insurance contributions.

A women's group in London quotes the following case. A woman was employed by a pregnancy testing agency to assemble urine sample bottles at the rate of £1.64 per 1,000. It took her and her two children approximately three hours to assemble 1,000 bottles, which were then used for pregnancy tests at £3 each. The homeworkers were not informed of the need for care in handling bottles and as a result of haphazard methods of assembly, the bottles were often contaminated leading to wrong results in pregnancy tests.

The group determined to expose this double exploitation of women. They set about getting information on the company; they advertised in local shops and on local and national radio to find other homeworkers doing the same work, and one of the group worked inside the laboratory for several days. Unfortunately just as they finished their research with evidence of low safety standards and wage rates, the firm upped and moved to Stevenage.

(Source: *Live Wire No. 2*)

The London Homeworking Campaign, set up in 1976, aims 'to bring homework out of the twilight world of semi-legality, where women frequently work long hours for little money under bad, if not hazardous conditions, by campaigning for the recognition of homeworkers as "employees" with the same rights as factory and office workers, and by fighting for decent social conditions to end the need for taking in homework.' Homework should be a real choice rather than a forced necessity.

The Campaign has brought together trade unions and community organizations; it does not anticipate immediate results, and it expects to have to campaign over a period of at least ten years.

They pledge themselves to agitate and organize for:

1. *Decent pay and conditions for those who work at home*

   Full status of 'employee' for homeworkers, and the extension of existing protective legislation to cover homeworkers (for example, Health and Safety at Work, Employment Protection Act).

   Extension of trade union organization to cover homeworking, and the full involvement of homeworkers in trade unions.

   Full information on homeworking, and the rights of homeworkers to be widely publicized.

   Enforced obligation on employers to provide statistical details of homework to the Department of Employment. Lists of homeworkers to be made available, through a responsible local agency, to trade unions and others concerned to ensure the rights of homeworkers.

   Pay equal to rates of unionized factory workers, plus a homework premium to cover overhead costs.

2. *Decent social provision to end the necessity for homeworking*

   Improved local authority provision for daytime care of young children, pre-school and school-aged children (after school and during school holidays), for daycare of handicapped and elderly dependants, and for English language training for immigrants.

   State benefits (Family Allowance, Family Income Supplement, Supplementary Benefit) to be raised to realistic levels to end the financial necessity of taking in homework.

   Extension of Government Training Programmes with pay.

   Enforcement of employers' disabled workers quotas.

A few campaigns are being launched in other areas. You may find details in your local community paper.

LONDON HOMEWORKING CAMPAIGN *214 Stapleton Hall Road, London N4*

Another contact is:

LOW PAY UNIT *9 Poland Street, London W1*
A group which has been compiling research on low paid jobs, including homeworking, and which now publishes a magazine for homeworkers and is attempting to organise them to press for more satisfactory levels of pay.

Wages for Housework

'THEY SAY IT IS LOVE; WE SAY IT IS UNWAGED WORK
THEY CALL IT FRIGIDITY: WE CALL IT ABSENTEEISM.
NEUROSES, SUICIDE, DESEXUALIZATION: OCCUPATIONAL DISEASES OF THE
HOUSEWIFE.'

(S. Federeci, *Wages against Housework*)

Women are all exploited in one fundamental way: they do unwaged work at home. Therefore some people are arguing that housewives should be paid. Women's housework is essential to the nation; it raises new workers and 'maintains' the others. But yet this work is not paid, it is seen as a 'natural feminine function'. Not for a man though; the British government allows a man a housekeeping tax allowance when he is caring for children alone. However there is no housekeeping tax allowance when a woman does the same, alone. The assumption here is that a man *must* go out to work to earn a wage and therefore the services of the wife should be replaced at least to some degree by the housekeeping tax allowance; but there is no such assumption for a woman.

A movement from America, called 'Wages for Housework', has spread to England. In 1976, the Wages for Housework Committee in London organized and launched a family allowance petition. The demands of that petition were: first of all, family allowances to be increased to catch up with prices; secondly, family allowances to be paid for the first child; and thirdly, that the family allowance be tax free (that the man not be taxed on the money that belongs to a woman). Finally, a wage for housework for all women to be paid by the government:

'Everywhere in the world women have been resisting the attempts of governments to lay the burdens of the crisis economy on the doorstep of those who already work so hard for so little — women. We have defended every penny that we and our mothers and grandmothers have won: family allowance, social security, grants, pensions, wages on our outside jobs. And every social service that we need to free us from a little of our workload, from being 'on call' 24 hours a day.

'The Wages for Housework campaign internationally (in England, Italy, Germany, Switzerland, Austria, New Zealand, USA, Canada . . .) has spearheaded women's resistance to these cuts. It has been successful in many cases in defending what we have and pushing for more. All of this is part of the campaign for a full wage for all women, with or without children, with or without a second job, a job on top of housework. We want this wage from the government, which depends on us to bring up and maintain every generation of workers, including ourselves.'

The following is a letter that was sent to the Chancellor of the Exchequer by the campaign in Britain. The petition referred to in the letter was circulated by women among neighbours and workmates, and at street events, where we got together to hear music, speeches and puppet theatre and discuss our situation. A deputation of about sixty women and children handed it in at Downing Street on Mother's Day 1977 with over 10,000 signatures.

February 22nd 1977

Dear Mr Healey,

We are writing to you on behalf of the thousands of women who have signed the enclosed petition demanding increased Family Allowance and wages for housework for all women from the government. We are writing to request a meeting with you.

Everyone knows that the social contract is now being challenged by thousands of paid workers. No doubt you will be meeting with trade unions and others who claim to represent these workers. But if you really want to know what is happening to workers in this country, you will have to meet with women.

The social contract has always rested on women's shoulders. You must be aware that when prices go up and wages are held down it is *women* who do the extra work of shopping around, cooking and stretching to make ends meet. When hospitals and nurseries close it is *women* who take over the nursing and caring — for free. And *women* are refusing to accept this 'contract' which is always at our expense. Those of us who live with men are pushing them to get more money. And women in every situation are demanding money in our own right for the work *we* do, the work which is always taken for granted . . . until it's not done.

You must be aware of women's widespread anger at the con of the Child Benefit scheme. What can a £1 rise mean nowadays, except that mothers are not worth very much? And what does £1.50 mean to single mothers, when most of it goes straight back to the tax man, *or all of it* straight back to the DHSS?

Year after year we women have been forced to fit our budget to yours. *We feel strongly that the time has come for you to fit your Budget to ours.* We will be coming together on March 20th to celebrate Mother's Day and to discuss the question so many women are raising: 'When's Pay Day?' A deputation from that meeting would be glad to meet with you any time the following week.

Please let us know as soon as possible what date is convenient to you as we will have to make arrangements for babysitters and to take time off from work.

Yours sincerely,

signed: Selma James (Wages for Housework Committee)

It is true that the role of a housewife must be recognized as a full-time job and not simply as an enjoyable way of spending one's life while the poor husband is slaving away at work. Child-rearing and housework must be re-evaluated and shared between men and women. But the slogan 'Wages for Housework' raises a lot of opposition. Many women are not interested in their household and child-rearing, at least as their only job, whether paid or not.

We reproduce here a paragraph on Wages for Housework written by 'A Woman's Right to Work' (one group in the Working Women's Charter Campaign) because it summarized briefly the opposition to Wages for Housework, which then gives its reply:

'The slogan "Wages for Housework" is an empty and defeatist one because it does not take up the questions of nurseries, equal pay, abortion on demand, extensive contraceptive facilities which are the necessities for equality, but it reinforces women's oppression in the home by confirming it. A wage, however minimal (or however generous for that matter), would simply confirm that a woman's natural place is to care for the worker and to bring up future workers. Rather than accept that a woman's rightful place is in the home and all that we are lacking is a state-paid wage, we must fight for housework to be socialized, for cheap communal eating places, laundry facilities, which will be linked to our demands for nurseries, and other facilities. We shall be fighting for women and men to collectivize work in the home and for the private burdens of housework and cooking to be social-ized.'

Wages for Housework's reply:

'The right to work is the only right women are born with. We start working from babyhood when they put a dust pan in our hands to "help mummy". And the first problem women face in demanding what we are due is that this work, housework, isn't seen to be work at all. Not by the man who comes home, puts his feet up and says "What have you been doing all day?" And not by those on the left, women and men alike, who say women should get out of the house and "into production".

'*From the moment we demanded a wage for it, housework stopped being invisible. Wherever the Wages for Housework campaign is, people are discussing housework. It can no longer be seen as a woman's nature to mop up spills, remember to buy the toilet rolls, comfort crying children, be the "office wife". The demand for money has made clear that housework is a job like any other,* that we can refuse like any other, *and that no one can take us for granted any longer.*

'*Like other workers, women are refusing more and more to work our lives away. In many ways we've cut down on the housework we do, refusing to get married, deciding not to have children, insisting that men pull some weight in the house, insisting on a washing machine. But all of us, married or single, are still housewives, and expected to mother everyone, at home and wherever we go.* And like every other worker we are using the work we do (and our increasing refusal to do it) to back up our demands for what we need.

'*The more money we get at home and the less we are forced to slave there, the stronger the position we are in outside the house as well. For generations we've had to fight employers, unions, and our own husbands for the right to go out to a paid job. But what we are after is not the work. We have plenty of that already, and anyway who* really *likes putting labels on millions of tins of beans, typing thousands of letters, changing hospital sheets as well as our own sheets?*

'*We go out to work for the company of other women and for the money. The job is hardly an ideal place for a social life but it's better than the loneliness we face a lot of the time working at home. And with inflation few women can manage on the money a man brings in . . . if there is a man. Often now even with a family, a woman has no choice but to go out to earn a wage; it's become an additional part of the housewife's job. But we also want the money for our independence. A wage of our own is the first thing we need if we want to live without a man. And as millions of women testify, if we live with a man, having our own wage is the best weapon to put him in his place and to break his power to make us do the housework.*

'*Yet everywhere the wage we women get is low (on average not much more than a half of what men get, despite what they call "equal pay" laws). This is not an accident, it is directly a result of the fact that we work at home for no wages. Our time is considered to have no value, our skills are not considered skills. We can't count on the men we work with to see our needs and our wages as important: they treat us as subordinates like they can treat their own wives and sisters at home. The unions think our right to work means the right to cheap labour. And above all, employers know, and never lose a chance to tell us, that there are thousands of women at home without a penny of their own who'd be glad to take our job if we don't like it. We've been forced to compete with each other and hang on to jobs we hate, as our only way to get the cash we need and our independence from men. And that holds wages down.*

'*Our strongest lever against this trap has been the money we've managed to win for ourselves independent of the outside job. The more wages we get without a second job the more we can win with one. Even the minimal wages for housework we get now in the form of Social Security has helped women who work outside the home to push their wages up. Employers know they're not a woman's only choice and women are making plain that they're no knights on white chargers. Of course, we have a right to go out to work, but many of us are in a position to make clear that we don't intend to be* forced *to do so, by lack of money or anything else.*

'*Just as Wages for Housework puts us in a stronger position to demand more in our waged jobs, it also strengthens our demands for nurseries, abortion, good health care, the right to live and sleep with other women. These are battles that have been sectioned off and isolated from each other, as for instance young mothers have been separated from pensioners, and lesbians from other women. But our basic weakness is the unpaid housework all of us do. Wages for Housework is a campaign for all women.*

'*We're entitled to nurseries not as a favour (the state is never 'generous', everything they have they got by robbing what we've produced), and not on condition we go out to a second job, but because like every other worker, a mother is entitled to time* off. *And when we fight for abortion, we're entitled also to the right to have children; which means first an end to forced sterilization in Britain and abroad, and second the right to the money we need to keep those children.*

'*Finally the "Woman's Right to Work" want housework socialized. Much of it already is. Schools, hospitals, restaurants, food factories are all housework factories where women are the main producers — at "housework wages", and women, children, and men are the products, and treated as such. If the Right to Work want to fight to extend the communal canteens that Chinese women and men have so roundly rejected, we're sure they'll find plenty of enlightened state planners who'll agree it's a good plan to increase productivity . . . and perhaps even "free" more mothers for the assembly line. Meanwhile the rest of us women will continue to fight, as the working class has always fought, for the money to socialize on* our *terms. Surely, if we have a right to go out to work we also have a right to go out somewhere other than work — and as everyone who's been on a bus lately knows, you need money to exercise that right.*'

The issue of Wages for Housework is very complicated. It is a debate worth expanding. To its credit we must say that it calls into question the notion of work and especially of 'productive' work, and that housework and child-rearing are productive work.

But there is a real danger that Wages for Housework would confirm women's servitude rather than eliminate it. It does not recognize *alternative ways of working* both inside and outside the home which would not be so oppressive. We should be fighting for a society where work is not just an unpleasant burden for which the only reward is *money*. A wage has never transformed a boring job into an exciting one.

WAGES FOR HOUSEWORK CAMPAIGN   *20 Staverton Road, London NW2*

And the campaign has two regional groups:

BRISTOL WAGES FOR HOUSEWORK GROUP   *79 Richmond Road, Montpelier, Bristol 6*

CAMBRIDGE WAGES FOR HOUSEWORK GROUP   *19 City Road, Cambridge*

For more information contact:

POWER OF WOMEN COLLECTIVE
64 Larch Road, London NW2
Read *All Work and No Pay*, published by the Collective, 70p

WAGES DUE LESBIANS
59 Wrottesley Road, London NW10

FALLING WALL PRESS
79 Richmond Road, Montpelier, Bristol 6
The press publishes and distributes information on Wages for Housework in this country and internationally. See in particular *Wages Against Housework* by S. Federeci, 10p, and *Power of Women and the Subversion of the Community* by M. Della Costa and S. James, 35p.

WOMEN AT WORK: OTHER RESOURCES

THE NATIONAL JOINT COMMITTEE OF WORKING WOMEN'S ORGANIZATIONS
Transport House, Smith Square, London SW1
The Committee is a representative body from the trade unions,the co-operative and Labour Parties. Its job is to work for the improvement of the status of women. The Committee sets up studies and will pressurize on any local, national or international committee established by the government or other authorities to deal with matters in which women have a special interest, for example women's education, Sex Discrimination Act, abortion, Social Security Pensions Act, value added tax on sanitary ware, health for women, energy prices, child benefit scheme.

WAGES COUNCILS
Wages Councils have been set up by government to establish a national minimum wage. They cover an enormously varied group of trades (mainly in the retail trade, catering and clothing industry) such as hairdressers, staff of work canteens, booksellers, bakers and newsagents. Contact the nearest office of the Wages Inspectorate or write to the Secretary of the Wages Council, 12 St James's Square, London SW1.

LOW PAY UNIT
9 Poland Street, London W1
As the name suggests the Unit mainly concerns itself with the problem of low pay for both men and women. Recent statistics released by the government show that 20 per cent of low-paid men and 40 per cent of low-paid women are employed in the forty-six industries covered by wages council machinery. This is despite the fact that these industries employ only one in eight of the total labour force. The Low Pay Unit is particularly concerned with the wages council industries, such as hotels and catering, laundries, hairdressing, etc. It attempts to assist the independent members of the various wages councils by sending them the Low Pay Bulletin which appears every two months and in certain cases more detailed studies of their particular industry. They have a series of memoranda, papers and pamphlets available.

NATIONAL ADVISORY CENTRE ON CAREERS FOR WOMEN
251 Brompton Road, London SW3
NACCW specializes in advising girls and women about careers and training. Schools are encouraged to join and seek career guidance for their students, and the service is also available to older women. They have published a book *Returners* which is useful to women considering re-starting or starting careers. Price 85p post free.

Although a charity, NACCW has no state aid and charges membership and advisory fees. It has a small loan fund which provides interest-free loans to students with special needs when state grants do not apply.

SOCIETY FOR PROMOTING THE TRAINING OF WOMEN
Court Farm, Hedgerley, Slough, Bucks
SPTW offers interest-free loans to women only, repayable when you start earning.

FURTHER READING

DANGER! WOMEN AT WORK
by Patricia Hewitt, from National Council for Civil Liberties, 186 Kings Cross Road, London WC1, 30p
This NCCL pamphlet is a report of a 1974 conference. It provides a summary of the arguments and ideas about women and work, and is a good handbook of information on the situation of women at work.

WOMEN AND WORK
RACISM – WHO PROFITS?
both from Counter Information Services, 9 Poland Street, London W1, 45p each
These are two of a series of special crisis reports on the economic cuts of 1975–77, produced by a group that specializes in providing the information normally left out of stories. The reports are full of statistics and facts, but not academic or boring. These two reports are extremely useful, and are recommended to anyone interested in the subject.

WOMEN WORKERS IN BRITAIN: A Handbook
by Leonora Lloyd, Socialist Woman Publications, 182 Pentonville Road, London N1, 25p
A handbook of information on the number of women workers, where they work, what they earn.

LIFE AS WE HAVE KNOWN IT
Co-operation of Working Women, Virago, £1.50
This classic first-hand account of working women's lives has just been reprinted by Virago. The lives, experiences and aspirations recorded here, spanning the 1850s to the early decades of this century, make fascinating reading.

SPARE RIB
27 Clerkenwell Close, London EC1
Spare Rib has published a lot of interesting articles on this subject. See in particular 'Women's Work' (No. 16 and No. 47), 'The History of the Housewife' (No. 26), 'Shared Housework' (No.25) and 'Asian Women Speak Out' (No. 52).

PROSTITUTION PAPERS
by Kate Millett, Paladin, 50p
This book is made up of outspoken discussions with prostitutes. It attacks the society which neglects the exploitation of women in prostitution: 'Masochism is part of the female role. It's feminine and I've been trained into it, even unconsciously.' Prostitution is not just a commercial transaction; the customer buys the prostitute's loss of free speech and her humiliation as well. A good book.

WOMEN'S TWO ROLES: HOME AND WORK
by A. Myrdal and V. Klein, Routledge and Kegan Paul, £2

WOMEN AT WORK
by Lindsey Mackie and Polly Patullo, Tavistock Publications, £2.20
'Most women workers are society's handmaidens: they make clothes not cars, care for the sick rather than cure them, serve in restaurants not parliament . . . We found very little evidence that enough effort is being made to change all this.'

NIGHT CLEANERS
a special issue of Shrew (Vol. 3 No. 9 Dec. 1971), from Shrew, c/o A Woman's Place, 42 Earlham Street, London WC2
A thorough and fascinating discussion of the campaign initiated by feminists to organize the women who work nights for London contract cleaners. A copy is also available at the Women's Research and Resources Centre, 27 Clerkenwell Close, London EC1. The Other Cinema distribute a series of two films made by Marc Karlin on the nightcleaners' struggle called 'The Night Cleaners'. The photography is a bit tricksy, but again this provides a fascinating first-hand account of the struggle with insights into the role of the women's movement in stimulating and supporting it.

WEDLOCKED WOMEN
by Lee Comer, Feminist Books, £1
This book describes the real mechanics of female oppression as it is experienced by the great mass of women in their role as housewives and mothers; highly recommended.

HOUSEWIFE
by Anne Oakley, Penguin, 80p
The phenomenon of 'housewifery' is a new one Never before, has work been split between home and outside the home as it is now. The author studies women's roles in pre-industrial society, and housewives and their work today.   An interesting book.

FINDING A VOICE: Asian Women in Britain
by Amrit Wilson, Virago, £2.50
A recent book on what it is to be an immigrant, a woman and a worker, caught between two cultures.

PATTERNS OF DISCRIMINATION AGAINST WOMEN IN THE FILM AND TV INDUSTRY
Association of Cinematographic, Television and Allied Technicians, 2 Soho Square, London W1
A report by Sarah Benton published in 1975.

RELATIONSHIPS & LIFESTYLES 3

RELATIONSHIPS AND LIFESTYLES

Beginning to take control of our lives must start in our homes. It is essential to live in an environment where we are respected, and where we have equal rights and responsibilities. This can give us the strength and support we need to face a world that generally does not grant us this equality. The traditional institutions of marriage and the family can deny us those rights and frustrate our attempts to become independent women.

Most people live in what is known as a nuclear family: a husband, a wife and two or three children. In this family, traditionally, the man goes to work and the woman is responsible for general household tasks as well as for childcare. (If the woman works outside the home, she is usually still responsible for housework as well.) The woman has been 'taught' to expect and enjoy this way of life, and therefore to find fulfilment in having nice children, a clean house and being a good cook. The family is where we learn our values and so ideas about the position of women are passed on from generation to generation.

Women who, either by choice, accident or necessity do not live within the pattern of the nuclear family are often punished by society and pay a heavy price for their non-conformity (for example: it is almost impossible for single mothers to find houses to live in; lesbian mothers are usually not allowed custody of their children; and it is *still* socially unacceptable for women to go to places of entertainment on their own, whether they be single, widowed or divorced).

This chapter attempts to show the positive steps women are taking towards controlling their relationships and the manner in which they live. The choices about who a woman lives with can be many and varied depending on the individual, and they need not be seen as situations that have to last forever. People change and, as their needs change, so will their living situations.

Many people are making fundamental changes within the structure of their marriages; some are choosing to forget marriage altogether and live as a group, and in some cases raise their children together; some women are finding that living with and loving only women is fulfilling in more ways than having relationships with men.

We have said that it isn't easy to live outside norms: people who do this can suffer. This has led to the growth of self-help organizations that are fighting for legal and social changes for groups such as single-parent families and lesbian mothers. These organizations recognize the importance of support from people experiencing similar difficulties with the authorities, with the law and in their homes.

Change is needed in all aspects of our lives. To change laws is simply not enough; attitudes must also be re-evaluated. Women should be able to choose their life-styles and relationships without having to combat unbearable social pressure.

MARRIAGE

One Woman's Marriage

Anna and Mark, who come from working-class backgrounds, have known each other for ten years, and have been married for seven; they live in a Yorkshire town with their five-year-old son, Andrew.   Mark works full-time as a community worker; Anna is very active in local women's movement activities.

Since they have been together their relationship has gone through many changes. We talked to Anna about her marriage:

'I never wanted to be a wife, I wanted to be an artist. I kept telling myself and my friends I'd never get married, marriage seemed really awful. Looking around at the married people I knew, it seemed like a recipe for hating somebody.

'But then I met Mark and we began to live together. I was pretty strong in myself when I first met him; I don't think I felt oppressed by him. I felt worse about the way I was, not getting things together, being really messy and sloppy. Everything we did, all the housework, was shared equally; Mark even did his own laundry. I was careful not to slot into the "wife" role, I wanted to remain an individual.

'When we did decide to marry it was basically for practical reasons. I was coming off the pill, and we thought that if I did get pregnant it would be better for the child if we were married; we didn't know other people who were bringing up kids without being married (if we'd had even one or two examples, we probably wouldn't have got married). At the time it seemed too hard, not to get married, too much to take on; we thought life would be easier if we were a bit more conventional.'

Soon after they married, Anna became pregnant; at this time she and Mark were making a living doing Punch and Judy shows on the beach. At first the birth of a child didn't alter their relationship too much:

'I didn't have anything like the post-natal blues because I wasn't left alone, we were sharing Andrew then. For the first two weeks I stayed at home while Mark went off, but I couldn't stand it, so I started going to the beach with him and that went well.

'He was more maternal towards the baby than I was. If the baby cried, he'd drop everything, whereas I'd often think, "Oh hell, what's it on about now". I think it's an innate thing in him; if we lived in a society where I could work for a decent wage, he'd be better looking after the child.

'Things began to change when Mark got a full-time job that he felt involved in and committed to. About a year or so later I suddenly realized that things had changed between us. We'd got into the usual stereotype of the man going out to work and the woman staying at home; all day long I'd be looking forward to him coming home, and when he did he'd feel drained and tired and would be very critical of me. For instance, in the past, if he'd come home and found me reading a book, he'd comment on what a difficult book it was and how he couldn't possibly read something that hard. Now he'd come in and say, "Look at the state of the kitchen, what are you doing reading?"

'At the time I didn't think things were terrible between us, I just used to make the best of it. I blamed myself for a lot of it: I thought if only I was tidier or a more together woman, I would get everything done. I was totally dependent on him, and the more dependent I became the less power I had. If he was critical of me I wouldn't answer him back, because I had no power, so he just got worse. I wasn't like the woman he'd first met; he'd respected me then because I'd stood up for myself, but now I was becoming the woman he definitely didn't want to know: the housewife.'

Anna sees her financial dependence on Mark as a central part of their problems:

'I don't see how I can have any freedom until I can earn my own living. But there's no sort of job I could get that would justify me getting it; I can't earn as much as Mark can. Since we met, he's done a lot of interesting things. When he fills in a job application, he's got qualifications and experience that he's gained while I stayed at home and looked after the child.'

Anna started going to a women's liberation group and began to realize that her problems were common to many women:

'I saw that the reasons why I was so fed up and couldn't cope with the housework were valid reasons. It was an impossible situation. I remember one day writing down how much work I did in a week. I was really amazed, it was something like eighty hours, and that was just the child care! I really am working hard, so how come I feel so guilty?

'Mark helps with the housework more now. He's always intellectually believed in women's liberation. He tried not to put me down, but it's hard if you're the person on top always to be aware of when you are being oppressive. It's not his fault, just an occupational hazard of being a man, I guess.

'Going to a women's group made our marriage better; it made me feel more positive, and in that way made our relationship more positive. This is quite different from the "Wife runs off with women's liberation group" attitude you sometimes read in the papers.'

Anna is now trying very hard to make herself financially independent by taking in lodgers and developing her craft skills. She has made many friends through the women's movement and gets a great deal of support from these friends. Nevertheless she feels that she still has problems to work on:

'I still feel that I don't assert myself enough, that I allow myself to be oppressed. There are things I do for Mark that I probably wouldn't do for a person I was living with as a separate individual. I think that over time this will happen less, but change is quite gradual.'

The problems of living traditionally as a couple are many, and some of these can be seen by the conflicts that Anna is faced with. Besides someone always having to take care of the child there is the cooking, cleaning, washing and shopping to worry about. Because it is usually the woman who stays home while the man goes to work, these jobs become the woman's work (though this is rarely acknowledged and she is never paid for what she does). Anna is fortunate in the sense that Mark is understanding and aware of the difficulties of their situation, and together they are trying to work out these problems; but for many women, there is not this support and understanding and they have to cope with these problems by themselves.

When the Going gets too much to handle by yourselves

No matter what life-style you choose, there is almost no way that you will escape having difficulties. If you live with other people as a couple or in a group there may be personality conflicts, or sexual problems that cause all sorts of other tensions. If you live alone this may cause a number of problems that you find difficult to deal with. Often these problems can be dealt with by talking to other people or sometimes by the passage of time. Sometime relationships are open enough for problems to be talked about freely, thereby alleviating tensions. But many people feel that an outside observer, a friendly ear, would be most welcome.

Until recently the National Marriage Guidance Council has been seen as a place to go only if you are having marriage problems. But most councils today are trying to change their image and deal with couples, married or non-married, heterosexual or homosexual, and groups and individuals as well. Most local Marriage Guidance Councils, although affiliated to the National Council, are financially independent and make their own policy. A unique thing that Marriage Guidance Councils offer is the opportunity for people in the surrounding community to get actively involved in counselling. The Marriage Guidance Council offers a very thorough and highly professional training programme for its counsellors.

'The commitment is tremendous,' says Dorothy Johnson, organizing secretary of the Leeds MGC, *'the training programme is officially two years, but in practice it takes about two-and-a-half. This includes six training weekends, in-service training, meetings with fellow counsellors, regular tutorials with a personal supervisor, and there is a reading programme to keep up with. In the booklet given to prospective counsellors, it says that the average time is seven or eight hours a week, but it can take easily twelve hours or more.*

'The type of person who approaches us to become a counsellor has changed. We used to have a high proportion of women who had no other job, but now we have more professional people applying, men as well as women. Also in the past if you were divorced or separated you had very little chance of being accepted, but now the criteria for selection have changed and your divorce, separation, single status or religious belief has no significance.

'We are looking for people with flexibility of attitude, approachable and sympathetic, with experience of other people and the problems they face. Age is important; we rarely select anyone under twenty or over fifty.

'After two local interviews, a candidate has to attend a rigorous day-long selection conference at the National Marriage Guidance College in Rugby.'

Even though Marriage Guidance Councils are willing to counsel anyone who comes to them, they see very few non-married couples and few individuals. In Leeds, out of the 800 clients in 1975, only twenty-seven were not married. The problems, whether married or not, remain similar:

'Generally the problem that is presented is a relationship difficulty, and nearly always there is an underlying sexual problem. Sometimes infidelity is the problem, but that is not as common as it was in the fifties. Nearly always there is a lack of communication between the partners.

'I think it is easier to counsel a couple, as there are many problems in dealing with face-to-face counselling if only one partner is there: the other partner is wondering what is going on, and the counsellor only hears one side of the story. The couple cannot escape the reality of the relationship if they are both involved in the counselling.

'Our first aim is to establish a relationship with the client; if that doesn't happen in the first interview, the couple may decide not to return. One aim in counselling is for the couple themselves to arrive at the decision that they want, and which is the right decision for them.

'A growing side of the Marriage Guidance Council's work is with groups, leading discussions. Counsellors who are interested have special training for this. They lead discussions in prisons, schools, borstals and youth clubs. We regularly have a counsellor working in Leeds prison, leading discussions on personal relations and problems with groups of about eight to ten prisoners. We have a group of counsellors going into a comprehensive school on a permanent basis to lead groups of fifth and sixth formers, and a tutor leads groups with the teachers, so that they can lead the groups when the counsellors withdraw.'

How to become a Marriage Guidance Counsellor

The majority of counsellors are women. This is very easily explained by the fact that marriage guidance counselling is a voluntary activity which takes up few hours in the week.

To become a counsellor you undergo two selection processes, one at a local level, one at a national level at the Rugby centre. First you apply to your local Marriage Guidance Council which will pay for your training at Rugby if you are accepted. Two counsellors will screen you and check whether your reasons for wanting to become a counsellor are valid and whether you'll be a good one. If they decide that they want you, then they recommend you for selection at a national level.

You'll spend one weekend at Rugby, where your ability to be a counsellor will be assessed by counsellors and by a psychiatrist. If you are accepted you go back to your local Marriage Guidance Council for part-time training. This can take any length of time but will be at least two years. During training you are under the supervision of a tutor. Training is completed by a few residential weekends at Rugby. One counsellor stated that: 'the training at Rugby is superb. It's experiential training and at least half of it is based on the personal growth of the counsellor. We all benefit enormously from it.' Advanced courses are also available on such subjects as psychosexual counselling.

What a pity that being a counsellor is not a paid job and so is confined to those who can afford the time for it.

There are many Marriage Guidance Councils throughout the country: for your local one check the phone directory. If you are interested in becoming a counsellor, drop into your local office; they are always looking for people.

NATIONAL MARRIAGE GUIDANCE COUNCIL *Herbert Gray College, Little Church Street, Rugby*

Some people choose to live as a single-parent family. But some do not; some become single parents by death, divorce or separation. Many people do not see single-parent families as a 'real' family, and believe the children are 'deprived' of a happy family background. A parent is also subject to pressure if she or he chooses to remain single. One woman we spoke to said: 'There's tremendous pressure to get married, everybody is in couples, so what is a single person to do, or where do I go?'

These pressures are increased by inadequate childcare facilities. Most single parents have to find part-time jobs, as few full-time ones allow for school holidays or conform to school hours; but the pay is inevitably low, and not enough to support growing children.

Single parents are often discriminated against by housing authorities, who consider that a single person with a child should share a bedroom, whereas two parents are entitled to a room of their own. A further housing problem arises for women who wish to leave their partners. They are not usually considered homeless and entitled to a council house, as most councils consider that the women have an adequate house with their husbands. The authorities will not bend the rules for single parents who have moved because either they or their children could no longer tolerate the conditions under which they were living. They may be able to evict their husband (or lover) and regain possession of their former home for themselves and their children, but this will involve going to court, and there is the problem of what to do in the meantime.

Lack of information is a chronic problem. Many single parents would be better able to cope if they were aware of the benefits available: supplementary benefit, family income supplement, rent and rate rebates and financial benefits for children at school. And isolation helps to deepen the desperation that many single parents feel. Groups have formed to help alleviate some of the loneliness that has become part of so many single parents' lives.

fighting back : Gingerbread

Gingerbread is a national organization run by and for single-parent families. There are local Gingerbread groups all over the country, with a central office in London, a national committee and regional committees. There is a local constitution for affiliated groups; if they do not abide by this constitution then they have no voting powers. However the constitution is not rigid and allows local groups to develop in their ways. The Keighley Gingerbread group has been active for two-and-a-half years. Sheila, one of the founders of the group, feels that single parents should not have to live with the loneliness and frustration that she felt after her marriage broke up five years ago.

'When my marriage broke up, I came to Keighley with Carin, who was four months old (she's five now), and lived with my step-father. Soon afterwards I got a flat on my own. Unfortunately I didn't have any friends here and very few relatives, and life was pretty grim. I was staying at home living on my maintenance plus social security; I was lonely and very isolated: even a trip to the butcher was quite exciting. I never had enough money to do anything, go anywhere or buy Carin the things I felt she needed. It was terrible for Carin as well, she didn't meet people, apart from her grandad, and consequently was frightened of other people.

'Everything in society is geared towards couples: you can't go to the pub on your own, you're just out on a limb and nobody wants to know you unless you are part of a partnership. I felt I really wanted to start a group or something, because I didn't think single parents should have to live in such a way.

'Also being a single woman I felt very much at a disadvantage. For a woman to survive on her own is very difficult. It was things like trying to rent a television, everywhere I went it was, "Will you take a form home and get your husband to sign it?". It was just one aggravation on top of another.'

Sheila started college to train as a teacher. She found she had more time because of this, and decided then was the time to do something. She heard about Gingerbread from somebody at college, got in touch with the central office in London and decided to start a group in Keighley.

'About twelve of us met at my house and discussed the aims and the objectives of the group. The first aim was political: to better the lives of single-parent families. We felt that central and local government should be doing a lot more to help single-parent families because single parents are not in a position to help themselves: if they have young children they must have daycare and after-school care in order to have a full-time job and become self supporting. The isolation that the parent suffers affects their relationship with the child. In the long run we felt it was in the authorities' interest to help *us because children were going into care and costing them a lot of money, when just a bit more at home would save the family from breaking up. The second aim was social: we set up a committee for fund-raising and to run social events for adults and children. We recognized that this met a need, because the loneliness can be absolutely devastating. But the secretary (Noel) and the chairperson (me) were both committed to the political side.'*

The group met weekly, and were given a lot of coverage by the local press, 'not always the right sort of publicity', but it got people involved. Soon the group grew to fifty or sixty people. There were certain issues that needed a great deal of attention from the group.

'Daycare facilities are absolutely crucial so that single parents can go out to work. It is no good providing this on a nine-to-four basis, it must be from about seven in the morning to six at night so that mothers with different jobs are catered for. Then there was housing: single parents are very much disadvantaged in getting council houses. We used to march down to the housing department and see the housing manager. We haven't failed once yet to get a house for somebody in need.

'Social Security is another problem. We found that people often don't get what they are entitled to; we found that as soon as we went with them to the Social Security office they'd get it without a fight. None of us had had any experience whatsoever with lobbying MPs, dealing with Social Security or the Housing Department; what is needed is not experience, but dedication and time.

'We organized one demonstration, where we handed our children officially into care. We explained to the rest of the group what we were doing and why, and because they had experienced the problems themselves, they understood what we were trying to do. We notified Social Services about what we would be doing. If all the children of single-parent families were taken into care (that is approximately one million, and growing) it would bring the system to a standstill. The point we were trying to make was that many children of single-parent families that end up in care might not do so if the parents were under less pressure. A bit more money in the home could relieve a lot of this pressure, and at the same time save the country money in providing other homes for children.

'The most constructive thing we've achieved is the nursery; although this is officially separated from Gingerbread, it is run by Gingerbread members. In September 1975 we heard that a factory nursery was closing down and our chairperson stepped in and stopped the closure. We took it over and ran it. We had a lot of opposition; the Social Services Department was very much against the project, even though they didn't admit it openly. The nursery is now running quite separately and we have charitable status for it; it has a special interest in single-parent families. Getting the nursery brought our Gingerbread group to its knees in a way, because the people who worked very hard (mainly our chairperson) transferred their energies into the nursery.

'Our social committee has arranged social events, Christmas parties, outings to the seaside in the summer, fund-raising events like fairs, jumble sales and sponsored walks. The rest of the group has a say in what is organized for them, but the social committee does all the work, and then comes back to us and tells us what they need: if they need people to work on stalls or to make things. All this is important, as each Gingerbread group provides its own funds, in one way or another.

'Obviously there are bound to be problems within any political or social group. A Gingerbread group, being both, has its share. One problem with single-parent family groups is that a single parent is doing the job of two people and consequently has only half the time, so their time is limited and their energy is even more limited. This is one of the basic facts that anyone starting a group for Gingerbread will have to face. And there is the disillusionment when people get to a point where they get fed up with banging their head against a brick wall and they then give up trying; all these things work against an effective pressure group.'

People sometimes think that women suffer the most from being a single parent, but the Keighley group has not found this to be so.

'I would never say it is easier for a man than for a woman to be a single parent, unless they are able to go out to work. The pressures are different: the man has to conform to a woman's role because in cases where a man can't work, he is then condemned as a scrounger for living on Social Security.

'The situation for single parents will not change for a long time, even with pressure from Gingerbread and the National Council for One Parent Families and the Finer Joint Action Group, who are all doing a great job. To get the Finer Report [on One Parent Families] implemented would make an enormous difference to single parents, but the government won't do it, and if the present one won't, I don't think any other one will.

'Gingerbread has done a lot for single parents in that it has brought a lot of the problems we face to the attention of the public and government, not that this has actually made a great deal of difference. But now instead of condemning us they say, "They have a rough time, but we can't do anything about it".

'The problem is much larger than just the problems of single parents. It's a whole way of life, it's society and the way in which society acts. We're geared as a society to the two-parent nuclear family as a consumer unit, and if we don't conform to this, then nobody is interested. While you have that sort of atmosphere, that sort of society, then many single parents are going to sink. I feel that the problems facing single parents are the symptoms of a disease, which is capitalism. Capitalism depends upon competition and where there is competition there are losers. Single parents are losers because they have not got the weapons needed to compete effectively. The most unfortunate result of this is the effect it has upon the children, when they have to grow up in deprived circumstances. When you have competition of this sort, you're not going to have people being willing to help each other.'

The national Gingerbread office can give information on local groups, and help in starting a group if there is no local one.

GINGERBREAD *2nd Floor, 35 Wellington Street, London WC2*

Housing is one of the most basic problems facing single parents. A woman can get stuck in the double bind of homelessness and joblessness, making life unbearable for her as well as her children. Another major problem is the adjustment to having to cope by oneself, to the aftermath of the divorce or separation, to trying to create a new life for oneself.

One woman, herself a single mother, has been involved in trying to alleviate these problems for divorced and separated mothers. Seven years ago Nina West started building flats for these women through Nina West Homes, a registered, charitable housing association. At the moment Nina West Homes has three small blocks of flats in occupation, one in the process of conversion, one being built and two in the process of being bought. She will then be providing a total of fifty-six flats for single mothers. Each project has no more than twelve women living in it at one time. The first, Fiona House, has a day nursery attached to it. The nursery is for children from the flats and from the neighbourhood, and is run by qualified staff, thereby allowing the mothers the freedom to go out and work. The blocks of flats are designed for children of specific age groups, allowing mothers to move to another block of flats when their children become old enough. Fiona House is for children under five; Craig's Court and Shirley Court are for children between five and sixteen.

In Fiona House each flat was designed with the kitchen windows overlooking the playground so that mothers could keep their children in sight. Each front door was painted a distinctive colour so that the children would know which was their home without any difficulty. An intercom system was designed so that if a mother wanted to go to evening classes, or go out socially, she could switch her intercom on so that a neighbour would listen for her children. She could go out, safe in the knowledge that her children were being listened for. A communal room was also provided.

In the most recent projects there are modifications. Most of the original features are included, but there is now a utility room included in each block with a washing machine and drying room. The communal room is being redesigned to be open-plan so that the problem of friends and relatives unofficially dossing down is avoided. Instead the room will be like a central open play space.

Nina has found there is a very high demand for the flats.

'Women go completely out of their minds trying to find a place to live. When they come to us they're filled with Valium and other tranquillizers. But once they move in, the Valium goes out the window, the woman begins to find herself again.

'The women provide an enormous amount of support for each other. One day a social worker walked into one of the houses and the women threw him out; they understand one another and don't need any of the social workers' theories. The friendships they develop are so strong that when Silvia wants to move, Vivian wants to move too, and that's that. So when their children are six, they will both move to Craig's Court, until they get married again and move out. Our one rule is no men are allowed to stay overnight. I'm running homes for single mothers and not their boyfriends and lovers.'

Nina West Homes as a registered housing association is supported through subsidies from local councils, the Greater London Council, the Department of the Environment and the Housing Corporation, providing accommodation at fair rents (which is slightly higher than council rents for equivalent accommodation). In the beginning Nina had a hard time convincing people of the need for the homes, but now the authorities give her a lot of support and financial assistance. Her secret?: 'I don't believe in fighting them. I just tell them what we need and ask them to help us. It's a different approach.'

Nina understands the situation that most divorced women face.

'I've been divorced twice and have been left with young children to support. I scrubbed floors at the age of nineteen to support my baby daughter. I know the despair and the depression that being divorced entails. I know the hopelessness of finding a home and the viciousness of being unable to get a job because of inadequate childcare.'

Nina West is interested in the problems of the divorced and separated beyond just providing housing. She has from time to time considered trying to establish a counselling service run along similar lines to Marriage Guidance Councils but after the situation has irretrievably broken down. It is interesting to note that housing association money (from local authorities and the Housing Corporation) is available to registered associations to meet special housing needs. Nina West established a housing association on her own, but others might try to work with already established associations. And loans are available from the local authority for the construction of the daycare facility; these are repaid out of attendance fees, themselves paid for by the local authority for low-income families. Dealing with the bureaucracies can be difficult and extremely frustrating, but the need remains and the subsidies are there. Nina West has shown what an enthusiastic and determined person can achieve.

NINA WEST HOMES *12 Hampstead Hill Gardens, London NW3*

Single Parent Families; Where to get Advice and Help

Having a Baby
Social Security, for maternity allowances, extra payments for baby clothes, etc.;
National Council for One Parent Families;
see also the section on 'Health and Childbirth' and read *Single Woman's Guide to Pregnancy and Parenthood* by Patricia Ashwood-Sharpe, Penguin, 95p.

Housing
Local Housing Aid Centres (HACs);
Tenants Associations, Community Associations or the Citizen's Advice Bureau for difficulties with repairs and rent;
Child Poverty Action Group, for information on housing rights;
Housing Department of your local council; don't let them forget about you, keep hassling them and keep a record of your approaches to them. Local newspaper for finding accommodation; always use a Box Number to avoid obscene calls; try looking for someone in a similar situation to share with;
see also the section on 'Crimes against Women' for what to do if you have to leave the man you are living with as a result of domestic violence.

Money
A local Claimants Union (if there is one) if you have trouble with Social Security;
Child Poverty Action Group, for information on your rights;
Citizen's Advice Bureau, a Law Centre or a solicitor for advice on what to do if your maintenance is not being paid.

Work
Department of Employment Job Centre; you should register if you are able and willing to work full time;
Employment Agencies for temporary work;
Local paper for job ads;
Department of Employment for information on TOPS retraining courses; where you can be paid whilst learning a new skill;
Think about a job with creche facilities provided, or a living-in job if you need somewhere to live;
see also section on 'Women and Work'.

Childcare
Local Authority Day Nurseries: most authorities give priority to single-parent families, but you may still have a long time to wait;
Social Services Department for a list of private nurseries, childminders and playgroups in your area;
Gingerbread, to make contact with others in the same situation to set up your own self-help childcare arrangements or a babysitting group;
see also section on 'Childcare'.

Divorce, Custody and other Legal Matters
See *Breaking Up* by Rosemary Simon, Penguin, and various guides to do-it-yourself divorce available in your local bookshop;
Citizen's Advice Bureau, Legal Advice Group or local Law Centre for legal advice, information on entitlement to legal aid, and where to find a suitable solicitor;
Action for Lesbian Parents for advice and help if you are a lesbian.

Useful Groups

NATIONAL COUNCIL FOR ONE PARENT FAMILIES
255 Kentish Town Road, London NW5
The Council exists to help individual one parent families who contact them for assistance, and to fight for the rights of one-parent families as a group. They have a welfare department (staffed by qualified social workers) to provide information and advice by letter, phone or private interview. They also try to improve the position of one-parent families in general by working with local government, and urging local authorities to provide necessary services.

FINER JOINT ACTION COMMITTEE
c/o 255 Kentish Town Road, London NW5
The Finer Joint Action Committee consists of nearly twenty-five national voluntary and professional organizations who are fighting for the implementation of the 230 recommendations made by the Finer Report on Single Parent Families. This report, which was issued in 1974, has still to have any of its recommendations implemented. These organizations include the British Union of Family Organizations, the Catholic Housing Aid Society, the Child Poverty Action Group, the Family Services Unit, the Family Welfare Association, Gingerbread, MIND, Mothers in Action, the National Association of Widows, the National Council for One-Parent Families, Prisoners Wives Groups and Shelter.

There are some recommendations out of the 230 that the Committee feels deserve *immediate* attention and implementation:

1. A special cash allowance available as of right to all one-parent families.
2. The abolition of the separate functions of the matrimonial jurisdiction of the magistrates' courts and the divorce courts and their replacement by single, unified system of family courts.
3. Statutory housing provision to ensure that all one-parent families have an adequate home.
4. Real choice for the lone parent as to whether or not to work; this involves effective equal pay legislation, better pay and conditions for part-time workers, adequate daycare facilities for children of all ages and better training and employment opportunities for women.
5. A service offering help, advice and information on all matters of concern to one-parent families.
6. A new scheme for the assessing and collection of maintenance. The amount of support which a man should pay his family should be a matter to be arranged between the supplementary benefits commission and himself. This would relieve the lone mother from the anxiety and distress of having to go to court and sue for financial support.

As it may take some time to introduce a special cash allowance, immediate reforms of the benefits scheme are urgently needed as one-parent families are especially hard hit by inflation.

SCOTTISH COUNCIL FOR SINGLE PARENTS
44 Albany Street, Edinburgh
The Scottish Council's aims are to bring together for consultation all bodies in Scotland concerned with the well-being of single parents and their children. The Scottish Council acts as a link between those needing advice and assistance and the organization able to provide the guidance and help required. It is open to phone and letter enquiries and will always have a cup of tea ready if someone comes to their office.

NATIONAL COUNCIL FOR THE DIVORCED AND SEPARATED
13 High Street, Little Shelford, Cambridgeshire
The National Council is a voluntary organization that assists in forming local clubs for the divorced and separated; it also provides personal advice through the 'Apart Aid Panels' that its members run in different parts of the country. It also acts as a pressure group on matters concerning marriage, matrimonial property, maintenance, income tax, children, etc. It publishes a regular news bulletin. There are both individual and corporate memberships.

CHILD POVERTY ACTION GROUP
1 Macklin Street, London WC2
CPAG, which has a national office and local branches, is a research, advisory and pressure organization for those on low incomes, and it has a particular concern with single-parent families.

CRUSE
c/o Cruse House, 126 Sheen Road, Richmond, Surrey
CRUSE is the national organization for widows and their families, making available a service of counselling, advice, help with children and social activity. Enquiries can come from the widow, widower or a referring agency.

NATIONAL ASSOCIATION OF WIDOWS
Chell Road, Stafford
A national pressure group to press for a better deal for widows. See also the *Handbook for Widows* by June Hemer, who founded the National Association of Widows, and Ann Stanyer, who is an adviser to the Association (Virago, 75p); this handbook includes advice on funerals, pensions, wills, supplementary benefits, tax, housing, legal aid, education and training, and it discusses some of the problems of loneliness, isolation, sense of loss, and lone parenthood.

Collective Living

Some people are finding it necessary to step out of the traditional framework of marriage and live with other people in larger groups. Collective households (sharing cooking, housework, shopping, washing, childcare responsibilities and money) are a realistic alternative to living as a couple for many people. Living in a collective on the one hand frees ones time, whilst on the other hand it is demanding in energy and in the support towards other people in the household. Collective living can be an important experience in growing and learning about yourself and about other people. Often when men and women live as a couple one or both of them may give up friends, education, training or a job to make that relationship work. Within a collective household where everyone cooks and cleans on a rota basis, each person is given the chance to develop relationships, skills and interests outside the home. Within the household traditional roles are usually broken down with men involved in all the responsibilities of the house, and both men and women making decisions equally regarding all household problems.

Although each collective household differs, we decided to look at one house in detail, to give a clearer understanding of what a collective is. Lisa lives in Manchester with two men and two women. Their house was started with the intention of living, working and raising children together. Lisa is twenty-nine, David is thirty-one, and Paul is twenty-eight; they have been involved with each other since 1971, and have lived together since 1973; Maria moved in in 1976 and Sheila in 1977. Also part of the household are Mischa (aged three) and Ben (aged four). All of the adults have had some sort of higher education; all of them are involved in various political movements. At this point in time David and Maria have full-time jobs, Lisa works part-time, and Paul is in his final year at university. We spoke to Lisa about their household, the practical set-up and some of her feelings about living with other people:

'We began to think about living collectively about 1971. Paul, David and I were living in Cambridge at the time. We'd been in a street theatre group and there were quite a few people with similar politics living near us. We decided that rather than cooking all our meals in our own bed-sits and flats, we'd each take turns at cooking the evening meal. This arrangement went on for eighteen months and grew to eight women and eight men, though we did have to divide up to eat. It made me never want to go back to cooking every night (or even every other night) again.

'In 1973 Sue came to live with us, and started sleeping with Paul. At this point Paul, David and I had decided to move to Manchester together. The idea was that we were going to live in a house together, take it in turns to share the housework and the cooking. It took quite a while to work out the housework business. It was allright with Paul, but with David it was a different matter. He really thought he was doing an equal amount, but when it came down to it he wasn't really. He'd wash up forks and leave dried scrambled egg on them, or wash clothes and not rinse them properly. But women on the whole would also have to learn new skills, such as putting up shelves, etc. I'm still pretty bad at most of that stuff, though it's slowly getting better.

'At first we shared incomes. When Paul and I were working we put more into the rent box, the food tin and bill box. You have to get on with everybody and be convinced that they're doing worthwhile things to do this. After a while this system began to break down as relationships started to change. If you're doing an alienating job you don't want to share the money you earn with someone who sits around the house all day and doesn't even do much housework. Someone who goes out to work and has to keep to set hours deserves extra money because it is more pleasant to be able to organize your own day. We did have meetings of the household about five times a year to ensure that everything was working smoothly.

'Just before the group moved to Manchester, Sue had a child. We decided that we would all look after it together: Sue wouldn't be the mother with prime responsibility.

It seemed a good idea for both the mother and the child. The mother wouldn't have to have the child all the time and get fed up, she'd be able to have her own life and have the child. People who didn't want to have children themselves but enjoyed children would be able to participate in a situation of equal power and have a close relationship with the child. It seemed like a healthy idea from the child's point of view, as many children get totally dependent on their mothers, getting upset when the mother goes out to the shops. A child can't be particularly happy if she's worried about somebody going away all the time.

'The idea was that there would always be enough people involved in the house: one or two could get full-time jobs, some could get part-time jobs and some not work at all. In this way childcare could be done equally as at that time there were a number of children around that we were sharing bringing up. We found that involving children in our living tied us together. It's like forming an alternative family; with families you always know that whatever happens they'll still be there. I think it is quite a good thing to set that up with people you get on with and care about. It is nice to know that people are committed to each other. In some cases it just can't work out, because people change and go in different directions. Even now that Sue has taken Ben, her child, and moved to Nottingham, we are still very involved and tied up in their lives, mostly because of Ben.

'At first in Manchester, neighbours were suspicious of us. We were living in a respectable suburban area and people saw us as hippies, partly because of the way we dressed, more because of the way we lived. Once we moved it was much easier. Here there are lots of people who don't live in strictly nuclear families; there are lots of extended families and single parents. At the playgroup that our children go to, elder sisters or childminders and not always parents pick up the children, so our kids are not so unusual. At first people in the playgroup saw us as weird. This was overcome because we were willing to work there and put an effort into improving the playgroup; people therefore became more tolerant. We also talked to other women at playgroup about what we were doing, so they got to know us as people.

'We found that it was very important for the people living in the household to have similar political views, otherwise it just doesn't work. When Sue moved out we wanted someone to move in in a hurry. We asked someone I was having a relationship with to move in. He was much younger than the rest of us, he had been to an approved school, he hadn't been through higher education; he was political, but from a working-class background; he was different in so many ways: age, class, experience, personality. It just didn't work. It's been much better with Maria and Sheila partly I'm sure because their age and background are much closer to David's, Paul's and mine.'

The emotional relationships among Lisa, David and Paul have gone through many changes. Lisa thinks that living in a collective provides a lot of support for the changes:

'I think our emotional relationships are enough to keep the house together. Since I came out as a lesbian, Paul and I aren't sleeping together any more (we have been involved since 1968). I feel we get on much better, we haven't had any big rows, whereas before most of our rows were tied up with sleeping together and my not being into it. I think things are much better now that none of us are sleeping with people in the house, it makes it easier on a day-to-day basis. It makes relationships between us more equal, whereas when there are two people sleeping together they tend to be closer and others feel excluded.

'I think jealousy is dealt with better in a collective situation. Say if I was sleeping with someone, Paul wouldn't have to sit in his room getting upset about it, he could go downstairs and have a cup of tea and talk about it with somebody in the house. It makes it easier to cope with if you've got other people around. Because you're all living in the same house you are committed to supporting each other. It doesn't always work out, though. If you are not getting along with anybody in the house that makes you feel really isolated. You can feel that everyone is against you: if four people are saying you're a shit because you do this, this and this, it is much more powerful than one person saying

you are a shit because you do this, that and the other. It has its good side as well: it makes you look at yourself and see if you really are a shit!

'I'd never go back to living as a couple again. People treat me as an individual now and not as one half or one quarter of a unit. There are always people to talk to and get support from. As far as I'm concerned I like living this way; I like groups. If it wasn't for the children we might have split up (who can tell?) but I don't think that would have been for the better.'

Stepping out of the traditional framework of marriage and family is not an easy thing. Some people have opportunities to set up alternative living situations that are supportive for them and the people they live with. If a collective household is chosen, problems such as childcare, housing, making ends meet and loneliness are shared with other people, sometimes making them easier to cope with (although this can also be true of couples).

LESBIANISM: COMING OUT

Over the last few years more and more women have been 'Coming Out', admitting to themselves and to others that they are sexually and emotionally drawn towards women. Lesbians don't come in any one shape or size, or from a particular class or family background. How we come out varies wildly. The women's liberation movement has helped many of us dare take risks and discover together what our own sexuality really is, instead of just fitting in with the heterosexual society we were taught to conform to.

Lesbians include travelling saleswomen, shorthand-typists, full-time housewives, teachers, nurses, workers at Women's Aid refuges, truck drivers, bus conductresses, assembly-line workers, secretaries, playleaders, shop assistants, students . . . Lots of us have children. Some of us have always known we were gay, though we might have taken years to accept it fully. Others only found out through meeting other lesbians, often through the women's liberation movement.

Claudette is twenty-two, a West Indian who came over to Britain when she was nine years old. She met her husband at fifteen and had two children before she was twenty. She's done various jobs, typing, shop and factory work. Now she shares a council flat in Leeds with her daughters and another woman and her child, and is studying for 'O'-levels at evenings classes.

'I haven't always known I was a lesbian. I didn't really know much about it. I was always interested in women's bodies, especially tits, I've always had a big thing about tits, but I didn't label my feelings as lesbian.

'I first met lesbians two years ago at Al's house. I was living next door in two small attic rooms at the time. I met Maria and then she kept coming round saying she fancied me. I was curious, and the first time I did it with her was out of curiosity, but then we started a big relationship. At that time I was married, I'd been with Vince for six years, I was twenty with two young children. He used to go with other women, and I with other men but we never let on to each other about it. Anyway I said to him I fancied Maria and he said why didn't I try it (actually I already had by then) so I did and he got really freaked out. Things hadn't been very good between the two of us for some time. After that he kept changing his mind whether to stay with me or not. I'd had it, I just didn't want him anymore so I packed up his things and left them in suitcases and went and stayed next door. He left in the morning and I didn't see him for two months.

'For the kids this meant they just didn't see Vince for a while but I think they were relieved in a way because they didn't have to see us having rows any more. I didn't hide it from them when I was with women and Maxine understood, Nicky was too young.

'Vince comes round now. He prefers me sleeping with women than with men; he doesn't seem to be threatened by it in the same way as if I was sleeping with men.

'I'm better off financially being a single woman with kids because Vince never gave me money, or I couldn't rely on it. I can depend on Social Security now, and it comes every week; it's regular and my own. In the past when I was still married I had to get a job to earn money, typing or factory or cashier work, and then pay out for a child-minder for the kids; the last one cost £5 a week each so I ended up no better off. I was working the night shift in a factory four weeks after Nicky was born to pay off the furniture, then when we moved Vince went and sold it to pay off his gambling debts. So I'm better off being a single parent.

'Yes there have been difficulties. People saw that I was different when Penny and I moved in here. I had lots of women friends coming round. The men neighbours were a bit shocked and the lady next door offered herself (but I wasn't interested)! But once you start you can never go back. I've had hostility only from men. I've had a bit of violence from men since I came out as a lesbian but not too much. One woman I met at Charlie's (the gay club) used to be beaten up by her boyfriend, and he came and threatened to beat me up. He thought all lesbians were mad and couldn't survive without a man.

'Charlie's is the only place to go, except women's liberation parties and discos sometimes. I liked it at first, very butch women kept chatting me up but I liked femme women as well. So the role-playing was fun at first and I played the good little lady but then it got really heavy, having to say where I'd been and to account for myself to some woman and her doing the whole protective bit, I got fed up with it. I suppose women get into being butch because at last they have a chance to be boss; they've taken shit all their lives and now they want someone else to take it for a change. I don't see why women should want to be men, it's terrible, but I get taken for a boy sometimes.

'I haven't found racism or prejudice among lesbians but people notice me, I'm the only black woman in Charlie's. I'm fed up with being the only black lesbian around and sometimes I've wondered if women only want me because I'm black. There seem to be very few black lesbians; I've met only about three in the whole country who have come out. There are plenty who won't admit it. I look different to the other black women my age round here, my hair's different, my posture and dress all tend to be more positive I suppose. I look like someone who knows where she's going.

'I do sleep with men sometimes but when I do I would rather be with a woman; it's much nicer. And I always tell the guy beforehand that I sleep with women, and if a woman I like should come along that'll be the end of our relationship. Why do I sleep with men? Well because sometimes I get pissed off with having relationships with women because it's all highs and lows and I like it smooth. Sometimes it's so easy with a man, it's no effort because I don't have to talk to him, tell him things and get to know him, he just does the obvious thing. I don't get emotionally involved with men, and I get fed up after a couple of weeks. I'm not bisexual — when I'm with women I'm really into them and when I'm with a man I'm really into women too.

'When I'm sleeping with a man it affects my behaviour in other ways, I have to be "A Woman" and wait on him a lot. I feel a lot stronger when I'm with a woman. Women are making slaves of themselves, they shouldn't regard men as being so important.

'I think more women should come out. More black women especially. It's there really in most of us, it just needs something to spark it off. I think all women should try sleeping with women, they'd understand each other better and wouldn't need to be on these anti-depression things, and women can give each other so much, much more than a man can ever give, except a baby I suppose. Women are looked down on by men. If women are together then we're not going to think about our make-up, doing our hair, having a bath; because all women have got similar problems, we can just enjoy life together.'

Lesbianism and Child Custody

Custody cases are sticky. Normally children are given to the mothers, because of the woman's traditional role of child-raising. In cases where the mother is a lesbian, custody is usually given to the father, regardless of his ability to care for the child. Lesbians who have fought child custody cases find that their lesbianism, no matter what the situation with the husband is, becomes the central issue of the court hearing. They are torn apart, asked questions that have no bearing on good parenting whatsoever. In some cases, where the women have no 'blemish' except their lesbianism, lies are woven to impress the judge with their inadequacy, sometimes creating conflicts between mother and child that never before existed.

It seems a terrible injustice that women (and men) must suffer for following life-styles that bring them happiness. A society that so blatantly discriminates against homosexuals must be in grave fear of its own sexual identity. A woman who chooses to be a lesbian should no longer be seen as a 'social deviant' or perverted; we include this section because it shows the hypocrisy of a society that claims to be just and fair, yet won't let people live in the way they choose: we feel that this hypocrisy is the sickness, not the homosexuality.

Trish and Gilly live in a rural area of the West Country. Trish, now a student taking a degree course in Behavioural Sciences, was married, with one child, when she and Gilly, a social worker, met. Trist felt that she could not live in a false relationship with her husband while loving Gilly, and decided to leave him. Andrew, her son, then three, stayed with his father, Steve, (who was involved with another woman), because everyone advised Trish that she had no chance of winning a court custody case. Soon Steve's girlfriend left, and Andrew was returned by his father to stay with Trish and Gilly. Andrew's father began living with another woman shortly afterwards and put in an interim custody order.

> 'We all went to court for the interim hearing. Steve came with his new woman. The judge said he didn't like "tugs of love" over children. He thought the status quo should be maintained and Andrew should stay with us. Steve's solicitor played their trump card and said: "You do realize this mother is a lesbian?" But the judge said: "Just because a mother is a lesbian doesn't make her a bad parent." '

Trish wondered why everyone had advised her of the hopelessness of seeking custody, she couldn't see what they were making all the fuss about.

But soon she was to find out. A couple of months later the divorce between Trish and Steve came through and two days later Steve married Mary. The custody case came to court three months afterwards. A Court Social Worker had in the meantime visited both homes and all four people had visited a child psychiatrist chosen by Trish and Gilly. Steven and Mary had also visited one to represent their side. The hearing was adjourned for a further three months to allow time for Trish and Gilly to visit the psychiatrist representing Steve and Mary. Trish and Gilly's psychiatrist was quite positive about their ability to care for Andrew and presented a fair and objective report. But Steve and Mary's put the two of them through a gruelling experience: trying to find some sort of defect in either of them, and when none was found they were invented.

> 'They were more interested in defining my sex, to find out if I was a "true" lesbian, a bi-sexual or just playing, they didn't even consider if I was a good mother or not. They ended up with the hypothesis that I must be bi-sexual, because "genuine" lesbians didn't love children, and they felt I would most likely return to a "normal" relationship given time. Their psychiatrist asked me: "How would you encourage Andrew's sexuality as he grows older?" I said, "I don't know if you can encourage anybody to be anything, but assuming you can, I think I'd encourage him to be heterosexual." The psychiatrist replied, "Oh! so it's all right for you to be homosexual, but not your son." I realized that no matter what I had said, I couldn't win. In his report he wrote that I'd said that I would encourage him to be homosexual. Other things we said were also distorted or simply lied about.'

The court hearing lasted six days. Gilly and Trish had an excellent team of lawyers and very good reports from welfare workers, their psychiatrist and character witnesses. Gilly and Trish had a lot on their side, along with an ideal setting for raising a young child, acres of land, lakes and countryside, while Steve and Mary lived in an urban area, with a garden the size of a 'postage stamp'. But still, lesbianism became the central point of the case, no stone was left unturned. 'They asked what magazines and periodicals we subscribed to, whether we went to any organized lesbian activities.'

Trish and Gilly did everything by the book, seemingly they had all the points in their favour.

'The sickening thing was that we went to the ends of the earth to think of all the good things on our side. We kept diaries of everything that happened, we got so much advice from every source we could possibly think of. And literally Steve and Mary just stood up and said "We're heterosexual", and the judge said, "Lovely, you must be OK", in a metaphorical way.

'The two cases that have been won since ours were both won by people who didn't play fair, who'd done the sort of things you'd suppose that a man would do. One woman just kept the child on one access weekend because the child said it was miserable with the father; the other one stayed in the marital home, and the father couldn't find another place to live. They were both won by people being really bloody-minded. That's what makes us so cross, we fitted into every requirement and did everything by the book, absolutely everything.'

One thing that works very strongly against lesbian mothers is that there is no research available on children being brought up in lesbian households, whether they turn out neurotic or sane and balanced. In Trish and Gilly's case their opponents dug up evidence about prostitutes' children, because that was the closest (in their minds) that they could get.

In the end Trish got joint custody of Andrew, but Steve was awarded care and control, so the child was removed from his mother's home. Trish has access every other weekend and half the school holidays. Already Steve is complaining about costs of transport for his part of the journey to where Trish and Gilly live. The closing statement by the judge summed up the general attitude of judges around the country, the idea that lesbianism must be hidden and is an abnormal 'condition'. This quotation is taken from notes made in court:

> Andrew might grow up to be ashamed and embarrassed by his mother; that would be disastrous. The most important objective is that Andrew accepts his mother; the second objective is to ensure that he is most likely to develop along strong, normal masculine lines; and the third objective is to decide where he would be happy and obtain the best outlook on life.
>
> Concerning the third objective, the two homes are fairly equal; for the second objective the answer must be the father's home. About the first, Andrew is more likely to accept his mother's lesbianism and her relationship with Gilly if he is not exposed to it and grows up in a home which he can describe to his friends as 'normal'. No one need ever know about the relationship his mother has entered, but he is bound to be subconsciously affected by it. These are difficult and uncharted waters and I'm not prepared to sail in them.

Andrew lived with Trish and Gilly for two years and was happy and settled with them. He went to school there and his close friendship with Gilly's nephew has been severed by the move. Gilly and Trish have had to adjust to life without him which is hard when their whole life centred on his happiness and well being. Trish feels a lasting bitterness about the price extracted by society for their love. She comments: 'You need a pretty strong loving relationship to withstand four court appearances and the resulting loss of your child. It is fortunate for us that our love is still as deep and happy as it was in the beginning. But we both feel angry about this injustice.'

Action for Lesbian Parents

The outlook for lesbian mothers seems very bleak. Trish and Gilly's case is quite a common one, and recent cases that have been won by lesbian mothers are only seen as flukes and not as setting the scene for more rulings in favour of lesbian mothers. A group of women from all backgrounds and sexual orientations has come together to attempt to find ways of combatting the prejudice which faces lesbian parents in custody cases. We spoke with a member of *Action for Lesbian Parents* about the group and their work:

'Action for Lesbian Parents *grew out of a group called* Gay Wives and Mothers. *This group discussed the problem of bringing up children, but more so, what to do when your husband suddenly finds out that you are gay and wants the children back. At the same time that* Gay Wives and Mothers *was meeting, a woman was fighting a custody case through the National Council for Civil Liberties, which received some publicity through an article in the* Guardian. *Soon after,* Action for Lesbian Parents *was set up with people from* Sappho *(a gay magazine), some women from* Gay Wives and Mothers *and other women who were interested.*

'The first thing the group felt necessary was publicity. People didn't know that these custody cases were happening; even though there were only a handful at the time, there were likely to be more, as more women began to live openly as lesbians. Also people didn't really know about the kind of prejudice that was obvious, let alone the more subtle prejudice. The total prejudice from lawyers in these cases was amazing. Even my mother, who isn't in the least bit progressive, was amazed that judgments about the future of the children were based on these wild myths and stereotypes that have nothing to do with the welfare of the children.*

'In March 1976 we had a symposium called 'Women Alone'. Margaret Bramall, the head of the National Council for One Parent Families, spoke. She talked about how in some ways the sort of prejudice against the lesbian mother functioned against all single parents, and that she had had cases of single mothers with children who had brought up the children, and then the husband remarried, set up house and was awarded custody, just because his life-style, his class and the rest of it was considered to be right and better than hers.*

'One woman spoke who was a counsellor at Friends, a phone-in service. What she had to contribute was that although at the moment not many cases are going to the courts, she has, through doing anonymous counselling, come into contact with enormous numbers of women who are terrified about the situation they are going into by declaring their lesbianism publicly. It is more than just the legal stuff, because most of the judgments are based on the premise that a lesbian by definition cannot be a good mother. A lot of women internalize this and actually do think they can't be a proper parent.*

'The other thing Action for Lesbian Parents wants to do is a research project, which is just getting off the ground. This will mean that when some lawyer, or the judge, says in court, "There is no way we dare risk awarding custody to a lesbian because we know nothing about the effects", or say "The effects will certainly be such that the child will turn out a monster", one can then stand up and say that a study has been done which disproves this. Even if it's just a small study, it is very important. One woman who lost custody of her five-year-old son last year believes that favourable research findings could have made all the difference in her case in counteracting judicial prejudice.*

'Maureen Colquhoun, an MP, got interested in Action for Lesbian Parents and started coming along to meetings. She suggested that we take a brief to the Lord Chancellor. So we had several meetings with lawyers to prepare this, and a delegation went in December 1976. He was pretty non-committal, but he was quite interested, people felt he was more sympathetic than they'd expected. He said he wanted Action for Lesbian Parents* *to monitor cases for the next six months and his office would do the same. He can't do much, that's what is so depressing about it.*

'*It's a question of attitudes really. All the custody legislation says is that the decision should be made with regard to the best interest of the children. So that means it is completely up to interpretation and attitudes. It is a fact that the attitudes of the judiciary tend to lag behind public opinion, and public opinion isn't that accepting. It is also to do with conformity, this is what comes through the most: being gay is seen as a deviation and therefore it is a stigma against the parent.*

'*It often seems that we're fighting a losing battle. But what's important is that even though things aren't going to be changed immediately, Action for Lesbian Parents give women who find themselves with the prospect of having to go to court some support; they aren't totally isolated if there is a campaigning group.*

'*It is also important to have the base of the campaign as broad as possible, because what we're really saying is not just that these decisions are anti-lesbian, which they are, but they're anti-women. They don't respect the rights of women to live as they wish and bring up their children.*'

ACTION FOR LESBIAN PARENTS *c/o 57 Maids Causeway, Cambridge*

SOME BOOKS ON RELATIONSHIPS AND LIFESTYLES

LIVING LIKE I DO
by Nell Dunn, Futura, 85p
An exploration of alternative life-styles. Through interviews (eleven adults collectively raising four children, one-parent families, etc.) Nell Dunn investigates financial arrangements of communes, bi-sexuality as a life-style, community pressures and so on.

WE'RE HERE
by Angela Stuart Park and Jules Cassidy, Quartet, £1.95
This is a book of conversations with lesbian women.

THE CAPTIVE WIFE: CONFLICTS OF HOUSE-BOUND MOTHERS
by Hannah Gavron, Penguin, 60p
Most previous studies of family life were completed in the early 1950s; they concentrated mainly on slum areas, only looked at middle-aged people, and didn't take into account post-war marriages. Hannah Gavron did this excellent study in the early 1960s looking at young mothers with young children, reflecting on the general changes that have occurred in the structure of family life, the family today, changing patterns of work. She talked with forty-eight working-class and forty-eight middle-class women about housing, marriage, mothers and work. Her conclusions were revolutionary in 1965, and still need attention

today: a re-analysis of education for girls; a re-analysis of women's roles and capacities as workers; the re-integration of the mother with young children into society.

MOTHERHOOD, LESBIANISM AND CHILD CUSTODY
by Francie Wyland, Falling Wall Press, 79 Richmond Road, Montpelier, Bristol, 40p
'*We are demanding not only the power to choose to be lesbian without losing our children, or the possibility of having them. We are also demanding the power to be with those children in a way that is not work. And we will apologize to no one for rearing children who are, like their mothers, making a ferocious fight to determine their own lives.*'

SINGLE WOMAN'S GUIDE TO PREGNANCY AND PARENTHOOD
by Patricia Ashwood-Sharpe, Penguin, 95p
This handbook aims to be a written companion to the single woman who finds herself pregnant, and without support. The book contains information on where to get a pregnancy test, what action to take if you are pregnant, including a chapter on abortion. It includes chapters on what it is like to be an unsupported mother, dealing with social security, hosuing daycare work, etc. Also includes chapters on adoption and fostering. Good examination of the law as it affects single mothers and what to expect. There ought to be a copy in doctors' surgeries, and all other places where women can have a look at it.

WOMEN'S ART

When we talk about women's art the first question is often: 'Why haven't there been any great women artists? Why no female Picasso, or Rembrandt, or Van Gogh?' There are two answers to this:

As we know, arts in Western society remain largely oppressive and closed to those human beings who don't have the good fortune to be white, preferably middle class and male. The conditions for producing art are very important; to write, to paint, one needs time, money, a room of one's own, and access to knowledge. These conditions have always been difficult for women to obtain, and obstacles to aspiring women artists were and are numerous. As Simone de Beauvoir puts it: 'To tell the truth, one is not born a genius, one *becomes* a genius and the feminine situation has, up to the present, rendered this becoming practically impossible.'

A few women have made it but they are exceptions – Virginia Woolf, Billie Holiday, Louise Nevelson, Agnes Varda, Marjorie Proops . . .

Nowadays, getting started as an artist is difficult enough for men, but overwhelmingly so for women. If preparing to be an artist is easier for women than it was, earning a living and gaining recognition is another matter. We could put the question in a different way and ask 'Have there really been *no* great women artists?' The answer will be found in *Art and Sexual Politics* by Thomas Hess and Elizabeth Baker.

The second answer to the question is that women have always been artists but our work has seldom been recognized as art. We knit, we sew, do crochet, pottery, make patchwork, bedspreads and rags, decorate our homes. These works of art are not considered important; they are considered just 'housewives' hobbies' without any artistic value.

Nevertheless, by getting together women are getting the confidence to realize that what we are doing is valid and beautiful, and it is 'art'.

We are slowly asserting (or re-asserting) our own culture. We certainly have plenty to say and to contribute to the artistic life of this society.

Women's Arts Alliance

'Formerly "The Women's Free Arts Alliance", we had our beginnings when a group of us, including some women artists and some community workers, met together to discuss our need and that of other women for self-expression outside the context of home, family and job. We decided to set up an arts centre, the first of its kind in Great Britain, where activities could take place to meet these needs. We found premises in King Henry's Road in Chalk Farm, London. We started workshops in theatre, dance and music, and soon other activities were added in response to local demand, such as yoga and painting classes and a creche. New premises were found and 1976 saw the establishment of the project at its current site at 10 Cambridge Terrace Mews, London NW1.

'The workshop programme, now called "Womenschool", was extended to cover ten areas of arts and crafts, counselling, movement and self-defence. The atmosphere in the workshops is open and supportive. A place where women can learn new skills in a non-competitive way, free of the constraints of imposed standards. Women are encouraged creatively to define themselves for themselves.

'The permanent exhibition space was initiated on 23 March 1976, with a display of women's crafts and was later formally launched with a mixed media exhibition selected round the theme, and entitled: "Images of Women". The idea behind the gallery is so

that it should not be merely a place to show an end product but should take its place as part of the total creative process. The need for an alternative gallery space for women was recognized when virtually all the artists expressed their experience of isolation in working alone and their need to share experiences of their work processes and to discuss directions and ideas. The elitist and commercialized gallery circuit had to be challenged.

'Responsibility for exhibitions, including promotion and publicity, stays with the women concerned. And, most importantly, the work of established artists, who have had training, and those who have had no training, but use art as a vital means of expression, come together under the one umbrella. Each woman is seen as being involved in an on-going art process, with plans and decisions about revealing their work in conjunction with each other, being shared. Since the opening of the gallery there has been a continuing programme of exhibitions, including both group shows and one-woman shows.

'Apart from Womenschool workshops and the gallery space, other important areas of work have been developing. The premises have been used for seminars and weekend activities, such as workshops in video and related media; plus a regular afternoon event called "Sundays at 3.00": an informal space for poetry readings and other performance-type events.

'A shop, known as "Womenshop", has been set up as a practical space where women can display and offer for sale the poducts of their work. This complements the functions of Womenschool, where women learn and explore constructive and creative mediums, and the gallery where they display and communicate the fruits of their work. The shop, by way of extension, supports women in their efforts to distribute their work and be financially independent and self-supportive.

'At the present moment the shop is largely a feminist bookstore and is attempting to contribute, through its small profits, to the financial independence of the Alliance, a situation necessitated by the structural and financial crises experienced at the beginning of 1977.

'1977 dawned with many problems to be faced. Grant monies were virtually exhausted and the director, Joanna Walton, was resigning and returning to the USA. Both herself and Kathy Nairne (involved from the beginning) had been enabled by the grant money to adopt positions of paid responsibility at the Alliance. They had borne all the weight of organization and administration with some voluntary help from time to time. Without funds this system couldn't continue. It was also generally realized that a close concentration of work responsibility in this way meant that other women had not shared the experience of this type of work. There was a gloomy sense that there would not be woman-power forthcoming to continue this work. Impending doom loomed large as plans were made for a general meeting to discuss the possibility of setting up a collective to operate the Alliance. About forty women attended the meeting on the 11 February 1977. Many expressed a strong sense of personally-felt alienation. The many elements of Womenschool and the gallery operated in isolation; fragmented one from the other. In the absence of general meetings there was no on-going dialogue or communication between the various groups. Without such a feature it was difficult to experience the Alliance as a place with an overall identity and extremely difficult to initiate new projects in what was effectively a vacuum.

'The general meeting expressed eagerness to get together in quite a different way; to evolve ideas and make decisions in an open collective. Responsibility for individual events and activities was to take place in the context of the Alliance as a whole, rather than disparate elements working in isolation. The board of trustees was dissolved and the accounts finalized.

'Six days later saw the first official meeting of the collective. About twenty women attended and a co-ordinating (administrative) group of five (later extended to seven) was formed. The group now meets weekly on Monday nights and is open to any or all of the general collective. Full-scale meetings occur monthly to discuss and share items of new and overall interest.

'As of mid-1977 the Alliance has no arts grants and no bank balance. But the Womenschool workshops have survived and indeed flourished. Many women have come forward to teach workshops, perfectly happy to take responsibility for organizing and promoting their programmes (as opposed to the old system of depending on a paid administrator at "the top"). The Alliance ekes a tiny income each week from this source (one-third of workshop income goes to Alliance, and two-thirds goes to the teacher). But this cannot even meet the weekly rent requirement of £15.00. However, progress is very real and very exciting where it counts. The advanced African Drumming class has just had its public debut at the "Women's Monthly Event". Workshops have expanded and now include: African Drumming, co-counselling, diary and writing, dance, karate, yoga, tai chi, life-drawing, poetry and screenprinting. The photography darkroom is now in full swing and can be booked by women at very low rates, in three-hour blocks. The gallery collective have been conducting weekend seminars. The two so far organized were entitled: "Women's Practice in Art" and "Female Imagery in Women's Art Practice".

'Another new feature has been the opening up of the Alliance's premises to other women's groups (payment is in direct accordance with ability to pay). The Women and Music group meet regularly on the premises (many of these women attend Womenschool workshops). Gay Sweatshop, the gay theatre group, who put on benefit performances for the Alliance, used the space for rehearsals of their play about lesbian mothers. And plans are underway for the Women's Art Slide Register group to take up permanent residence. Mutual support between women's groups was also in evidence at the bookshop's launching of the new Virago publication Life as we have Known it, by Co-operative working women at the Alliance with Virago directors and women from the Women's Co-operative Guild.

'Financially, the future is very insecure indeed. But the period of time since the collective has been in operation has been one of unprecedented growth and excitement — one that should not be allowed to be threatened by the minimal financial needs required to cover basic operating costs. The energy and the commitment is there, and hopefully it won't be compromised.'

(Report by a member of the Women's Arts Alliance)

WOMEN'S ARTS ALLIANCE *10 Cambridge Terrace Mews, London NW1*

See Red Poster Workshop

Throughout this book we have discussed how women are organizing in collectives, and how feminists stress the importance of a group working together, sharing both skills and the decision-making. However, this concept of sharing does not usually apply to art. Usually it is regarded as heresy to share *your* piece of art with someone else, and the tradition is of the 'artist as individual'. *See Red Poster Workshop*, a group of four women, is challenging this concept and beginning to produce artwork collectively.

'We started two-and-a-half years' ago, but it has taken us a long time to evolve to where we can produce a collective poster. In the beginning, we did discuss what we were doing, but not enough. Things have been printed, which we have later had rows about. We have been really careful since then to discuss our work before it is printed. It is much easier to discuss a finished painting than an abstract idea. But now we discuss the idea, then bring in sketches and everyone talks about it. People laugh at collective art work; they say: "Do you all hold the same pencil?!" But in fact, it sometimes does happen that one of us is erasing what the other has drawn.

'Our posters are always screenprinted. We feel it is an ideal process for communal work. We all have individual skills, but the process itself needs three or four people.'

See Red prints feminist posters. They do pictures for women's publications and posters that are sold at women's meetings, conferences, by mail order, at women's centres; they also send out displays of about eight or ten posters for people giving talks about Women's Liberation.

The group feels very positive about the integration of their traditional art skills and the work they are doing.

'When we started we had a series of meetings where we just talked. It was exciting because we realized that we could use the skills that we had learnt at art school and combine our feelings about the women's movement and women's struggles in some positive way.

'We started from nothing but free time: we all have other jobs to maintain us. We first squatted a shop in Camden Road, which was sordid, to say the least. We bought, borrowed or were given, all our equipment, and received small donations like £20 of supplies. At the end of 1976, someone threw a brick through the window, so we had to move. The South London Women's Centre gave us some space, where we just worked in the evenings. They didn't charge us rent, but only what we could afford to pay. That way we could sell our posters very cheaply, just covering our costs. Now that we've moved once more, we have to pay rent, so our prices may go up.

'Most of our ideas for posters come out of what people are feeling strongly about at the moment. In the beginning, we tended to do ones which we had personally experienced: the double life women lead, children, domestic labour. It is hard for us because we want to present a really positive image of women, and we find that difficult. There just aren't any; they need to be re-invented. But we don't want to get into producing an image of women as "super heroines". We are really working in a void in that respect; to find positive images in our society is almost impossible.

'Our posters are sometimes depressing. But that's because all the things we've done have been derived from our own lives and our own problems. Therefore, they are something about all women's problems, and they are terribly depressing. But we decided that by presenting a negative image for scrutiny, it may be positive in the long run. Like the poster that says "My wife doesn't work", which shows that she does work twelve hours or more a day. Although this is a negative statement, you can get a positive message from it by realizing "What am I doing, wasting my time?".

'We'd like to get the posters to a wider audience. We have got some into places of work, but this is not extensive. We are working on some posters about health care, and we'd like to get them into health centres. The posters should be able to say something to all women.'

See Red is willing to teach women to screenprint. They have held quite a few workshops, and have taken their equipment along to other groups. They have done printing with local playgroups and are running a class, one night a week, at a local battered women's refuge.

SEE RED POSTER WORKSHOP *16a Iliffe Yard, London SE17*

Feministo: A Postal Event

At the beginning of 1975 a group of women gradually started sending each other small artworks through the post to keep up their friendship. The originators involved their friends, and this core of women now extends all over England.

Each person replies to the artwork she has received by making either an image/object that reflects something of her perspective on life or that responds directly to the image she has received. Of course, work has to be small to be posted, but small scale has an added dimension:

'Women's life-styles tend to contain small time-scales, brief moments; we need flexibility to deal with the tiny important moments that children, friends, or lovers present. This is often reflected in the work. We are so busy with our children, our jobs, and our domestic life that time for artwork has to be slotted in between tea and the ironing, or whatever.

'It is a really important part of the postal event, that it is an extension of what you've always done, using the kind of skills you use in the house and the same materials. We use "female", "domestic" skills, such as crochet, knitting or sewing, as well as the more traditional "arts" skills. We have very few physical resources, and this is reflected in the artworks. Many of them use old packaging or clothing; we recycle lots of things.

'Because "feminine" skills are integrated into everyday life they have low prestige value; you can't stick your knitting in a frame and sell it for £3,000. The postal event is about challenging those kinds of values.'

The postal event has been a real support for many women and helped them tremendously by breaking their isolation and making their artwork important in their own eyes. It has helped them change their life and their ideas. We talked to some of them in Birmingham:

'This search for images to do with being a woman is, for many of us, an attempt to find a feminist perspective and to put art into a directly political sphere. We are trying to unite apparently disparate aspects — the private, domestic and personal with our political and social understanding. Some of the things that have been made and sent fall into rough categories. Some are about food: boxes of chocolates using parts of woman as the sweets; or a plate of salad with the meat on the lettuce. There's a papier mâché woman. Some are on childbirth and our ambiguous relationship with our children. There are works expressing suffocation and isolation in personal life. And there are a great number on marriage. It's really like a fantastic diary in some ways, bits of people's lives. It's like talking to somebody else in a visual way. One day Sue sent a crocheted cactus to Kaye and received a crocheted plant the day after.'

'On the whole, the postal event has changed a lot of things, given us confidence. Before, some of us were doing little bits here and there but you never had the time within the domestic situation to do a big painting or anything like that, and besides what would you do with it when it was finished?

'It's easy to get into the trap of thinking, "I'm only doing little things", and shove them out of the way. You need support to carry on, but with the postal event you feel your work is valid; you've got the right to take the time you need to work, specially when you have to reply to a work you've received. Sometimes it's very urgent, the images are very personal; they are about things that are going on in the person's life at that time, and if you waited six weeks then it would in a sense be a rejection of the person. The standards about the way you make your work change. It's very much about executing the idea. You could wait six weeks or three years and make it perfectly, but the important thing is to do the idea and build up a visual communication. Sometimes it works, sometimes it doesn't. When you find somebody that you've really got something going with, you tend to concentrate on her; but there are bound to be times when your work doesn't strike a chord or spark off a visual discussion in any way.'

'The postal event means that other people too take your work more seriously; parents, children, husbands stop assuming that you are going to be there all the time. They stop treating you like a mother with a hobby, and begin to perceive that you might possibly be a person.

'When we started doing the postal event, we really were just a bunch of housewives. Even though we had a women artists group in Birmingham, we were still fairly isolated with all the problems of childcare and housework. Now, those women here in Birmingham who have children are all involved in taking care of each others' children (through playgroups, baby groups, etc.). During our time off we don't do the housework or mend socks. It is our free time.'

'Making things is another way of sorting out our lives. It can revolutionize the ideas in your head in a matter of months. For example, those from art schools have a tendency to do their own motif and their own work, but if a postal event arrives, they need to reply even if they want to carry on with their other work. Then people begin to question the whole process of their individual work. Images are reiterated in different people's work, images and ideas aren't private property. In fact ownership of the work is totally ambivalent: does it belong to the person who made it or the person who received it?'

Though originally Feministo had the vague idea of doing an underground exhibition of all their works within the women's movement, pushed by a friend of theirs, they ended up with an exhibition in relatively big galleries with tremendous success. Their exhibitions have toured all over England, visiting Birmingham, Manchester, Liverpool, and London. In 1976 they got an Arts Council grant which allowed them to carry on exhibiting.

'When we got a postcard from a friend in London saying, "Go to the Ikon Gallery in Birmingham and get an exhibition", we were wetting ourselves with fear. It's really hard to describe what it was like at that point; we could do it only because we were backed up by many other women. Going to one of these classy little places to ask for an exhibition by yourself would be absolutely terrifying, but when there's a group of you and you are all committed to what you are doing, you all believe in it, then they can't put you down and don't try to.

'The Berlin exhibition, "One hundred years of women's art", was a completely un-looked for and unsought opportunity. They got in touch with us, and we were so surprised that we ignored the letter for a whole year, we didn't believe it was meant for us! First we thought it was going to be a small feminist thing, but when we got there it turned out to be a huge, international exhibition for established artists. Here we were, putting up our little tiny artworks made out of household rubbish in half an hour here and there, and here they were, all these professional artists with their great technical sculptures and huge paintings.

'Defining ourselves as artists is difficult, especially for those who have no training — the Berlin exhibition brought up all sorts of feelings of paranoia: what right have we got to be here? What are we aiming at? etc. Making changes in art is not just about making changes in content or form; if it's going to be a really revolutionary kind of art and a woman-defined one, then everything has to be changed.

'Putting up the exhibition is like doing a collective piece of work because when it is all up together it really does look like one gigantic piece of women's work, one woman could have done it all but in fact twenty have. The work is not judged at all, everything in the postal event goes into the exhibition. So it's getting bigger all the time and it's a tremend-ous amount of work — 300 tiny pieces — to put up. It takes two days. Somebody from the group has to go and do it because things are fragile and relate to each other in ways that aren't apparent if you just pick it up out of a crate. This work is crucial since it's a very important part of the show that it does not come over as a collection of art pieces but as a "conversation".'

Not all the women involved have been in the women's liberation movement. Women get to know about the postal event from the exhibitions, from the radio and through knowing other women. It has a tremendous appeal to them because they realize that what Feministo is doing is just an extension of things they've always done secretly and do everyday as part of their lives.

'There doesn't seem to be any danger of us getting cut off from other women as "artists" to be looked up to, because when women actually see the work they feel involved, it speaks to them. We try as much as possible to reproduce the atmosphere of the home in the gallery, so that the work isn't alienating, it's just the sort of thing you might have lying around in your kitchen.

'When I first heard about Feministo, I didn't get involved because I thought they

must be doing something incredibly clever. I just admired them from a distance. Then I went to an exhibition and realized that in fact what they were doing was just an extension of things I've always done like embroidery. I felt incredibly involved with it and it was an amazing experience.'

The notion of visual contact as a network of relationships is one the group would like to see extending very widely. This is what you do:

1. Get excited at the idea of a postal visual communication event.
2. Write to Phil Goodall, 14 Valentine Road, Kings Heath, Birmingham 14, who will send you a list of people already involved in this.
3. Pick a name, or if you've seen their work, choose someone who does work which means something to *you*.
4. Use one of the ideas or situations that make you angry or sad, and put it into a *visual form* before it's forgotten or buried or passed over. This could be any form at all using one of your skills, or the odds and ends you've collected that seem relevant.
5. Pack your artwork with a note, and post it. Please don't forget the stamp and also a stamped addressed envelope.
6. Soon you'll get a reply in the form of another piece of work which will be the start of your communication/relationship, (get in touch with Phil Goodall if you get no replies to your communications). This is the beginning of a dialogue; two people have got some clues about each other.

A set of postcards of the postal event travelling show on the theme, 'Portrait of the Artist as a Young Woman', are available in a set of twenty at £1.50 including postage from Lyn Foulkes, 65 Livingstone Road, Kings Heath, Birmingham 14.

WOMEN'S THEATRE

In the spheres of theatre and poetry, as in so many other areas of creativity, women are at last discovering talents and getting together to bring them out. The results are specifically feminist forms of art, revealing the trials, and the joys of women's everyday lives. Here, a member of the Women's Theatre Group describes how the group came to be formed and the work it is doing:

'The present group came together at a season of women's plays at the Almost Free Theatre in London in the autumn of 1973. At that time, there was a larger group, run as an open collective, meeting every Sunday. This became a difficult, unwieldy system and caused a split in the group.

'Seven of us were left wanting to work in a similar direction, away from established theatres, in search of new audiences, and seeking an efficient and creative way of working as a small feminist collective. Our aim is to explore social and political issues from a feminist viewpoint in a theatrical context. We do everything — act, make costumes, write publicity material and of course write and produce our own shows.

'Our first work was the dramatized readings from New Portuguese Letters by the Three Marias, to help publicize the cause of the Three Marias being tried in Portugal.

'Fantasia, our first real show, a half-hour play with slides and music, is about women's fantasies. It set us on our feet and helped us get an Arts Council grant.

'In the autumn of 1974, we wrote My Mother says I Never Should, a play about the sexual problems of teenage girls. The show has been on the road since then, playing in schools, youth clubs, colleges of further education, teacher training colleges, conferences, and other venues. Every show is followed by a discussion and with young people, and we often include role play in the discussion session.

'Our 1975 output consisted of Work to Role, a play dealing with the areas women are likely to enter after they leave school, experiencing pressures at home and at work to conform to certain accepted roles and the conflicts this can present. It raises questions about work, trade unions, marriage and the family, telling the story of Rose, a school-leaver who is bullied for "her own good" by her far-seeing over-worked mother; and for "his own good" by her selfish fiancé. It also shows Rose's friends and relatives: the unmarried mother, the college educated feminist, the exploited workers and the freezer-worshipping, pill-popping wife. "The play was aimed at an audience of school leavers, but we have also shown it to trade union and teacher audiences, as well as to theatre-goers." '

The Women's Theatre Group's latest play, Out on the Costa Del Trico, deals with the twenty-one week long strike for equal pay by the women at the TRICO windscreen wiper factory in West London in 1976. Like all their plays, it links the struggle of women against oppression with the struggle of the working class against big business, showing that the same forces are active in both, in a non-propagandist, fast-moving, slick and very funny play.

The shows are about an hour long. Fees start at £50, and are on a sliding scale; transport costs outside Greater London are extra. Financial assistance towards putting on their plays can sometimes be obtained from the Greater London Arts Association, 29—31 Tavistock Place, London WC1 (not available to schools). Scenery and sound equipment are provided; the group can work without lighting but need two square pin power points and space for staging. All shows are followed by a discussion.

THE WOMEN'S THEATRE GROUP 27 Stepney Green, London E1

There are several other women's theatre groups, including Monstrous Regiment, the New Gay Sweatshop and the Coventry Lesbian Theatre Group. For details of these and other groups, and contact addresses for making a booking, see the listings in either Spare Rib or The Leveller (available from some newsagents or from 155a Drummond Street, London NW1).

FEMINIST WRITING

The work and views of writers can only reflect the breadth of their own knowledge and experience. Women have traditionally been denied any wider knowledge than what's necessary to run a household, any broader experience than love, marriage, children and dull narrowing paid work. Small wonder that female writers and poets of the past could not express the wealth of culture available to men with education, who could travel and mix with many different people. Of course we are talking of the upper and middle classes here; working-class men and women were equally deprived of this experience.

Thus women poets and writers have traditionally written of what's laid down for us, our allotted sphere in life: love, the beauties of nature, powerlessness. It's hardly surprising that much of the poetry is depressing; women saw how limited and restricted their lives were, chafed against them but had no option but to accept.

To be allowed to write at all, a thoroughly unladylike occupation, was in itself an achievement. Emily Dickinson was forced into obscurity and religious symbolism in her poetry to hide the love for another woman she wished to express (see: *Women Remembered*, edited by Charlotte Bunch, Times Change Press, £1.50).

When Sylvia Plath started writing, in the 1950s and early 1960s, women's lives had changed but not enough. We were still programmed to see our main, if not only, creative act in life to be finding a man and bearing *his* children. Secret rebels found no support in a society geared to the maintenance of romance and true love forever after. Women who fixed their eyes upon a star were frowned on as freaks and given the brides bouquet. Sylvia Plath could not take the contradiction. Married to a man, Ted Hughes, whose poetry while arguably inferior to hers was yet lauded to the skies, she was castigated for not gracefully accepting the back seat, the role of a great man's wife. Like so many other great creative female artists she took the only way out open to her spirit, she committed suicide. Another factor holding women back has been the male standard imposed on writing: it's been male poets who have set the standard of poetry, and male critics who've cemented it, and within their poems, women are defined as anything from Tennyson's weepy Mariana to Dylan's Bad-Eyed Lady of the Lowlands: beautiful, passive creatures who live only for love and men's inspiration.

We aren't supposed to want to ride the railroads, stride down the road with the sun in our eyes, a song on our lips and the whole free world in our hearts. If we were to try this, we would face rape, pregnancy and worse before the day was out. Adventure is not for us as Tennyson clearly states in 'The Princess':

> 'Man for the field and woman for the hearth,
> Man for the sword and for the needle she,
> Man with the head and woman with the heart,
> Man to command and woman to obey,
> All else confusion.'

And then, we wrote of what we knew and understood, knowing that any experience is valid, that small too is beautiful, that poetry is in the eye of the beholder even if what she beholds is potato peelings (Al Garthwaite).

Feminist Poetry

Ruth is a poet. She told us what *she* thinks about feminist poetry, and then talked about *her* involvement with the Sheffield Poetry Group:

'Many women who write don't publish anything, don't show it to anybody; their writing is kept secret. It's only recently that more women have admitted that they write poetry

about their daily life, their feelings, their pains . . . Can you write something which feels like a poem to you and yet is about the washing up? Of course you can, and you should not feel ashamed of it.   There are books of feminist poetry written by women about themselves and their feelings at a particular moment; and these stuck in the bottoms of drawers.   Poetry is a very good way of expressing oneself and expressing one's anger.

'*Everybody can write a poem. I call a poet anyone who says she is one. I had a friend in London; some editors of a magazine asked if they could publish some of her poems. She went home, took out a few pieces of her writing. And on the back of one of these pieces of paper, she had a shopping list: "Make sure to write to my mother, don't forget the guitar, buy two toothbrushes, etc. . . . " Surprise, surprise! They published the shopping list thinking it was feminist poetry. She didn't know what to say, and eventually she* pretended *it was a poem. She actually got some fan mail asking who the second toothbrush was for.* Poetry can be your shopping list!

'*Mind you, this makes poetry very suspect as well. I could sit down and write a list of books I read last year and say that was poetry. Feminist poetry is a question of how you write a poem which says what you experience as a woman, in a way which cannot be interpreted as anything else. It is therefore very limited, because when you read it back you may realize that it can be interpreted in a completely different way. Whatever you write, in any language, you come up against this linguistic barrier. You've used a phrase because it's the conventional way of expressing what you wanted to express. But it's alien to you, it's loaded with images you didn't mean. Take a flower for example; a dictionary of poetic images will tell you that it symbolizes a whole list of stuff you would have never thought of, but a lot of people who have done A-level English will know these symbolisms, and will start interpreting the flower as "Jesus Christ and his crucifixion" or whatever.*

'*Images have all sorts of different connotations and the inherent sexism in the words we use is very difficult to avoid.* The Lesbian Body *tries to get over the problem of male sexist language by splitting the words, putting little lines underneath, inventing others. I think sometimes they end up being equally female-sexist and incomprehensible. You can change "History" into "Herstory" but you have to decide when you are being pedantic and when you are not, and when you want to be understood by other people. We must not forget that poetry is about* communication.

'*As a feminist, should you only write poems about changing society? If you start doing that, you will get very idealistic; and if you always try to be realistic, to say how women are oppressed, your writing will not be spontaneous anymore.* The Ideal Feminist Poetry will be written only in an Ideal Feminist Society. *Otherwise it is impossible. I know somebody who wrote a poem about a guy she really liked. Everybody tore it to bits saying that this guy was in fact a sexist pig. Do you have to put an apology at the end of the poem saying, "This was how this guy was on the 4th of March between 6pm and 8pm, but he is in fact a sexist shit"?*

'*These problems of self-doubt, language, sexism, are difficult to solve and can undermine women's confidence deeply. They are best tackled in groups, and this is what the Sheffield Poetry Collective does.*

'*I had been in a poetry group in London before and thought it would be nice to start one here in Sheffield. I put a notice in the Women's Movement newsletter and the group started.*

'*It's not a formal group, we don't have membership. It's made up of women who write or read or are interested in poetry. Since we all know each other, we meet whenever we want to. We mostly talk a lot and criticize each other's poetry.*

'*Personally, the group has given me a great sense of despair and disillusionment about poetry. In the sense that we really cannot overcome the limitations of our conditioning or our language or the society in which we live. You suddenly realize that because you have had a special kind of education your poetry is bound to be elitist and not understood by people walking out of a factory and vice-versa.*

'But being in a group also encouraged me to write, and made me very critical of what I wrote. In that sense it is quite like a consciousness-raising group. Poetry can help you to express a feeling that you don't want to admit, but would like to talk about. You can write a poem about some mythical person without admitting that it's you. When other women come up and say "It's exactly how I felt two days ago" you feel relieved to be able to share your feeling with somebody else. It helps you to get rid of some pain that you've internalized, but does not pressurize you into admitting it openly.

'This therapeutic function of poetry could be more exploited by the women's movement. The experience "that's me too" is very often as good as "that's me". I once read in a play the phrase "paper blusheth not". That phrase is absolutely true; how many times have you seen a piece of paper turn red because it's ashamed of what it said? One day a woman wrote a poem about an amazing cure for headaches; it was entitled "Maggie's headache" and went something like this: "Masturbation, morning, noon and midnight; you come, and it's gone." That is a genuine feeling, this is somebody saying, "This is how I got rid of my headache; it worked for me, you can try it."

'Sometimes it's easier to write a poem than a letter. You don't have to punctuate, or tie things up. In poetry, the male myth of perfection and order is not so relevant. You can be very honest, it does not have to be logical nor need it make sense.

'As a group we worry far too much about what people are going to think and how they will interpret our poems. In a way, we are falling into a trap because we are trying not to write poetry like men do, nor to think on their terms, but to discover things in our own way. But you cannot normally live up to these ideals, other people are going to read what you write, and will interpret it the way they want it. At one stage we even came up against this horrible feeling that one cannot communicate anything to anybody. It was getting very heavy and we decided not to talk about it ever again, but the feeling keeps cropping up.

'Another major problem is the political implication of writing. Is poetry a kind of cop out? For example, we decided to write collectively about the obscenities shouted by men as we walked past a building site. But should we write our feelings down or tell them straight to the men? In a poem you can say what you wanted to say instead of screaming at these guys; you may be putting your anger in the wrong place. Is poetry a defence against having to take action? Can you take action and still write poetry? Well, I'm afraid we still don't have the answer to these questions.

'On the whole the group is really positive. It does encourage us to be creative, and may encourage other women too. Perhaps everybody is not going to turn round and say, "That's a great poem", but nobody is going to criticize you personally. That criticism is impersonal. Criticism is important as long as it is not destructive. It makes you think in a different way. Everything you write is somehow going in the right direction and you find that you are getting more honest, more free. It gives you an amazing confidence. Most people think that people are born and trained for some skills but this is not true. Everybody can write poetry. People are just put into boxes and told "these are your limits" (e.g. because you are a woman you'll be a washer-up all your life). That's not true. In the group we had somebody who always wanted to play the cello but was told she could not. When she realized she could be a poet, that she was a poet, she stood up and said, "Right, maybe I can be a cello player too!" She became a cellist.

'Somehow when you admit that you can be creative outside the boundaries which you have been confined within, you suddenly find that you are breaking down more than one barrier, and can go through a lot more. That's a political function of feminist poetry.'

WOMEN AND MUSIC

All music says something; it is an expression of feelings, a powerful means of communication, and it contains a certain view of life, supports a certain order of things. Unless we use music to express women's fight against oppression, to encourage other women to stand up with us, it will always support the established order of men as the stronger and women as the weaker, passive sex.

(Northern Women's Liberation Rock Band Manifesto)

In the past all 'young ladies' learned to play the piano and sing, but they were meant to use these skills to entertain others, not to make a career of it. At a time when higher education for women was very rare, it was extremely difficult for a young woman with talent to leave her home to go and study music and develop her skills. Many women who succeeded in the literary world had to write their novels in secret but you can't compose music secretly; it makes too much noise! If you did manage to write some music, there was still a fight to get the male musical world actually to play it. So, women who did compose stuck to songs and short pieces, which were considered more 'feminine' than the long orchestral works that make a composer's name. In the same way, it would have been extremely difficult for a woman to follow a career as a performer in classical music (there were of course women music hall singers, but they were not considered at all respectable!). She would not have been able to get the training she needed and would have been barred from jobs.

This situation still exists today; women are allowed to fill 'feminine' musical jobs like teaching music to children or amateur choral singing, but are not encouraged to join the professional music world. More than 50 per cent of all music students are women, yet women make up only 15 per cent of the Central London Branch of the Musician's Union. In 1975, the London Philharmonic Orchestra had seven women out of eighty-nine musicians, and the BBC symphony orchestra sixteen women out of 105 musicians. On the whole, women tend to get jobs in touring ballet and opera orchestras where the pay is comparatively low and they have to go on endless tours around the provinces.

In pop music, sexual discrimination is the same if not worse. A female singer's reason for existence is her voice *and* her sexuality. Not only has she got to be a good singer, but the press coverage she will receive will depend on whether she is attractive and sexy. Her success does not depend solely on what she is worth as a singer, but her worth as a sexual image as well. Why? Because record companies, themselves male-dominated, are well aware that their best vehicle for publicity, the press, is still a male stronghold. They will *watch* her rather than listen to her and will judge her fate according to their traditional male attitude.

The music industry has certain images of women and women singers have to conform to these images if they want to succeed — the 'earth-mother' folk singer or the glamorous female, who's there to be looked at rather than listened to. When they do make it, women performers tend to confine themselves to 'romantic' songs which correspond with the image of sweet, pretty women that men want to see. You rarely hear women performing the more aggressive kind of pop music.

Rock music is especially male-dominated. Women are mostly put down as too stupid to get a band together, and men think only *they* can handle the complex electronic equipment. No self-respecting woman would want to sing the words of most pop-songs; many of them are positively insulting:

> Pop lyrics present women as sex objects for men. Nowadays no one would dare insult blacks by singing songs about golliwogs, but men think nothing of singing about women as 'baby', 'doll', 'my girl', in other words as their playthings, their possessions. Women are not encouraged to be strong and independent beings in their own right. Instead commercial pop songs present for them a world in which true love is their only goal and men are the only source of sadness, joy or meaning in their lives. These songs help to keep women in their accustomed roles as wives and mothers, dependent on men, because they hide the real conflicts in women's lives and relationships with men and so prevent them understanding their oppression.
>
> (Northern Women's Liberation Rock Band Manifesto)

But more aggressive, positive women singers are appearing and becoming well-known, women like Joan Armatrading, Dory Previn, and Patti Smith. Specifically feminist singers and bands are emerging who try to create music that expresses the new values of women standing up for themselves: 'Our songs are about women's hardships in the home, at work and in their social life, about women fighting back, having a good time together without men, about how *we* want to be' (Northern Women's Liberation Rock Band Manifesto). Women's bands are forming and playing, writing new songs that we can sing and really identify with.

We as women are discovering the importance of music in our lives and are creating our own music. Frankie Armstrong, the folk singer, says:

> '*Music has an incredibly vital role, in terms of actually being able to express and convey aspects of experience which require immense subtlety. As a speaker I don't have that gift but I have it as a singer. When I sing, I know I can involve a particular kind of experience about what it's like to be a woman. Some people after a performance say to me, "For the first time, I really understood something", or "My husband has at last understood what I have been saying for five years". Somehow songs leave you a lot more open. There's a lot of work to be done in relation to conveying ideas amongst ourselves, amongst women, and songs, music can make a fantastic contribution to it. For example the music of our ancestors put me in touch with a sense of women's history and women's roots that no history books will ever do. There's nothing in history books about the experience of poor peasants or working-class women. The only place you are likely to find that, although obviously still very selectively, is in the songs that they sang and continued to sing right up to this century.*
>
> '*With songs we can learn about our roots. This has been a great revelation about who I am and what I am and what I want to sing about . . .*'

Music is not something that belongs to a few people who are allowed to stand up on a stage, *music belongs to all of us.*

Positive Happenings

1. Several women's bands have formed over the past few years and have been much in demand to play to women all over the country. These include the *Northern Women's Liberation Rock Band*, the *Stepney Sisters* (both now disbanded) and *Jam Today*. In Germany there are *The Flying Lesbians*, whose record is for sale in Britain. Groups change and break up over the years, so contact WIRES (Information Service) for current information.

2. Women in the States are starting to set up their own recording companies, such as Olivia Records, producing records by feminist singers and also trying to work in a more collective, less competitive way than conventional recording companies. Records on that label by singers like Cris Williamson, Meg Christian, Holly Near, are becoming more widely available in this country.

3. In order to gain access to knowledge of the technical side of recording and production, women in this country are trying to set up some sort of recording facilities, and also to organize a course so that women can learn the skills themselves. Both projects are quite enormous and a lot of money

will be involved in trying to set up the recording facilities, but it's one way that women can get to know what other women are doing musically. All over the country, women are very isolated and to make cassettes would be at least a start to break this isolation.

4. Women are organizing around trying to encourage women to take up instruments (see: Women's Arts Alliance). A music register at the Women's Arts Alliance in London keeps a list so that women interested in certain instruments can contact other women.

5. Monthly women's music events are held in cities all over Britain to bring musicians together and create a regular setting for women to discuss and share ideas, and perhaps play together or have women's bands playing. There have been several women's weekend music workshops in Liverpool.

6. At the grass roots, music is being written and performed around specific issues like National Abortion Campaign songs, songs about women's strikes, and so on. Women sing on demonstrations; at the May 1977 NAC demonstration, *Jam Today* played on a lorry throughout the March attracting many more supporters than shouted slogans have ever done.

For more information contact: **WOMEN'S LIBERATION MUSIC PROJECTS** *c/o Women's Arts Alliance, 10 Cambridge Terrace Mews, London NW1*

BOOKS TO READ

WAYS OF SEEING
by John Berger, Pelican, £1.25
'The way we see things is affected by what we know or what we believe.' Full of reproductions, this book is a bit difficult to read but quite fascinating. It contains a very good section on the way women are being seen or, rather, used.

MAMA! Women Artists Together
by a collective of women based in Birmingham, from Birmingham Women's Artists Group, Flat 2, 20 Valentine Road, Kings Heath, Birmingham 14, 50p
This brings together articles on women's art that have previously appeared elsewhere, particularly 'Some Thoughts on Feminist Art' and 'Towards a Revolutionary Feminist Art', both edited by Monica Sjöö, and a detailed report of the Feministo Women's Postal Event. There are pieces on the Women's Arts Alliance, Women's Posters and a useful resource list including some US contacts and publications. It is an excellent starting point for exploring the role of art in society, women's art, and how this relates to their lives as women. This booklet is now being distributed by the Publications Distribution Co-operative and is available from some bookshops.

WOMEN ARTISTS
by Karen Peterson and J.J. Wilson, Women's Press, £3.95
A recognition and reappraisal of women artists from the early Middle Ages up to today, with lots of illustrations.

ART AND SEXUAL POLITICS: Why have there been no great women artists?
by Thomas Hess and Elizabeth Baker, Collier Macmillan, £1.50
The other question raised is 'Why have there been no great women artists even though women have produced great works of art?' Who knows that a painting attributed to J.L. David is now considered to be by Constance Marie Charpentier, who worked

in David's studio? It was purchased in 1917 for $200,000. This book is interesting with pleasant illustrations.

TOWARDS A NEW EXPRESSION
by S. Santoro, Rivolta Feminile, 70p, available from Feminist Books
A slim volume of photographs of the portrayal of female genitalia in art and culture.

WOMEN AND THE ARTS
Spring-Summer 1974 issue of The Arts in Society *from University of Wisconsin-Extension, 610 Langdon Street, Madison, Wisconsin, $3.50*
The Arts in Society is an excellent US magazine which covers aspects of social, community, political and educational uses of art in contemporary society. The Spring-Summer 1974 issue was devoted to women's art, and is well worth reading. A quote from Elizabeth Janeway writing in that issue: 'Because women have let the false images stand as our representatives we have falsified ourselves, chosen to divide ourselves and exist in hopeless endless stasis, unable either to act truly or to be ourselves in freedom and enjoyment. What can we do? We must change our image instead of merely withdrawing inside it and denying that it represents the self.'

OUR HIDDEN HERITAGE: Five centuries of Women Artists
by Eleanor Tufts, Paddington Press, £5.95
To the familiar 'Why have there been no great women artists?' the author prefers 'Why is so little known of the great women artists of the past?' Many women had quite a successful career but there is no record of it — the Bolognese Elizabeth Siram supported her family with her income from painting during the Renaissance. This book calls into question the value and methods of art history as a whole. It is highly recommended to read but unfortunately highly priced too. Ask your local library to get it.

WOMEN'S LITERATURE

We recommend the usual writers: Jane Austen, Simone de Beauvoir, the Bronte sisters, George Eliot, Mary Gaskell, Ursula le Guin, Doris Lessing, Anais Nin, Jean Rhys, George Sand, Olive Scheiner, Virginia Woolf. It is impossible to give all the contemporary writers but here are a few good titles:

A ROOM OF ONE'S OWN
by Virginia Woolf, Hogarth Press, £1.75

LES GUERILLERIES
by Monique Wittig, Picador, 40p (poetic novel)

RIVERFINGER WOMEN
by E. Nachman, Daughters Press, £2 (feminist classic)

RUBYFRUIT JUNGLE
by R.M. Brown, Daughters Press, £2 (feminist classic)
(Anything published by Daughters Press is usually worth reading. Details of their publications can be obtained from Daughters Inc, 22 Charles Street, New York, NY 10014.)

THE LESBIAN BODY
by Monique Wittig, Peter Owen, £3.25 (poetic novel)

THE THREE MARIAS: The New Portuguese Letters
Paladin, £1.50

DAUGHTER OF EARTH
by Agnes Smedley, Virago, £1.95 (feminist classic)

DOWN AMONG THE WOMEN
by Fay Weldon, Heinemann, £2.00

FEMALE FRIENDS
by Fay Weldon, Heinemann, £2.75

REMEMBER ME
by Fay Weldon, Hodder and Stoughton, £4.25

THEATRE

SINK SONGS
by Michelene Wandor and D. Brooke, from Feminist Books, 45p
A collection of seven short feminist plays.

FEMALE TRANSPORT
by Steve Gooch, Pluto Press, 75p
A play about six female convicts transported to Australia in the early nineteenth century.

Comprehensive book lists on Feminist literature can be obtained from *Compendium Bookshop, 240 Camden High Street, London NW1*, or from *Feminist Books, PO Box HP5, Leeds 6*.

See also **WOMEN AND LITERATURE: an annotated bibliography of women writers** *by the Sense and Sensibility Collective, 90p, from the Corner Bookshop, 162 Woodhouse Lane, Leeds 2*. This bibliography deals exclusively with fiction, and twentieth-century authors account for over 80 per cent of all entries. The introduction states that it will be useful to women wanting to study the female experience as it has been portrayed through literature, as well as for the individual simply looking for good reading. It includes a cross-referenced index.

WOMEN'S POETRY

SEVEN WOMEN
by Women's Literature Collective, 70p

CUTLASSES AND EARRINGS
edited by Michelene Wandor and Michel Roberts, available from Feminist Books, 60p
A collection of feminist poetry by Astra Blaug, Alison Fell, Michele Roberts, Sheila Rowbotham and Michelene Wandor.

MONSTER
by R. Morgan, Vintage, 44p
An American feminist poet published by women in the British Women's Movement.

WOMEN AND THE MEDIA

A Woman's Own Thoughts

'A woman is a sometime thing.
Sometimes a mother,
Sometimes a wife,
Sometimes a sister, a nurse with your life
In her hands.
Sometimes a lover, sometimes a worker,
Often a listener, occasionally a shirker.
Sometimes this and sometimes that
(Usually the lady who feeds the cat).
A gossip, a poet, a cook . . .
Declaim it:
She's whatever is needed. You name it.
And sometimes I think, with this incredible range,
Wouldn't it be nice to be ME for a change?'
J.J. (First published in *Woman's Own*)

The mass media — television, radio, newspapers and magazines, films, advertisements, popular art and sculpture — all portray women in the same way; and by presenting us over and over again in the same limited roles, they contribute to and reinforce our images of ourselves, our expectations and our fantasies.

Whatever form the medium takes, whether it is spoken, written or visual, the relationship between the sexes remains the same. As John Berger says in *Ways of Seeing*: 'Men act and women appear.' The social presence of a man symbolizes power, something he is *doing to you*. By contrast, 'Woman's presence expresses her own attitude to herself and defines what can and cannot be *done to her* . . . To be born a woman has been to be born within an allotted and confined space.'

This 'allotted and confined space' is forged by a male-dominated society. Within it there are several roles we can try to slot into, either one at a time or together: the housewife, the sex object, the mother, the whore, the virgin; but they all have one thing in common: dependence on male approval. This has many painful consequences for women. Since we exist only through our image we have to watch ourselves continually and are not allowed to express ourselves as we really are:

Me, myself is dead.
I am wife to my husband
I am mother to our sons
I am mistress to our dog.
And there is nothing else of me,
Nothing left of me
Me, myself is dead.
(anonymous poem sent to Mary Stott, and quoted in her book
Forgetting's No Excuse, published by Virago)

Let's try to analyse this unequal relationship between men and women and how the media will emphasize and play with it.

According to the ad-men, a housewife's reason for her existence lies in her ability to cater, polish, scrub and care passionately about the quality of the weekly wash. Her reward for doing all this work will be love from her husband and children. Therefore, on television we are bombarded with model housewives in immaculate houses, coping smilingly with all the demands made on them. The message is clear: 'Women, this is your only aim and wish in life. If you can't attain these heights, your family won't love you anymore. Only our products can help you find happiness.' What makers of advertisements do is simply to reinforce the traditional stereotypes of women in order to sell products. They know that a woman has been taught to think that her family's pleasure is the way she can be fulfilled, and therefore they play heavily on this.

Now women are campaigning against these female stereotypes.

Women have also had little access to the technical knowledge which is indispensible for learning many media skills, skills which at the moment are monopolized by men in a male-dominated media industry (in newspapers, in printing, in television, in film production, in recording facilities . . .).

We are now beginning to set up our own facilities, and organizing our own courses where we can learn these skills ourselves. We are learning to make films, to print, to publish by ourselves, and in doing this we are expressing our own personalities and defining our own images.

Women in Media

Women in Media Group (WIM) is an organization for women only, most of whom work in some branch of the media, in television, broadcasting, advertising, public relations. Their main aims are to work actively towards increasing women's opportunities for careers, for promotion and for general employment in all levels of all the media. They are also active in bringing pressure to bear on the relevant bodies to improve and demystify the media image of women. And they are also more generally trying to improve the legal position of women in this country.

In 1972, the group started a campaign against the advertising of vaginal deodorants on television. They wrote to Sir Brian Young, Director General of the Independent Television Authority (now called the Independent Broadcasting Authority), protesting against the acceptance of advertisements for vaginal deodorants, because of their harmful effects on the body. They stressed that they found it quite extraordinary that the Authority should allow the advertising of such a socially useless and medically harmful product while continuing to maintain its ban on the advertising of contraceptives.

Two months later, after another exchange of letters, the IBA announced that it was banning all television advertising of vaginal deodorants and sanitary protection under the 'good taste' section of the code. The IBA's comment was that 'it considered the views of WIM alongside much other evidence and in the context of wider issues', but obviously the WIM campaign was successful. 'This shows what an organized, determined group of women can achieve with or without media expertise. The secret lies in assembling the evidence, stating it lucidly, addressing it to the top authority with copies to all the key people, and never accepting the bland brush off.'

Since then the group has worked hard. They have actively supported the first Women's Rights candidate in the General Election of 1974 (Una Kroll, in Sutton and Cheam); and they played an important part in the drafting of the Sex Discrimination legislation, advising the Select Committee, making submissions, organizing witnesses to appear before the Committee, briefing MPs to ask questions in the House of Commons. Submissions have also been made to the Annan Committee on the future of Broadcasting, to the Royal Commission on the Press and to the Heilbron Committee on the law on rape.

From time to time WIM organizes conferences and seminars on particular themes such as 'Packaging of Women', or how women are portrayed in advertisements.

WIM hold monthly general meetings, but most activities are organized by sub-groups which meet more frequently. These are set up informally to deal with specific objectives such as organizing a seminar or pursuing a particular campaign. Other sub-groups are more permanent and are set up to educate WIM members as well as to monitor events. An example of this is the sub-group on racism in the media.

WIM sub-groups often seek help from, and give help to, other specialist groups for particular campaigns and longer-term investigations. WIM has helped the National Abortion Campaign with publicity and has been instrumental in helping set up the Sex Discrimination Act 1975

Group which is composed of representatives of the Child Poverty Action Group, the NCCL, the Women's Liberation Campaign for Financial and Legal Independence, and Rights of Women, and which, in consultation with members of the Equal Opportunities Commission, is looking into how the tax and Social Security system penalizes women.

WIM has also organized a seminar for writers to discuss, among other things, feminist writing and whether 'female' writing exists. It has also applied for a grant from the Equal Opportunities Commission to make a video film on images of women today, for use by feminist groups here and abroad. Their latest achievement has been the publication by Virago of a book entitled *Is This Your Life?* on images of women in the media (see: Books), written by various WIM members.

WOMEN IN MEDIA GROUP *c/o Sandra Brown, Flat 10, 59 Drayton Gardens, London SW10*

For more information about discrimination in particular media, see:

IMAGES OF WOMEN: Guidelines for Promoting Equality through Journalism
a report by the NUJ Equality Working Party, from the National Union of Journalists, 314–320 Grays Inn Road, London WC1, 20p
'Don's Wife Wins Award' . . . 'Blonde bombshell Margaret Bain . . . took over as the glamorous face of Scottish Nationalism from party pin-up Margo Macdonald' . . . 'Custom Car wants a features writer . . . he (or she – state bust size) . . . ' . . . 'Another food price shock for the housewife' . . . There are very many ways in which journalists perpetuate the image of women as second-class citizens by stereotyping them or simply ignoring their existence. This short guide looks at some of the ways that the press – and this includes the quality press – does this, and suggests some ideas for avoiding this. (See also: Sexism in Children's Books.)

PATTERNS OF DISCRIMINATION AGAINST WOMEN IN THE FILM AND TV INDUSTRY: A Report
by Sandra Benton for the Association of Cinematographic, Television and Allied Technicians (ACTT), 2 Soho Square, London W1

Some Useful Addresses

AFFIRM
35 Coleherne Road, London SW10
AFFIRM is the Alliance for Fair Images and Representation in the Media. This group is 'interested in combatting offensive stereotyping of women (including hostile treatment of lesbians) in any of the media, whether advertising, broadcasting or the press. AFFIRM is *not* a research organization, it's more of a pressure group that express the views of those at the receiving end of prejudice and misrepresentation.' They have produced a leaflet explaining the methods they have found best in expressing disapproval of unsatisfactory treatment of women in the material put out by the media. In their five pamphlets, they give addresses to write to, and suggest the emphasis to make your letter more effective.

ADVERTISING STANDARDS AUTHORITY
15 Ridgmount Street, London WC1
For complaints about advertisements, though they are notoriously unresponsive to complaints on grounds of sexism.

INDEPENDENT BROADCASTING AUTHORITY
70 Brompton Road, London SW3
For complaints about advertisements on independent television.

Further Reading

IS THIS YOUR LIFE? Images of Women in the Media
edited by Josephine King and Mary Stott, Virago, £1.95
In this book, a group of women investigate the attitudes and images the media offer readers, viewers and listeners. They look at the myths perpetuated about women and try to find new possibilities. Some chapters are better than others but it makes very good basic reading for anyone interested in the media.

WOMEN IN FILM

London Women's Film Group

'The London Women's Film Group is a film-making collective which came into existence in 1971–72 with the aims of making films for the women's liberation movement and generating interest and discussion about the relationship between feminism and the cinema.

'The film industry has always been dominated by men. Within the industry, discrimination is overt. Jobs such as camera operator and sound recordist are still almost exclusively male preserves, although a few women are just beginning to break down those barriers. In general, women have been relegated to the traditional areas of "women's work" within the industry, to being secretary, production assistant, researcher, etc.

'One of our central aims is that women should be able to acquire those skills denied them by the industry, to work collectively sharing both skills and ideas, introducing politics into the practice of film-making itself.

'Only when women have access to film technology can a genuinely feminist cinema be generated, a cinema reflecting the political needs and desires of women.

'We would also like to show our films in as wide a variety of contexts as possible, to factories, housing estates, schools, colleges and women's groups. In this way we could begin to break down the traditional division between work and leisure activities and the passivity of the spectator.

'We prefer to send speakers out with our films so that the films can be accompanied by a discussion of the issues, both political and aesthetic, raised by the films.

'The group's most recent film, The Great Equal Pay Show, was finished in 1975. The major protagonists of the film are all played by women caricaturing various stock types: "a woman Cabinet Minister", "a male trade union convenor", "a typical male fantasy housewife". The film sets out to show how the Equal Pay Act, introduced by Barbara Castle and the Labour Government in 1970 with an eye to the elections and finally phased in by 1975, will not necessarily improve the wages and working conditions of women.

'Spring and summer 1975 were spent scripting and shooting a film about abortion. This is a forty-minute film, part-fiction, part-documentary, financed by a small grant from the British Film Industry.'

For further information and speakers write to:
LONDON WOMEN'S FILM GROUP 42 Earlham Street, London WC2
Their films are distributed by the Other Cinema, 12–13 Little Newport Street, London WC2. Seven other short feminist films are also distributed by the Other Cinema:

Serve and Obey (3 mins) by Linda Love and Sheila Malone. The film about girls in school takes its titles from the appalling motto of a school in London.

Women against the Bill (20 mins) directed by Esther Ronay and members of the Notting Hill Women's Liberation Group. This is a series of interviews with women shop stewards discussing the Industrial Relations Bill and the reasons why they are against it, how they joined the union and the strength it has given them.

Fakenham Film (10 mins) by Susan Shapiro with Socialist Women. The third and fourth months of a successful six months work-in by women workers at Sextons Shoe Factory, Fakenham, Norfolk. The issues raised are woman's right to work and the relationship between women and trade unions.

Miss/Mrs (6 mins) by Linda Love and friends. About the reality of being a woman contrasted with 'Woman' as she is presented by the media.

Betteshanger (10 mins).   The first film in England to be crewed entirely by women.   About a woman who was involved with other miners' wives in an organization formed by the women to support their husbands' demands during the miners long and successful strike in 1972 and how their own lives improved in the process.

Women of the Rhondda (20 mins) by Mary Capps, Mary Kelly and others.   Interviews with three women, daughters, wives and mothers of miners in Wales who lived through the epic strikes of the 1920s and 1930s.

Put Yourself in my Place (20 mins) by Francine Winham.   Husband moans to his wife 'put yourself in my place': she does and puts him in her place and they view the world from each other's standpoint.

(*For more feminist films see:* **Selective List of Women's Films Available in the UK**)

Sheffield Film Co-operative

At the moment (1977) this is the only women's film group in existence outside London.

Though the group started in 1973, they only took the name of 'Sheffield Film Co-operative' in 1975.   The group now consists of four women, all from the Sheffield Women's Liberation Group.   They have five children between them and are very concerned about the everyday problems women face.

In 1973, the Women's Liberation Group made a series of six schools programmes on women for the local BBC radio station.   The series was entitled 'Not Just a Pretty Face'. They were given complete control over the programmes, and for most of them recording, editing, and mixing sound effects was new and something they enjoyed getting to grips with.   To their surprise, the programmes were not only well received and repeated the following school year, but they subsequently heard that 'Not Just a Pretty Face' was quoted in the BBC handbook in 1974 as a good example of imaginative local radio broadcasting.

By 1974, the group had largely dispersed.   At the same time, a local and experimental cable TV service had opened in Sheffield operating as 'Your community TV station'.   Four of the original group approached the manager and said they'd like to make some programmes about Sheffield from a woman's point of view:

> '*To our amazement he said: "Right, fine, get on with it." At that point we almost got cold feet; we knew nothing about TV equipment, had no experience at all in video, and all of us had pre-school-age children. However, in the end we decided that anything we did had to be at least as good as the awful programmes they were doing, so we went in head first.*
>
> '*We made the programmes about "the problems of shopping in the wonderful new shopping centre if you were so odd as to have prams, pushchairs, young children and so on." This meant taking the outside broadcast van to the city centre. We were incredibly ambitious at that time, but one of the advantages of knowing nothing before you start is that you have no idea of the problems involved — you just have to find ways of overcoming them as they present themselves. It also means that you are learning a great deal very rapidly (a technician accompanied us too).*'

The programmes took four months to be finished.   They never reached a lot of people because the cable station only serviced a small proportion of homes in Sheffield.   Nevertheless the group decided to make another programme on childcare facilities for working mothers, which later proved useful to the Working Women's Charter Group in Sheffield.

The group made their break with the cable station when they decided to tackle the subject of abortion.   At this time, the National Abortion Campaign was at its height, and NHS abortions were notoriously difficult to obtain in Sheffield.   The group decided that it would be possible to show a film much more widely than a video recording.   Moreover they would have complete control over a film, whereas the manager at the cable station was more cautious, and kept reminding them that his licence to transmit came from the Home Office.

So the Sheffield Film Co-op was formed in May 1975.   The abortion film, *A Woman Like*

You, was completed in December of that year. 'Although technically there's a lot wrong with it, particularly regarding the sound quality, we were all going through the process of using new equipment again.' The film has been shown widely by the women's movement. Four copies were sold to the British Pregnancy Advisory Service in the summer of 1976 and it won an award in the Derby Independent Film Awards.

For their next film, they were given £750 by the National Women's Aid Federation to make a film on battered women, and got a further £150 from the Yorkshire Arts Association. *That's No Lady* is a fifteen-minute colour film dealing with the myths and prejudices surrounding the subject of battered women; it is available from the National Women's Aid Federation, 51 Chalcot Road, London NW1.

The group has formulated two main aims:

'Firstly to establish ourselves as a competent film production group in an industry domin- ated by men (even amongst independent film-makers women are thin on the ground!); and secondly to make films that the women's movement find useful or that treat subjects from a woman's perspective (for example we would like to make a film about the way women are treated by the National Health Service).

'Money is hard to come by. The Regional Arts Associations and the British Film Institute are the only public funding bodies and they have very little money. We are in the process of applying to the Gulbenkian Foundation for money for equipment. It would be used by us and other film-makers in Sheffield. If we are successful that will be a big step forward as the other problem is always access to equipment. It's very difficult to make plans for the future. We just try to keep all our options open, follow up any- thing that sounds interesting and wait and see.'

SHEFFIELD FILM CO-OPERATIVE *13 Taptonville Road, Sheffield 10*

Women and film Group

The Educational Advisory Service of the British Film Institute, together with the Society for Education in Film and Television, an organization it grant aids, are both concerned with the development and promotion of media studies in schools and colleges. A few women who work for BFI and SEFT have tried to launch a theoretical and educational debate focussing on questions of ideology and the relationship of film and media to society:

'As feminists we are concerned to use this theoretical knowledge by placing it within an ideological perspective drawn from the women's movement and to see how far the theories produced by film and media studies can be made to work for feminist analyses.

'Summarizing this work very briefly and therefore crudely, in the first instance it is concerned with art and/or entertainment as products, rather than as creative expressions of the human spirit (what we are taught at school). Works of art and media products are produced by a specific kind of human labour using various technologies, techniques and artistic devices, themselves produced as tools by a particular society for particular needs. By saying this, we take art out of the realm of the eternal and put it firmly back into history.

'We feel that this change of emphasis from the what *to the* how *is very important to feminists. Usually we tend to think that if only women could get behind the camera, sexism would disappear from films and TV, or that all we have to do is to go through media programmes and excise the sexist images and replace them with "true" feminist ones. However, we have not only to gain control of the equipment, but also to under- stand the techniques, the forms and conventions of story-telling, the language of the*

image and make them work for us, rather than allow them so insidiously to subvert our good intentions.

'*It was these ideas which we saw as crucial to the work of analysing images of women in the media. We formed ourselves into a non-institutional ad-hoc group, and in July 1975, we organized a one-day workshop on Images of Women to raise these questions on how images are constructed. Subsequently, two issues of an* Images of Women News-letter *were produced which aimed to make more generally available information on groups, events and materials collected by us and others.*'

The group wants to develop resource materials for use in schools and colleges on women and the media, and for their work with women's groups. To make this possible they have produced various publications:

1. *Film Study Extracts:* a number of extracts were selected for the BFI's Distribution Library from films by women film-makers and some titles concerned with the treatment of women in Holly-wood. A list of these extracts is included in the Women's Film List; and details of plot and extract synopses and discussion points are available in the extract supplement.

2. *Film Availability:* this is a list of films made by women or concerned with women's issues which are available on 16mm and currently in commercial distribution. The group also tries to bring pressure to bear on distribution companies to make available 16mm prints of films made by women. So far they have succeeded in the case of Dorothy Arzner's *Dance Girl, Dance*. They are now pressing the BFI Distribution Library to take Nelly Kaplan's *La Fiancée du Pirate*. They welcome suggestions or requests for other titles around which they could mount campaigns; it makes it easier if you can also make a promise of a booking for the film should it become available.

3. *Images of Women in Film and TV Study Guide:* a project on which they collaborated with a number of other women working in the area. As well as giving an introduction to feminist film criticism, this covers a number of topics, outlining the basic principles involved, and various strategies for working them through. These topics include: (a) the image of women in media (slides and documentation to raise questions about the construction of images and how sexist ideology operates within them, using images from advertising, magazines, newspaper photographs, film posters, agitprop material, accompanied by notes for teachers indicating the kind of points the group had in mind when making the selection plus ideas for work which students might do); (b) women in Hollywood (case studies of three or four films, with slides and sample shot break-downs); (c) women in television; (d) history of women film-makers; and (e) women's independ-ent film-making.

4. *Women and Film Resources Folder:* a collection of information and documentation relating to the area, including film availability lists, course outlines, bibliographies/filmographies and other related material.

5. *Miscellaneous material:* (a) BFI Book Library Bibliography No. 51, *Women and the Cinema*; (b) a bibliography prepared in conjunction with an Images of Women course run at the Polytechnic of Central London; (c) Images of Women workshop documentation; and (d) a collection of Women and Film/Media course outlines.

WOMEN AND FILM GROUP *c/o Educational Advisory Service, British Film Institute, 81 Dean Street, London W1*

SOCIETY FOR EDUCATION IN FILM AND TELEVISION *29 Old Compton Street, London W1*

Selective List of Women's films Available in the UK

We thought it would be useful for women who would like to see some good women's films but 'don't know anything about it' to have a pre-selected list.

This one is purely personal in that it's based on our and other women's opinions; it's never-theless a good base to start from. Summaries have been taken from the BFI women's film list. For an exhaustive list, write to the Educational Advisory Service, British Film Institute, 81 Dean Street, London W1. All films are available in 16mm, except where otherwise stated.

FEATURE FILMS

Arzner, Dorothy: *Dance Girl, Dance* (USA, 1940, 90 mins, Kingston): chorus girl film with woman's picture. Important for Arzner's treatment of traditional Hollywood female stereotypes.

Breien, Anje: *Wives* (Norway, 1975, 95 mins, colour, Contemporary): three former school friends now married and in their late twenties meet again at a reunion party. They decide to prolong their fiesta and set out to leave everyday existence behind.

Kaplan, Nelly: *La Fiancée du Pirate* (France, 1969, 106 mins, CIC, 35mm only): story of young woman exploited and ostracized by inhabitants of French provincial town, who finds her revenge by becoming local prostitute.

Loden, Barbara: *Wanda* (USA, 1968, 100 mins, colour, Columbia Warner): Wanda is divorced, out of a job, drifts from man to man and becomes involved with a bank robber.

Micklin Silver, Joan: *Hester Street* (USA, 1975, 86 mins, Connoisseur): New York 1896, Lower East Side. An emerging community of Russian Jews is portrayed through the activities of immigrants.

Red Sisters Collective: *Take it Like a Man, Ma'am!* (Denmark, 1975, Other Cinema): a middle-aged woman finds no meaning in life, finally finds work and becomes involved in a strike, discovers her strength in solidarity with other women. Sex role reversal sequence.

Rothman, Stephanie: *Student Nurses* USA, 1970, 85 mins, Tigon, 35 mm only): film in soft porn genre made by declared feminist, telling the various stories of four student nurses.

Varda, Agnes: *Le Bonheur* (France, 1965, 79 mins, colour, Harris): bitter sweet story of a man who loves his wife, children and mistress. The wife is found drowned after she has learned of her husband's affair and a new family is set up when husband and mistress marry.

Zetterling, Mai: *The Girls* (Sweden, 1969, 93 mins, Contemporary): first film of 1960s to display militant feminist position.

WOMEN'S SHORTS

Nelson, Gunvor: *Take off* (UK, 12 mins, Spare Rib): ironic comment on truth behind phenomenon of stripping.

Severson, Anne: *The Big Chakra* (UK, 10 mins, Spare Rib): meditation on the human vagina.

WOMEN'S MOVEMENT AND AGIT-PROP FILMS

All the London Women's Film Group films and those listed by them (*see:* London Women's Film Group) and the Sheffield Film Co-operative (*see:* Sheffield Film Co-operative).

Crockford, Sue: *One Two Three* (UK, 1975, 32 mins, Liberation Films): Dartmouth Park Hill Children's Community Centre showing the nursery at work.

International Women's Film Project: *The Double Day* (USA, 1972, 52 mins, Other Cinema): scientific and historical analysis of conditions of working women in Latin America.

Mackenzie, Midge: *Women Talking* (UK, 1970, 90 mins, Liberation Films): Jane, an American woman and mother of five children, talks about her life and family and the changes she has gone through.

Newsreel: *Miss America 1968* (USA, 1968, 7 mins, Liberation Films): Women's Liberation Groups disrupt annual pageant in Atlantic City, New Jersey.

Price, Victoria: *A Woman's Place is in the Home* (UK, 1974, 20 mins, colour, Liberation Films): part documentary, part drama about a couple tracing problems in their relationship to the conditioning of their upbringing.

San Francisco Newsreel Group: *The Woman's Film* (USA, 1971, 42 mins, Liberation Films): women talking about how they gained strength by uniting in women's rights campaigns.

Sydney Women's Film Group: *Film for Discussion* (Australia, 24 mins, National Film School): a film about two young women considering the contradictory facts and fantasies associated with being female.

Thompson, Hilary and Sheldon, Caroline: *Two Plus Two or Death of a Bullfighter* (UK, 1974, 25 mins, colour, 8mm): comment on sexism in Spain.

Tufnell Park Women's Liberation Workshop: *Woman are you Satisfied with your Life?* (UK, 1969, 10 mins, Liberation Films): silent film contrasting real life struggle of women with the image of women as purveyed through advertising.

Winham, Francine: *Careless Love* (UK, 1975, 10 mins, colour, National Film School): a drama in which a woman finds her lover unsympathetic to marriage because her children aren't his. She resolves the situation in a dramatic way.

Winham, Francine: *Hell Girl House* (UK, 1974, 12 mins, National Film School): fantasy horror film about women's conditioning in relation to make-up.

FEATURE FILMS MADE BY MEN OF FEMINIST INTEREST

Biberman, H.J.: *Salt of the Earth* (USA, 1953, 94 mins, Contemporary): reconstruction of Mexican miners' strike for equal pay and conditions and how the women begin to assert their needs for equality.

Karmitz, M.: *Coup pour Coup* (France, 1972, 90 mins, colour, Other Cinema): reconstruction of a women's strike in clothing factory in France, very moving and very funny.

Kluge, A.: *Occasional Work of a Female Slave* (Germany, 1974, 90 mins, Cinegate): Roswitha Bronski supports her children and her husband by performing illegal abortions.

ADDRESSES OF DISTRIBUTORS

Cinegate, *70 Portobello Road, London W11*
Contemporary Films, *55 Greek Street, London W1*
Connoisseur Films, *167 Oxford Street, London W1*
Columbia-Warner Distributors, *135 Wardour Street, London W1*
Robert Kingston Films, *645—7 Uxbridge Road, Hayes End, Middlesex*
Liberation Films, *2 Chichele Road, London NW2*
National Film School, *Beaconsfield, Bucks*
The Other Cinema, *12—13 Little Newport Street, London WC2*
Spare Rib, *27 Clerkenwell Close, London EC1*
Tigon Films, *103—109 Wardour Street, London W1*

SOME USEFUL ADDRESSES

BRITISH FILM INSTITUTE
81 Dean Street, London W1
The BFI has a number of sections relevant to any-one interested in images of women. The Still Department, National Film Archive and Book Library all have useful and important material but only to members of the Institute. In the Educa-tion Department, the Film Material Section is very anxious to make it widely known that they have resources and services available for women's studies and film (*see:* Women and Film Group).

FILM WOMEN INTERNATIONAL
Svenska Film Institutet, Box 27126, 10252 Stock-holm 27, Sweden
The first worldwide association of women working in films was founded by twenty-five directors, producers, actresses and critics in July 1975. The aims and activities of the new association include among other things: supporting and encouraging the production of films made by women, films creating a new and more truthful image of women, films condemning discriminatory attitudes and behaviour of a 'sexist' character; cataloguing and collecting archives of films by women; helping to organize festivals, congresses, seminars and helping to widen contacts between women working in films throughout the world.

WOMEN'S CINEMA
Drill Hall, Chenies Street, off Tottenham Court Road, London WC1
A cinema club for women only.

TELEVISION : WOMEN IN FOCUS

The 'Women in Focus' programmes were made as an experiment in Community Television in the Vale of Leven, an industrial area fifteen miles to the west of Glasgow. They are an attempt to bring out the reality of women's lives in the area and to point to facilities, groups and local activities that are available to women.

The emphasis is on what steps women can take to help themselves and improve their situation, because very often they find themselves desperately isolated. The main material of the programmes is drawn from individual women's personal experiences, supported by statistics or more general points.

Most of the women involved were local, the majority being young mothers; Women's Liberation and other groups from Glasgow were drawn in to help with specific programmes. They all took part in the planning, filming and editing. The whole project, from making first contacts to producing six finished programmes, was completed in four months. None of the women had had any previous experience of video or film-making; they learnt as they went along and acquired the skills needed as quickly as they could, but 'any problems encountered through lack of expert help were offset by the advantage of having a collective effort in which we taught ourselves.'

'Women in Focus' started as an adult education project, but grew into something much wider. In the course of the project, two babysitting groups started and many long discussions developed around the themes of the programmes; a group sprang up consisting of women willing to act as leaders in discussions round the programmes.

'We are six in the group; three of us are mothers of children under five. We are all of differing religions (protestant, agnostic, catholic) and of varying political affiliations (one of us is a communist, the rest agree to differ on many subjects). In fact, it is our agreeing to differ that seems to hold us together because in spite of the differences, we all have the same common purpose and we have all suffered common problems. We could probably write three chapters of your book telling the story of bloody housing schemes, the isolation, the widespread depression, and so on, and the parallel story of how we each became involved in our project and how our attitude progressed from "What the hell" to "Christ! we must do something about this".

'Our main objective at the moment is to have our films shown to as many people as possible, to men, women and teenagers, both to individuals and to members of organizations. Through this, we hope to voice the opinions of the ordinary individual, often as isolated woman, and gain recognition of the problems facing that woman with a view not to raise a battle cry, but more to promote a desire for individual and mutual self help, which very often sets the pace of those in authority or at least acts as a stimulus for them to look seriously at the problems facing women in society.

'As a group, we have decided to form ourselves into a branch of the Workers' Educational Association. This is to give us an identity, a means of self-education (the more knowledge we acquire the better we will function), and it will also provide us with a practical link with the body which holds our tapes. The benefits to each individual member of our group during the programmes have been immeasurable and these we hope to be able to pass on to each and every housewife/mum/worker who sees our films. We hope they'll make people think deeply and not in a despairingly shallow way.'

The tapes include 'Just a Housewife', 'Under Our Feet', 'Women and Childcare', 'Women at Work', 'All Equal Now', 'Bodytalk' and 'Images of Women'. They may be hired from the Workers' Education Association at a cost of 50p per tape.

For further information write to: *Jenny Bale, Workers' Education Association, 212 Bath Street, Glasgow 2 or Jane Heslop, 351 Redburn, Bonhill, Dunbartonshire.*

PHOTOGRAPHY: HACKNEY FLASHERS COLLECTIVE

'Keep young and beautiful . . . ' sings Radio One.
'Can men cope with the shopping?' a serious question in a family magazine.

The Hackney Flashers Collective replies:

'Can a woman be young and beautiful and cope with the shopping, the cooking, the cleaning, the laundry, three children and work the 6–10pm industrial shift while her husband looks after the kids? Who looks after the children if she doesn't live with a man, or alternatively, how does she earn her living if there is no one to help look after the children? What are women doing? What do they think they are doing? What are they told they should be doing? . . . '

These are some of the questions occupying the Hackney Flashers Collective. The Hackney Flashers Collective is a group of ten women who use the tools of the popular media — documentary photography, commercial advertising images and statistical information — as a means of investigating how women are conditioned into accepting the duties of wives and mothers. They also aim to explore how women's work, both in and outside the home, fits into the structure of capitalist society. As well as exhibiting their photographs, they put on shows that include other media (e.g. advertising). All the women in the collective work in visual communications, some professionally.

The event that set the group off was an exhibition on women at work in Hackney, a large borough in East London, in 1975. The recently formed women's sub-committee of the Hackney Trades Council had insisted on having a section of the Trades Council's 75th Anniversary Exhibition devoted to women workers. They asked the group to do the photographs for it, and wanted this exhibition to show what sort of work women were doing in Hackney and wages they got for it to drive home how little the trade unions had done for them.

It became very clear how appropriate the demand was when the Trades Council chose as their theme for the whole anniversary celebration: '75 years of *Brotherhood*'.

'Women — Work in Hackney', an exhibition of some 200 prints accompanied by statistics on pay, promotion prospects and the union power of women both nationally and in Hackney was shown in Hackney Town Hall in 1975. The kind of work and working conditions pictured, with the pay scales accompanying them, attested to the fact that the unions had paid little attention to sisterhood in those seventy-five years of activity in Hackney.

The exhibition has been very successful and is still on tour in Britain. Statistics are kept up-to-date by one of the women in the collective who's a statistician. This first experience taught the group a lot:

'When we started in 1975, we were dissatisfied with several things. First with the way photographs and women were used by the press or rather misused; the photos we really believed in were never displayed. We also wanted to crack the myth of the isolated professional and learn a subject together in a group. We don't deny that our professional position helps us. It enables us to get high quality results, photos of good quality, properly printed and mounted. We want to share our skills.

'The group is now a skill-sharing group as much as anything else. We work in small groups with our different skills, or one of us runs a workshop on a particular topic she knows well, for all of us. We might not all become so good at it, some may be more expert, but at least we try not to be elitist.

*'Politically, we have changed a lot too. At the beginning we just considered our-
selves to be feminists, but gradually we came round to being anti-capitalist as well. We
got very angry very quickly, going round with the bosses. They assumed we were doing
it from their point of view and were rather naive with us. They told us amazing things
like why they couldn't be bothered to open creches, for example.*

*'We got into the factories through our connection with the Trades Council. If they
didn't fall for that one, we said we were trying to present a panorama of all the work
women did, and did they want to be included among the employers that were offering
work! Nobody turned that down, even the most fascist firms thought they'd get a bit
of free advertising.*

*'The other problem we have come across is the problem of power or censorship.
Any group who puts its services at the disposal of the community, has to make sure it
establishes who has the say over what happens to the work; otherwise you are back in
the same situation as in the media — you are used as a commodity, someone asks you to
do something and it's used out of context. We learned how to remain in control of our
work. In the beginning, the Trades Council didn't understand what we were talking
about, until we explained that all we were asking for was what they were fighting for
in the unions: the right to control our own labour. This is a very important point.*

*'How to get publicity on our terms was another one of our discoveries. It's import-
ant to have it, but not the wrong kind. Some newspapers wanted us to come along and
talk about the "poor deprived people" we'd seen, whereas we said: "We can't talk about
women working in Hackney, we are not experts in this matter, but what we can talk
about is how we work, and what we are doing with our photographs."*

*'Another thing we found out in dealing with the formal media is that they are always
in a rush. We had become a news item so they wanted to get us now! We were about
to be consumed by the news-hearing public, and they were in a fantastic rush to get us.
We, as a collective, take a long time to do things. Our decision-making structure is time
consuming. It took us a long time to discover that the media structure was different from
ours. At the very start we were willing to give in to their rush; now we tell them that if
they want to interview us it will have to take time and we are able to say no if necessary.
We've worked out exactly what our relationship to the media is and have a policy towards
it.'*

The second project of the Hackney Flashers Collective was on collective childcare. It was completed in 1977 and was very different from the first exhibition. Besides being more agitational,
it showed that people are involving themselves and doing something about the lack of childcare
facilities.

Money is the eternal problem. The Flashers get a little back from the first exhibition, but
they need grants to continue their work. They have had one grant from the Greater London
Arts Association, but unfortunately do not generally fall into any of the GLAA's categories.
The collective does not present its work as 'Art' yet it is not a community arts project, because
it is not run by people in a particular neighbourhood.

The Hackney Flashers Collective is now really stable.

*'We find it an amazing support group; that seems to come from working together and pro-
ducing something. We feel a responsibility for the exhibition but not the same heavy,
pressing weight that you get if you are working on your own. You know that if you
cannot cope, somebody else will share the responsibility. It's a great incentive, and the
result is that we all work harder.'*

The Hackney Flashers exhibitions are available for hire at a small fee.

HACKNEY FLASHERS COLLECTIVE *c/o Michael Ann Mullen, 7 Archibald Road, London N7*

Other groups to contact are:

PHOTOGRAPHY WORKSHOP
c/o Jo Spence, 152 Upper Street, London N1
This group has been interested in the use of photography as a means of developing people's images
of themselves and of society. They have run a
number of interesting courses, including a successful women's studies programme for fifteen-year-
old girls. They are collecting and analysing images
from the media, and are preparing slide sets on
sexism, racism, and classism. They would be
pleased to meet with others who are interested
in these or other projects.

HALF MOON PHOTOGRAPHY WORKSHOP
27 Alie Street, London E1
A photography workshop and gallery in the East
End. They have produced a number of photo-
graphic exhibitions including 'Men photographed
by Women' and 'Women: Who are We?', which
are available for hire.

WOMEN IN PUBLISHING

Virago

Virago is a feminist publishing company which produces books for the general and educational
market on subjects highlighting all aspects of women's lives.

Virago began in 1975 as an associate company of Quartet Books, and published nine books
in its first eighteen months. They are now a completely independent company, run by a small
group of women who deal with everything except sales and distribution. In addition they have
an advisory group of about thirty women, working in a wide variety of fields, who help with
the formation of their book list.

Virago was set up:

to encourage writing on women's issues for the widest possible audience;

to provide a service for women writers;

to encourage new writers as well as publish established ones;

to publish books for use in schools, colleges and universities;

to commission new books, but also to produce paperback editions of hardbacks already published elsewhere;

to publish books simultaneously in hard and paperback editions, in order to reach a mass audience
immediately;

to publish books at reasonable prices and to support the book trade by offering realistic terms and by
providing an emphasis on promotion and publicity;

to publish transactions which represent the best of women's writing from abroad;

to sell books through new outlets as well as the traditional ones, (through mail order conferences, women's organizations, schools, alternative bookshops, clinics, community centres, etc.).

They have already published books spanning a wide range of subjects, including archaeology, autobiography, communications, fiction, history, oral history, politics, religion, sexuality, sociology, school and reference books.

Their plans for the future include more emphasis on practical handbooks, pamphlets, folders, illustrated books, translations and reprints.

In 1977 they started two new series: a reprint series of out-of-print classics written by women and a series of pamphlets on practical subjects.

VIRAGO *4th Floor, 5 Wardour Street, London W1*

Feminist Books

In 1974, Feminist Books published *Wedlocked Women*, a book all about the plight of housewives. This was the first publishing house set up by women, with the aim of helping women to have their work published. By 1975, a second publication, a collection of articles concerned with women's liberation called *Conditions of Illusion* was published.

Though both books were well received, they did not cover the cost of their production; Feminist Books still prints few pamphlets but can no longer afford to be a publishing house. So, it has embarked on a new project with all its efforts now being directed towards distribution.

'*We started in 1973. There was a consensus that there ought to be a feminist publisher in England.* Wedlocked Women, *written by one of us, sparked off the whole thing. It had previously been commissioned by another publisher and though it was submitted on time, they turned it down because of its political content. They thought that feminism and women was a sort of "coffee table" subject and wanted all the polemics of the book taken out. The author refused to let them publish and went to established left-wing publishers. Similarly, they liked it but wanted some alterations to put the book in line with their politics; once more she refused. We then decided to publish it ourselves.*

'*We had a run of good fortune; first of all, two or three of us had already been involved in one form or another with editing a book, either working in a bookshop or on the publishing side. Then we met a person who was prepared to back us and gave us some money. Being a small group and starting to print a book is quite an adventure. The first book was already in the process of being printed so we had to take on the existing printing commitment. It was not exactly what we wanted and was expensive, but as it happened it was a very good job. The second time* (Conditions of Illusion) *we decided to do the whole process ourselves, to keep the book as cheap as possible. The only way to keep costs down was for us to do all the typing and layout ourselves; the printer let us use his facilities. This was a large undertaking with 400 pages of text, and only two people to do the work! One of us was a fast typist but had never done typesetting. We hired a composer for a month which meant that she had to type the whole book in one month. The other one was a "mathematical genius", good at numbers, shapes . . . she did the layout and things like that for the first time in her life. She did a marvellous job!*

'*It took us a month to type it, six weeks to paste it up and make corrections. By the end, the two of us were really tired and ill from the effort.*'

To publish a book costs between £2,000 and £3,000 and this is going up all the time because of the price of paper. Feminist Books refuse to let themselves get into the common business practice of being in debt all the time, getting loans from banks, not paying the little group that they buy pamphlets from, increasing prices in expectation of inflation (this itself being a source of inflation!).   So they are not publishing any big titles any longer, but have now become a flourishing distribution network.

'We are still able to publish small pamphlets but the distribution side of Feminist Books is by far the most successful and is a very necessary service.

'Strangely enough, we had no problem in setting it up.   Because the two previous books were successful they generated a whole distribution network; people and book-shops ordered them.   Since it worked so well, we decided to take on other feminist literature and distribute that.   In the women's movement there were a lot of people publishing their own pamphlets but unable to sell them.   A group who would print only 500 pamphlets without a distribution service can now publish 2,000 and we'd take 1,000 of those.

'We distribute almost any feminist literature which doesn't have a very big distribution organization of its own.   Our aim is to help people who can't otherwise distribute their books.   So, we tend to do NCCL stuff, women's groups, women's literature, etc.   We don't do feminist periodicals because that's too complicated.

'There are now two women involved in the distribution network, two days a week, on very low pay (in fact just enough to pay the rent of a room and the van which are absolutely necessary for storage space and heavy weights).   But it's worth doing.   The success has been tremendous.   The network is now international.   Because it is a sort of self-generating system, when we send our new list to all the little alternative feminist bookshops all over the world, they just order whatever we've got; they trust us and know we have the kind of stuff they want to buy.

'We don't distribute only to bookshops.   We seem to be the only people who would supply women's groups at a discount.   For example, in Ireland groups are starting all over the place, they want bulk supplies, but cannot get them there; so they write to us.

'We service the women's movement and that's one of our main achievements.'

Feminist Books' list includes: *Conditions of Illusion, Wedlocked Women, Sexism in Children's Books, Abortion on Demand, Little Girls, The Moon for Dinner, Sex Race and Class, Out of the Pumpkin Shell, Sink Songs, Female Transport*, and many others.   In all there are thirty-four titles available.   Ask for their list.   Women's groups get a 25 per cent discount on orders of £5 or more.

FEMINIST BOOKS *PO Box HP5, Leeds 6*

Other Feminist Publishers

THE WOMEN'S PRESS
12 Ellesmere Road, London E3
The Women's Press is a new feminist publisher, launched in February 1978. Their aim is to provide women writers and readers with an attractive alternative to conventional publishing, but at the same time distributing their books to the widest possible audience.   They guarantee anti-sexist content and presentation, feminist sympathies and feminist priorities.   They aim to give strong personalized support to working women writers and also to bring back into print neglected works by women writers of the past.   All books will be published in paperback editions, and their prices will be as low as economic survival allows.

The Women's Press is associated with Quartet Books, as was Virago when it first started.   And like Virago, it draws ideas and support from an editorial advisory group.   It intends to publish a slightly different mix from Virago, with over half its titles consisting of fiction, plus literary criticism, art history, and books on psychoanalysis, therapy, mental health and politics.

FALLING WALL PRESS
79 Richmond Road, Montpelier, Bristol 6
This is a small publisher of socialist and feminist books, pamphlets and periodicals.   It also distributes foreign publications.   It produces its own *Falling Wall Review* which details the new publications it has available.   It publishes and distributes material for 'Wages for Housework' and the 'Power of Women Collective'.

ONLY WOMEN
c/o 4a Queen's Road, London SE15
This is a publishing house run by women and for women, and it has chosen the difficult path of all production carried out entirely and solely by women.

WOMEN'S LIBERATION PUBLICATIONS

Spare Rib

Spare Rib is a women's liberation magazine, launched in June 1972 and produced by a collective of ten women. It comes out monthly, costs 30p, and sells about 18,000 copies. But because so many copies are passed on and filed, the readership figure is far higher per copy than most other magazines. It is financially independent, deriving its income from sales and advertising.

By rejecting the traditional hierarchical structure of one editor and subordinates, *Spare Rib* is demonstrating in a practical way that the democratic principles of the women's liberation movement can work not only on a small scale but also commercially.

'We see Spare Rib *as an alternative to traditional women's magazines, which reflect and reinforce women's oppression and inequality in all kinds of ways, whether by assuming we're all housewives and mothers or by objectifying us as "liberated" swinging sexpots. We're trying to challenge these male-defined fantasies, and give women a place to express their own identity and visions of a different future. To do this, we need to document the changes that are taking place as part of the movement of women taking control over their lives.*

'Because Spare Rib *is the only feminist publication which is commercially distributed and on sale in shops and news-stands throughout the country, it reaches many women who may not have had any previous contact with the movement. So we try to make the ideas and concerns accessible and exciting for all women, not just for committed feminists, and we try to do this without watering down our political perspective. How best to do this, and all the problems involved, are things that we constantly discuss in our collective meetings.*

'The magazine started with two editors, then one, and after a couple of years it evolved into the collective structure we have now, with everyone sharing responsibility for all the decisions that need to be made. People have a variety of special skills and interests, and the routine work is rotated. While there is far more sharing of skills than in a traditional set-up, the pressures of putting out the paper each month with such limited resources mean that we have to have our own areas of responsibility, so that deadlines are met and the work gets done. Right now we're scrutinizing the collective model and all its implications, so that we can develop it to meet our own needs as workers and the changing needs of the magazine. As the movement grows and the magazine expands, so the pressures increase and we have to figure out how best to adapt this.*

'Part of the pressures are, of course, financial. We are now just about breaking even, but can't pay proper wages or pay contributors. We hope this will have changed by the time this book is published! We only survive by tapping a pool of committed supporters who donate their work and energy because they see the need for such a magazine and want to contribute to it (ironically we have to exploit women in order to produce a paper which fights against this kind of exploitation!). Money from advertising is slowly increasing, as are sales; and of course we try not to take adverts that contradict the politics of the paper (just where that line is drawn is worked out in discussion in meetings, often too late!). When we make mistakes angry readers soon let us know.

'We try to keep in touch with readers, and encourage them to contribute ideas and news of what they are involved with, and hold regular readers meetings which are attended by women from all over the country. Since we're based in London, and don't have money for travelling, it's easy to become "London Chauvinists". To combat this we have regional pages in the magazines, which focus on what's happening in different cities and areas. And the noticeboard pages, "Shortlist", to help to keep people in touch with each other.

'Spare Rib is sometimes criticized for being depressing and heavy, and we're always trying to find ways of making it lighter and more humorous. But we don't aim to be "entertaining" and escapist like Woman's Own, and often being a woman in this society is not that funny. Nor do we want to encourage the stereotype of the "liberated woman" competing with men on their terms. We believe the whole power structure needs to be radically changed to abolish the oppression which, despite token improvements, still exists and permeates all aspects of our lives and our sense of ourselves.'

SPARE RIB 27 Clerkenwell Close, London EC1

Women's Report

Women's Report is a bi-monthly feminist news magazine packed with information. Less glossy than Spare Rib, Women's Report is a different kind of magazine. It gives excellent feminist analysis of current issues and events, and its feature articles are often very well researched.

'Women's Report is in its fifth year of publication. It was started with a gift of £200 from the Fawcett Society, to which we were loosely associated at the beginning. Since then, the magazine has been completely financially self-supporting, relying on its subscriptions and bookshop sales for income.

'As Women's Report developed a more radical feminist analysis, rather than being simply a disseminator of information without comment, the politics of the two groups diverged and we amicably agreed to sever the ties.

'Nowadays, the magazine usually contains one or two longer feature articles, where some attempt is made to articulate the politics of the group, as well as the shorter news items, which are divided into broad categories, such as legal issues, education, health and our image in the media, and given separate pages.

'We collect news from a variety of sources, including national newspapers, the "alternative" press, feminist papers, press releases from government and other bodies, readers' letters and so on. The distinctive aspects of Women's Report are that we publish news about all women (not focussing exclusively on the women's liberation movement) filtered through a feminist perspective; and we aim to represent the mainstream of feminist opinion, rather than having allegiance to particular sub-groupings or formal political sects. Thus to some readers, we are cautious to the point of being non-committal (and by extension, non-comitted), whereas to others we are almost outrageous.

'*The magazine is used by women in different ways. As well as providing the individual with up-to-date information on what is happening to or for or against women in the world, and how this has been presented in the media,* Women's Report *is used as a source of information by other feminist magazines, and for teaching (e.g. Women's Studies courses), and as general reference material, and also as a source of ammunition against those who say the battle is won and to provide the anger (and humour) to go on fighting.*

'*Between fifteen and twenty women are now in the collective. In the early days several members were professional journalists, but none of the present collective was a writer before joining* Women's Report, *although some women have become professional writers as a result of this experience. A few of us had written nothing since school (and little then) until joining the group, and thus have gained invaluable confidence and expertise. New members come originally either as personal contacts of existing members or in response to occasional advertisements in the magazine. They are integrated into the group gradually, through being assigned to helping write a page with older members and through being present through the cycle of production. There is no selection made on the basis of clarity and details of ideology, but we would all call ourselves feminist. The political differences between us come out over specific issues and can either inject or absorb energy. The women in the group do have quite different life-styles, backgrounds and perspectives from each other. How constructively these differences are being used is one measure of how well the collective is working, as it is easy to gloss over differences when we are caught up in the technical process of producing the magazine.*

'*The group meets one evening a week, when we exchange news about administrative progress and hold-ups, as well as discussing the last issue of the magazine, what we will write as feature articles for the next one and so on. These discussions give rise to argument of current news in the mass media or around the women's liberation movement. We compete in the big weekly hand-out of new books sent us by publishers — racing to grab the literary critiques and biographies and trying to persuade everyone else to review heavy sociological and political tracts or "meaningful" but tedious works on essential theory! To be present at Monday meetings of the collective (numbers averaging about ten) is to experience the circus, the board (bored?) room, the intense family dispute and the hospital ward (sometimes all of these simultaneously!). Hence the need for pub adjournments!*

'*Administrative jobs rotate between collective members: one woman deals with subscriptions, another with the money, another with ordering review copies of books and so on. Because some women have been in the collective much longer than others, we are making attempts to share our practical knowledge, so that we all know all the procedures involved; no one is regarded as the "expert" at one job. The nature of these jobs has evolved over time, to cope with the increase in circulation, now about 2,800 copies (by direct subscription, through bookshops and women's centres, and by sales at conferences, meetings and so on). We each volunteer to read a particular publication or two or three to gain our basic information. We aim for continuity over several issues of* Women's Report *so that we can get more familiar with health problems or whatever, and perhaps build up useful personal contacts. Book, film and event reviews are written by whoever read, watched or participated.*

'*After we have each written our material, we all meet for a weekend to sub-edit each others' work. This consists of reading and correcting for sense and political content, as well as for economy of expression. Feature articles are also written as collectively as possible, with everyone involved in discussions before and during the writing of successive drafts. Never is only one person responsible for the whole of an article.*'

WOMEN'S REPORT *14 Aberdeen Road, Wealdstone, Harrow, Middlesex*

Livewire

Livewire is a free newspaper for women in Lewes, a small town in the South of England. It was started in November 1975 by women who wanted to do something in the women's movement, but didn't know quite what. A successful consciousness-raising group was coming to a halt and fight against an Anti-Abortion Bill, which had taken up all their energy for a while, had stopped as the Bill was no longer before Parliament. Twenty women decided to do a small, compact paper directed towards women only. It would be a news-sheet for local women, informative and practical, but at the same time it would put across feminist ideas. The main aims of the paper are:

1. to provide information relevant to women in the town and surrounding villages;
2. to provide a way of looking at the community through women's eyes;
3. to try to break through some of the isolation that women experience by giving them adequate contacts.

The first *Livewire* came out early in 1976. It was devoted to the under-fives, in order to attract women with children. Since then, *Livewire* has been published every four months; issue 2 was on 'Our Health', issue 3 was on 'Women and Work'.

All the issues are packed with features, articles and useful information; for example 'Our Health' includes 'Self-Help', 'Tried and Trusted Remedies for Thrush', 'How to Complain', 'Psychiatry', 'The Need for Community Care', 'Preventive Dentistry', 'Medical Treatment Abroad', and 'GPs in Lewes'.

A thousand copies are published each time and distributed to launderettes, main bookshops, cornershops, clinics . . . Some are put in letterboxes to reach women who do not go to these places.

The group received a grant a year ago from the Social Services Department. Because they were quite pleased with the issues produced, the grant has been renewed, but it costs more than the grant to produce the paper and the group is now debating whether to charge or not.

One of the main characteristics of *Livewire* is its simplicity. It manages to get ideas across without being mystifying or full of jargon. The paper is now quite a success with local women.

'We don't get much written feedback, but we do get a lot of sympathetic support when we talk to women. Most of them are really happy with the paper and feel friendly and positive about it. They welcome the opportunity to talk about themselves to people who are interested. One of us, one day, was chatting with her neighbour who's in her seventies and a retired headmistress. She found Livewire *interesting but added that "all these things were already said when I was young". We are trying to get her to write something for the next issue.'*

Because it had to attract local women, it was important to concentrate on a few issues at the beginning and stick to them. But now the collective would like *Livewire* to become more of a newspaper.

'We should have more topics relevant to this town; but then we would become a community paper. It has to be worked out. We must involve more local women, get them to write in, to make comments, to tell us what is happening in their neighbourhood, it must be their *newspaper.'*

A particular feature of *Livewire* is that it is duplicated not printed. It is produced on A4 sheets of paper, collated, folded once and stapled to produce an A5 magazine. Text is typeset in a 10-point typeface and in two columns; headlines are typeset in an 11-point bold typeface. And the front-page logo remains the same for each issue. This makes the magazine extremely cheap to produce, whilst at the same time looking readable, professional and well-produced. The magazine's designer, Liz Bennett (Cottage No. 3, Northease Manor, near Lewes) would be happy to share production/design details.

LIVEWIRE *c/o The Information Centre, Lewes, Sussex*

Manchester Women's Newspaper

This newspaper was started by a small group of women in 1975, to try to reach women outside the women's liberation movement. The paper comes out every two months and the collective meets every week to keep in touch with one another. Various national and local newspapers are monitored between them and each article is read and criticized by the whole collective. On top of that other people are asked to write reports of projects they are involved in.

The collective tries to have a balanced paper: a few pages of news which is either local news, or national news affecting every woman; a health article over two pages; a big feature article over four pages which covers various subjects like prostitution, rape, clerical workers, childbirth, etc.; and a story.

The typing is done mainly by two women who volunteered to do it because they could attend meetings; two Sundays in the second month are put aside for layout which is done in people's houses. None of the women get paid though they spend quite a lot on phonecalls, bus fares, and other essential expenses. They have set up an original distribution network; sellers (men or women) willing to take a bunch of papers each time, sell them at work. Each woman in the collective has built up over the months a list of so many people who will take so many papers. This way they sell 800 copies, and 500 are sold through bookshops and newsagents.

'We started the paper because we wanted to reach women who weren't highly educated or middle-class, and also to present a kind of alternative to the usual women's magazines which churn out the same stereotypes and put women back in their usual place. But we don't want to be heavy and turn people away from us; this is our main problem.

'For the first issue, we got together articles which we thought might be interesting like health, and a handy women column, but not of the sort you can see in traditional magazines. We emphasized things women tend to leave to men, not because they cannot do it, but because they think they can't do it. We had a story that we invented ourselves, but it was not very good! It was about a woman who had an argument with her boyfriend about an evening she planned to spend with a girlfriend she had not seen for a long time; her boyfriend had planned previously to go out to a concert and she didn't want to go anymore. We wrote about the thoughts of this woman and how she was scared to lose him and at the same time found him a bit piggish; she decided eventually to see her friend whatever the cost. It was too dogmatic a story and did not leave much space for the readers to make up their own minds.

'It took four months to complete the first issue because none of us had had any previous experience; we had contributed to the women's movement newsletter but that was all. We did not do a lot of abstract talking at the beginning, we sorted problems out as we went along. An alternative bookshop and vegetarian shop gave us £50 and that covered the cost of printing 500 copies (sixteen pages).

'We put it in the usual easy places, alternative bookshops, university union bookshop, newsagents. We tried hard to get the paper outside (for example, on council estates) because you have to find women where they are, and not only those who are in touch with feminism anyway. The success was tremendous and we had to print 500 more. Now we produce 1400 copies and sell around 1300.'

The collective's attempt to put across feminist ideas in such a way that people are not going to be alienated or just turned off is a difficult one. Their university background does not help, in fact it hinders their efforts at communicating with other women. This is a common problem amongst feminists; how did the collective cope with it?

'Whoever sells the paper in council estates will always ask how the women find it, but it's very hard to get an answer. Most of the time they don't really say much. Sometimes you get a nice response like this woman who declared that she has to hide the paper at home because she is married to "a right chauvinist pig!" When asked if she would hide Woman's Own *she answered "Oh no! it's different, isn't it. This one is telling you how to help yourself".*

'Few women would actually say that they were married to "chauvinist pigs"; but on the whole there seems to be a new spirit around, a new awareness (although its origin in the women's liberation movement goes largely unrecognized, needless to say). Even things like the Sex Discrimination Act, although it changes so little, have given women a new confidence, at least the law appears to support their claim to be "equal".

'Many women who read the paper don't think of themselves as feminists. One, a clerical worker, told us that she tried to join a women's group but was really put off because they were all teachers and their experiences were so totally different from hers. She complained that Spare Rib *had no chance of getting through to the ordinary woman in the street and added that we, the* Manchester Women's Newspaper, *were a bit better but still had a long way to go!*

'Recently, the paper has become much more of an overtly feminist paper and we are not very keen on that. The women's movement in Manchester hasn't got a newsletter and we are becoming more and more of a clearing house for them. Too many advertisements for women's meetings are irrelevant for most of the women we want to reach. We do a back page though, which is very useful, lots of contact addresses: abortion, contraception, law centres, single parents' associations.

'We get criticisms both from feminists and from other women. To find the balance in between is very difficult.'

Originally the paper was set up with the idea that it would be *used by women.* They would feel part of it and contribute to it. To fill thegap between women in the women's liberation movement and other women is the main concern of the collective. In order to do this they watch their language, trying to avoid jargon, sounding intellectual or making assumptions, and giving the paper encouraging touches like the story of a woman bus-driver. But this is obviously a very long-term aim and the group has other problems to face: financial and collective.

'The cost of paper has gone up so much, we will have to raise our price from 8p to 10p — still we must be the only commodity which has not gone up for fifteen months. To do the layout in people's houses is not a long-term solution. Every time it's a panic to gather all the bits and pieces from everybody.

'As far as working as a collective is concerned, we have felt that our meetings were very businesslike. We had too much to get through to talk about personal problems and some of us belong to the same women's group which gave the others a feeling of exclusion. Now we meet first over a meal and then have the meeting. It works much better this way.'

MANCHESTER WOMEN'S PAPER 4 *Bednal Avenue, Manchester 13*

National feminist Magazines

Many of these are available from alternative bookshops, as well as from the address given. You can usually get a sample back copy free if you send a large stamped addressed envelope. Prices do not include postage, if ordering direct.

BANSHEE
c/o Irishwomen United, 10 Parkview Place, Ringsend, Dublin 4 (monthly) 25p
Irish women's liberation magazine, with news, articles, reviews, cartoons and jokes.

BREAD AND ROSES
4 Ridge Mount, Cliff Road, Leeds 6 (two to four issues a year) free — relies on donations
each issue is devoted to one theme such as rape, women and paid work, or lesbianism, with contributions in prose or poetry from many different women. Much attractive artwork.

CATCALL
37 Worthley Road, London E6 (bi-monthly) 15p
This duplicated magazine was set up to provide a non-sectarian forum for the discussion of theory and exchange of ideas between and for women in the women's liberation movement. Always includes funny cartoons.

LINK
16 King Street, London WC2 (quarterly) 20p
Professional-looking magazine put out by women in the Communist Party, aimed mainly at women within the Party though of interest to others, usually on one particular theme each issue, like 'Women in History', or 'What is Feminism?'.

MOVE
The Other Image, c/o 32 Hill Street, Totterdown, Bristol 3 (monthly) 20p
A lesbian feminist magazine put out by the Bristol Gay Women's Group, with most contributions coming from the West, South-West and Wales though they will print news, articles, letters and poems sent in from women anywhere. Useful addresses of lesbian groups and meeting places included, attractive drawings and a friendly style.

RED RAG
207 Sumatra Road, London NW6 (two to four issues a year), 30p
A socialist feminist discussion magazine, consisting mainly of fairly long articles, with a few shorter letters and reviews, and some interesting/funny/ attractive photographs or drawings.

SAPPHO
The Basement, 20 Dorset Square, London NW1 (monthly) 40p
One of the earlier lesbian magazines, with articles, letters, poems and reviews, also useful addresses. It also publishes audio-tapes.

SHREW
c/o A Woman's Place, see Stop Press (occasional) 30p
The first magazine to come out of the women's liberation movement in Britain, *Shrew* ceased publication around 1972 for several years to re-appear late in 1976. Each issue is written and produced by a different group of women and concentrates on a different theme. In the latest series, madness and matriarchy have so far been covered, and a working-class women's *Shrew* is on the way.

SCARLET WOMAN
5 Washington Terrace, North Sheilds, Tyne and Wear (occasional) 20p
Duplicated newsletter of the socialist current in the women's liberation movement, intended as a forum for discussion of difficulties and exchange of news.

SOCIALIST WOMAN
c/o Dodie Weppler, 182 Pentonville Road, London N1 (occasional) 20p
Magazine put out by women in the International Marxist Group.

SPARE RIB
27 Clerkenwell Close, London EC1 (monthly) 30p
The feminist magazine with the largest circulation.
See interview with *Spare Rib* collective.

WOMEN AND EDUCATION NEWSLETTER
*c/o 4 Cliffdale Drive, Crumpsall, Manchester 8
(quarterly) 20p*
Especially aimed at women involved in education,
whether as students, teachers, or parents; includes
pre-school section.   For more details see:
Education.

WOMEN'S REPORT
*14 Aberdeen Road, Wealdstone, Harrow,
Middlesex (bi-monthly) 20p*
A feminist news magazine; for more details see
interview in Images of Women.

WOMEN'S STRUGGLE NOTES
*c/o Rising Free, 182 Upper Street, London N1
(bi-monthly) 15p or 10p for wageless*
Designed as a magazine contributed to, by and for
working-class women. Some women in the editorial collective are in the organization Big Flame.
Produced alternately in the North and the South
of England.

WOMEN'S VOICE
*10 Kempton Court, Red Hall Estate, Darlington,
Co. Durham (monthly) 10p*
Magazine put out by women in the Socialist
Workers' Party.

WIRES NEWSLETTER
32a Parliament Street, York (every 2½ weeks) 15p
The National Newsletter of the Women's Liberation Movement Information Service.

ZERO
*c/o Rising Free, 182 Upper Street, London N1
(monthly) 20p*
An anarchist/anarcha-feminist monthly produced
by a collective mainly from East London. National
and international news and reviews.

Women's Libraries

FAWCETT SOCIETY LIBRARY
*City of London Polytechnic, 117 Houndsditch,
London EC3*
This library is one of the few collections by and
about women. It contains papers and books on
the issues and organizations of the feminist movement. It was established in 1926, and examples
of women's history have been gradually donated
and bought to make a highly interesting collection.
For information about the work of the Fawcett

Society and details about membership, contact
the Fawcett Society, Parnell House, 25 Wilton
Road, London SW1.

WOMEN'S RESEARCH AND RESOURCES CENTRE
27 Clerkenwell Close, London EC1
The Centre has a library and acts as a reference
centre for women's studies. It also produces a
useful reading list.

6

HEALTH AND CHILD BIRTH

SELF-HELP HEALTH

Something new and exciting is happening. Women are coming together and learning about their bodies in self-help health groups. We are attempting to break down traditional ideas about the relationship between doctor and patient; we are learning about how to treat infections before they become dangerous; but most important, we are working together, which must be a positive step in our struggle for control of our bodies. We are also beginning to challenge the present structure of health care, demanding to be given information where hitherto we have been denied it by doctors who feel that they 'know it all'.

The present relationship between a doctor and his (we use the male pronoun because the majority of doctors are male) patient is almost that of a child and her father. The doctor is seen as all-knowing and he usually does not have to justify himself to his patient. Patients often don't question a doctor's diagnosis because most people believe that after a doctor has had all that training 'he should know'. Women in particular suffer from being passive patients. Women consult doctors more than men, either on our own behalf or concerning our children. Gynaecological problems abound: women suffer from itches and discharges whose source we never see. We have no idea what is up ourvaginas since our reproductive organs are not on display as men's are. Since we don't look up our vaginas, we expect the doctor, who does, to know what is healthy or unhealthy without question or comment on our part. Many women suffer from this: cancer of the cervix can be improperly diagnosed, hysterectomies are carried out for no reason (as are mastectomies where the whole breast is removed) and women die from cancer and kidney diseases after being told 'not to worry' by their doctors.

Medicine today is not organized on a preventative basis in Britain: it is used to treat infection, which is often caused by carelessness or lack of knowledge. We are not given adequate information to help control infections such as thrush by ourselves. We also are given pills for almost any symptom. Often outside pressures tend to come out in physical symptoms such as over-eating or headaches. Often valium is prescribed as a cure-all, but valium is not the answer for a woman who is frustrated with her life, or who is having trouble at work, or with her husband or children.

With all this as background, some women understandably began to feel that something must change. We felt it was important to understand how our bodies worked and what they looked like. We started meeting in small groups, first to talk about our bodies, and then, when the group had built up a measure of trust, we each got hold of a speculum and began to explore our vaginas. Most women who see their cervix for the first time feel exhilarated. Finding out that we all look practically the same is a comforting thought if we have been told by our doctor that we had a retroverted uterus or something else that made us feel that we were odd or malformed. We worked best in small groups because we could compare inner and outer colours, kinds of cervix, kinds of discharges and share our feelings about our bodies in an intimate group.

Self-help health groups are helping women to demystify health care, question the role of doctors, and come to terms with and understand our own bodies. They challenge the existing structure of health care, cut doctors down to size, and make us question possibly for the first time what kind of care is best for women.

There are now many self-help health groups throughout the country. They differ in what they do depending on the needs of the women involved, but they very often begin with self-examination (looking at our cervixes) and go on from there to discuss health care in general and its relation to women. The Leeds Self-Help Group is a good example of a self-help health group:

Leeds self-help group

'The Leeds group started after many of us had heard a talk by two women at the University. Some of the women were interested in forming a self-help group, so along with some women from a women's group that was folding up, we started meeting regularly. In the beginning we did self-examinations; most of us found that even though we had done this on our own, we had never done it regularly, so we never knew what we looked like at certain parts of our cycle. For some women it was the first time that they had ever looked at their cervixes. Most were really scared, not knowing what to expect: maybe something would be wrong; but for them it was really important to have other women around who would give support, and perhaps say "yes, it's great; you're OK!"

'Now our group does many different things. Some women are not involved in self-examination on a regular basis, some do articles on health for local papers, some do research on different aspects of health care. We have begun to fit caps, now that we have the equipment. It is much better for a woman to come to us for this because she'll be more relaxed and we'll do it better. Also we are using a microscope to look at ovulation. Books will teach you up to a point, but just seeing erosion, or the cervix of a woman who is pregnant, or thrush, is the best way to learn. It is legal for us to do all this. Here in Britain we don't have a "practising medicine without a licence" law like they do in the US. The two laws affecting health practice here are the Dangerous Drugs Act (say if we had heroin and gave it out, it would be illegal) and the Abortion Act.

'It is very important for us as a group to discuss self-examination and its relation to existing health care: how it's working or not working and how we can change the situation. One of the most crucial things to deal with is how women are mystified by doctors. We notice when we talk to a woman who hasn't done self-examination that they still are in awe of doctors. Doctors can still frighten you by saying they see erosion or a lump on your cervix . . . and if you can't see it, how can you possibly have an equal discussion with that doctor about it? It is vital to challenge this, in small groups and individually, to be honest (even though it is hard) when you go to the VD clinic or your GP, and to say that you have examined yourself with a speculum and have seen something wrong. At first doctors are shocked. Some doctors might be pleased and suggest that if you have any more problems to come along. If they're not being nice: well, you won't get that far.

'Knowing about the processes of our bodies makes us less frightened of our health, and less afraid to deal with doctors. We also read medical journals and books; we feel that we have to know what doctors are reading, not because it is right, but because doctors are reading it and forming their ideas from it. We have to know what we're up against.

'Women's health groups can also act as pressure groups. The group in Manchester was the force that made the British Pregnancy Advisory Service open a centre there.

'Hopefully in the future women's health groups will get together and set up a women's clinic, so people could go there and learn skills from other women, like IUD fitting. But now, with the economic situation, it is hard to find the money.

'We are now beginning to come to some conclusions about our health and health care generally. This increased knowledge is a great source of strength, and powerful in changing the ideas and practice of doctors.'

There are many things that individual women can do, if there is no self-help health group in your area, with the help of a friend or on your own.

When you go to see the doctor, go with a friend
This can be a help; because if you are scared about asking questions on your own, your friend can ask them. Or her being there can give you the courage you need to ask these questions yourself. At first doctors may not allow a friend come in to the consulting room, but be firm, and he should let you.

Read about your problem, before and after your visit If you know what your problem is, get a book and read about it so that you can ask questions about it, or know when the doctor isn't giving you the best advice. Put yourself in a position of knowledge. Once you get home start reading as well. Maybe you will find other ideas about cures, or you may discover new questions you need answers to.

Write letters If you feel that a certain doctor or clinic is particularly harmful or detrimental to your health, write letters, get your friends to write letters, relating your personal experiences with individual doctors or staff. Sometimes this does help.

Enrol on a Women's Health Course Some women's groups are now running classes for other women. This is obviously very important in letting a lot of women know about the women's health movement. Ask your local authority, Worker's Education Association or Community Centre if they have a class; and if not, why not run one yourself. There is no need to be an expert, we all have to learn somewhere. Try it!

Women's Clinics

Women in other countries are asking the same questions about health care as their British sisters, but some are going one step further and setting up their own self-help health facilities run *by* women *for* women. In these centres questions of birth control, pregnancy and infections are treated on a sharing and equal basis; instead of being *told* what is wrong, the patient learns along with another woman about her problem.

With a paramedic (a woman who's had some medical training but is not a fully qualified doctor) you can learn how to do breast and cervical examinations, perhaps looking at her vaginal infection inside the patient and then smeared on a slide under a microscope. You will also be able to learn to take blood pressure, do tests for anaemia and get samples for cervical cancer and VD tests.

Quite often, there is a doctor available if needed and you will be referred there if a major problem is diagnosed. In America a few clinics do outpatient abortions, with counselling; and though fees are kept down as much as possible they are not free.

An English woman who spent some time in Sydney was very impressed with the Women's Clinic in Leichardt, a district of Sydney. It is simply a house that has been converted into a women's health centre:

'The first time I went I had thrush. The woman who saw me wasn't a doctor, she was a paramedic. She asked me if I had ever used a speculum and let me insert it myself. She took a swab and told me all along what she was doing and explained everything.

'The second time I went I made an appointment to see the doctor: I had a cyst growing on my face and pains in my breasts. A woman came in and said her name was Ann and that she was learning about what the doctor did and would be there with me and the doctor. She took me into a room where there was this woman sitting in jeans and a tee-shirt. I wondered where the doctor was! She said she was the doctor and her name was Pauline. It wasn't intimidating at all. She had a look at my face and told me about that. Then she asked if there was anything else I wanted to talk about. I told her about the pains in my breast, and without me having to ask, she explained what it was, and why, and what I should do about it. She asked if it was allright for Ann to have a look, as it was a good example of something. This was so different from being examined by an ordinary medical student who just pokes you without asking.

'It's just like going to an ordinary GP, except you get much better treatment. They have really good leaflets explaining things. When I got thrush they gave me one explaining what thrush is; it listed all the medicines you might be prescribed and what they all were, which were good and which weren't. They also had lists of all the self-help things

you could do. They had leaflets on many other subjects: trichomonas, pregnancy testing, abortion, menopause, painful periods, all done in the same form.

'It gives you a good feeling to be examined by people who really care, and want to share information with you. You don't feel so mystified; you feel just a bit stronger.'

Urinary Infection

'The U and I club has now been in existence for over four years. We work within the confines of conventional medicine but instead of "cures" we teach prevention and management of the various forms which cystitis and vaginal thrush can take. For many women our self-help procedures have eradicated years of cystitis and thrush and for everyone the pain and frequency of an attack can be eliminated by our now famous management process.

'Success from cystitis comes from three sources: urological and gynaecological investigations and self-help. All three are absolutely essential to eradicate your attacks. Thrush is entirely preventable by self-help unless diabetes is present, so if this is your problem our booklet, not our book, applies to you. Cystitis patients must have both.

'The advice in all our literature is not just medically approved, most of it comes from main London teaching hospitals, and all I have done is to write it down in understandable English.

'We have no membership but for any personal queries we charge £1 and also have a private counselling service at a modest fee. Our booklet Self-help in Cystitis and Thrush *costs 80p. Our book* Understanding Cystitis *published by Heinemann costs £1.20.*

(Angela Kilmartin)

U AND I CLUB: Urinary Infection in Your Home *9e Compton Road, London N7*

BOOKS ON SELF-HELP HEALTH

OUR BODIES, OURSELVES
by the Boston Women's Health Book Collective, Simon and Schuster, £3.95 (to be published by Penguin Books)
'Our Bodies, Ourselves is written by and for women in response to an imperative need for women everywhere to learn about our bodies in order to have control over them and over our lives. We seek to communicate our excitement about the power of shared information to assert that, in an age of the professional, *we* are the best experts on ourselves and our feelings, and to continue the collective struggle for adequate health care.' This is a very practical book and full of information from childbirth to rape, venereal disease and sensible diet. All through the book, women's own accounts of their experiences are included (see: Feminist Classics for more information on this book). The Collective now publishes *Women's Health News Briefs*, a monthly collection of Xerox reprints on women's health. For details of this and subscription costs, write to: Boston Women's Health Book Collective, Box 192, West Somerville, Massachusetts 02144.

WOMEN'S HEALTH HANDBOOK
compiled by Nancy MacKeith, Virago, £1.95
Most ideas and practical books on the women's health movement have come from the US; many are hard to get and expensive. In this book, women have got together and written articles about self-examination, period pains, menstrual extraction, contraception, abortion, pregnancy testing, childbirth, cystitis, vaginal discharge, breast examination, drugs, nutrition, and comments on the National Health Service, Social Security and Supplementary Benefits and a useful list of health groups. The book is an important handbook for women concerned about their bodies. The book has a large section about using a speculum, what you see and what to look for when you do use one. The diagrams are clear and helpful. There is also a six-week chart to help you look for certain vaginal colours, secretions, discharges. It is a very good handbook. It has been written by twenty women from all over the country; contributors includes a GP, a pharmacologist, two journalists, an osteopath, a midwife, an acupuncturist and the chairwoman of the Patients

Association. In its original form it was published by Nancy MacKeith (details from 16 Methley Terrace, Leeds 7), but in 1978 it was updated and re-published by Virago.

VAGINAL POLITICS
by Ellen Frankfurt, available from Compendium Books, 240 Camden High Street, London NW1, £1.50
Although much of the material in *Vaginal Politics* is related to the American system of medical practice, the discussion of the doctor/patient relationship is one of the best to be found. The book was fundamental in making American women aware of the need for changes in their health system. It can be instrumental in Britain for the same reason. The author talks about what should happen during a medical examination, the chemical dangers of feminine hygiene deodorants, the psychiatrist/sex-power syndrome, the economics of abortion, and how self-help health is a very important political statement from women. The book is useful in understanding why the women's health movement is necessary for improving the health of all people.

EVERYWOMAN: A Gynaecological Guide for Life
by Derek Llewellyn-Jones, Faber, 95p
Professor LLewellyn-Jones wrote this guide with the intent to minimize the fear of the 'medical unknown' that many women experience. He includes information from birth through pregnancy and discusses the medical aspects of birth control, infertility, breasts and breast feeding and various 'things that happen to women'. The chapters on pregnancy are very thorough and well presented (there are ten on this subject). The book is by no means a self-help guide, but does explain the basic facts about our bodies in understandable English.

FIRST WOMEN AND HEALTH CONFERENCE REPORT
from Rose Star, 4 Burngreave Bank, Sheffield 4, or from alternative bookshops, 25p
The first English Women and Health Conference was held in October 1974. The three-day conference included workshops on self-examination, childbirth, contraception, nutrition, menopause, VD, health and education and women and the Health Service. The report discusses what went on in its workshops, and contains ideas and practical advice for setting up groups and dealing with doctors. It also has an extensive interview with one women's centre that is very involved in the women's health movement.

COMPLAINTS AND DISORDERS: The Sexual Politics of Sickness
by B. Ehrenreich and D. English, Writers and Readers Publishing Co-operative, 85p
　　'The medical system is central for women's liberation. It is the guardian of reproductive technology, birth control, abortion and the means for safer childbirth.'
Medical science has been one of the most powerful sources of sexist ideology in our culture.

CIRCLE ONE: A Women's Beginning Guide to Self-Health and Sexuality
available from Compendium Books, £1.50
Besides organizing groups around the ideas of self-health, it is important for us to have books and other resource material to help us in our search to understand our bodies. As any woman involved in self-health will tell you, it is not solely using a speculum that is important. *Circle One* gives a thorough background for self-health, and basic techniques, but goes into abortion, 'Birth Control Blues', lesbians and self-health, masturbation and sexuality. It is important for women already involved in self-health, as it puts the women's health movement in a wider perspective. It is also useful for women who have yet to use a speculum, as it is clear and easy to read. It is an overview, just a starting point for further exploration.

WITCHES, MIDWIVES AND NURSES
Feminist Press, 70p
This is a history of women healers. Women have always been healers; they were nurses, abortionists and counsellors, pharmacists, etc. They cultivated healing herbs and exchanged the secrets of their uses. Medicine is part of our heritage as women.

MIDWIVES AND MEDICAL MEN: A History of Inter-professional Rivalries and Women's Rights
by J. Donnison, Heinemann, £6.50
For those who want to know more about midwifery and its male take-over. Quite scholarly but full of fascinating details of when medicine was based more on superstition than science.

VD HANDBOOK
from Montreal Health Press, PO Box 1000, Station G, Montreal, Quebec, Canada, available from alternative bookshops, 20p
This book covers all sexually-transmitted diseases giving clear descriptions of symptoms, how and why you'll be examined, what the doctor is looking for, what treatment you'll get. It stresses the disadvantages of some forms of treatment, such as the development of penicillin-resistant strains of virus. It emphasizes the value of asking your doctor questions and demanding information about what is happening to you.

FURTHER INFORMATION

HEALTH CHARTER
129 Spencer Lane, Leeds 7
Health Charter intends to link up all the areas in which women are organizing around health: self-help, fighting cuts in the Health Service, fighting for better treatment by the medical profession, etc.

WOMEN'S HEALTH HANDBOOK GROUP
c/o 16 Methley Terrace, Leeds 7
They will provide information about your local health group.

ALTERNATIVE MEDICINE

The aim of alternative practitioners is to encourage people to learn about their bodies and why they get sick, and to understand how to remedy their ailments, in other words to *take responsibility for their own health*. In this respect there is much in common between the women's self-help movement and alternative medicine.

The basic distinction between orthodox and alternative medicine today is that orthodox treatment relies mainly on attacking disease with the help of drugs or surgery, whereas the alternative approach concentrates on stimulating a patient's constitution to fight on its own behalf. This re-emphasizes the old adage that 'prevention is better than cure' and treats the individual as a whole, both mind and body, and in the context of their physical and social environment.

Unfortunately, the cost of receiving alternative treatment is still far too high for most people. In China, it has proved possible to combine traditional with orthodox western medicine in a nationalized system of health care. It would be of great benefit if alternative and orthodox medicine could complement each other in a national organization that offered every individual a variety of practitioners and techniques depending on their particular illness and their informed free choice. Here are some of the alternative approaches currently available in Britain:

ACUPUNCTURE

Our body has twenty-four meridian electrical lines of force. Some are positive (yang) and others negative (yin). By inserting gold and silver needles into the skin along these lines, one creates stimulation or sedation. For a list of good acupuncturists write to:

ACUPUNCTURE ASSOCIATION *34 Alderney Street, London SW1*

HERBALISM

The National Institute of Medical Herbalists publishes a free list of qualified doctors. The Society of Herbalists provides information on herb cultivation, books and suppliers, and will recommend practitioners.

NATIONAL INSTITUTE OF MEDICAL HERBALISTS *68 London Road, Leicester*
SOCIETY OF HERBALISTS *65 Emmanuel House, 18 Rochester Row, London SW1*

HOMEOPATHY

Homeopathy was founded on three principles: 'like cures like'; treatment is tailored to meet the needs of each individual patient; and substances which are lethal in large doses can stimulate the body to health when applied in minute doses. Homeopathy is covered by the National Health Service. The British Homeopathic Association can recommend a local qualified practitioner; ask for one on the NHS. The Royal London Homeopathic Hospital has an out-patient clinic where you can get free treatment without a reference from your doctor; but book well ahead.

BRITISH HOMEOPATHIC ASSOCIATION *27a Devonshire Street, London W1*
ROYAL LONDON HOMEOPATHIC HOSPITAL *Great Ormond Street, London WC1*

NATUROPATHY

Naturopathy is based on the belief that by eating natural wholefoods and avoiding harmful substances in food and the environment, the body will be better equipped to resist disease, and it will be able to cure itself with the help of biochemical, herbal and homeopathic remedies. For 30p you can obtain a list of practitioners from the British Naturopathic and Osteopathic College and Clinic.

BRITISH NATUROPATHIC AND OSTEOPATHIC COLLEGE AND CLINIC *6 Netherhall Gdns, London NW3*

OSTEOPATHY AND CHIROPRACTICE

Both Osteopathy and Chiropractice maintain that anatomical faults in the back cause functional disorders in the body. Manipulation by correcting the spinal joints allows the blood and the nervous system to function more freely and so enable the body's own resources to recover health. They are available on the National Health Service after conventional diagnosis and a reference from your GP.

BRITISH CHIROPRACTITIONERS ASSOCIATION *120 Wigmore Street, London SW1*

RADIOTHESA

Radiothesa is based on the idea that every form of matter radiates energy on its own wavelength. The human mind is capable of tuning into these energy waves and registering them by means of a pendulum or a 'black box' as in water dowsing. Thus practitioners are able to diagnose and treat the disturbance manifested in a person's body. A list of practitioners is available from the Radionic Association and the De La Warr Laboratories.

(by Celia Unsworth, first published in Live Wire)

RADIONIC ASSOCIATION *Field House, Peaslake, Near Guildford, Surrey*

DE LA WARR LABORATORIES *Raleigh Park Road, Oxford*

BOOKS

LIMITS TO MEDICINE: Medical Nemesis
by Ivan Illich, Penguin, £1
This book shows how medicine is organized to create disease, and in the interests of doctors, hospitals, pharmaceutical companies and against the interests of people. People should be given back the right to self-help and to determine when they are ill. It is one of a series of publications from the Center for International Documentation on education, transport, health and other sacred cow services in contemporary society. It has been an influential book.

AWAY WITH ALL PESTS: An English Surgeon in People's China
by Joshua Horn, Monthly Review Press, £2.40
This book describes a fifteen-year stay in China by a British doctor and shows how medicine, to be effective, not only has to take account of scientific advance, but also fit into the culture of society incorporating its traditional ways of healing, and be accompanied by a political understanding of what medicine is to achieve and why.

Valium

(The first verse of this song is sung by a worried 'patient', the second by the doctor, and the last by a representative of Roche, the firm that makes Valium.)

(Mum)

I can't get work, the money's short,
The children need new shoes
Times are hard, my nerves are taut
I don't know what to do
Help me doctor, don't you tell me no
I'm under pressure, I'm about to blow
Feel like jumping off a window ledge
I need something — just to dull my edge

(Chorus)

Valium helps to ease the pain away
Valium, help me cope another day
Valium, when it's all too much to bear
It won't pay my bills
It won't cure my ills
It'll teach me not to care.

(Doctor)

There's nothing wrong that I can see
For medicine to solve
But nonetheless I'll give you these
I just can't get involved
My waiting room is full of anxious lives
They want freedom from a world of strife
I've no cure for all these social ills
I'm a doctor — all I have is pills (*Chorus*)

(Roche)

It pays us well when times are rough
To keep your system oiled
'Cause we're the firm that makes the stuff
That keeps you off the boil.
Prisoners of a world of stress and strain
When you're feeling wild we can make you tame
We're making millions from our enterprise
We've got you permanently transquilised . . . (*Chorus*)
(words by Malcolm Reed, sung to music by Ian Heywood)

CONTRACEPTION AND ABORTION

The one biological factor we cannot escape is the fact that it is women who get pregnant and bear children. In our society we are also expected to look after the children once they are born. This means that although it takes two to make a baby, the responsibility for ensuring that children aren't conceived unless they're wanted usually falls on the woman: after all, she has the most to lose.

Contraception

All the more reliable methods of contraception available at the moment are those that must be used by the woman: the cap, the IUD or the pill. Little research is done into possible male methods, although the male reproductive system is not as complicated as the female. Men sometimes seem reluctant to interfere with their 'virility', despite the fact that production of sperm has nothing to do with satisfactory sex.

Even if the men we sleep with can't take complete responsibility for contraception, there are ways in which they can help; they can ask if we are using contraception *before* having sex, rather than assuming that this is up to us; they can discuss the different methods and be sympathetic to the difficulties involved; they can avoid putting pressure on us to have sex when no contraception is available.

Finding a reliable method of contraception that suits your needs and your body is still not easy. To begin with, it can be hard to get the information you need to make a sensible choice. It is still not completely accepted that children should learn about contraception at school, and parents sometimes know too little themselves to provide adequate information for their kids. Doctors frequently have no special training in this area and tend to be unsympathetic, regarding the side-effects of the pill or the coil as the price you must pay for freeing yourself from the fear of unwanted pregnancy. Family Planning Clinics usually give you better advice and follow-up care than a GP, and have more training and experience of dealing with contraception. (You can find the address of your nearest clinic in your telephone directory.)

Many women's groups have concentrated on learning about the different methods of contraception for themselves, and making this knowledge more widely available. Several groups have produced booklets on contraception, at least one group has written a series of articles for a local paper explaining the different methods without using mystifying medical jargon, and several groups have organized women's health courses.

Once we know more about our bodies and how contraception works, we are then in a much better position to ask questions and make our own choices.

HANDBOOK OF BIRTH CONTROL
from Edinburgh University Student Publications Board, 30p
This book contains clear diagrams of the different methods of contraception, some information on the advantages/disadvantages and possible side-effects, and sections on abortion and sexually-transmitted diseases.

CONTRACEPTIVE HANDBOOK
from Montreal Health Press, PO Box 1000, Station G, Montreal, Quebec, Canada, or available from alternative bookshops, 20p
This book contains thorough information about'
how different methods work, the possible dangers, who should not use certain methods, and so on. Some of the information does not apply to this country, but most of it is very relevant.

THE PILL: On or Off Prescription?
A report of a 1976 Conference from the Family Planning Association, 27–35 Mortimer Street, London W1, 30p
An interesting discussion of the pros and cons of making the pill available without a doctor's prescription. It includes some useful statistics about the relative safety of the pill. The FPA also has other information and educational material available.

Abortion

Almost every topic discussed within this book assumes that a woman should have the rights and needs of a full human being. She should no longer be confined to the home or her children, she should be free to begin to explore the world around her, making friends and joining together with other women to change the many written and unwritten laws and ideas that are hurtful to her. Abortion is one issue that deserves all our attention. The inadequacies in the present law, and the fear that even this law may be repealed, are of extreme importance to many women.

The reasons to permit free, legal and safe abortion are many, and have been dealt with in numerous books and articles (not enough money; inadequate childcare facilities; the woman's desire to carry on with her job or education; an unsatisfactory emotional climate in the family; and many other reasons). The supporters of abortion tend to be practical; they look at a woman and her life and see how a pregnancy and child would affect the woman and the development of that child. Anti-abortionists tend to forget about the woman; they often do not regard her as a feeling person with rights. Many women see it as totally wrong for others to restrict a woman's freedom to choose what is right for her. The arguments go on and on.

Many groups have formed around the issue of abortion. Two main groups are now in existence: *A Woman's Right To Choose* also known as the Abortion Law Reform Association (ALRA) mainly deals with the parliamentary fight for legal, free and safe abortion. The *National Abortion Campaign* (NAC) was formed in 1975 to fight the anti-abortion campaign which was sparked into action by James White's Abortion Amendment Bill.

A Woman's Right to Choose

The Abortion Law Reform Association has its offices in a small room in London. Its walls are covered with posters and books; there are typewriters on the tables; and all this gives the feeling that a lot is going on. Sue and Keith were in the office when we came to talk to them about ALRA, its past, present and future.

'ALRA was formed in 1936; fighting for abortion reform as a social and political pressure group has been a historical thing: We differ from the National Abortion Campaign, in that they are more of a grass-roots militant action group, concentrating on small regional groups, and large-scale demonstrations. We aren't concentrated in small units, although we do, like NAC, hope to work more within the regions; we are a membership organization, co-ordinated from London, with policy agreed upon by an executive. In some respects we have built up an "establishment" image. This is in many ways unfortunate, as we have been closely tied up with the legislature and fighting for actual reform in Parliament. We see ALRA and NAC as different but complementary units working together.'

ALRA has approximately 1,000 members and an executive committee of twenty-two. They are financed solely by private donations, membership fees, sales of literature and fund-raising; they are usually in some sort of financial difficulty. Keith, as the administrator, and Sue, the political organizer, are the only paid workers. Keith sees it important for men to get involved in the abortion campaign . . . 'I know it's not men's bodies, but we're half the problem in the first place!'

Abortion on request for every woman is ALRA's ultimate goal; working with Parliament has taught them many things, though.

'It is a question of practicalities: we haven't got a hope in hell, in the foreseeable future of getting any law through Parliament that would allow abortion on request past twenty-four weeks, or for social, physical or mental reasons, past twenty-eight weeks. Therefore, we don't see any reason to go all out for reform beyond that; this would waste a lot of our energy and resources that probably wouldn't have any pay-off in the near future. So ALRA's target is twenty-four weeks (the same as the Lane Committee set up by the government to look into abortion), whilst keeping viability at twenty-eight weeks, complying with the 1929 Infant Life Preservation Act. We think that is realistic.

'We are campaigning for more effective abortion through the NHS; we are interested in abortion daycare centres, we believe this is absolutely crucial especially as far as allegations of draining resources in the NHS is concerned. It's not just the question of doing the abortions but also of providing counselling and other services surrounding it.'

There are a lot of things that individual women can do. Even though ALRA does not work mainly on the local level, it does realize the need to keep pressuring MPs and Area Health Authorities.

'We'd love people to collect petitions, disseminate information, and to write to us with suggestions for pamphlets. The major thing, one that we cannot stress enough, is for women to write to their MPs; you would not believe how MPs are influenced by letters they receive. A lot of them still haven't formulated their ideas on abortion, so if they get a lot of anti-abortion letters it really does make a lot of difference. Also, people can help by writing to the local health authorities and asking what the situation is as far

as abortion is concerned (finding out information for us is very important: how easy is it to get an abortion in certain areas) and also by lobbying for a daycare abortion centre to be provided locally.

'We are not just a pressure group to maintain the 1967 Act, although we vigorously fight any threats to it. We want us to become a more broadly-based pressure organization: putting pressure on the media to make knowledge available, to stop the idea that abortion is one of those things you don't talk about. We would like to see abortion get to the stage where contraception is now. Social education is important, making people aware of the issues. We should be speaking in factories and trade union branches, trying to reach the "woman on the street". We want to keep pressure on Parliament, and also get more doctors involved publicly.

'We must educate women, teach them what their abortion rights are, then maybe they'll help us fight for better ones.'

A WOMAN'S RIGHT TO CHOOSE The Abortion Law Reform Assn, 88a Islington High Street, London N1

National Abortion Campaign

The National Abortion Campaign has groups all over the country fighting to bring awareness of the abortion issue to as many people as possible. Although the campaign started in response to the MP James White's Abortion Amendment Bill (which has now been dropped), it is still strong in many cities. NAC is fighting for local outpatient abortion facilities, talking to groups and preparing for any more campaigning that may have to be done to save the woman's right to choose an abortion insofar as it stands presently; and when the time is right, NAC plans to go ahead and make *abortion on demand for every woman* no longer a dream, but a concrete and important reality. NAC was formed nationally as 'a mass campaign which had never been tried before; it was felt NAC could do this mainly by focussing particularly on abortion and not on broader issues like contraception.'

On a national level NAC has been quite effective.

'It has had an effect on people in the labour movement, people in the constituencies, who have listened to NAC and had NAC speakers. People have thought about abortion more and realize that the 1967 Act isn't the utopia that was envisaged.

'The British Medical Association came out against the Select Committee on James White's Bill and that was due to NAC supporters occupying their offices and making them come out against it. We also have had a lot to do with changing attitudes so that women actually are able to say publicly, "I agree with abortion!" '

The policy-making bodies of NAC are meant to be the *planning meetings* which are held every three months, which is where the main decisions come from; and there is a *steering committee*, which meets once a fortnight (these meetings are open to anyone) and takes day-to-day decisions and communicates with local groups. There is also an annual conference which is based on specific themes or problems. The national headquarters sends out a newsletter which includes the minutes of the steering committee and articles about what local groups are doing and national events.

In Sheffield, where 60 per cent of all abortions performed in 1974 were done privately, there is a very strong NAC group, which has met for two years. They have been active in many areas of the fight for abortion. They talked with us about the campaign.

'Originally we were a Women's Abortion and Contraception Campaign (WACC) group, which was a women-only group. The NAC group developed out of that in order to involve men and women, and to draw in delegates from the labour movement. At that time it was felt that WACC would still continue campaigning around abortion and contraception, and carry on meeting, (but in fact it didn't).

'On a national level we have supported the campaign through demonstrations. We have sought support on a local level through speaking at trade union branches, to women's groups, housewives, schools, scouts and at two public meetings in Sheffield. We are campaigning for an outpatient abortion centre. There was one planned, but for various reasons it was cut, so we've got a petition going around asking that it be reinstated. We've held meetings on housing estates and organized a "day of action" in town, using the petition as a focus. A film has been made about abortion facilities in Sheffield: it follows one woman trying to get an abortion through the NHS and failing, and then having to go to the private sector. We have shown this film at meetings and at schools; it's a nice opener for discussion.

'We are trying to raise the issue among people who wouldn't hear about it if we weren't here, such as trade union branches and housewives. Our trips to schools have been successful, we have had a debate with "Life" (an anti-abortion organization) at a sixth-form college and the pupils were right behind us. We also spoke to some adventure scouts (whose group included girls), who got in touch with us through the Pregnancy Advisory Service. This was another debate with "Life", who always seem to make themselves off-putting. For example, a girl asked "What if I get raped?" and the Life man said, "Well, after all, all you have to do is to wait nine months and you can have the baby adopted." There was an uproar! The scouts later asked the Pregnancy Advisory Service to send someone to talk about contraception, which is a good follow-up.

'An important thing is to involve people who are not usually involved. By taking petitions to housing estates, we have met a lot of women who won't come to meetings regularly, and it's important for us to go around to them and raise the issue locally. We now know that we could count on these women if there were ever another anti-abortion bill.

'We have produced a bulletin of basic information about contraception and abortion, who to contact, where to go. We also detailed who the NAC group was, its aims and how to work with it.

'We have had trouble finding out what's happening locally with regard to abortion, which is just as necessary as applying pressure nationally. There are people in the group who are doctors and nurses and that way we find out a bit, but we don't accumulate as much information as we should.

'Sustaining a group is a problem. A lot of us have other involvements and jobs, which means you get to meetings tired; and when you think about organizing things you can't quite see where to fit the time in. We're quite good at putting specific projects into action, but we're not so good at evolving a long-term perspective.

'We've also had some problems with the local Trades Council with our last public meeting, which was organized by the Trades Council and sponsored by us. We went to speak to them and they agreed to plan a big meeting. There were about ninety people there, but mostly people we knew, not many new people or labour movement delegates. The problem was that the Trades Council didn't publicize it; even though they produced leaflets these weren't distributed. They are willing to give support on paper, and the Sheffield NAC group particularly has a lot of trade union support. But when it comes to mobilizing people it is usually left in the hands of the bureaucrats who are not willing to do it.'

NAC works closely with the Abortion Law Reform Association, but the Sheffield group thinks there is a major political difference between the two groups.

'It is in terms of how you see things in society being achieved and changed. Many of the women involved in NAC feel that change in society will come only by involving the masses of people in deciding and implementing that change, whereas ALRA has been a campaign aimed at the government creating that change.'

NATIONAL ABORTION CAMPAIGN 30 Camden Road, London NW1

Getting the facts on Abortion

Being able to use facts and figures in campaigns has always been an impressive weapon; this is no less true in regard to the campaign for better abortion facilities. It is important that facts be known about abortion in all areas: how easy it is to get an abortion, how many beds are available, who gets National Health abortions. Some groups are compiling booklets or pamphlets that are relevant to women in their areas, selling them to shoppers, trying to bring an awareness of abortion to as many people as possible.

In Leeds, the NAC group found that before they would campaign around abortion issues locally, they needed to know the facts.

'We didn't know how many beds there were in Leeds or how easy it was to get an abortion on the NHS. What we knew was all hearsay, and different people had different information. So we decided to go into it a lot further and write a pamphlet about it, which would be a very factual thing, and once completed, we would be better able to assess what needed to be done.

'We met to discuss the aims of the pamphlet, the content and how we were going to put it together. Each person was given a section to outline and then, after the group approved, went on to write it. When each section was finished we would read it aloud in the group and criticize it. We would either rewrite it alone, or a few of us would get together and do it. Sometimes we would swap sections.'

The final contents of the pamphlet are: an introduction, explaining why they did the pamphlet; an explanation of the 1967 Abortion Act; general information and history of NAC and its struggles; a general outline of the anti-abortion movement; abortion in Leeds, discussing the NHS; BPAS in Leeds, giving statistics of how many women came for counselling; a piece about a private nursing home in Leeds that does abortions; a local doctor's views; a section on contraception (proving that abortion is necessary) which includes a bit about FPA's; information about abortion and how it's done; what to do if you think you're pregnant; and at the end, lots of addresses. Throughout the pamphlet there are the personal experiences of women who have tried to get abortions on the NHS and failed, of those who have succeeded, and of someone who had to have a back-street abortion.

'All the sections were edited by two people, so there would be a similar style throughout the pamphlet. We raised money from discos and various other NAC fund-raising activities. We had 1,000 pamphlets printed by Moss Side Community Press, which we sold for 15p each, and we're now considering a reprint.

'We have sold pamphlets in town, outside factories and on housing estates. The response has been very good. People have shown a lot of interest and enthusiasm, and we have had requests for information from women seeking abortions.

'The pamphlet is a necessary tool to bring a national campaign to a local level; for people to be able to see its relevance to them — abortion is no longer an abstract issue.'

Compiling information in this way also helps NAC and ALRA when they present evidence to Parliament. To have a pamphlet of this sort in every city, town or area would be an important resource for any student, MP, doctor or abortion campaigner. It isn't difficult, but as the Leeds group found, it is time consuming. But in the end the results are important: it's a good way to get people interested in abortion, and educate them at the same time.

ABORTION IN LEEDS *from Leeds National Abortion Campaign, 94 Royal Park Road, Leeds 6, 15p*

FURTHER INFORMATION

ABORTION IN DEMAND
by Victoria Greenwood and Jock Young, Pluto Press, £1.65
A very well-written book that puts the abortion issue in its historical and political perspective. It talks about the 1967 Abortion Act, the consequences of the Act, the Abortion Amendment Bill, the ideas of all the different groups fighting around the abortion issue. An easily read book, worth reading.

ACTION GUIDE: A Woman's Right to Choose, *21p*
CAMPAIGNING FOR BETTER ABORTION FACILITIES IN YOUR AREA, *35p*
both from the Abortion Law Reform Association, 88a Islington High Street, London N1
Practical involvement is a very important aspect of the abortion campaign; letting people know about 'the situation', explaining about the laws and lobbying MPs. The *Action Guide* gives suggestions of all sorts of campaigning that can be done: petitions, letters to newspapers, letters to the Queen, street theatre, fund-raising, morale raising, pickets and sit-ins and suggestions for talks. Also tells how to go about starting a group — it's never too late! *Campaigning for Better Abortion Facilities in your Area* sets the stage for campaigning for outpatient abortion clinics, packed with facts to use, has sample letters, campaign tactics, also a summary of research done here and in the US on the safety of abortion, outpatient abortion, cost of outpatient abortion. The two pamphlets in combination would be useful for any group campaigning around abortion.

GROUPS CONCERNED WITH CONTRACEPTION AND ABORTION

FAMILY PLANNING ASSOCIATION
Margaret Pyke House, 27–35 Mortimer Street, London W1
The FPA is a voluntary organization which aims to help people to have children only when they want them. Over the past fifty years they have built up a network of clinics, most of which have been handed over to the NHS since contraception became free (for addresses of these, see your telephone directory). They now provide a national information service on birth control and related subjects and produce a wide range of leaflets, fact sheets and other publications. There are youth projects for contacting young people with information and help with sexual relationships and contraception, and an education unit running courses on personal relationships and family planning for people involved in sex education or other youth work. The FPA has been, and still is, a major force in making contraception and reliable information available to everyone.

WELL WOMAN CENTRE
Marie Stopes House, 108 Whitfield Street, London W1
This provides a wide range of services: birth control, vasectomy and female sterilization, abortion counselling and referral, special sessions for women experiencing physical and emotional difficulties at the menopause, and so on. The clinic is also concerned with investigating new methods of contraception and research into the practical aspects of birth control. As it is a private clinic they charge fees, but emphasize the friendly and informal atmosphere that they provide.

BRITISH PREGNANCY ADVISORY SERVICE
First Floor, Guildhall Buildings, Navigation Street, Birmingham 2
BPAS is a non-profit making charitable trust which has clinics in a number of cities offering free pregnancy tests, and counselling on abortion, contraception, vasectomy, and sterilization at low prices.

PREGNANCY ADVISORY SERVICE
40 Margaret Street, London W1
Similar to BPAS.

WOMEN'S RELEASE
1 Elgin Avenue, London W9
Part of *Release*, the drugs advisory group, they offer pregnancy counselling and advice on obtaining an abortion, contraception and sterilization.

NATIONAL ASSOCIATION FOR THE CHILDLESS AND CHILDFREE
318 Summer Lane, Birmingham 19
The Association helps women to have children or to come to terms with not having them. It provides information on infertility problems and adoption and sets up self-help groups for people who are depressed and desperate about their inability to have a child. They hope to exert pressure to change advertising bias so that the happy family with two kids isn't the only life-style represented. The 'childfree' (i.e. those who have chosen not to have children) form only a small proportion of the members, and the Association helps by putting them in touch with each other for support, as people in this position are sometimes isolated and feel that those around them are hostile.

CHILDBIRTH

'Pregnancy, if no longer described explicitly as a disease, is still treated like a medical problem in exactly the same setting and by exactly the same personnel used for the treatment of actual disorders.'
(from *Complaints and Disorders*)

Pregnancy and delivery was once a women-only business. Delivery took place at home with the help of an experienced midwife and women relatives. Skill, learnt through experience, has become the preserve of male practitioners. One can argue that the number of live births has risen since this take-over, but this is mainly due to improved medical care for difficult deliveries and better hygiene.

Nearly all deliveries nowadays are performed in hospital. Childbirth is being treated in the same way as disease, and women are being excluded from their traditional role as midwives. But childbirth is a *perfectly natural phenomenon*, which, if the woman is healthy, can safely be carried out at home without any trauma either for the child or the mother. In Holland, where more than half the babies are born at home, the mortality rate is 40 per one million births whereas in Britain where nearly all births are in hospital, the rate is 150.

Women are organizing around two issues concerned with childbirth: the first issue is a woman's right to choose which kind of delivery she wants, including the right kind of information about this. If she is healthy and no complications are foreseen, she should be able to have her baby at home where lover, husband or friends can support her.

And the second issue is to improve conditions of delivery in hospital. At the moment deliveries resemble an assembly line where speed and efficiency have priority. Each is forced into the same pattern although individual needs may differ considerably. Many women do not need any drugs, but even so they are given them. Many complain that, completely numbed, they miss the whole experience of childbirth (as does the father waiting in another room).

Women during pregnancy and childbirth ought to be treated as intelligent and feeling human beings; childbearing should once again become a straightforward, healthy process that most women can handle perfectly well if provided with the right information and the right help.

WHOSE CHOICE ?

Some people are trying to demystify the process of pregnancy. Either in informal groups or organizations, people are publishing pamphlets to help pregnant women by giving them information not otherwise available, and they are holding classes which will help women understand what's happening to them during pregnancy and tell them the choices that they can make. In this section we describe the work of two groups, the Sheffield Childbirth Group and the Leeds Pregnancy Handbook group.

Sheffield Childbirth Group

This is a group of about eight women who are campaigning for home confinement, and for the provision of better childbirth facilities in general. Their main aims are to inform women of the choices open to them and to give advice and information to women wanting a home confinement; to help improve the quality of a woman's experience of childbirth; to campaign for an increase in resources for the domiciliary and midwifery service and a change in policy on home births; and lastly to support family, friends and others who wish to play an active and informed part in the process of childbirth. Here they describe what they are doing:

'Hospitals vary a lot; some are better than others. Nevertheless we feel that they are just too scientific, and geared up to cope with the highly abnormal. But virtually everybody is getting hospital treatment; it requires a great deal of stamina to resist this or to have a "normal" delivery there.

'Each delivery is forced into the same pattern although the needs of women do differ (for example, it is very difficult not to be given an episiotomy, the cutting of the skin between vagina and anus, though this means a lot of discomfort and many women don't need it).

'There is just too much pressure put on a woman and she is trapped in a vicious circle (for example, she is unable to relax her breathing because she is surrounded by so much equipment that she cannot move, so she is handed over to a machine ... a ludicrous contradiction!).

Delivery at home, if it's a normal one that is, can be a very enriching experience. Unfortunately it is nearly impossible to get booked for home confinement in Sheffield because there are three hospital maternity units which, with the falling birth rate have many empty beds. Consequently doctors are very reluctant to perform home deliveries. Our first priority was to compile a list of sympathetic doctors. This we did in two ways: firstly, through people we knew who had had home deliveries, friends, friends of friends, etc.; and secondly, as a result of our own pressure, the practitioner committee sent a circular to GPs asking them whether they were willing to do home confinements. We thought this list would have around half a dozen names but in fact we gathered fifty-one. Mind you, it included GPs who in practice were refusing home confinement because their criteria were so high that nobody qualified. Doctors' criteria vary a great deal; some may accept virtually anyone, given that she has not got a deformed pelvis or something strikingly wrong with her, whilst others may give it only on the birth of the second or third baby if the first one was OK and so on.

'The main consequence of this is that our list is not as accurate as we hoped that it would be. Nevertheless it does allow us to give some practical help to a woman who has been refused home confinement. We give her the name of a doctor nearby. For the reason given before it does not always work and we have had a few failures, but hopefully our group will get bigger and our list longer.

'We are just beginning to undertake more public action. Recently we rang up The Star, a local newspaper, because the GP unit was closing. A GP unit is a kind of bridge between hospital and home deliveries; it is a fully equipped unit where a woman can deliver assisted by her GP and a district midwife. Unfortunately the unit did close, but we took the opportunity to write an article on all the options for childbirth locally, emphasizing home confinement and how you can get it, and what you can do in case of a GP's refusal (when you can either ask him to refer you to somebody else or write to the family practitioner committee). We gave a list of reasons why doctors might refuse to give a home confinement. And we described what we were trying to do.

'We are still very much a small group started by word of mouth. We did not feel we could advertise until we were sure about what we were doing. We put an advertisement in the Association for Improvements in Maternity Services, but our first big step will be a big article in the local paper when we should get inundated by calls afterwards which worries us a bit.

'The Sheffield Childbirth Group includes three midwives. It's very unlikely that this gives us any extra clout in the medical sphere. Midwives as a body, though they would not admit it, have been done out of a job and pushed into a very humble status. But within the group, it helps tremendously since we can give better support to each other, and it certainly gives us much more confidence in our ability to cope as a group and help other women. Childbirth is (for three of us) our job, and we have all experienced it and we all want to share this knowledge.'

For the future the group is hoping to be able to give more practical help to women, for example by going to ante-natal care with them and by producing a really good list of doctors.

'We are trying at the moment to decide what we can do on a consistent basis. We hope the group will get bigger and bigger. It would be a kind of network of mutual help between people who had the same experience.'

Secondly, and of a somewhat lower priority, they hope to set up a midwifery practice to enable people to have the sort of birth they want. Whether this will come about or not depends largely on the midwives in the group, who are very tormented about going outside the NHS, to which they are politically committed. They feel that it is a very big decision to step into private practice even for the highest motives. And so, this is a quite distant project.

SHEFFIELD CHILDBIRTH GROUP c/o 4 Burngreave Bank, Sheffield 4

Leeds Pregnancy Handbook

The *Leeds Pregnancy Handbook* contains all the information that a Leeds woman having a baby needs. It includes sections on ante-natal care, the rights of a pregnant woman, home births, hospital births, labour, feeding, the post-natal period and other services. It was compiled by a group of women all of whom have had their babies in Leeds.

'The pregnancy handbook was one of these ideas that many people were interested in but which had never actually got off the ground. During a complete year a lot of information about pregnancy and particularly about the process of birth were collected by a local women's group. In 1975 three of us, all very pregnant, decided to put a deadline on the handbook and we spent three months compiling it.

'Our reasons were numerous. We believed that it was up to the individual woman to determine the sort of pregnancy and labour she wanted. To do this she needed facts *about pregnancy, facts about the medical facilities available and facts about her rights. She also needed the confidence to act upon her knowledge. For many of us pregnancy meant our first close and lengthy contact with the world of doctors and hospitals. They often treated us as if our bodies were separate from ourselves, and we were not told what is happening to us or why. Even less were we consulted in any decision making.*

'Most of us have some idea how we would like to be treated during pregnancy and labour. We must be informed about what alternatives are available to us and demand the service that we want. We are aware that for a lot of women it is a luxury to have a partner who is able to help share the responsibility, particularly in the first week after childbirth. Our choices seem rather unfair, either we have the child at home where we need a lot of support which is not provided by the state or we have it in hospital with more support than we need (in fact we would say interference).

'People do not have a free choice, but we wanted to say that whatever the particular situation, there are certain things that a woman can press for.

'We spent quite a lot of time on the section of the actual process of labour. This knowledge should be available to all women; it actually helps if you know why you are having a pain or contractions.

'We also discussed breast and bottle feeding because women are again put into a situation where they don't make their own choice. In hospitals, either breastfeeding is not encouraged since it cannot be easily routinized or scheduled and this goes against the grain of hospital administration, or a woman can be made to feel guilty because she has chosen a method of feeding which involves the baby being able to be fed by the father or by other people.

'We talked about post-natal depression and tried to fit this into a social context as well as just an emotional and physiological context. People talk about post-natal depression as a pure chemical change; we stressed how almost inevitably some period of gloom would set in when a woman was trying to cope with her new life. (For example, if it's a working woman our society demands a total change in her life-style in order to have a baby. We wanted to stress how the lack of socially shared housework facilities exacerbate this problem.)

'We got a lot of help from a woman involved in the National Childbirth Trust who gave us a lot of case studies. We went through these to try to give a fair comment on each hospital. We felt that it would be irresponsible simply to dismiss a hospital if some women were going to have their babies there.

'Our basic aim was to produce a handbook which was not superficial, and which contained enough information for a pregnant woman to get by, and to produce something visually interesting and easily readable. We spent a lot of time on the layout and graphics and we had the pamphlet properly printed. Our finances came from the local health group and also from a local women's group; and there were a few small donations.

'We printed 500, priced it at 20p, and sold out; and we have covered our costs from sales. We distribute through alternative bookshops. The handbook got a review in Leeds Other Paper, Spare Rib *and the* Yorkshire Evening Post, *and it also got mentioned on local TV programmes. We could have been much better at publicity but did not have the energy. And we ought to have sold it at the gates of maternity hospitals.*

'Interestingly enough, the Area Health Authority and Hyde Terrace (which is the biggest maternity hospital in Leeds) asked questions about who dared produce this handbook. They did not want this sort of information in the hands of pregnant women. It challenges the hospital's right to make decisions, decisions on whether you are going to be shaved or not, or whether you are going to have an epidural or not. The handbook stresses what is really necessary and what is only convenient for the hospital. They did not like it at all, which proves our point that information is the basis for struggle.'

LEEDS PREGNANCY HANDBOOK GROUP *c/o Harehills Housing Aid Centre, 188 Roundhay Road, Leeds 8*

WHICH TECHNIQUES?

Different techniques are now being used to alleviate the pain of delivery. One of the National Childbirth Trust's main aims is to propagate these techniques amongst women, and it holds classes all around the country. The Leboyer method is also starting to spread in England and is used to help women, and more particularly babies, during the process of childbirth.

National Childbirth Trust

In 1956, a number of women joined together to form the Natural Childbirth Association (now known as the National Childbirth Trust). They were mainly mothers who felt that all was not as satisfactory as it could be for women in childbirth. Some of these women had used a relaxation method in childbirth and found it so beneficial that they wanted other women to know about it. They began to hold classes for pregnant women to prepare them for labour.

The idea snowballed; and now, though the headquarters are in London, the organization has many branches throughout the UK with a local organizer for each area. Here a woman who runs National Childbirth Trust classes talks about these classes and the specific methods of the Trust:

'A course includes eight to twelve classes and are taught during the last three months of pregnancy. They are quite cheap (between £5 and £10 depending on the family income) and may even be free if you cannot afford to pay.

'The main techniques have the barbaric names of "Psychoprophylaxis" and "Psychophysical Ante-Natal Preparation"; it originated in France during the 1950s, with doctors like Dr Lamaze who used the knowledge gained by Pavlov (famous for his experiments on the conditional reflex), in an attempt to reduce the pain of childbirth. Psychoprophylaxis is a method of preparation for childbirth, basically it means a conditioned reflex, whereby you train a person to react to given signals in certain ways. It's like teaching somebody to drive and stop at the red light; you train a pregnant mother to recognize what a contraction is and to respond to it immediately, using certain methods which will enable her to cope with it. If she does not recognize those signs, then labour dominates and she won't be in control; fear and anxiety will overcome her and the pain will become unbearable.

'Therefore, during classes, a pregnant woman will learn how to gain physical and mental control of the activity of childbirth. This conscious controlled activity is twofold: first she learns neuro-muscular control and muscular dissociation. She discovers that during labour there is only one huge muscle working (the uterus provokes the contractions). This is a kind of demystification of the whole process of childbirth. Then she'll have to learn how to relax other muscles while this one is working so hard. Since there is no control over the uterus (you cannot make it contract at will), a substitute is used. Someone will squeeze her arm or leg very hard and meanwhile she will breathe in such a way that she will relax the rest of her body and thus cope with the pain. This skill does not come easily and it requires concentration and practice at home.

'Second she learns special breathing. This helps her to stay calm; it also raises the pain threshold and aids comfort. It is a form of deep breathing which becomes shallower and lighter as the contraction intensifies, thus maintaining the maximum amount of oxygen for mother and baby. This whole method of conscious activity and breathing will help a woman in labour to regain control over her body and all the painful and strange sensations of labour.

'There are two other aspects of the National Childbirth Trust's classes emphasizing the support group and the partner's presence. For many women, the small group they are involved with rapidly becomes a supportive group, and this is far more important for many people than anything you can teach about labour. A good group will continue afterwards into a post-natal group where mothers can gather, babies play together and babysitting be arranged.

'The other important aspect is the idea of the partner's presence. It is comforting to have a husband, a best friend or a relative to share the pregnancy and delivery. For many men this teaches a lot about the female bodily function and they feel very emotionally bound up with the child. Hence, the partner is encouraged to come along to the labour rehearsal as well as the breathing exercises in order to know what the mother is expected to do.

'Childbirth should be a shared experience; that's why we would like very much to see husbands or relatives accepted more readily in maternity wards. With a good preparation and a lot of support, childbirth need not be an unbearable shock, but rather an amazing and unforgettable experience.'

NATIONAL CHILDBIRTH TRUST 9 Queensborough Terrace, London W2

The Leboyer Method

In France, Dr Leboyer has promoted a method in which a child is born into a silent and soft environment. He claims that babies are very sensitive to being born and conditions of delivery in hospital only aggravate the shock. From a very cosy womb, the child is suddenly thrown into a world of bright lights and clinical techniques.

Amongst his followers in England, two midwives have opened a private practice in London where they prepare women in pregnancy and deliver their babies at home. The Leboyer method appeals to both of them:

'The "Leboyer method" is a misleading term; it is not a method, but an attitude of sensitivity to the baby and the mother. Dr Leboyer does not want this whole new awareness to be called a method.

'Bright light and new techniques make birth a very traumatic experience; it does not have to be. Take, for example, the cutting of the umbilical cord which is usually done while it is still pulsating. Leboyer has proved, as a result of three years of research, that this causes the loss of red cells and that the real moment for separation is when the cord stops pulsating. We have experienced babies screaming when the cord is cut too quickly.

'Leboyer recommends us always to be very gentle, very quiet and to allow the baby to absorb its first moments of life rather than pressurize it into a world of clinical techniques and impersonal feeling. Mainly, the process of birth depends on the mother, the father or helper, and the midwife.

'The attitude of the mother during pregnancy and labour, how well she accepts the pain of labour and goes with it rather than against it, makes the birth easier. Leboyer once said that you must think of a birth as a love story, as an orgasm, not as something painful and dreadful. In fact, when he was making the film A Child is Born, *some people in the next room thought it was a blue movie hearing the sound of the mother's breathing.*

'A birth is a love story not only between the mother and the baby, but between the father and the baby. It is vital to have that immediate contact with the father.

'The role of the midwife, if it's a normal delivery, is more that of a helper than anything else. A midwife cannot practice *the Leboyer method; she can only have a different way of looking at a birth. Personally, I started changing when I went for a year to the Arctic to work as a midwife in an Indian reservation. My attitude then was that delivery was the midwife's responsibility. When the first woman came to the clinic, I immediately started getting things ready and putting her into bed. But she got out of bed and squatted on the floor. I was trying to catch the baby but she pushed me more or less away. I just delivered the head and she delivered the whole body herself. It was only after this experience that I realized she came in only for shelter basically because it was warmer than inside her tent. She did not need a midwife.*

'We want to encourage an attitude to birth where the mother is taking responsibility for her own child, and as a midwife we are here only to help and to be present in case of any difficulty. Once the midwife has delivered the head, you can deliver your own baby. One mother even cut the cord herself as she thought this was her feeling of separation from being pregnant. Mothers do go through amazing swings in their hormone changes, more sensitivity towards the child and the mother would undoubtedly help a great deal.'

BIRTH WITHOUT VIOLENCE *by Dr Leboyer, Fontana, £1.50*
This book, originally published by Wildwood House, introduced the Leboyer approach to Britain, producing a quite substantial impact on attitudes to childbirth.

Other Childbirth Groups

ASSOCIATION FOR IMPROVEMENTS IN THE MATERNITY SERVICES

West Hill Cottage, Exmouth Place, Hastings, Sussex

AIMS was formed in 1960 as a result of letters in the national press by Sally Willington (now president of AIMS) who spent ten weeks in a maternity hospital before her second baby was born and didn't like what she experienced there, nor the lack of aftercare. People wrote in with offers of help and money, and asked her to do something. She organized a meeting in London and AIMS began. (It was originally suggested that it should be called the Society for the Prevention of Cruelty to Pregnant Women.)

Peak membership was about 1,000, with groups all over the country; it declined rather badly in the late 1960s, but began to revive in the early 1970s, particularly when induction began to be the big issue. It has now about 420 members.

Their main objective is spelt out in their name and they try to do this by developing communication between those who give and those who receive maternity care. Much can be done at local level, and AIMS has now several members on Community Health Councils; other groups' activities include conducting surveys, arranging meetings between the public and maternity care staff. Their current concerns are the closing of small GP units as an economy measure, the decline of home confinements, the continuing stress in the medical world on childbirth as a purely physiological event and the lack of medical interest in non-technological developments (for example, Leboyer).

Most of their members are mothers, with a scattering of midwives, sociologists, and even one or two obstetricians. They maintain good links with related groups (National Childbirth Trust, for example), and keep abreast of research projects. A quarterly newsletter is published in which new developments are covered and the views of mothers represented.

SOCIETY TO SUPPORT HOME CONFINEMENT

c/o Margaret Whyte, Oak Tree House, High Shincliffe, Durham

This society has been active for over two years in supporting women if they choose to have a home confinement. They also pressure the DHSS to maintain a home confinement service. They have no office as such or official membership but have set up a network of contacts in many areas. Each area establishes an independent local organization, trying to find out which doctors are sympathetic to home confinements and refer women to them.

They have produced a large pamphlet which gives advice for home confinement, a highly informative precis of obstetrics in the Netherlands and details of the respective safety of home and hospital confinements. If you opt for a home confinement they give you the following advice:

1. To obtain the services of a midwife, write to the area nursing officer and the area medical officer stating one's intention of remaining at home. Ask if they will give a written refusal of service if difficulties are encountered here.

2. To obtain the services of a GP, contact the GPs on the obstetrics list. It is better to ask the help of the secretary of the local Community Health Council to do this, having of course first made sure that your GP really does refuse absolutely to attend you at home. If he does so refuse, do not sign the form EC 24 and if you have already signed, give him notice that you are breaking the contract. Make sure you have not been booked into hospital at any stage of the proceedings.

3. Next send a letter to the Area Medical Officer informing him (or her) of the situation and to the Secretary of the Family Practitioners Committee asking for their advice.

BIRTH CENTRE
188 Old Street, London EC1, 01-251 0768 (1pm to 4pm only)
This offers advice and support on alternatives in childbirth. They run preparation and yoga classes and also have an education programme for CSE and Further Education students studying child care, pre-nursing and residential care, showing Leboyer's *Birth Without Violence*.

ROYAL COLLEGE OF MIDWIVES
15 Mansfield Street, London W1
The College will give you names and addresses of midwives to attend you at home.

LA LECHE LEAGUE
c/o Valerie Bresnihan, 199 Weedon House, Du Cane Road, London W12
> *'Breastfeeding is a simple normal function . . . It has now become complicated; only our attitudes towards it have created problems. It was to help solve those problems that the La Leche League came into being.'*

For women who wonder whether to breastfeed or not, or don't know how to do so.

BOOKS ON CHILDBIRTH

THE RIGHTS AND WRONGS OF WOMEN
by Ann Oakley and Juliet Mitchell, Penguin, £1.25
This contains a very good article, 'Wise Woman and Medicine Man'.

CHILDBIRTH BOOK
by Christine Beele, Turnstone Books, £2.10
Everything you need to know from a feminist point of view.

THE EXPERIENCE OF CHILDBIRTH
by Sheila Kitzinger, Penguin, 65p
A guide to relaxation and breathing exercises for labour.

GIVING BIRTH
by Sheila Kitzinger, Sphere, 50p
This explores, with the help of labour reports written by women and their husbands, what it feels like to have a baby. The book stresses the relationship between husband and wife through the whole process of childbearing.

EMERGENCY CHILDBIRTH
by Gregory J. White, available from Compendium Bookshop, 240 Camden High Street, London NW1, 40p
This little pamphlet has been republished by a group of women in the women's liberation movement because it contains very interesting medical information on birth and how to help in an emergency childbirth.

TWO BIRTHS
by Lesser, Mines and Bwyn, Wildwood House, £1.75
Words and photographs of two women having their babies at home.

NATUREBIRTH
by D. Brook, Penguin, 90p
This book describes how birth has been mechanized and how you can fight against this; quite a useful guide to get prepared for a natural, healthy delivery, though the author is over-confident and skips many problems women might experience in a hospital.

YOGA AND CHILDBIRTH
by T. Crisp, Sphere, 65p
This book has a very good section on diet, but is disappointing for women who want to carry on yoga during pregnancy.

SAFE ALTERNATIVES IN CHILDBIRTH
from NAPSAC, PO Box 1307, Chapel Hill, NC 27514, $5
A collection of papers on the pros and cons of different birthing practices based on a conference in the USA organized by the National Association for Parents and Professionals for Safe Alternatives in Childbirth (NAPSAC).

BABYHOOD
by Penelope Leach, Penguin, 90p
This book covers the expected stages of a baby's development from birth to two.

THE KNOW-HOW OF BREAST FEEDING
by Sylvia Close, J. Wright and Sons, 75p
Sound practical guidance on how to deal with the problems of breastfeeding.

MY NEW SISTER
by Bo Jarner, A. and C. Black, £1.25
Clear and interesting photos tell of Sarah's happy birth and of where first born fits in. Strong features are the very real midwife and supportive nappy-changing, bottle-feeding dad.

CHILDLESSNESS: Its Causes and What to do about them
by Elliot Philipp, Arrow, 70p
A straightforward account of the questions and examinations you're likely to face if you want to have a child and can't, and the possible treatments for infertility.

MATERNITY: Letters from Working Women
edited by M. Llewellyn Davies, Virago, £1.75
Useful to remind us of the gains we've won by fighting for them.

GETTING OLDER

Menopause

During the menopause there are drastic hormonal changes occurring in the body. This can bring physical discomfort to many women, and may cause or aggravate emotional problems. The menopause often coincides with the time when a woman's children are leaving home; if most of her life has been taken up with childbearing and child-raising, adjusting to the fact that this part of her life is over can bring many problems. For the woman who has never had children the menopause means that she never will, and she may regret this or feel she has failed in some way. Other women who have looked forward to freeing themselves of childcare and re-establishing their own lives may find that they have to care for older relatives and once more lose the chance to do what they want to do. And because our ideas of beauty are based on youth, the menopausal or older woman may feel that her sexual attractiveness is at an end.

Doctors are becoming more aware of ways of treating the physical effects of the menopause, but can still be very unsympathetic and too ready to blame everything on a woman's 'change of life'. They shy away from dealing with emotional problems and dispense pills instead. Far too little research has been done into how much of the emotional problems of the menopause is really caused by physical changes, and how much is caused by social attitudes to older women.

The specific health problems of older women have tended to be neglected, even though women are working for better health facilities in general. Much of the activity has come from younger women; there are many groups campaigning about abortion and childbirth, but very few working for better treatment for menopausal women, or better health care for old people.

Older women may find it more difficult to get in touch with other women in the same situation, and they may be more reluctant to talk about their bodies and their personal lives. Yet it is only by getting together and discussing our problems that we can begin to work towards solutions. Local women's health groups may be dominated by the problems of contraception and childbearing, but this will only change when older women make their voices heard. Local women's groups or centres could put menopausal women in touch with one another, and local women's newsletters or the WIRES news service could provide a contact point for older women who want to discuss their problems with others who share them.

PUBLICATIONS

NO CHANGE: A Biological Revolution for Women
by Wendy Cooper, Arrow, 60p
Ms. Cooper is a leading proponent of Hormone Replacement Therapy for menopausal women. Here she sets out the reasons why she considers it so valuable.

SISTER GIN
by June Arnold, Daughters Press, $4.00 (available from some alternative bookshops)
A very positive novel about women growing older, changing and developing. The central character is undergoing the menopause and though it's often uncomfortable, she comes through it to start a new life.

MENOPAUSE
from Health Rights Inc., 175 Fifth Avenue, New York, NY 10010 (available from alternative bookshops), 30p
A pamphlet about the physical changes of the menopause, the symptoms this might produce and the available treatment.

GROUPS

WOMEN'S HEALTH CARE
16 Seymour Street, London W1
Women's Health Care was set up to publicize information about the menopause and Hormone Replacement Therapy (HRT). They hope to open a Women's Health Care consulting clinic in London and eventually in other towns. At the moment they send literature and lists of NHS and private menopause clinics to women who want to know about HRT; they tend to see HRT as a cure-all for menopausal problems, and gloss over any possible side-effects, so it may be as well to get hold of the other viewpoint before deciding if HRT is what you want.

MENOPAUSE CLINICS (National Health Service)
Many large hospitals have special clinics for women with menopausal problems. You have to be referred to them by your GP. They seem to concentrate on the physical symptoms rather than any psychological difficulties that may arise. To find out where your nearest clinic is, ask your doctor or your Area Health Authority.

Cancer

Two groups of interest are:

WOMEN'S NATIONAL CANCER CONTROL CAMPAIGN
1 South Audley Street, London W1
'Women should have a cervical smear test regularly because cervical and breast cancer can be treated very successfully when diagnosed in the early stage. This is the message which must be got across.' The WNCCC is trying to educate women through working closely with Area Health Authorities and recognized bodies in health education and preventive medicine. The WNCCC runs a mobile caravan unit which travels all over the country taking part in screening programmes. For more information about their screening and education programmes, contact the Campaign.

MASTECTOMY ASSOCIATION
c/o Betty Westgate, 1 Colworth Road, Croydon
The Mastectomy Association was formed in response to needs expressed by women who had had a mastectomy. Their main aim is to help women who have recently had, or been advised to have, a breast removed. The services provided are non-medical: giving information about bras, different types of prosthesis and swimwear. They also offer emphatic understanding and support. They feel that a woman who herself has experienced a mastectomy and coped with the various problems it poses, can best offer assistance.

7
WOMEN AND

CONDITIONING

THERAPY

WOMEN AND THERAPY

'The psychiatric ward is a factory for the combine (society). It's for fixing up mistakes in the neighbourhood, in the schools, in the churches.'

(Ken Kesey, *One Flew Over The Cuckoo's Nest*)

Before this century 'madness' was seen purely as a physical illness, often hereditary and nearly always incurable. Now the social factors contributing to people's mental troubles have begun to be taken into account.

We are brought up with certain assumptions of what our roles ought to be as individuals, as women or as men. Some people accept these roles and never challenge them; others do not adjust to what is expected of them, even if they cannot articulate their dissent. Generally they express it through depression, mental illness or alcoholism.

Specific goals and models have been set up for women. I.K. Broverman is quoted by Sue Sharpe in her book *Just Like a Girl* as saying that stereotypes and clinical judgments of mental clinicians 'are more likely to suggest that healthy women differ from healthy men by being more submissive, less independent, less adventurous, more easily influenced, less aggressive, less competitive, more excitable in minor crises, having their feelings more easily hurt, being more emotional, more concerned about their appearance, less objective and disliking maths and science. This constellation seems a very unusual way of describing mature, healthy individuals'. A woman must be a caring, loving mother and wife, a good cook, a perfect housekeeper and an exciting sex partner. If she fails to cope with these 'natural' demands, she is seen as a failure by her partner, her family, her doctor and, worse, she *feels* like a failure.

When she complains to her doctor 'Something' is wrong with her, and that she can't manage, he usually gives her valium. This won't cure the isolation, the feeling of uselessness or the sheer mental and physical exhaustion brought by the care of three kids and a husband. It is the condition of being a woman in this society which drive women to depression. Lee Comer in *Wedlocked Women*, puts it this way: 'It must be remembered that it is the same forces which drive one woman to be excessively houseproud that will drive another to alcoholism, agoraphobia (a rapidly growing condition almost wholly confined to housebound women living on suburban estates), dependence on tranquilisers or pep pills, physical cruelty to her children or any of the other manifestations of stress.' Emphasizing this point a woman psychiatrist in Leeds declares: 'Being a housewife with two or three children and being cut off from your relatives and other people in a suburban estate, is a very good recipe for getting depressed or having trouble.'

The different norms expected from men and women mean that aggression is not acceptable as an outlet for women. Violent men seem to end up in prison and violent women in a mental hospital. One woman in nine is expected to spend time in a mental hospital at some point in her life; in 1968 out of 58 million prescriptions for mood-altering drugs, three-quarters were handed out to women. Obviously for many women life is not the cosy domestic dream they were persuaded to expect.

Though many doctors still believe that mental illness or depression is the manifestation of a physical disease, there exists another category of psychiatrists who believe in the primacy of social factors such as family and society. The methods they use are grouped under the name therapy.

Therapy rejects treatment by drugs and bases itself on a long series of talks between the doctor and the patient, where together they will explore the patient's past and his or her present life. Different doctors have different methods according to the 'school' of analysis they subscribe to.

Freud was the first person to propound this method. Now many methods are available including: psychoanalysis, co-counselling, encounter and psychodrama. Many schools have emerged, Freudian, Jungian, Gestalt, Transactional, Behaviourist . . .

Therapy is normally a long and expensive process (for example, between one and five sessions a week at £5 each, for up to seven years); but people have organized alternative forms of therapy which do not depend on being able to afford such a high price.

An Experience of Therapy: Opening Myself to Change

Assessing her own therapy, Frances describes how it can be used by women to change deeply rooted destructive patterns of relationships, and how she emerged from therapy more profoundly political:

'When I decided to do therapy, I was depressed, withdrawn and sexually frigid. And although I'd tried very hard talking, thinking and reading about it, I could do absolutely nothing about it. At one point I had even managed to make a list of eight possible explanations but I was absolutely trapped and controlled by something that I did not understand and could not alter.

'I read all I could about psychology, which only provided me with a series of labels to describe my state and, more seriously, literally to hide behind. Even when I read Karen Horney's Feminine Psychology which provided illuminating and basically feminist analyses of frigidity in the reproduction of the family structure in adult couple relationships, I did not find the means to solve those well-documented problems that I was so intimately experiencing. It was only when I went to a therapist with my neatly labelled "problems" that I discovered I could no longer hide behind them. The pain was real and the labels irrelevant. I had to react to my pain either with masochistic self-pity or with a determination to change. I had to decide to go through to a new future or submit to the tyranny of my past and present.

'I found my therapist through my University Health Service where the GP referred patients only after discussing the individual's case with the staff therapists and selecting the most suitable combination. I asked for a woman partly because I could not really talk to a man about sexual problems, and partly out of simplistic feminism.

'When I first started I encountered opposition and discouragement as well as support and understanding. The most immediate support came from friends who had been in therapy. It was really helpful to share this alarming process with others who were familiar with the jargons of patterns, syndromes and neuroses.

'Other friends were frankly horrified or embarrassed by what seemed an admission on my part of a terrible disease or deforming blemish. We are all expected to cope, and not to admit failure, although I am sure many of us have sufficient pressures in our families, relationships and work to make it very difficult to function well. Unhappiness bordering on depression or intense anxiety is seen as shameful or a kind of illness. It's repressed lest our admission of it threatens everyone else's precarious facades of coping. However I did see my decision to go into therapy as an admission of weakness. I was ashamed that I could not work things out for myself or within the structure of a women's group.

'By admitting my need for some sort of help I began to learn important things. In the first place I had always appeared to others as strong, productive and together — a competence which was rather daunting. Once I was able to admit my own vulnerability to myself, many relationships became more equal. No longer did I always put myself into the unconsciously superior role of supporting others, instead we were able to share both our strengths and our weaknesses. I believe that women are conditioned into two conflicting roles; one tends to dominate and dictate the nature of relationships. There is the

"Big Mother" role and the "Emotionally Dependent Child". I had been trying to be the first and forcing close friends into the second. With my image of myself as a strong type, I experienced shame in having to admit need and dependence. We are all distorted by the inherent contradiction of these exclusive roles and a lot of work needs to be done to understand the way women relate to each other.

'I learned that to seek help was not an admission of abject failure, but the first step towards taking responsibility for myself, and freeing myself and others from the tyranny of my past. It was a matter of coming to a realistic assessment of my capacities and recognizing my healthy need of others.

'It requires strength to go through therapy and abandon all such defence mechanisms and behaviour patterns which had got me through in the past. Opening myself to change required an often painful process of self-discovery. I had to come to terms with feelings from which I had hidden, like fear of abandonment and strong self-hate, as well as those I could not allow myself, like happiness and the capacity to love others and myself and the expression of my sexuality.'

(part of an article written by Frances Seton for *Spare Rib* No. 44)

Co-counselling

Although co-counselling has not specifically a feminist approach, its non-hierarchical structures and group techniques have attracted many women. One of its attractions is that it avoids the power relationship of conventional therapy, where the patient is dependent on the doctor or therapist.

Co-counselling does not set out to be an alternative psychiatric system. But its method and theory differ completely from conventional analysis. The theory assumes that everyone is born with tremendous intellectual potential, natural zest and lovingness, but these qualities have become blocked and obscured in adults as the result of accumulated distress experiences (fear, hurt, loss, pain) which begin in childhood. The method, then, is to teach a person (the client), with the help of another person (the counsellor). A woman counsellor tells us more about it:

'Co-counselling is to do what children do naturally and what adults who have not had this ability stamped out of them can do: to turn to another human being and to use their awareness and their love and acceptance to go over the distress and to discharge the hurt, the painful experience. These have certain physical manifestations, people will shake and tremble or be embarrassed and laugh.

'The basic thing in co-counselling is not the learning of a new skill; it is to recover a skill we are born with and which society pushes out of us by making it socially unaccept-able to cry and to laugh, to shake and show fear or emotion. What we believe and put into practice is that people have innately in them a way of recovering from distress, from the hurt which they accumulate through life.

'This is not something you have to learn, it's something you have to re-learn, and which does come naturally. What we are trying to do in co-counselling is to help each other recover this ability and we use each other's free attention to do it.

'Therefore co-counselling is a system based on a concept of equality. The people involved take turns to be counsellor and client. Although we use the terms "counsellor" and "client", we try to get away from the traditional relationship of therapy where the counsellor is in possession of a body of knowledge and understanding of the way people work, and where the client is helpless and goes to the counsellor to have things made clear. In co-counselling both counsellor and client have this knowledge and understanding.

'We say very strongly that the counsellor's role is not to guide, to direct, to take charge of the session. The counsellor is only there to attend to the client who decides what material to work on and the way to work. You ask the counsellor to help you in the way you know is best for you. The counsellor will act on your suggestion, perhaps making suggestions of her or his own.

'Someone who has been counselling for a long time will be experienced, will have got rid of a lot of distress and will probably have more free attention for the client but this will not necessarily make a better counsellor than someone who is just beginning.

'The discharge is the most important thing about co-counselling. It is not cerebral, it is nothing to do with theory, coming to understand in your head what your problem is, which is why it is distinct from therapy. It is simply to use the loving attention of another human being to recover from your own pain. This requires that people are handling their own lives at that moment with a certain degree of success, and although they have their own distresses they are not so distressed that they function primarily as a client. In classes people are taught to be a client, by being taught to let go of the inhibition that stops them crying and laughing; but also they are taught to be a really effective, thinking, caring counsellor for someone else. They must have the ability from *the beginning to lift themselves above their own distresses and preoccupations and be there for the other person's benefit. That's why co-counselling can take off so easily in a class; we teach people how to gather all the attention that is free of distress and how to use it for themselves and for one another.*

'*Introductory meetings for people who want to get involved in co-counselling are held fairly regularly by counsellors and teachers (a teacher is an experienced counsellor who has recovered the ability to discharge, who has read and understood the theory and is involved in workshops). After this a class meets once a week for two or three hours. The theory and practice of counselling are reviewed.*

'*People choose a co-counselling partner from the class and the two will meet at least once a week between the classes. In their sessions they will have to divide their time equally so both are alternately counsellor and client during the same session.*

'*Part of the class is taken up by session reports where people explain the difficulties they have encountered and try to sort them out. Classes usually run for sixteen weeks with a break and after that for as long as people want to go on. Very often, those who have counselled for a while will go back to a different class which will help them grasp better the basic idea of co-counselling. After that, they join the community of co-counsellors, who meet regularly for workshops and gatherings.*

'*Co-counselling is noticeably female. It seems that two-thirds of the counsellors are women and the leadership is predominantly female. Men have far more severe social restraints put on them about feeling and expressing emotions. Women have a great deal of licence in our society in being emotional creatures, therefore it is easier for them initially to achieve some kinds of discharge like crying and shaking. But once men recover this ability there is no difference between the sexes.*

'*But the female majority has had at least one great influence: the issues of feminism and sexism have been taken up in co-counselling. We don't only look into personal distresses which we accumulate in our own private life but we also look into social distresses brought about by our sex. This is becoming predominant in co-counselling. Instead of thinking "God I will never go through that!", once you realize that your distress is socially enforced and approved, then it makes it clearer how you can work on it.*

'*In Yorkshire we've just started to have a lot of women's events and had a couple of all day workshops for women. We try to meet once a month to concentrate specifically on women's issues. But it is different from a consciousness-raising group. I think it is more positive. In a counsciousness-raising group people may feel depressed and won't know what to do with their depression because nobody knows how to handle it, whereas co-counselling has a very clear understanding of what you do with feelings, how you discharge the pain so that you re-evaluate the knowledge and experience of the pain. It works much faster than a consciousness-raising group. There is no fear of the problem being too big to bring out.*

'*If everyone is in a position of fully understanding emotions that are expressed and knowing that all distress can be removed, it brings hope and tremendous power. The most important thing to me has been watching the women that I've known in counselling emerging to an almost unrecognizable degree in an incredibly short time. By focussing on certain issues, they have taken charge of their own lives, they are more vibrant, open, energetic, much more powerful. They actually look quite different.*

'*As we recover strength, we begin to put it straight into everything we are doing so that we become more effective. Our power to effect changes in all aspects of our lives increases tremendously. Co-counselling is not like a refuge that you run to from the world; it is a support system so that you can operate more effectively in the world. The women who are co-counselling in this area are also doing an amazing number of things as well. They've realized that all problems can be resolved, that all feelings of powerlessness and helplessness can be overcome, and they act much more positively. Distress is both personal and cultural: once we have realized this we can work on both aspects simultaneously and much faster.*'

Feminist Therapy

The feminist critique of conventional therapy is twofold. Firstly, psychotherapy exists basically to reinforce the idea that if a person cannot adjust to her social role, it is she who is wrong, not society. Therapists argue that women want to be mothers and wives; they make women believe that this is all that a healthy, normal female should desire and they are quite ready to help them when they don't. Secondly, feminists have attacked the patriarchal character of a therapeutic situation. Most of the time, the therapist is male and the woman will once more enter into a dependent relationship with a man, repeating her social, economic and emotional dependence on her father, husband, boyfriend, boss. Often therapy seems only to reflect the power relationships that already exist in society.

Convinced that people are oppressed and not sick, that therapy should aim to promote social change and not social adjustment, two women have opened a women's therapy centre in London. The *Women's Therapy Centre* opened in 1975. It was conceived as a place where women could come to get therapy that would be more sympathetic and supportive to women who were trying to gain control over their lives, rather than pushing them back into a traditional family situation and therefore compromising their needs. In the centre a new 'feminist therapy' is evolving. The roots of this began in New York when Susie Orbach and Luise Eichenbaum were involved with a group of feminist psychotherapists:

> *'For two years the group discussed the social expectations that women are presented with all the time, what are their experiences as mothers, wives, daughters, lovers, sisters and workers, why they share feelings of powerlessness, helplessness, rage, guilt, self-hate, sexual frustration. These so-called "neuroses" are in fact based in social reality; therefore we tried to understand the underlying causes. We attempted to define new goals, new models for women in therapy as opposed to traditional ones.*
>
> *'Traditional therapy aims to reinforce the family as it is in society today and a woman's role within the family. Also therapists have particular models of what is "correct" feminine and masculine development in the socialization of children. The power relationship between the therapist and the person is very rigid, whether it is the Guru model of Gestalt or the cold one of analysis. The therapist is meant to be a powerful, authoritarian figure.*
>
> *'Feminist therapy is trying to understand the deep roots of conflict, a social understanding of family pressure and the pain a woman might feel as a consequence of it. The family in capitalist society socializes the child in certain ways; although there is a unique experience within one's own family, that family unit is supposed to fulfil a definite role.*
>
> *'Our idea of what is useful for women, or what's going to be satisfying for them, is not the resolution of conflicts but the understanding of where the roots of the conflicts come from. The roots may get transmitted through the family by the idea that you resolve your problems by getting married and then life will become terrific. We must understand the pressure on the family and be aware of the pain a woman might feel every time she steps out of that model and away from those expectations. Another difference is that we try not to escape the problem of the power relationship within analysis, but will talk with the person of their experiences of powerlessness and validate these in the therapy. We will not negate the reality.*
>
> *'The difference between feminist therapy and consciousness-raising (CR) is that the latter is pinpointing the underlying structures in society. Women find out through their common experiences how patriarchal structures work and why they make us feel certain ways. Politically this is very important. However the unconscious is not simple and even if we understand the basic principles underneath the problem, we may not know very well how it works exactly for each of us; and that's where therapy comes in. For example, a CR group might help us to understand where jealousy comes from, but we may still feel it very strongly, and feel guilty about those feelings. This kind of problem*

occurs throughout the women's movement and is very difficult to handle in CR groups. Thus, whatever feminist therapy is able to bring to the understanding of the situation is useful; it would help to find out how deeply we have internalized the barriers we are trying to break.

'It is wrong to elevate therapy to something that it is not. All we try to do is understand our situation; to talk of therapy as a political movement is wrong, we would like to see a very active mental health movement.'

In the Women's Therapy Centre, women can find not only individual therapy, but different kinds of self-help groups: a compulsive eating group, a pre-orgasmic group, fantasy therapy, etc. There are frequent seminars and regular supervision for therapists. The workers in the Centre have started to compile a list of sympathetic therapists all over the country. They hope eventually to get a grant, but at the moment the Centre is financed by the people who use it. They pay according to their income.

THE WOMAN'S THERAPY CENTRE *19a Hartham Road, London N7*

PRE-ORGASMIC GROUPS

A significant percentage of women have never had an orgasm; Kinsey's survey on 5,940 women in 1938—49 showed that 55 per cent of the women *never* or *rarely* experienced orgasm. The 1972 Playboy Foundation study showed a slightly lower figure.

For those who want to have orgasms, the kinds of help available are limited to conventional psychotherapy and the more practical Masters and Johnson couple therapy. Success is not guaranteed, and the treatment is time-consuming and usually expensive. So what else can be done?

In 1975, feminists in California and New York developed a completely new approach to this question which was based upon the changed attitudes to female sexuality which have come out of the women's movement. They set up institutes which organize groups for women to explore their sexual responses and discover for themselves how to have orgasms.

The term 'pre-orgasmic' is preferred to the medical term 'non-orgasmic' because this approach pre-supposes that every woman with a clitoris can become orgasmic given the right kind and amount of stimulation. A frigid woman is one who has not had an orgasm yet. The concept of frigidity is a male-defined one, and it's a way of making women feel inadequate. Most women who believe they are frigid can change this by getting the correct information and by trying to get rid of their deep-seated fears and shame. And almost all women have some sort of shame and guilt about their body and their sexuality.

Pre-orgasmic groups in the US are led by experienced counsellors who have been trained in this work; fees are normally on a sliding scale and are covered by medical insurance. Ninety-five per cent of the women who attend the group learn how to have orgasms by the end of the five-week session. And this is the first step to sharing an orgasm with a partner.

Eleonor Stephens, who has been involved in a pre-orgasmic group, described this new work and how two years ago she started the first pre-orgasmic group in England:

'In America we held a series of discussions on women and our bodies, and the material for this was later published in the book Our Bodies, Ourselves. Of the ten topics covered in the course, the three which concerned female sexuality were most popular. At the end of the last session, a shy woman in her thirties with three children came up to me to tell me how useful she had found this and how much she had enjoyed it. But she wanted to ask me one last question: "What does it feel like to have an orgasm?" For her and many others I knew that we had failed. Yet we had talked frankly about childhood experiences and attitudes to our bodies, discussed Freud and other theorists, reviewed Masters and Johnson, extrovert women had compared positions that suited them best, and so on. Yet basically we'd missed the point, and it was very likely that a lot of women coming to our groups were not experiencing orgasms.

'Two years later in Berkeley in 1973, I became involved in a pre-orgasmic group. When I came back from America, I wrote a series of articles for Spare Rib on this subject. I did not intend to set up a group but so many women wrote in saying, "We must have a group here, we are desperate," that I decided it was essential to start a pre-orgasmic group.

'Many women join pre-orgasmic groups as a last resort. Previously they would have gone from one relationship to another looking for the right lover who would teach them the secret of sexual satisfaction. This after all is an important aspect of the "Romantic Myth of the Ideal Lover", which has prevented women from taking responsibility for their own sexuality and has maintained their dependence on men. Romanticism is large-ly responsible for keeping people in ignorance about sex. The truth is that many women need a lot of stimulation to get an orgasm, and that it is very difficult to reach a climax through penetration of the penis. Yet the contrary has been taken as a norm.

'Our view is that sexuality is something a woman must find for herself. She must understand her individual needs before she can effectively communicate to her partner her likes and dislikes and what she finds sexually exciting. Masturbation is the best way for a woman to learn and teach herself about herself. By teaching women to give them-selves orgasms, the whole process is demystified, and orgasm is seen not as something beyond our control, something "done to us" but something which we can cause to happen.

'There are several variations on how the groups and workshops are organized, but in general they follow a similar pattern, based upon the method developed by Lonnie Barback and Nancy Carlsen, two therapists who worked at the University of California Medical Center in San Francisco. Each group has two co-ordinators who lead the discussions, and not more than ten members; they meet for two hours, twice a week for five weeks. The woman contracts to undertake one hour's homework each day, which is essential despite its heavy time commitment.

'The techniques used come from a variety of sources: Masters and Johnson; Lo Piccolo and Kegel, whose specific exercises for controlling the muscles of the pelvic floor are practised; relaxation exercises and massage are initial parts of the homework helping women to explore and feel comfortable with their bodies in general, and sexual areas in particular, as a preliminary for masturbation.

'The first sessions introduce women to physiological and anatomical aspects of human sexuality, about which many women are ignorant; some feel their genitals are abnormal and it is reassuring to look at pictures and to look at themselves in a mirror.

'Detailed discussion of the process of masturbation is introduced through several short films which have been made for this purpose. One shows a woman taking a shower, enjoying soaping herself and touching her body, then going on to masturbate to orgasm. Another film shows a woman using a vibrator. However strange this sounds, in practice the films work beautifully. They are sensitively produced and their explicitness makes them far more useful than books or lectures. (Most young boys have seen each other *masturbate, but very few women have ever shared this.)   Another film shows a hetero-sexual couple making love with both of them concentrating on the woman reaching orgasm by manual stimulation, not through penetration.   In this film the woman has an orgasm, and the man does not, and both appear happy and satisfied with this.   Women are so used to the opposite situation that it is gratifying to see an alternative.   This film raises discussion of the problems associated with simultaneous orgasm.   The idea that both partners must have an orgasm at the same time is a very entrenched myth, very frustrating to women.   Except in the situation where both people stimulate each other orally, it is very hard for partners to give sensitive and rhythmic stimulation when they are on the verge of an orgasm themselves.   In most heterosexual situations, the man becomes distracted from the woman's orgasm and the woman gives way to male orgasm.*

   '*A great deal of time in each session is devoted to sharing feelings about sex in general. The fear of being out of control is very common, so that when women feel themselves close to a climax, some deliberately resist the sensations.   Some worry about looking funny or making too much noise.   Lots of these aspects of self-consciousness are relieved by the privacy of masturbation.   We all have so many "shoulds" about sex, so many imperatives which we have been socialized to accept, that it is hard to find out what we are really like.   This is the importance of the hour's daily homework; it gives women a chance to explore their own potential for sexual pleasure without pressures to conform to external standards.   Many women find it hard to put aside this time for themselves because they feel they don't deserve the attention.*

   '*This is why the group structure and the support it gives is so crucial.   Groups are the best therapeutic situation because the main thing that women feel is isolation; they feel that they are abnormal and never talk to anyone about their sexuality.   The discovery that ten other women are in the same situation is tremendous.   The process involves so much courage and trust, that without encouragement many women would not continue.*

   '*The leaders, some of whom have clinical group experience, are all trained, and they meet together to discuss the progress of their different groups.   They bring to each group the experiences of many women they have worked with, and also share their own personal feelings.   In the traditions of the women's movement, the groups are non-hierarchical and everybody is encouraged to participate.*

   '*Women have to create their own sensuality.   We need a feminist eroticism; we need to know what gives us pleasure and turns us on.   Right now women are in a difficult situation because they are trapped into two conflicting systems.   One is the Victorian Puritanism, which says that sex is bad and dirty; it should not be enjoyed: "Shut your eyes dear and think of England."   The other one which sprang up in the sixties with the trend of sexual liberation says that women must be sexy and have multiple orgasms otherwise they are not liberated.   So now women feel either guilty or inadequate, but these feelings are once more dictated by male sexuality.*

   '*Our work is not at all to push the stereotype of the Liberated Woman with multiple orgasms.   We want women to discover their own sexuality, for themselves, free from pressures of stereotypes.*

   '*My vision of what's needed in England now is some sort of Feminist Sexuality Centre where we can develop this work further, train more of us in this approach and help set up groups outside London.   Everywhere I've been to talk to women about this work, there's been enormous interest and obvious need.   Until this need is met, women are at the mercy of myths, misinformation and the subjugation of their own needs to those of men.*'

(by Eleonor Stephens and including parts of her *Spare Rib* article
'The Moon Within Your Reach')

PRE-ORGASMIC GROUP *c/o Spare Rib, 27 Clerkenwell Close, London EC1*
The group has published a pamphlet on pre-orgasm.   See also *Spare Rib* No. 42 'The Moon Within You
Reach', No. 44 'Opening Myself to Change', No. 48 'Self-Help Therapy'.

FURTHER READING

WOMEN AND MADNESS
by P. Chessler, Allen Lane, £4
This book examines

> 'the forcing of women into rigid pre-deter-
> mined feminine roles and what relationship
> this bears to the fact that the great majority
> of psychiatric patients are women. Married
> women are especially vulnerable. The way
> the feminine role fits women alarmingly
> for the equally passive role of mental
> patients, the double standard operated by
> psychiatrists (alert, vigorous and frustrated
> women are disturbed and unfeminine) is
> interestingly presented.'
>
> (*Women's Report* May 1974)

PSYCHOANALYSIS AND FEMINISM
by Juliet Mitchell, Penguin, £1.20
The author sees how the work of classic psychoanalysis (Freud, Reich, Laing) can be used in a
specific feminist context. A very difficult book
but rewarding, perhaps best tackled in theory
groups or seminars.

NOT MADE OF WOOD
by J. Foudrane, Quartet, £1.75
The author, a psychiatrist, denounces the psychiatric ward which duplicates the hierarchy of the
outside world. Patients are *made* helpless and
passive, while doctors and nurses are in charge.
He describes his experience when he set up a
ward where patients are encouraged to take charge
of themselves and help each other. A fascinating
book.

I NEVER PROMISED YOU A ROSE GARDEN
by Hannah Green, Holt Rinehart and Winston,
$6.95
A young woman's journey through schizophrenia
and out the other end, helped by a female psycho-
therapist, but hindered by the rules of a rigid
mental hospital ward. A very powerful novel.

FAMILY LIFE
a film by Tony Garnett and Ken Loach
How an ordinary family destroys the mind and
spirit of a young woman; alternative Laingian
therapy starts to help but when this is withdrawn
conventional methods take over and the once
lively, energetic girl becomes a passive vegetable.

COMPULSIVE EATING
Spare Rib articles: No. 52 'The Feeling Behind the
Fat'; No. 53 'Why do we Starve or Stuff Ourselves'
Fat is a way of saying no to powerlessness and
self-denial. This is a feminist issue.

SOME OTHER SUPPORT GROUPS OF INTEREST TO WOMEN

ANOREXIA AID
1 Pool End Close, Macclesfield, Cheshire
An anorexic will systematically starve herself even
to the point of endangering her life and yet remain
obsessed with food. The vast majority of anorexics
are adolescent girls but boys of ten to twelve years
old can be anorexics too.

Anorexia nervosa is a complex problem, bound
up with the values of society (feminity is being
thin, fragile, etc.) and a rejection of dependency
towards the family, but at the same time it is a plea
to stay dependent. Each case is unique and symptoms vary from individual to individual.

Anorexia Aid is a mutual support society for
anorexics and their families. They have approximately a thousand members, they send out a newsletter annually and hold meetings in several areas,
where anorexics can share their problems. They
also circulate a National Register to enable individuals to contact each other when they wish to talk
with others in the same situation.

DEPRESSIVE ASSOCIATION
*c/o Mrs Janet Stevenson, 19 Merely Ways, Wim-
bourne Minster, Dorset*
This group denounces the lack of understanding
of many people including doctors and psychiatrists
towards depression. What depressive people need
is care and help. They try to organize support
groups and send out a newsletter.

ALCOHOLICS ANONYMOUS
11 Redcliffe Gardens, London SW10
There are half a million alcoholics in the UK of
whom at least 150,000 are women, and there are
probably another 4 million affected indirectly by
alcoholism.

Research has shown that in the last ten years
the ratio of women to men alcoholics has increased
from about 1 to 8 in at least 1 in 3. The National
Council of Women suggests that this number
might be even higher since alcoholic women from
the upper classes would be said to be suffering
from a liver complaint.

Most of the time a woman will start drinking
through loneliness, boredom and frustration, but
a new category of alcoholics has appeared, 'the
lace curtain drinkers', respectable women who
drink alone in the quiet of their suburban homes.
The new availability of alcohol in supermarkets
makes the path to alcoholism much easier.

The major organization that deals with alcoholism is Alcoholics Anonymous. Like all the groups
above, they are not feminist but might help. An
ex-alcoholic woman said that it has been for her
the best way of dealing with alcoholism, in spite of
its male orientation: 'At a group everyone relates
through their experience of alcoholism. This
breaks down class divisions and sex divisions as
they talk about their problems with it and they
discover what they have in common.'

For more information read **Alcohol Problems of
Women and Young People** from the National
Council of Women, 36 Lower Sloane Street,
London SW1 and **Spare Rib** Article No. 22, 'The
Ideology of Alcoholics Anonymous and the Isola-
tion of the Alcoholic in Women's Liberation'.

LESBIAN ALCOHOLICS
*c/o Sappho, Basement, 20 Dorset Square, London
NW1*

CHILDCARE AND WOMEN

The family structure that most of us have grown up to accept as 'normal' is one where the man goes out to work and earns money, while the woman stays at home looking after children, and is kept by her husband in return for her work in the home.

Although many women do go out to work, childcare is conventionally thought of as a woman's task, and any paid work she undertakes must be fitted around the needs of the children who are seen as her major responsibility. Women are faced with the choice of parenthood or a career, whilst men can, and usually do, have both.

Social and technological changes in the past hundred years or so have made this position illogical. The development of reasonable contraception and the trend towards smaller families means that many women have finished childbearing and got their children off to school by the time they reach their early thirties; greater life expectancy means that a woman can look forward to another thirty or so years of active life after her period as a 'full-time mother' is over.

Yet motherhood is still used as an excuse for not training women ('you'll be getting married soon and having babies; what's the point then of training you?'), and for not giving women responsible jobs ('you'll always be taking time off for the children . . . '). Women who want to retain and develop their skills need the opportunity to work outside the home. Women need a genuine choice, a choice between full-time childcare, or full-time work or a satisfactory combination of both. That is why we need nurseries, playgroups and other means of providing care for our children outside the home for a few hours or a full working day.

It is not impossible for this to be done. During the war, when women workers were essential to the national war effort, the state provided much more extensive childcare facilities than it provides at the present time. In 1944 there were 67,749 places in local authority day nurseries; in 1974 there were just 24,772.

Nevertheless, some women enjoy their role of full-time mother and do not wish to work. But many feel lonely and isolated, stuck at home with their children for most of the time. In our more mobile society many people have moved away from the area where their parents and relatives live; women often have little contact with the rest of the community and no one to rely on for babysitting and mutual support. Playgroups and mother and baby clubs can and do give these women the opportunity to enjoy the company of other women and develop interests outside their home.

So far we have talked mainly about the effect of full-time motherhood on women. But this situation can also be far from ideal for the children. Few families can afford the variety of playthings that a nursery or playgroup can provide, and a woman who is tied down with mundane, repetitive tasks will find it difficult to be a stimulating companion for her children.

And children do benefit from being with other children. They learn from one another and they learn to work and play together and share things co-operatively. They also learn to be less dependent on their mothers. By spending time with adults other than their parents, they come into contact with a wider range of personalities and behaviour and acquire more experience on which to base their own future development. For example, children who are brought up in the conventional way may never see men doing the day-to-day tasks of childcare, so they grow up with the idea that childcare is exclusively women's work. In a society where the importance of what you do is judged by what you earn, children will also get the message that caring for children is a low-status job.

And, of course, these ideas are reinforced by the books that children read and the way boys and girls are differentiated at school.

So women are concerned not only with the provision of childcare for their children outside the home, but with the provision of 'alternative' forms of childcare; these are not only concerned with the problems of women stuck at home, but by involving men and by trying to change what children are taught, they are attempting in the longer term to alter commonly held ideas about childcare and about the roles of men and women in society.

Who pays for Childcare?

It is likely . . . that the problem facing women workers . . . in relation to day care have been increased dramatically in the last decade. We must decide whether such 'non-priority' demand is simply to be ignored because we disapprove of women going out to work; or whether we decide that the purpose of social and educational policy is to alleviate these problems in a positive fashion.

(from *Social and Educational Provision for the Under-Fives in Britain*, Labour Party Under-Fives Working Party)

Anyone who has looked after small children knows that it is work. Of course children can be a great source of pleasure, but often the sheer physical effort involved swamps the enjoyment. Children make a million and one demands and can drain your physical, mental and emotional energy far more than any other job.

Yet *this* job is unpaid, and is made compulsory for many women simply because no alternatives are provided. Many groups are campaigning to get the state to provide more childcare facilities, so that women can choose how much of their energy they devote to their children. And other groups want the state to recognize that childcare is work; that they should be paid for the work of caring for their own children in the same way that other working people are paid; some are concerned to increase the rate of Child Benefit and to see that it is paid direct to the mother, whilst others under the banner of 'Wages for Housework' want a state-paid wage for their role of housewife and mother.

Child Benefits

For many years, a married woman who stays at home to care for children has had no income in her own right except Family Allowances, now known as Child Benefit. Although this is pathetically low (£1 per week for the first child, £1.50 per week for any other children in April 1977) it does give a woman some control over her weekly budget, and can be crucially important if her husband doesn't give her enough housekeeping. When the government tried to take family allowances away from women in 1972 there was so much opposition to the plan by women that the idea had to be dropped.

Families with children tend to be worse off than those without, because although a man is expected to support his children, he is *not* paid more to enable him to do so. Originally, family allowance was meant to cover the cost of caring for a child and so relieve family poverty. But the rates have never kept up with inflation; they rose only once between 1968 and 1977, so the allowances are now way below what it would realistically cost to keep a child, and until 1977 no allowance was paid for the first child. Family allowance was taxed; the families with the lowest incomes who don't pay tax, benefit most from it.

A proposed Child Benefit scheme would provide a tax-free cash allowance for *every* child, to be paid weekly to the mother. It would replace family allowances and cut out the tax allowances for dependent children that are normally paid to the wage-earner in a family. The scheme was due to begin in April 1977, but in 1976 the government decided to drop the plan. One reason for this was that the scheme would mean a redistribution of income from men to women; because child tax allowances would stop, the man's take-home pay would be reduced, although in fact, including the benefit paid to the woman, the family as a whole would be better off. At a time when wage increases were being held back the government was afraid that the trade unions (dominated by men) would not accept this proposal. Instead they proposed to introduce a £1 family allowance for the first child, which would be taxed and worth far less than the proposed child benefit.

At the moment (March 1977) the government has accepted a compromise plan, suggested by a joint Labour Party/TUC working party, to introduce the original scheme in stages: but unless they agree to make more money available, the child benefit will still only be £2.70 in 1980! Hardly enough to feed a child for a week! Although the compromise plan will establish the principle of a tax-free child benefit, it won't mean any extra money for families in 1977, and doesn't guarantee an adequate benefit after that.

Only the pressure of public opinion persuaded the government to accept even the compromise plan, so it is important to keep up that pressure if we want to get realistic benefits. The *Child Benefits Now Campaign* is a loose association of organizations concerned with children and families, such as Gingerbread, the National Council for One Parent Families, and the Child Poverty Action Group. They feel that families with children are suffering most from inflation but receiving least support from the state. Adequate child benefits would provide some independence for women unable to work because they are caring for children, and would help the very poorest families — the 200,000 working families that they estimate are too poor to pay tax. The campaign wants child benefits to be reviewed annually and to be kept up with inflation.

Of course the government will still say they can't afford to put the full scheme into operation, but most of the cost would be met by money saved when family allowance and child tax allowances are withdrawn. The rest of the money needed was originally provided for, but is now being spent on other things. The government's compromise plan is not good enough. Women and their children need benefits high enough to give them some sort of financial security when their husbands can't or won't give them enough money.

The *Child Benefits Now Campaign* is petitioning and generally applying pressure to get the position improved. You can get posters, leaflets, petitions, badges, and find out what you can do to help from the campaign.

CHILD BENEFITS NOW CAMPAIGN *c/o Child Poverty Action Group, 1 Macklin Street, London WC2*

Some other organizations to contact:
GINGERBREAD
2nd Floor, 35 Wellington Street, London WC2
Gingerbread is an organization set up by single parents to press for more realistic financial support for single parents. There is a network of local groups where single parents can offer one another mutual support and advice, and organize locally and nationally for better provision.

WAGES FOR HOUSEWORK CAMPAIGN
20 Staverton Road, London NW2
The campaign is concerned with analysing the position of women as wageless workers in a waged society. This includes all aspects of women's work, and not just child-rearing.

EXISTING PROVISION

The Different forms of Under-Fives Provision

HOME

Eighty per cent of women with dependent children under five stay at home with their children. They don't have much alternative. But some are evolving new family structures or creating self-help networks in the community to make things easier for both parents and children.

CHILDMINDING

A childminder is defined as anyone receiving reward for looking after one child or more under five for more than two hours a day. Officially a childminder must register, but it is estimated that there are more unregistered minders than there are registered. And childminding represents the most used form of full-time daycare today.

DAY NURSERIES

These are provided by local authorities for children between the age of 0 and 5 whose parents must work. A matron or nursery nurse is in charge. There is a small fee. They remain open during working hours and the school holidays. In actual fact, they are available to only very few children. Some workplaces and colleges provide day nurseries, and there are also privately run day nurseries which charge high fees and so are available only to those families that can afford to pay.

NURSERY SCHOOLS

These provide nursery education for children between two and five free of charge. The schools are run by the Local Education Authority and are staffed with at least one nursery teacher. They are open during school hours only, and are closed during school holidays. There are enough places for about 5 per cent of children in the age range. There are also privately run nursery schools, kindergartens and pre-preparatory schools which take young children at a price. Nursery classes, sometimes called rising-fives, are sometimes attached to infant schools. They are much the same as nursery schools, except that the children are at the bottom of a big school rather than in an environment of their own.

PLAYGROUPS

These provide the opportunity for creative play for children aged between 2½ and 5 for two or three mornings a week. Some playgroups also give grounding in reading and writing. Playgroups are mostly formed and run on a voluntary basis by the parents themselves. Their primary concern is the development of children through play rather than through education. Unlike other facilities for the under-fives, parental involvement is encouraged. However, they do not usually meet the needs of parents who wish to (or must) work, although a few are open all day.

MOTHER AND BABY CLUBS AND ONE O'CLOCK CLUBS

Generally these consist of a clubroom where mothers can bring children too young for a playgroup. There is usually someone responsible for watching the children, so they provide an opportunity for mothers to relax their vigilance. But the mother (or guardian) has to come with the baby.

CRECHES

A creche generally refers to a childminding or drop-in centre provided on the premises where a mother is working part time or visiting. We are using the term *creche* to refer to casual provision, though it is sometimes used to refer to all-day provision at the workplace or in a college.

For further information, see:

BUT WHAT ABOUT THE CHILDREN? A Working Parent's Guide to Childcare
by Judith Hann, Bodley Head, £4.95
This discusses the advantages and disadvantages of childminders, nurseries, the extended family, playgroups and other forms of childcare. It acknowledges that women often want, as well as need, to work; so it's fairly unmoralizing.

WHERE?
from the Advisory Centre for Education, 32 Trumpington Street, Cambridge
This monthly magazine often contains articles and information on under-fives provision. ACE also publishes *The Best of Where on Pre-Schooling* at £1.50.

EDUCATION AND PLAY
by Barbara Dinham and Michael Norton, Wildwood House, £4.50
Volume One of the Directory of Social Change which contains an extensive first section entitled 'One to Five'.

Childminders

Childminders are people (almost exclusively women) who are paid for looking after other people's children in their own home for more than two hours a day. Nobody knows how many childminders there are in Britain; although by law they should register with the local authority, many don't bother because they wouldn't gain anything from it. However, a recent report (*Childminding in London* available from the London Council of Social Service, 68 Chalton Street, London NW1, £2) found that registered childminders provide more than half the official full-time daycare places for children under five in London, and estimates that illegal, unregistered minders provide possibly twice as many places as registered minders. If these figures are similar all over the country (and other studies suggest that they are) this means that childminding is by far the largest sector of the market in full-time daycare for the under-fives.

Yet until recently there was very little official concern for providing facilities or decent pay for the women who carry out this work. Most childminders charge between £4 and £7 for looking after a child for between forty and fifty hours a week, and usually less for a second child from the same family. Out of this they have to provide the children's meals and toys, bus fares if they take them out, wear and tear on their homes, and extra heating and lighting.

The London Childminders Branch of NUPE (National Union of Public Employees) has calculated that a minder's 'residual earnings' after taking these expenses into account amounts to approximately 3p per hour per child. If she registers with the local authority she will also have to provide safety equipment like safe heaters, fire-guards and stair-gates, and will often be limited to looking after three under-fives including her own. A few local authorities help minders with equipment, toys and books, and in Lambeth there is one experimental scheme where minders are employed by the local authority. But the majority of minders get no help or support at all.

Recently childminders have begun to organize together to improve their conditions. In 1971 the Child Minders Action Movement was formed in the London Borough of Sutton, and since then more and more minders have been joining NUPE, who have produced a Childminder's Charter of demands. Its main points are:

1. Employment of childminders by local councils throughout Britain, with a standard rate of pay set by national negotiations.
2. Substantial improvements in pay and better conditions of service for all childminders.
3. Training for childminders in all aspects of childcare: first aid, behaviour problems, emotional developments, etc.
4. Greatly improved communications between local councils and the childminder, to include a central register of information concerning parents (e.g. home and work phone numbers) and problems affecting particular children.
5. Proper guidance to be given to both parents and childminders on their respective responsibilities.
6. NUPE's working party at national level to examine the educational and legal setting in which childminders work.

A NUPE official says:

'We have concentrated our attention over the past three years in attempting to change the policy on under-fives at national level as we believe that only through this medium will it be possible to organize groups like childminders, who are at present not employed by anyone.

'We have a small membership base amongst childminders in London and West Yorkshire and we intend to maintain this base as far as is possible in order to ensure that our knowledge of the childminding scene is continued.

'We believe that there will be substantial advantage for childminders in joining our union when they become employees of the local authorities. It is quite clear that the issue of childminders has been made a major national issue in the social policy area by virtue of the Trade Union Movement's involvement; without our participation and our efforts to ensure that a comprehensive under-fives policy is developed, both the Labour Party and the TUC would not have developed their policies on the under-fives, and would not have discussed childminders with the same priority.

'The advantages for childminders in supporting the Childminder's Charter that we have outlined is that it will involve a substantial increase in their rates of pay, which I believe will be welcomed by the community at large if it means an improved standard of service; and it would bring minders fully into discussions about the development of under-fives policy with each local authority through the union structure. I cannot over emphasize the importance of this last point as all too often minders are treated as second-class citizens by some of the professional social workers (particularly the more senior social workers in each locality). Only through collective strength will minders be taken seriously by the planners and social workers, and I contend that this will be a major advantage for minders after unionization.'

NATIONAL UNION OF PUBLIC EMPLOYEES *Civic House, Aberdeen Terrace, London SE3,*
or get the address of your local branch from the phone book or library

The following contacts may also be useful:

NATIONAL CHILDMINDING ASSOCIATION
c/o Joan Jay, 137 Little Breach, Chichester, Sussex
A recently formed childminders' group, it publishes a newsletter entitled *Who Minds?* and is looking at the law relating to childminding and the terms and conditions under which childminders work.

NATIONAL EDUCATIONAL RESEARCH AND DEVELOPMENT TRUST
Longroyd Bridge, Huddersfield, West Yorkshire
They have been active in promoting the interests of minders and have a Childminders Research and Development Unit.

COMMISSION FOR RACIAL EQUALITY
Elliott House, 10–12 Allington Street, London SW1
They have information on the importance of childminding to black and immigrant communities. They have published *WHO MINDS?*, a study of working mothers and childminding in ethnic minority communities, 1975.

BRITISH BROADCASTING CORPORATION
Broadcasting House, London W1
In 1977 the BBC broadcast a series of twenty TV programmes designed for childminders. A book for childminders was published to coincide with this series: *Other People's Children: A Handbook for Childminders*, £1.

LOCAL AUTHORITY REGISTERS
Registered childminders can always be contacted directly, and addresses can be obtained from the local authority register.

See also:
MINDER, MOTHER AND CHILD
by Berry Mayall and Pat Petries, University of London Institute of Education, £2.25
This is a detailed study of the quality of care provided by childminders, showing that even with registered childminders, children often experience cramped or crowded conditions and too few facilities for play. It recommends that childminders be employed by local authorities.

PAYMENT FOR CHILDMINDERS

Growing evidence of the numbers of children being cared for by minders, and greater militancy from the minders themselves, is forcing local and central government to recognize that a problem exists. There are beginning to be moves to give more help to childminders. (A recent Labour Party Under-Fives Working Party report suggested new legislation obliging local authorities to employ childminders, provide them with services and equipment, and train them.) However, this is not entirely out of the goodness of their hearts; with Social Services expenditure drastically cut, subsidies to childminders, or even employing childminders, is a cheap alternative to providing proper nursery facilities for all those who need them. The Community Relations Commission (now called the Commission for Racial Equality) has calculated the cost per child per year at £350, paying childminders £6 per week and providing supportive services run by social workers. This compares with an estimated cost of £500 per year for a day-nursery place, excluding building costs of the nurseries. Of course childminders should be properly paid, but this should not be used as an excuse to cut down on nursery provision for those who need or prefer this kind of daycare.

One of the most interesting things about the current debate on childminders is that it shows up very clearly the contradictions in official thinking about payment for childcare. The woman who stays at home and cares for three children of her own is doing exactly the same amount of work as the woman who cares for one child of her own and two of somebody else's. The Labour Party report and many other organizations are suggesting that the second woman should be paid and provided with toys, equipment, support and so on, while the first woman struggles on unpaid and unsupported. The logical conclusion must surely be that *all* childcare should be paid for, whoever does it and wherever it is done.

Nurseries

Women who demand more nursery provision are often accused of being selfish and wanting to 'dump' their kids; they are even threatened with the idea of their children growing up to be hopeless neurotics if they leave them to go out to work.   Not everybody yet accepts that women have as much right as men to a life outside the home; but even leaving this aside, in an economic climate where many women are forced to do paid work, to deny them nursery provision on the grounds that they ought to be at home is pure hypocrisy.   Failing to provide proper nurseries does *not* stop women from going out to work, it simply means that we have to make unsatisfactory childcare arrangements which certainly does not benefit our children.

A good nursery can be a positive influence for a child, whether her mother goes out to work or not.   If you live half-way up a tower block with nowhere for your child to play or meet other children, then a nursery is obviously a much-needed facility.   But even if your material conditions are fine, for a child to spend the first five years of its life tied to just *one* human being can't be very good, especially if that adult isn't totally happy about the situation.   The experience of being cared for in a stable, secure way by other adults can be very important in making children feel more secure about their own identity, and experiencing the world as an affectionate and warm place.

It is not simply a question of women's rights being in conflict with children's rights; after all, it is ludicrous to imagine that something which has a bad effect on an adult can possibly be good for the child that's with them.   Yet state nursery provision is still based on the assumption that a woman's duty, like it or not, lies in the home.

THE HACKNEY NURSERY CAMPAIGN

The situation in Hackney is not unusual.   Hackney Borough Council has a waiting list for day-nursery places of over 900 children.   This probably represents only a fraction of those who want and need daycare provision: according to the 1971 census there were 3,556 under-fives in the borough whose mothers were working (this includes only married women), and there were 2,479 under-fives in single-parent families — (recognized as a priority group for day-nursery places).   But since many people see no hope of getting a nursery place through the council list, their names are never put on.   At present there are 471 day-nursery places in the borough, and the council plans to expand this to 809 by 1983, which is surely nowhere near enough to meet the needs of mothers and children.

The Hackney Nursery Campaign developed from the women's sub-comittee of the Hackney Trades Council, but it decided to campaign independently when working through the Trades Council became too frustrating.   They are campaigning to get the council to provide more nursery places:

'There isn't enough of any kind of under-fives provision, but the worst shortage is in full-daycare.   We'd like to see day nurseries for all mothers who want them, and part-time care for others.   We estimate that perhaps two-thirds of the under-fives in Hackney want full daycare, but at the moment provision is based on the assumption that only a very small proportion will want it.   We reckon that thousands of children here are being cared for by childminders or by parents working shifts.   It's impossible to say what the true demand for nursery places is; at present women don't go out to work because they can't get nursery places, but with more provision women could work out the best solutions for themselves.   Now they mostly have no choice.   It's certainly a common practice in this area for people to end up doing home-work or shift work as a solution, which of course is very bad for the parent and the children.

'One of the first things we organized was a Mother's Day march, to draw attention to the fact that there were people campaigning for day-nursery provision.   This was held on a Saturday and the route went through the main shopping centre.   The march was quite well supported; we started with about a hundred people and ended up with a lot more.   We got a lot of abuse down in the south of the borough where the fascists are very strong, but on the whole the march made a good impression.

'We discovered an empty property, Clifton Lodge, that used to be a day nursery just

after the war; there were thirteen nurseries in Hackney then. This place was leased by the council and had been empty for about three years. So we launched a campaign for the council to reopen it as a nursery. We held public meetings, put up posters, spray-painted the outside of the building; it certainly brought attention to the issue, and made the campaign more and better known, with articles in the local papers and so on. We even all agreed that we should use occupations and sit-ins as a means of getting things done, but one part of the group thought we should occupy straight away for the publicity, while the rest of the group felt we should widen our base first and obtain a lot more support before we went into anything like that.

'What happened in the end was that the council ditched their lease on Clifton Lodge after telling us that it would cost too much to repair. They gave us an inflated figure for the repair cost of about £100,000, which was just ridiculous, and they continually said it was totally out of the question to provide any more daycare. Hackney Trades Council are going to buy Clifton Lodge now, so we're pressing them to provide a permanent creche there.

'The most recent thing we've done is that we have managed to get our views to the Policy Committee of Hackney Borough Council, which is basically a group of top councillors sitting round deciding what policy they're going to put forward. They said they were very impressed by our evidence, and referred the matter to the Social Services Committee. But their whole line is "Where are we going to get the money from?"

'At the moment we're also supporting NUPE at Moorfield's and St Matthew's Hospitals. There's a nursery closing there soon, and we're hoping they'll work out some sort of occupation to keep it open, and to extend the nursery to all hospital workers, because at the moment it's for the children of doctors and nurses only.

'We've always said we are a campaigning group, and not a self-help group, so we wouldn't consider setting up a nursery ourselves, even with council money. We believe that the council should provide nurseries, and that nursery provision shouldn't be left up to self-help groups. We do have qualms about the kind of care that local authority nurseries tend to provide, but the quality of care is really another issue . . . you've got to have the nurseries first.

'One of the demands of the campaign is pay parity for all nursery workers; that is, pay parity with nursery teachers, who are paid higher rates than nursery nurses, and parity of education, which would mean a whole new study programme. At the moment the NNEB course (the training course for nursery nurses) doesn't go very deeply into educational standards, it's mainly concerned with health and hygiene, whilst nursery teachers courses are purely educational. What we want is a welding of the two, to improve the quality of childcare; at the moment if you try to organize some kind of integrated daycare, with both nursery nurses and nursery teachers, you run into problems, because you're paying people different rates to do what is basically the same work. There are also problems about hours, because teachers work shorter hours and have longer holidays than nursery nurses. We don't want nurseries that close during the school holidays or that open for morning and afternoon sessions like nursery schools, because these are useless for women at work. What is needed is a unified training system and unified salary scales, to combine the best aspects of nursery schools and day nurseries.

'It's also important to have enough nursery places and to have proper community nurseries, so that each child can go to a nursery just around the corner in company with other children who live nearby, in order to get continuity between home and nursery. That's an additional argument against workplace nurseries, over and above the way they can be used to exploit women. Although we insist that all funds for nurseries should come from local authorities, we emphasize parent and worker control in nurseries. We've had a few arguments about that; there are some teachers in our group who don't agree with parent control because parents have been known to do things like insisting that all the kids have Chopper bikes instead of educational toys, of objecting to the kids getting *dirty. But parents should be involved in how the hours are arranged, what facilities are provided, and the general conditions of the nursery.*

'A frustrating thing during the Clifton Lodge episode was leafleting a local estate to try to get people along to a meeting. We got a tremendous amount of sympathy, practically everyone we spoke to said: "Yes, more nurseries, that's a fantastic idea", but we didn't get any response in terms of people actually coming to the meeting! We talk a lot about how to get more ordinary people involved in the campaign, but one of the problems of this kind of campaign is that women with small children are not in the best position to get out to meetings and help with our work, especially if they go out to work as well. And sometimes their husbands don't like them going to meetings. So the people most affected by the problem are often just not able to do anything.

'The other thing is that mothers of under-fives are a transient group: by the time women realize that there are other people they could get together with, that they can organize, by the time they've become most aware and confident, their children aren't under-fives any more. Because it's a continuously moving group we don't think it's realistic to base a campaign wholly on those women, though some people think we should. We firmly believe that the condition of children should be everybody's responsibility, not that everyone should be able to interfere just when they want, but that it's everybody's responsibility to make sure that the people bringing up children have the best conditions to do this in.

'For quite a while now we've been pushed into a defensive role of trying to stop existing nurseries from being cut, rather than campaigning for more nurseries. Playgroups and day nurseries have had the axe waved over them for the past eighteen months; but the fact that we and similar campaigns exist in this area (even though we haven't got enough active members to keep up a continual barrage of pressure) does mean that the council feels less able to make drastic cuts. They have at least to pretend to take some notice of local groups.

'The effect of the economic situation, rather unfortunately, is that we're too late. If we had the economic climate of five years ago, they would probably be willing to expand their day-nursery provision. You can really see the effect of attitudes about childcare operating at local level. There are people on the council who would have tried to get services provided, at a time when finance was a bit easier, if they had recognized the need for it. But because the idea that women shouldn't go out to work, but should stay at home and look after their children, had permeated the Labour Party and the council, they didn't do anything at that time. And now we're in a really weak position.'

HACKNEY NURSERY CAMPAIGN *c/o Hackney Under-Fives, Centerprise Bookshop, 138 Kingsland High Street, London E8*

For nursery campaigns in your areas, contact your local women's centre, or WIRES. If a community newspaper is produced in your area, this may also be a useful source of information.

Playgroups

Not all women want or need full-time care for their children; but they would like to have a break from them sometimes, and they want their child to have the benefits of being with other children. For them, playgroups can be a solution. They provide facilities for children from 2 to 5 years old to play together under supervision. But, unlike nurseries, playgroups are usually open only for a few mornings or afternoons a week.

Whilst there are playgroups that are run fully professionally, using trained staff on a five-day-a-week basis, these fall into two types: they are either established with local authority support in areas of particular need, or they have to charge quite high fees to cover their costs, and thus can only exist in better-off neighbourhoods. But most playgroups are run on an extremely low budget using a great deal of voluntary help. They may employ a supervisor, and there are now quite a lot of adult education centres that provide short courses in the basic skills for this, and besides the relatively low supervisor's fee, there are other costs such as the hire of the hall, heat and light, play equipment, consumables such as paint, paper and other materials, and insurance. These costs are usually met by a small attendance fee and small grants from the local authority (either to start up or towards running costs as well) and small-scale local fund-raising.

Playgroups now represent probably the largest single element in under-fives provision, and the Pre-School Playgroups Association (PPA) calculates that its playgroups serve upwards of 400,000 children. The Association now has a team of national advisers and training officers as well as its own voluntary network of local branches and regional associations. It also works closely with county and borough Social Services Departments, many of which now have play-group officers and are active in promoting and providing some support for playgroups.

The PPA stresses parent participation in the management and running of playgroups, although not all of its member playgroups subscribe to this. It also has a concern for developing playgroups in areas of special need and for the handicapped. It has recently branched out into 'mother and baby clubs' for very young children. And it is concerned very much with parent education and development, through its courses run in conjunction with the Open University through encouraging mothers to become active in the playgroup movement, and through its magazine *Under-5*. It also has an extensive publications list covering children's play and running playgroups.

Although the growth of the playgroup movement has widened the range of care available to mothers, and has been enormously beneficial to them and their children, it has to some extent let the state off the hook financially, and reinforced the idea that looking after children isn't work, and doesn't need to be paid. While the number of playgroup places has risen, nursery places have fallen; it's far easier to give a hundred pounds or so to a playgroup for equipment than to provide and run a nursery with paid staff. And so the very real need for much greater full-day nursery provision is just not being catered for as it is more expensive in comparison with 'cheap' playgroups.

In many areas where there is little provision for the under-fives, there is enough demand for playgroup places to keep them open five days a week, morning and afternoon. Mothers who work outside the home are often forced to use playgroups because there is nothing else available and if they are working they will have to make complex childcare arrangements which involve neighbours, grandparents or childminders collecting the kids and looking after them until the parents get home. These women are not in a position to work on a rota at the playgroup. And although the opportunity for mothers to come and play with their children, and be involved in the playgroup, is very desirable, many women don't *want* to spend time with thirty noisy children; they want a break from childcare and they feel they have a *right* to it.

The present self-help, unpaid emphasis of playgroups is not necessarily ideal for the children either. For 'disadvantaged' children (for those whose first language isn't English, or who don't have enough playspace at home, for instance) a playgroup can be a chance to catch up before they start school. But to do this successfully they need a stable group of workers prepared to put a lot of effort into the playgroup, and few people can afford to make this sort of full-time commitment of energy without being paid for it.

Getting money to pay playgroup staff is far from easy. The areas where there is the greatest need for playgroups are also those areas where family money is short; fees have to be kept as low as possible so as not to keep away the children and parents who would benefit most. Certainly fees that covered wages for workers would exclude a great many children. Unfortunately local authorities are unlikely to question the idea that playgroups should be run voluntarily, when it is obviously to their advantage.

Your local *Social Services Department* can give grants to playgroups, but is unlikely to give you enough to pay workers. They usually have someone in charge of dealing with playgroups, as you have to be registered with them; this person may be able to suggest local sources of money.

The *Pre-School Playgroups Association* sometimes gives small sums of money, but again this won't provide wages. However, it does produce some useful pamphlets on fund-raising for the playgroup.

You can apply for *Urban Aid* for money to pay staff or provide equipment. There is the main Urban Programme and also a separate programme for holiday play-schemes both of which come out annually. Applications have to be sent in at particular times of the year, and you have to provide exact details of what money you want, what for, and why you think you deserve it. The Social Services Department may give you a hand with filling in the form; it looks difficult but in fact most of it is quite straightforward. However, Urban Aid is getting more and more difficult to obtain; 75 per cent of the grant comes from the Home Office, but the other 25 per cent has to be paid by the local authority. Now that they're all cutting down spending, local authorities aren't so keen to put forward Urban Aid applications because they don't want to pay their 25 per cent.

A few playgroups have managed to get their workers paid for a limited period under the *Job Creation Programme*. In its present form this ended in March 1978, but it has been replaced by a similar scheme which has a greater emphasis on training. The programme is intended to provide jobs for unemployed people, especially school leavers. Contact your local office of the Manpower (what about Womanpower?) Services Commission for details of how to apply.

(For tips on completing the Urban Aid application form you could contact a playgroup which has done this successfully. Contact Chapeltown Community Playgroup, Chapeltown Community Centre, Reginal Terrace, Leeds 7.)

PRE-SCHOOL PLAYGROUPS ASSOCIATION *Alford House, Aveline Street, London SE1*

Besides PPA's own publications, the following are useful practical handbooks:

THE PLAYGROUP BOOK
by Marie Winn and Mary Ann Porcher, Fontana, 70p
How to organize a playgroup, and suggestions for activities. It's helpful to have around . . . if you are involved in a playgroup, you need as many new ideas for activities as you can get. But, it's a good example of 'hidden values'. Children are referred to as 'he' throughout; the authors assume that playgroup workers will be unpaid and always women, that boys and girls have different toys, that all children live in nuclear families. For example, they suggest using books about what people do: policemen, firemen, postmen, shopkeepers, etc. Don't women do anything worth mentioning?

THE PENGUIN BOOK OF PLAYGROUPS
by J. Lucas and V. McKennell, Penguin, 50p
Another book of practical advice on organization, financing, staffing and running a playgroup. It suffers from many of the same assumptions as *The Playgroup Book.*

INCREASING PROVISION FOR UNDER-FIVES

Although there are many conflicting views as to the way under-fives provision should develop in the future, there is little disagreement with the fact that there is not enough of it. In this section, we look at three groups campaigning for more provision of all forms, nationally, city-wide and locally, and at a fourth group that is campaigning for provision after school has finished for women with school-age children.

A National Campaign

The *National Campaign for Nursery Education* began in 1965, to press for a rapid increase in the provision of educational and play facilities for children under five, with special (though not exclusive) emphasis on nursery schools and classes. Such provision should be planned nationally by the Department of Education and Science and locally by the Education Authorities, in consultation at both levels with the authorities responsibile for Health and Social Security and with concerned voluntary organizations.

Their suggestions for what people can do in their own areas are:

— Find out what is happening in your local authority.
— Contact your local councillors and education officers, and organizers or advisers for nursery education.
— Find out what local support you can get by contacting nursery schools, playgroups, health visitors, teachers' organizations, trade union branches, women's organizations, etc.
— Talk about nursery education with them. Invite representatives and parents to informal meetings to discuss the possibilities of planning a survey of local provision and demand, or of holding an open meeting with representatives of your local authority.
— Keep your local press and radio informed of your activities.
— Contact the National Campaign for Nursery Education for advice and information, and let us know what is happening in your area.
— And make sure your local authority knows that you are there!

NATIONAL CAMPAIGN FOR NURSERY EDUCATION *67 Woodland Gardens, London N10*

A City-Wide Campaign

The *London Nursery Campaign* is intended to operate as an information point and support group for all the nursery campaigns operating in London in each borough. Pressure on local authorities comes from local groups, whilst the London Nursery Campaign acts at national level. The campaign believes that priority must be given to the question of under-fives within the four major unions involved, around the following principles:

1. Every child has the right to a full-time daycare place.
2. Under-fives provision must take into account the needs of working parents.
3. All under-fives provision should be financed by central government.
4. All under-fives provision should be under one government department.
5. Unionization of all under-fives workers under one trade union.
6. All under-fives workers to be employed under the same conditions and pay scales by the local authority.
7. Equal training facilities for all under-fives workers.

They feel that the Equal Pay Act and Sex Discrimination Act become meaningless without the enabling facilities of adequate daycare provision for children under five, and point out that nationally there are only five day-nursery places for every 1,000 children under five.

LONDON NURSERY CAMPAIGN *26 Lovelace Road, London E8*

A Local Campaign

(*A Look at Hackney Under-Fives*, by Liz Chambers,
who was part of the group from its beginning)

'*An under-fives association works to improve all kinds of provision for under-fives in a borough, in any way it can — largely by providing support to projects, an information network and a platform for action. The key factors in the development of Hackney Under-Fives Association (HUF) have been: firstly, the fact that there has been one person working* full-time *on building up contacts with individuals and groups, both statutory and voluntary, all over the borough for most of its life span; and secondly, this fact has enabled HUF to develop a* proper *information service for everyone needing it, since without proper information there is no basis for real action.*

'*HUF came into being in early 1973 at a public meeting on the Nursery Expansion plans for the borough. The idea of an action group on under-fives was born at that meeting. It was a fair time before the group actually* did *anything, other than sound out various patches of ground with Hackney Council and the ILEA and write innumerable letters to all kinds of people on all kinds of scores. Looking back over the minutes and copies of letters of this first eighteen months, one realizes the opportunities lost due to lack of real information about, and therefore understanding of, the situation. A sense of self-belief is essential in the early days of any organization. You have to look as though you know what's going on until the time that you* actually *do.*

'*The second secretary of the Association took on the job full-time after HUF had been in existence for eight months. After six months of intensive care, the phone calls and the ideas started flowing in. More effort and bureaucratic efficiency was needed to ensure that everyone knew what was happening. Certainly, the general level of awareness about the under-fives in the borough began to creep up. HUF have always believed in a lot of publicity and fortunately had a sympathetic reporter on the local paper who came to meetings and generally kept up a fair level of interest. This was instrumental in reaching people who were not reached by personal contact.*

'*Since then, the influence of HUF is evident in certain things; the increasing sympathy that the officers and some members of the council have shown towards the needs of under-fives and their families; the growth of community groups with special interests in the under-fives; for example, groups for handicapped children and their families and for children in hospital; toy libraries for all under-fives; childminders support and action groups; mothers and small children groups (twenty new groups have been formed since 1974); shared care groups all round the borough; a Nursery Campaign (specifically for the development of daycare in conjunction with the Working Women's Charter Campaign); and a Health Visitors support group. Many more people are now aware of and doing more things for under-fives in Hackney.*

Lessons Learned

1. Facts, not feet, first. Don't expect anyone to listen to you if you're badly informed.
2. Don't take the initiative away from other groups; you can support them, but not negotiate for them.
3. Realize that still an awful lot of people (some of them the ones you would most like to reach) don't know what's available for them and their kids, or what their rights are, or what they could fight for if only they knew.
4. Understand the need to involve council members as well as the officers in the workings of the association.
5. Realize that getting any credibility at all, either with local people or with the council, is a delicate, hard and long-term task.'

HACKNEY UNDER-FIVES *Centerprise, 136 Kingsland High Street, London E8*

Latch-key kids

Provision for the under-fives may be hard to find, but for the over-fives it is almost non-existent. Once your children go to school you may have more freedom to go out to work, but you still have to fit your working hours into school hours, and make arrangements for your children to be cared for in the school holidays. This can cost £9 per child per week.

For one-parent families this often means remaining stuck on supplementary benefit after your children have gone to school. A part-time job during school hours is unlikely to bring in as much money as social security, and there is still the problem of school holidays. Paying for your child to be cared for outside school hours, while you return to full-time work, could cut such a hole in your earnings that, once again, you'd be better off on supplementary benefit. The only alternative is to leave your kids to fend for themselves or each other until you get home from work; the so-called latch-key kids.

The Croydon branch of Gingerbread, the association for one-parent families, set out to solve this problem with their 'latch-key' project. The aim of the project is to enable lone parents to continue full-time employment, or to return to work and so get out of the supplementary benefit trap.

They began by doing a survey into the need for such a project, contacting infant and junior schools in the area to establish statistics. The cost of the project was thoroughly worked out and submitted for an Urban Aid grant, but the application was unsuccessful. Then the EEC Committee to Combat Poverty in Europe took up the project and, much to the group's surprise, agreed to give them £12,000 a year for two years; beyond that their financial future is uncertain.

Having got the grant, the next step was to find a suitable house. Three members of the group met the Borough Surveyor, and the council found them a house comparatively quickly. It had been completely stripped of its plumbing by vandals, all the fittings were wrecked, and the windows were blocked up with corrugated iron. But it was large, it was two minutes from East Croydon station, it was approached by subways under the main roads, and it was accessible from all bus routes. Gingerbread pay nearly £2,000 a year rent and rates on the house.

The council said they hadn't the money to repair it, so Gingerbread members set about restoring it themselves. They turned out to have a wide range of skills; urgent phone calls produced a glazier, painter, bricklayer, lawyer, carpenter . . . On 6 January 1976 they got the keys and for several months the house was full of volunteers working non-stop, in the first instance to get the ground floor ready in time for the Easter holidays. Forty 5 to 11 year olds turned up; there was little need to advertise as the news had spread and there was great demand. Gingerbread Corner was under way! With continuing non-stop voluntary work, the house, which is on five floors, was completed by the summer holidays.

A year later, forty-five children come to the house every day after school; nearly all are collected from their schools by the centre's mini-bus or their car system. There is a resident playleader, two paid staff and a volunteer to provide the children with interesting activities. One hundred and ten children are registered for the holidays, with about sixty on the waiting list. During the holidays there are two playleaders; each works five hours a day with four paid helpers each, so that the centre can be open from 8.15am to 6.15pm. School and college students have worked there voluntarily during the summer, helping with outings and with swimming. The playleaders try to make the holiday programme as varied and flexible as possible. All the children are from one-parent families, but need not necessarily be Gingerbread members.

In the evenings and at weekends the house functions as a social centre for all Gingerbread members. Social events are planned by the Group Social Committee and are listed in the group's newsletter. Teenagers have organized a regular club night, and on family nights or afternoons there is plenty of entertainment for all ages.

Gingerbread Corner has been a success because the group has worked hard over many months to make it so. They hope that the success of their project will mean that more grants are made available in the future to fill the desperate need for after-school and holiday care for 5 to 11 year olds, although there is no further funding available from the EEC at the moment.

Economically, it would make sense and save the state money if they provided facilities like Gingerbread Corner and enabled single parents to go out to work. The group estimates that the supplementary benefit which would be paid to six one-parent families, each with two children, in one year, would more than cover their year's playschool expenditure. In fact the playschool allows about fifty families to return to work and stop claiming supplementary benefits, and is thus saving the state around ten times what it costs to run the centre. You'd think even the government would recognize a sound investment when they saw one!

GINGERBREAD CORNER *21 Fairfield Road, Croydon CR0 5LJ*

GINGERBREAD *2nd Floor, 35 Wellington Street, London WC2*

STUCK AT HOME

For most families, a woman has no choice but to stay at home and mind our children full-time (barring perhaps a few hours when her children are at playgroup), whilst her partner goes out to work.

Some families have organized babysitting clubs or co-operatives. Anything from two or three families with young children up to thirty can be involved. The idea is to share baby-sitting between parents with payment in time rather than in money. Each group decides its own rules: e.g. how many tokens or points each family will start with, how many hours of babysitting each token is worth, and whether that value is increased after midnight or during mealtimes. Some of these clubs also offer the opportunity for women to get together to talk about their problems. A description of the Working Association of Mothers shows how such a project can develop and grow.

Working Association of Mothers

The problems of coping with children are not confined to working-class areas, and can't always be solved simply by having more money: it's no use being able to pay for your child to go to nursery if the nurseries don't exist! In particular, the isolation experienced by women who stay at home with small children extends across class barriers, from smart suburbs to inner-city slums. One group which arose directly out of women's need to get out of the house is the Working Association for Mothers in Brighton; WAM is a self-help organization run by mothers to help each other overcome the day-to-day problems of bringing up children, and to provide support and friendship on a practical basis:

'We concentrated mainly on babysitting and childminding to start off with, and one or two holiday activities where a few women took everybody's children to a circus on the front, that sort of thing. Everybody was very scattered then, we were travelling miles to babysit for each other, but we were really keen, fantastically keen, because we all had this need — what had prompted us was that we wanted to get out at certain times, or for an evening, and this seemed to be the answer, so we were prepared to work damn hard for it! We sat up till all hours getting enrolment forms done and so on; we worked with that sort of enthusiasm.

'The name's confusing: we're not just for working mothers, and men can join in their own right. To join you have to have a child under school-leaving age. You pay 75p and get ten one-hour tokens; these can be used like money: if someone babysits for you for three hours you give them three tokens, if you go to a coffee morning you pay tokens. And to get any tokens back you've obviously got to do something for somebody else. It doesn't have to be the same person who babysat for you, it can be anybody in WAM. You can earn tokens in all sorts of ways: you can dig gardens, do someone's shopping, take their children to school. Some people even do hairdressing or dressmaking for tokens. The 75p pays for six months membership, and covers the cost of the newsletter and administration. The newsletter comes out once a month and lists dates of coffee mornings and any other activities.

'Each area of Brighton has a contact who organizes things there, and it's up to them what they do. Most have coffee mornings and evenings, some have speakers, parties and so on. Different areas develop different identities. We insure all our members for accidents when they're babysitting or doing other WAM activities, which costs a lot, and now that we cover such a wide area, running costs are high. Any money you spend on WAM business is paid back to you, plus tokens for the time you spent doing it, so you can earn your tokens by doing administrative work for WAM.

'The majority of WAM mothers have pre-school kids; they're attracted by the baby-sitting and their common experience, especially if they've just had their first child. Lots of women join when their babies are about six months old; when you first have a baby it's all new and exciting, but after six months the novelty begins to wear off! You begin to miss the friends you had at work and feel the need to talk about things not connected solely with nappies, and bottle versus breastfeeding (although all these things are important to WAM members). People seem to work through WAM, taking from it what they need at the time. You join when your child is very small and you're interested in the coffee morning, babysitting circuit, then when your child gets to school you're interested in the holiday activities.

'Last year we ran a playscheme for 5 to 11 year olds. It ran for five weeks, with two paid playleaders and about six WAM helpers every day; we organized lots of indoor activities, games and outings, and it went extremely well. It was financed through a grant from the council and the money that WAM had built up, and the children paid 25p

a day, which included the outings. We hope to be able to open it more widely to work-ing mothers this year, and now we know it works we'll try to encourage other people to do similar things in other parts of the town. There's ample need for it. The difficulty is getting hold of schools: we wrote to thirty-six, and only the one would have us for the full five weeks. But the more successful the playscheme is, the more pressure there'll be on the schools to let us use their premises.

'Last year we were approached by Social Services about a woman who'd had a nervous breakdown and just couldn't cope with her ten-year-old child during the summer holi-days. They had plenty of money; that wasn't the problem. They could pay for the child to go somewhere. There just wasn't anywhere for him to go. Our playscheme helped there, and we believe there are many other people in Brighton (and all over the country) in a similar position.

'We've also managed to press the local authorities into running creches for daytime classes at adult education colleges here. WAM started them and proved that it worked, and now the local authorities have taken them over, and creches are opening in nearly all the colleges in this area.

'Although WAM is going so well, it doesn't seem so popular on council estates. This is possibly because most of the women there are native to Brighton and have family and friends around. Probably the women who need WAM most are mothers new to Brighton. They don't have the support of friends, neighbours, family, and need to make new contacts. But there are, of course, many native Brightonians in the group.

'For the last couple of years we've had a grant from the local authority towards our running expenses. We have always had support from the Social Services and from the Further Education Department (formerly the Youth and Community Service) and most of us feel we could do more to help them in return. Our playscheme is a good example of WAM helping the community in return for financial assistance. Social Services think WAM is a good organization because we promote self-help, and encourage mums with difficulties to help themselves as well as providing friendship and practical help. It's difficult to imagine the volume of letters and phone calls we get from people who are really desperate for help, and it's not just a question of money. Mostly it's a question of loneliness and lack of facilities. Some of our members feel it's not WAM's job to act as a branch of the Social Services and that our self-help status means that only people capable of returning services, babysitting, etc. should be allowed to join, but these are only a small minority. The majority of WAM members also work for other organizations such as PTAs, local playgroups, NSPCC, Adult Literacy, and have a strong appreciation of the difficulties of life in 1977.

'Many of our members have been trained for a career and have worked for some time before marriage and children. Many feel they would like to get back to some kind of full or part-time work as soon as the children are old enough. WAM helps to give the motivation — it gets you out of the house for a few hours, if only to a coffee morning, it encourages you to go to further education classes, introduces you, and your children, to new people. If you'd been stuck at home on your own with children for three years without having any way of meeting people, you wouldn't have much energy or initiative, or confidence to go back to work. You feel by-passed sitting at home looking at nappies. Being involved in WAM gives you something else to think about. You have your own lives and your own interests and your own friends in your own right, and are not just the wives of your husbands' friends. You're a person.

'However, we do have a large number of members who are perfectly happy to stay at home and look after their children and have no great desire to get back to work. WAM helps them in exactly the same way — it brings them into contact with other mothers at home, helps them to keep in touch with activities in the town, encourages them to organize activities for themselves and their children, and so on.'

WORKING ASSOCIATION OF MOTHERS *c/o Lynda Kinsella, 37 Millcroft, Westdene, Brighton*

Creches

'Creche' is the general term used for childcare facilities provided on the premises, where parents are working or visiting, though not many exist for male workers. Generally it refers to provision for children of women attending courses, conferences, meetings and casual provision at shopping centres or special events, and the term is used here in this sense.

A permanent creche is usually registered with the Social Services Department under the Nurseries and Childminders Regulation Act 1948, as amended by Section 60 of the Health Services and Public Health Act. It need not be registered if it runs for a maximum of two consecutive hours and without charging; and there is also no need to employ qualified staff in this case. A nursery nurse is generally in charge, although some creches operate with volunteers. Creches in schools need not be registered.

It is essential to provide creche facilities at any major event, otherwise many women are effectively excluded. The women's movement has had considerable influence, and it is now much more common to find creches provided. In 1975, the Association of Scientific Technical and Managerial Staff took the lead in becoming the first major national union conference to offer a creche.

Anyone can operate a temporary creche, or you can employ a childminder or nursery nurse. Advertise in the local newspaper or through *Nursery World*, available at newsagents, or ring a nursing agency or even a babysitting agency.

RUNNING A CRECHE

1. Try to tell people something about the creche in the advance information so that they can make a decision on whether to come to the event or not or whether to make other arrangements, etc. Many people have had bad experiences with poorly organized, ill-equipped creches and don't want to trust their children to a creche, unless they have some indication that it'll be satisfactorily run.
2. Try to find out in advance from as many people as possible how many children they'll be bringing, what ages they are, etc. Indicate whether they need to bring their own food, drinks, nappies, etc.
3. Provide toys, disposable nappies, potties, some clean pants in case of 'accidents', and somewhere for younger children to have a nap. Make sure there's somewhere you can heat bottles or baby-food. A large supply of toilet paper for wiping noses, bums and spilt orange-juice is essential.
4. It's always better to have too many helpers than not enough. Aim for at least one adult for every five children.
5. Give all the children and helpers badges with their names on.
6. If possible, organize separate activities for older and younger children. If you can't get more than one room, or there are only a small number of children, try at least to take the older ones out sometime during the day.
7. Keep a register, so you know how many children you've got, who they came with, any special requirements or arrangements.
8. Ask people who bring children whether they want to eat together with them at lunch-time, or if they would prefer their children to stay in the creche.
9. Don't assume that only *parents* bring children to conferences. Don't ask *'Where's your mummy?'*; instead ask *'Who did you come with?'*
10. Be prepared to be patient. Some children are used to creches; others aren't, and may find it hard to cope with separation from someone they normally spend their whole time with.

Mother and Baby Groups

Following the rise of playgroups came a realization that there were particular needs of children under two-and-a-half — and more often of their mothers who may be isolated, lonely, depressed or bored, whilst spending their days continuously with a young child. Mother and baby clubs provide the opportunity to meet other people in a similar position, as well as an opportunity for children to play together. As the name implies, the mother (or guardian) must come with the child.

There are a number of starting points for forming a mother and baby club. Playgroup supervisors may give over a morning or afternoon for a club. But more often, women form their own by knocking on doors in their neighbourhood and opening their own houses to those who wish to come. For ideas on starting a club, see *Starting a Mother and Toddlers Club*, from Scottish PPA, 7 Royal Terrace, Glasgow G3 7NT, 10p.

Information about mother and baby clubs locally can be obtained from the local authority Social Services Department or from PPA, whose Area Organizers have information on play activities locally.

In some areas, health clinics run classes for women with baby clubs attached. Some groups also organize classes for themselves which include facilities for young children through adult education institutes, local community centres and arts centres.

Some Other Initiatives for Women stuck at Home

Community education projects are becoming increasingly aware of the needs of women with young children and have been putting on programmes which cater for both women and our children. This type of provision was pioneered by the Allfarthing Institute in the London Borough of Wandsworth which successfully organized play activities for young children and activities for women ranging from craft workshops to talkshops, where they could discuss their mutual problems, and determined by women themselves. Now this formula is being repeated quite widely. Those interested in seeing similar courses run by their local adult education institute might first contact Allfarthing for a report on their work, and then could with this go and talk to their adult education institute; some institutes employ 'outreach workers' specifically to match educational provision to community needs.

Another interesting project is being run by the educational department of BBC Radio London. Originally called 'Stuck at Home', the programme invited women stuck at home to come into the studio for a morning. A creche was provided by ILEA, and this was crucial to the project. The women (and some men) spent an hour getting to know one another and chatting about their problems and views, and then participated in a half-hour broadcast, largely determined by the discussion that had gone on before. Two booklets have emerged from the project, one a handbook of ideas for playing with children, and the other containing some of the conversations that were broadcast. Anyone can appear on the programme provided they register in advance. The organizers see great potential for this kind of project, which could be taken up by other local radio stations in association with the LEA.

Finally a project which has been devised as a hot-line for helping parents with problems; this is the 'Child Care Switchboard' organized as a pilot project in Nottingham by the National Educational Research and Development Trust. Here the idea was to provide advice and help to parents, linked to a local radio programme. The hot-line number was well publicized, including being printed on the back of beermats. Again this is an idea which is replicable elsewhere.

ALLFARTHING COMMUNITY WORKSHOPS *Allfarthing Institute, Battersea Town Hall, Lavender Hill, London SW11*

RADIO LONDON *British Broadcasting Corporation, 35 Marylebone High Street, London W1 (contact Sarah Lovegrove)*

NATIONAL EDUCATIONAL RESEARCH AND DEVELOPMENT TRUST *Longroyd Bridge, Huddersfield, West Yorkshire*

CHANGING CHILDCARE

Besides fighting for better childcare facilities, women and men have begun to question the way children are treated, and how this can be changed to everyone's advantage.

Women who want to change conventional attitudes to our sex have been concerned with finding ways to avoid passing on these attitudes to future generations. Boys and girls learn what is expected of them very early on. Playgroups and nurseries can help to change this by allowing and encouraging *all* children to join in *all* forms of play; by involving men in childcare so that children don't see it as 'women's work'; by presenting the world as a place where women go out to work, do interesting things, make choices, and lead their own lives; by counteracting the view of women as weak and passive wives and mothers that children get from the television and books (and unenlightened people!).

Children of both sexes are oppressed by the way adults generally treat them. They are seldom allowed any choice about what happens to them, and they are expected to be dependent on adults rather than learning to do things for themselves. Because we live in a competitive culture, children are not encouraged to co-operate and help each other. They are taught to do things the 'right' way rather than thinking for themselves. These attitudes are also being challenged by new ideas about childcare, not only in playgroups and nurseries, but by people trying to find new ways of organizing their own family life.

Children's Community Centres

One group which has consciously tried to change *attitudes* to childcare, as well as provide more nursery places, is the Children's Community Centre at 123 Dartmouth Park Hill. The centre is a parent-controlled nursery financed by a local authority grant, and provides free daycare for about eighteen children. There are two paid workers, but the majority of workers are parents who come in unpaid on a rota basis.

The first idea for the Centre came from a group of women in the women's liberation movement. Their aims in setting up the Centre were:

1. to obtain a parent-controlled daycare centre for pre-school children that was not too large, so that families using the Centre were within walking distance, children were in a 'home'-size environment, and with easy communication between all workers on the policies and running of the centres;
2. to involve the immediate neighbourhood, from old age pensioners to teenagers at school, and to provide a meeting-place for parents and others in the neighbourhood;
3. the responsibility of running the Centre both practically and ideologically to be shared among all workers and parents;
4. eventually all workers including parents to be paid;
5. to break down the stereotype of sex roles for both adults and children by involving fathers and other men, and by providing situations and activities that question what boys and girls have been traditionally expected to do.

And finally they were also concerned with the quality of daycare they would provide for pre-school children. They hoped to give them the opportunity to question, to make choices and to learn to live and share with others.

The Centre tries to work against competition and individualism, to encourage the children to turn to each other for help and to work together ('at school they call this "cheating" '). They actively encourage the girls to use tools, to fight back when attacked, to be adventurous and curious. Of course this can be immensely difficult when what a child learns outside the Centre is so often directly opposed to what goes on inside. But it's not impossible to make a start.

Their pamphlet, *Children's Community Centre: Our Experience of Collective Childcare* (15p plus postage), gives a very thorough explanation of what the Centre is trying to do and how they have gone about it. It deals realistically with the difficulties of attempting to care for children in a new way, as well as the practical problems of starting any kind of daycare project. However, it manages to be inspiring rather than off-putting.

CHILDREN'S COMMUNITY CENTRE *123 Dartmouth Park Hill, London N19*
The Centre has also made a sixteen-minute film about themselves, which is available for hire from Concord Film Council, Nacton, Ipswich, Suffolk.

Birmingham Women's Liberation Playgroup

There is only one playgroup in this country which was set up specifically to apply the ideas of women's liberation to childcare:

'*Some women in the women's movement who had small children started a baby group in 1970, child-sharing between themselves. When they wanted to extend this group there was a campaign for a Women's Liberation Nursery, but it soon became obvious that it wasn't going to succeed — the council wouldn't give us premises or any other kind of help. So the women involved started a playgroup in somebody's house, one morning a week. They also began a discussion group on childcare at the same time. Eventually a Parks Department Playhut was obtained, the playgroup was then expanded and opened four mornings a week.*

'*The aims of the playgroup, as set out in 1973, are: to provide safe and satisfying group play for children between the ages of 2½ and 5 years, to counter positively the conditioning of children into restricting sex roles, and to encourage the formation of strong friendships among the children, and between the children and adults other than their own parents. We see this as a way of providing a more communal type of childcare which will benefit both children and parents by offering them a wider experience than in the family and home. We wish to encourage both men and women to join in the activities and support the playgroup as a practical demonstration of alternatives to the usual pattern of childcare.*'

The playgroup wasn't set up because there were no existing facilities, although there was some dissatisfaction with the sort of childcare provided by conventional playgroups. But the main reason for setting up the group was to put new ideas about childcare into practice:

'*It was a new thing to start childcare sharing at a much younger age, so that a very close bond grows up, not only between children, but between children and other adults, so that they're not just relating to their parents.*

'*Originally we set out to have half women's liberation children and half local children, but the area we were in was very well provided with nurseries, and the local children who came got nursery places very quickly and left. Now we've moved to another playhut in a different area. We started off without a supervisor, but found that it was very hard for new children to come in and see different faces each day, so now we have a paid supervisor, plus four or five other adults each morning.*

'*We did get a grant initially, but haven't had any other grants. We charge very low fees — 15p a day at the moment — and those who can afford it pay a subscription of £3.50 a term. But this means we can only pay the supervisor £7.50 a week, which we feel very guilty about. Nursery care and childcare are so badly paid anyway, and the women's movement is supposed to be fighting this, so it's just not right that we should pay badly too.*

'*At first the playgroup was organized very much like any other — there was an elected closed committee, and a lot of the routine business was done by the committee, though we still had open meetings which included everybody in the playgroup. Since last summer the structure has altered, because there was a feeling among some people that it should be run on a more communal basis. So the committee was dropped and everything was decided at open meetings. Now we've narrowly decided to go back to having a committee, but an open committee that anybody can attend, and it's not elected, it's on a rota basis. So it's still more communal than it was originally. There seemed to be a fear that a committee would somehow take over; but if you can trust your children in a collective childcare set up, you ought to be able to trust other adults to organize it.*

'*Our discussion meetings are one of the most important features of the playgroup; we've had meetings on things like the new Dr Spock book, childcare in Russia, aggression, competitiveness. Sometimes we discuss changing the structure of the morning, and more recently we've had discussions about individual children at the playgroup. We've been quite successful in getting parents involved in discussion meetings, though less so with local parents, especially Asian women. Many women's liberation women are used to going to meetings, but for some women this is a new experience. They feel put down at first because we're all university educated and so on, but some get over that barrier. Although the women who come may not have been involved in the women's movement before, we feel there's been a lot of progress in getting new women involved in the women's movement.*

'*One of the ideas of the playgroup has been that there's a much higher parent involvement than is usual; most parents do one morning a week. You are expected to be very committed to it, because you're expected to be committed to alternative childcare; you're very much encouraged to come to the meetings and so on. Nearly all the parents put in time at the playgroup, including quite a few men, who are unemployed or have jobs that enable them to do it. Some people obviously just can't. We've had very few non-parents involved, but it's difficult to keep their interest, although two men non-parents have been pretty regular over the years, which is very good.*

'*There can be a problem with men in the playgroup, because quite often they do boisterous things; it's the sort of image men usually have of childcare, coming home in the evening and getting the children all excited, and its the same in the playgroup. They like playing rough and tumble games, whereas women just aren't conditioned to do that and some women feel very inhibited about doing that kind of thing. We've had a lot of discussion about that; how the men ought really to be in the kitchen doing all the domestic things for one morning. But it's also a matter of liberating ourselves into trying to do more active games, and not just letting the men do that, because it's not really good for the children to see that.*

'*We always advertise ourselves as a Women's Liberation Playgroup. But the majority of people who get involved come through knowing someone who's already in it. This means that most of them are already concerned with combatting sex roles and so on, but the playgroup extends the opportunities to do this, and the discussion with other women is very fruitful, even to people who are already committed. I think a lot of women come to us because we do a lot with the children, and only marginally because it's women's liberation. There's an incredible amount of activity and commitment. It's more stimulating for the children than many other playgroups. We try to encourage children to take initiatives, express themselves, and in that way gain independence.*

'*The actual structure of the morning at playgroup is much like any other, except that we have a project. We have a theme for the week like women at work, colours, music, shapes, and within that theme each adult takes it in turns to do a project. That's a good time to bring in ideas. We also do plays; we did one recently about an Easter egg factory,* with women working. The boss and foreman (both men) got custard pies in their faces. Plays are an extremely good way to get across ideas.

'There's disagreement within the playgroup about how far we should fight sex roles. For instance, one woman feels we should be non-sexist but not feminist; that boys should be encouraged to play with stereotyped 'girls' toys and vice versa, but that we shouldn't deliberately set out to change things in a propaganda-ish way. Whereas others would argue that there's so much conditioning from outside, and television, and children's books, that you've got to fight it all the time.

'We try to encourage non-sexist books, but that's very difficult because there are so few. If a book was very anti-women or really showed girls in very traditional roles, then we would censor it. We have written our own stories, but that's dropped off a bit recently. Sometimes when the story is read at the end of the morning, the character is changed from male to female, especially if it's an animal.

'The playgroup is carried on into lunch groups. The children are split into groups after playgroup and go with their group to different people's houses every day, until about 3 o'clock in the afternoon. That seems to work very well; they get used to going to other people's houses, socializing with other adults and children. And it frees parents until mid-afternoon. A lot of the children who go to lunch groups mix well with other adults, because they get so used to it. My children, who've been through playgroup and lunch groups from 2½ up to school age, have, I think, really benefited from the early socialization.

'Children who've gone on to school do still see other children and adults from the playgroup, but through the friendship network rather than in a structured way. Quite a lot of people keep up the connections.

'But the playgroup is such a small part of their lives compared to all the other conditioning they get. Really you've got to keep going at it all the time. I think the playgroup in conjunction with parents talking about things all the time might have some effect. It does work reasonably well at the stage when they are actually at playgroup, but then they're faced with school, which is so grim, and everything we've done is undone within about a term. It's not just that they're meeting children who haven't been to a women's liberation playgroup, it's what they're told and how they're treated — girls one side, boys the other. I try to keep talking to my children and pounce on any sexist comments, like "You can't do that, you're a girl". I would like there to be a group that concerns itself with schools and what we can do to try and influence them. It would be a very difficult thing to do, but we ought to try.'

BIRMINGHAM WOMEN'S LIBERATION 65 Prospect Road, Mosely, Birmingham 13
The group has published Out of a Pumpkin Shell: Running a Women's Liberation Playgroup; this also includes children's stories and rhymes, and a good bibliography.

Three publications which would be of interest are:

LIBERATING YOUNG CHILDREN FROM SEX ROLES
by Phyllis Taube Greenleaf, New England Free Press, 60 Union Square, Somerville, Massachusetts 02143 (available also from Rising Free, 142 Drummond Street, London NW1)
Very good for pointing out the difficulties of running a liberated playgroup, and giving examples of how to cope.

CHANGING CHILDCARE
from Writers and Readers Publishing Co-operative, 9 Rupert Street, London W1, 30p
This pamphlet describes pre-school education in China and Cuba, and discusses the hidden and explicit values of childcare in this country. There, children are treated as a group of people with a responsible part to play in society; here, children learn authority relationships, competitiveness and sex-role stereotyping. This pamphlet attempts to define some of the values and aims of a socialist approach to childcare.

THE DAY CARE BOOK
by Vicki Breitbart, Knopf, £2.50
The why, what and how of community daycare. An excellent publication available in many bookshops in Britain, or try Compendium, 240 Camden High Street, London NW1.

CHANGING THE FAMILY

> For the ego, for the personality to develop, the infant needs to experience satisfaction and challenge at his (her) own pace. But nowhere has it been demonstrated that for survival, or mental health, the satisfactions, challenges and frustrations must all originate in the same person.
>
> (Bruno Bettelheim, *The Children of the Dream*)

A growing number of children are brought up outside the context of the 'normal' two-parent family. Often this comes about through divorce, death of a parent, or because the parents never married. But some people are deliberately choosing to set up different structures to care for children, because they find the conventional family set-up unsatisfactory for both adults and children. The claustrophobic relationship between a woman and her children, when she is forced to spend all her time caring for them, can stifle any other interests and activities which are important to the woman's development as a person, and limit the child's opportunities to form relationships with other adults and children and learn from them.

In the past few decades, Western psychologists and sociologists have emphasized the importance of the exclusive, one-to-one, mother-child relationship, and the damage caused to children who are deprived of this. But this arrangement is *not* biologically determined. In other cultures children are cared for from an early age by a wide variety of adults and older children, by aunts, uncles, cousins, grandparents, etc. Children can form close relationships with more than one or two adults, and certainly benefit from doing so.

Family patterns are determined by the material situation that people are in rather than by psychological necessities; different family set-ups may produce different characteristics in children, but there is no reason to suppose that our way of doing things is necessarily better than any other. (For a more complete discussion of this see *The Myth of Motherhood* by Lee Comer.)

'Alternative' childcare arrangements usually grow naturally out of the situations people live in, rather than being set up for ideological reasons: two women with children who have left their husbands may decide to live together and share childcare; a group of people who live together may decide to take part in caring for a child born to one of them; two families living close to each other may arrange to care for the children of both families in turn, freeing the other adults to do other things. The possibilities are endless.

The advantages for the mother are obvious; instead of spending all her time with her child she is freed to develop her own interests, perhaps take a job, or simply have some time off to enjoy herself. She no longer has to bear the whole burden of responsibility for the child, and can discuss her worries and difficulties with other adults. Many people are astonished at the idea of non-parents voluntarily taking on some of the work involved in childcare; but women or men who have chosen not to have children of their own, or who intend to wait for some time, or who are infertile, may nevertheless want to be involved in caring for children and forming loving relationships with them. They can share the pleasures of childcare, as well as taking their turn to wash the nappies!

How are children affected by being brought up by larger numbers of adults, or adults who are not their parents? It's strange that people always ask this question about 'different' family set-ups, but never think to ask it about their own conventional nuclear families. Children brought up by larger groups are not totally dependent on their mothers as many children are; they know that several adults love and care for them, and will provide them with their material needs. They have a wider variety of relationships, more choice about who they are with, and often have a much more interesting life. Because the adults have their own lives and are not with children all the time, they have more energy and imagination to give to the child than even the most dedicated full-time mother. And now that many parents choose to have only one or two children, a child can only benefit from close contact with several other children its own age. Setting up alternative family structures is not easy. We all tend to see our children as possessions, and find it threatening to allow them the freedom to form relationships with others. Suppose your child actually prefers someone else? Parents often feel guilty or unsure about 'depriving' their child of a 'normal' family life; any tantrums or bad phases that the child goes through can easily be blamed on the different family structure, whereas nuclear families rarely blame their children's neuroses on the nuclear family.

Non-parents have the constant insecurity of knowing that they have no legally or socially recognized right to carry on seeing a child, even when they have cared for that child for many years. If their relationship with the parent breaks down, they cannot go to court and demand access, and most of the people around them will find it hard to understand how painful it can be when that child disappears from their life. There are also the problems of maintaining relationships between a group of adults who are all involved with the same children. Then there's the problem of finding jobs that give them time to be with children, and trying to deal with a society that makes no allowance at all for family structures that don't fit into the normal framework.

But despite the very real difficulties, more and more people are trying to set up childcare structures which do not perpetuate the power structure of the nuclear family, and do not produce children who are totally dependent on one or two adults for their well-being. They want children to have the freedom to choose their relationships for themselves; to have the security and resulting independence of knowing that many people care for them and feel responsible to them.

Sarah's Family

Helen is thirty-three and has a three-year-old daughter, Sarah. They live with three other women, Barbara, Carol and Mary, all in their mid-twenties, who share in caring for Sarah. Helen and Mary have part-time jobs, Carol works full-time, and Barbara has recently started a college course.

Helen was married to Sarah's father, Kevin, when the marriage began to break down. She talked about her problems with the other women in the conciousness-raising group she was in. This helped her to find a more satisfactory solution than a mother's usual choice of staying with her husband or bringing up a child on her own:

'Barbara was in the same conciousness-raising group when I was thinking about leaving Kevin. We were quite close, and she said she'd like to live with me and share the child-care. We were looking for somewhere to live when Carol decided she'd like to come and live with us too: she spoke to me and said she'd live with me on one condition, and of course I thought that meant she didn't want to have anything to do with Sarah, but the condition turned out to be that she should share the childcare!

'We talked quite a lot about our ideas on how children should be brought up, and fortunately it turned out that our ideas were similar, so there weren't any great conflicts about that. And as far as the practical aspects of it went, like getting Sarah to playgroup in the mornings and babysitting, we simply stuck rotas on the wall.

'Sarah was two at this time; she had only ever lived with me and Kevin, but she didn't mind being looked after by other people. I used to really worry about the rota business because I thought Sarah saw herself as someone who was just passed around, and that people only spent time with her because they were down on the rota to do it, But I soon realized that she actually enjoyed it. She loves getting you to look on the rota to see who's getting her up the next day, and she'd like to be on it herself; she wants to be on the cooking rota too!

'I couldn't really believe that women with no children of their own would actually want to do this. I thought they were just doing it for my sake. They did want to be with Sarah, but were worried in case they made me jealous! We kept talking it over and assuring each other that we'd stop feeling that way, but nevertheless this carried on for a while.

'I don't remember ever getting annoyed by the others treating Sarah differently from how I would have done; there have been conflicts over things like food, what we thought Sarah should eat and so on, but we discuss problems as they come up, or arrange a time to get together and talk about things. There was a stage when Sarah got quite manipulative; if one person wouldn't give her something she'd rush off and ask someone else. I thought that was going to be a big problem, but it didn't last long. At first if she was going through a difficult patch I used to blame it on the way we were living. She used to get upset about wanting to be with Kevin, and I felt guilty about depriving her of that. But now I think she just uses it; if she's upset with me she's just as likely to say "I want Barbara, or Carol" as she is to say "I want Kevin". She tends to use Kevin as a last resort when everyone's fed up with her.

'I'm really pleased that Sarah now has strong relationships with other people, besides me and Kevin. She's changed tremendously, she's far more outgoing, she's much more able to cope with different situations and doesn't run to me and expect me to deal with things for her. Since we've lived communally like this, I've seen her with adults who are really difficult for a child to cope with, and she's actually been polite to them, because she's been aware of the situation and confident that she could cope with it. Instead of running and hiding behind me, she handles it all herself, which she would never have been able to do before. Her vocabulary's improved too; before we all moved in together all the words she used were ones I'd taught her, so it was just like hearing myself talk. Now she learns different words from all of us.

'My family disapproves of what we're doing. My sister thinks Sarah's going to grow up very insecure and messed up; she thinks children need one stable relationship and no more, and that they just get confused otherwise. I think that's rubbish. Even Kevin quite appreciates our set-up now. To begin with he was very sceptical and expected me to be unable to live with other women, and that he would be able to say how bad it was for Sarah, but he just hasn't had the chance. Even he's seen that she's changed for the better.

'I think the other parents at the playgroup are quite disapproving too. We live in a fairly respectable area, so most of the other children come from very conventional families. Sarah had a birthday party and when we invited one little boy, whom she really likes, his mother said: "Oh! She must come to Edward's party next week." But when they came here I noticed the parents looking round; they were obviously aware that something strange was afoot. And Sarah never got invited to Edward's party. I felt really upset for her.

'There probably will be problems when Sarah goes to school; by that time children have stronger ideas about what families should be like, with one mummy and one daddy, and she'll have to cope with that. At the moment the other children she talks to don't really understand what it's all about, so they just accept what she says about our family set-up.

'My situation is so much better now: I do much less childcare, I've got much more freedom, and I get a lot more support. It means that if I want to do something I feel I've got the right to do it, the right to some time to myself; whereas when I was with Kevin it was always a question of him doing me a big favour and allowing me to do things. I think that if I hadn't got together with Barbara and Carol, I would have stayed with Kevin because of Sarah. I've never, ever wanted to be on my own with Sarah; I find that a very depressing situation to contemplate.

'Barbara and Carol may both have to move away next year, to go to college, and that'll cause difficulties. We three have been the core of the household, the people with the commitment. If I can find two other women that I know and that I think it'll work with, I'll try and keep things going. But if not, I'd rather give it up than have it working differently.'

Bringing up Children together

Brenda and Marion have lived together for nearly five years. For the past three years they have been involved with Eva, a child who is not 'theirs', and now each has a child of her own, both of whom are cared for collectively.

Eva, now three years old, was born into a household of five adults and one child; all the adults took part in caring for her right from the start. Brenda and Marion were friends of this household, and began to see Eva regularly when she was very young. Eva's mother has since moved out of the household that Eva was born into, so Eva's time is now divided between three households: the house where she was born, her mother's house, and Brenda and Marion's house.

Brenda and Marion talked about how they got involved and how they feel about the situation now:

'It started off when Eva was about three months old, she would come here for a few days at a time. We were just part of the friendship network, we'd looked after kids before and had expressed an interest in looking after children, so this just happened. We had had other kids living here, so we were used to the idea of looking after someone else's child, and aware of the fact that their parents might take them away eventually.

'Then we started having Eva one day a week and one weekend in four. It's been very regular since then, because it is easier if you always have the child on a certain day. We had very little say in what happened to Eva when she wasn't here; our communication with the other people involved was fairly informal. We just went on seeing her and insisted that we should. I don't think we saw it as a long-term thing when it started — if you only see a child one day a week you don't feel that involved. We didn't really think about it all that much.

'We feel we've got more responsibility for Eva now, we've felt closer to her over the past few months, and she obviously likes being here. Sometimes I feel very secondary to her; but then we see her as much as most of the adults involved with her, so perhaps everyone feels like that about her. If we decided to move or something, then Eva would be a part of that decision. It's impossible to say whether our relationship with her will go on for years and years.

'It doesn't seem to be a good idea that Eva doesn't have one particular place as a base. But having got into this situation it's difficult to get out of it. I think Eva's now getting to the stage where she's going to start protesting more and more about anything she doesn't like; maybe she'll demand one home if she gets the chance. At the moment no one's interested in letting her choose. All the adults have got a stake in it. They're all involved with her and don't want to see less of her. Certainly when she starts going to school she'll probably want to have a base, it'll be really weird for her otherwise.

'It's hard to tell whether Eva has benefited from this set-up, because you don't know how much is her and how much is what's been done to her. She seems quite independent. She probably enjoys having lots of people to relate to, but not having them so spread out and dislocated (the adults don't really see that much of each other). She likes having other children around, and it's very sad that she doesn't have more stable relationships with other children; moving around all the time, she doesn't get much chance to know the other children in the street, for example.

'She seems to like us quite a lot, and likes coming here. If she was obviously miserable when she came here we'd get upset about it, but she likes seeing us as much as she likes seeing anybody else.'

Eventually both Brenda and Marion decided that they would like to have a child. Tom, Brenda's child, is now one year old, and Joe, Marion's child, is 10 months.

(Brenda):

'I thought I'd like to have a child at some stage, so when I thought it would be a good time, I went round asking people if they thought it was a good idea. I don't know what I'd have done if they'd said no! I was quite surprised when Marion seemed to think it was OK. She'd always sworn she never ever wanted to have children, so it came as a great shock when she said she'd decided to have one as well; and then it was a race to see who got pregnant first!

'We talked a bit about how we were going to organize the childcare, and who would be involved. We assumed there would be some kind of collective arrangement; in fact, Tom was conceived on the condition that he be brought up collectively, on his father's part. At first it was just us two and Mike (Joe's father) who were going to be involved. Gordon (Tom's father) was going to be a definitely non-involved biological parent. I don't think I believed this actually. It would have been impossible for him to be involved with me and not be involved with the child.

'There are six people involved in looking after Tom and Joe now. They both spend more time here than anywhere else, but they do stay at other houses during the week. It's on a rota basis, definite days with definite people. At the weekend, each of us tends to have our "own" child. Marion and I spend the most time with the children and have the most responsibility. We've never tried to assume that everyone would be equally close, because it just doesn't work like that.

'We did have one or two meetings of all the people involved, but mostly we just talk to each other informally. You do need to spend quite a lot of time just keeping in touch. I don't really like the children to be with someone I don't feel in touch with, though maybe I'm just trying to keep control. We have arguments about what happens to the children; up to now it's been mostly practical things, but now we are coming on to how they're treated, how liberal we should be and so on.

'I'm beginning to feel more worried about what'll happen in the future, because Tom and Joe are very used to one another now. I suppose it wouldn't really damage them to go off now and never see each other again, but the longer it goes on, the more upsetting it would be for them. I worry a bit about what would happen if their relationships with other adults broke down. But at the moment you only see the positive side — I can see who they like being with, but I can't see who they would miss.

'It's a severe limitation on your own freedom if you've got to stay around with the other adults; that's the big drawback. If any of the adults left, we would try to have other people around, because otherwise there'd be so few of us; it would become just like a nuclear family.

'I think the children have a nicer life now than they would have if they were just with one parent. They're quite happy and they thrive on it at the moment. The next two years are a bit dodgy; they're old enough to be aware of what's going on, but not old enough to say what they feel about it really. If they decided at some point that they wanted to spend more time with someone else, it would be upsetting, but that's going to happen anyway at some stage in their lives, so you might as well get used to it. If they really don't want to be with you then there's no point being with them.

'I feel that I'm better off than I would be in a couple situation, and better off being on Social Security than living with a man who supported me. I've got financial independence. But we're lucky, not everyone can get SS, especially non-parents who want to be involved with childcare. Three of the people who look after Tom and Joe work, either part or full-time, and the others are unsupported mothers.

'We've benefited a lot from the situation. Children take up such a tremendous amount of time, so the more the load is spread the better. For instance, Joe's never been very good at sleeping; a night with him is totally exhausting. If that's spread between four or *five people it's not so bad, but if it was just Marion, she wouldn't be able to do anything else; she'd just sit around yawning all day!*

'*I feel that other people having them sometimes is a safeguard against them becoming too dependent, or us becoming too possessive. It's built in that they know more people than children usually do, so to that extent they'll have more choice than most of the children they spend time with and who they form relationships with.*

'*I do feel possessive about the kids, but I never want them to stay here if they're going somewhere else that day. I don't think it's good for them to be with one adult all the time. And if a woman doesn't want to be stuck at home all the time, it can't be good for the child. So this way has advantages both for the children and for the mother.*'

If you knew, Kids

If you knew just how small you are
If you knew how big it all is
And that Mammy isn't so big
And not always right

If you knew what they think of you
If you knew how they despise us
And that we can't fight them all
Because we depend

If you knew how it hurts me
If you knew that it's hard to say no
You'd never again look in toy shops
Or listen for the ice-cream van

But you don't know how small you are
And you don't know that I'm small too
To you all the world is a playground
And I'm the best mam in it.

by Cassidy

BOOKS

THE MYTH OF MOTHERHOOD
by Lee Comer, Spokesman Pamphlet No. 21, 12p, from Bertrand Russell House, Gamble Street, Nottingham
A short, readable attack on the assumption that motherhood is a woman's true purpose in life. Examines the concept of 'maternal deprivation', the dangers of excessive mother/child attachment, and the violence we do to children in the name of love. Lee Comer presents some very important ideas in an accessible way. This pamphlet is well worth reading.

LIVING LIKE I DO
by Nell Dunn, Futura, 85p
This book consists of interviews with people bringing up children outside the normal family situation, talking about how their lives are organized, why they chose to do it, and how they feel about it.

DEATH OF THE FAMILY
by D. Cooper, Penguin, 65p
This book examines the stresses of the modern family and how it destroys the sexual and social independence of the individual. Discusses alternatives to the family and the difficulties involved. Not exactly an easy read, but worth it.

WOMEN AND CHILDCARE IN CHINA
by Ruth Sidel, Penguin, 70p
This is an interesting account of a visit to China, concentrating on the position of women and how children are cared for in nurseries, kindergartens and other places.

THE TWO WORLDS OF CHILDHOOD – USA AND USSR
by Uri Bronfenbrenner, Penguin, 80p
This book compares family upbringing and children's groups in the USSR and USA, the effects of each on the children, and what kinds of adults they are aimed at producing.

CENTURIES OF CHILDHOOD
by Phillippe Aries, Penguin, (out of print)
This is a detailed examination of the ways children have been regarded and treated over the last 500 years. Aries shows how much less has been expected of children over the centuries, and how childhood (which now officially goes on for longer than ever before) has become institutionalized.

CHECKLIST OF ORGANISATIONS CONCERNED WITH THE UNDER-FIVES

Advisory Centre for Education *18 Victoria Park Square, Bethnal Green, London E2 9PB*

British Association for Early Childhood Education *Montgomery Hall, Kennington Oval, London SE11*

Child Poverty Action Group *1 Macklin Street, London WC2*

Commission for Racial Equality *Elliott House, 10–12 Allington Street, London SW1*

Gingerbread *2nd Floor, 35 Wellington Street, London WC2*

National Association for the Welfare of Children in Hospital (NAWCH) *Exton House, 7 Exton Street, London SE1*

National Campaign for Nursery Education *67 Woodland Gardens, London N10*

National Children's Bureau *8 Wakley Street, London EC1*

National Children's Centre and the National Educational Research and Development Trust *Longroyd Bridge, Huddersfield, West Yorkshire*

National Council for One Parent Families *255 Kentish Town Road, London NW5*

National Council of Social Service *(for details of local Voluntary Service Councils) 26 Bedford Square, London WC1*

National Council of Voluntary Child Care Organizations *Turner House, Highbury Park, London N5*

National Society for the Prevention of Cruelty to Children *1 Riding House Street, London W1*

Nursery Education Research Group *c/o DES Oxford Pre-School Research Group, 28 Norham Gardens, Oxford*

Pre-School Playgroups Association *Alford House, Aveline Street, London SE11*

Save the Children Fund (SCF) *57 Clapham Road, London SW9*

Thomas Coram Research Unit *41 Brunswick Square, London WC1*

Toy Library Association (TLA) *Seabrook House, Wyllyolts Manor, Potters Bar, Herts*

Voluntary Campaign for the Under-Fives (VOLCUF) *c/o PPA or National Children's Bureau*

Women's Royal Voluntary Service (WRVS) *17 Old Park Lane, London W1*

Working Women's Charter Groups *address from the local Trades Union Council*

CRIMES AGAINST WOMEN 9

CRIMES AGAINST WOMEN

The first International Tribunal on Crimes Against Women was held in March of 1976. In various countries women have always united to fight against the open oppression that is directed towards us. But often these groups are more or less unaware of each other; and for the first time in Brussels, they came together from all over the world and found out about the scandalous conditions they share in common and that they are fighting against.

The structure of the five days was planned so as to give women a chance to contribute personal and spontaneous testimonies, to speak about their oppression to an international audience; it also allowed time for reports on campaigns so that women could learn about feminist strategies in other countries. Each country was responsible for discussing particular crimes that affected them specifically. Some of the thirty countries represented at the Tribunal were: Australia (Aboriginal women); Austria (Abortion); Chile (Women Political Prisoners); Denmark (Pornography); Germany (Discrimination against Lesbians, Psychiatric Treatment of Women, Gynaecological Crimes); Northern Ireland (Position of Women under Army Occupation); Israel (Family Law in Israel); Japan (Forced Prostitution); Puerto Rico (Forced Sterilization); South Africa (Position of Black Women); Spain (Women in Prison); Yemen/Arabia/Syria (Position of Arab Women).

The overwhelming impression from the Tribunal was that much of women's oppression is enshrined in the law (forced sterilization, pornography, anti-abortion laws). It is not only attitudes that are involved, but the *legal suppression* of women. One cannot help feeling after reading some of the testimonies from the Tribunal that there is a deliberate policy to keep women down, to keep women powerless; to trample to death any creativity, strength and talent that women around the world possess.

The crime which English and Scottish women spoke about was battering — the beating of women by men. Many women are battered by their husbands or fathers, and there are some cases of sons battering their mothers. There are no class barriers to battering. It happens in families of mechanics, labourers, miners and also in families of doctors, lawyers, teachers, social workers; in fact, everywhere. Battering is a crime: it is destructive violence against women, landing many women in hospital with broken jaws, ribs, arms, burns, concussions . . . and many women die. Yet even so, authorities and neighbours turn a blind eye.

Another crime, rape, was discussed by the American delegation. Many people do not believe rape is a British crime; for years and years it has been ignored. Victims of rape are afraid to report it, and even when reported are often not believed. Slowly British women, through our own or through other women's experiences, are realizing that rape exists in Britain, and in no small way. It is a real threat and fear that lingers in the back of women's minds and cuts us off from the freedom of action that men enjoy.

More investigations have been carried out recently to try to fathom the reasons why men rape so viciously, why they batter women so violently. The answers are many and varied. This chapter will not dwell on the whys, but on the ways in which women are organizing against this violence. Women are fighting back against these crimes, with precious little help from any official bodies, and, indeed, finding obstruction and hindrance from some. A Rape Crisis Centre with an emergency twenty-four hour phone has started in London. Hopefully others will arise throughout the country. Battered women's refuges are helping women to pick up the pieces and start over again; to begin a new life.

Maybe one day Social Services Departments will provide money, without strings, for battered women's refuges; and the police will co-operate with the Rape Crisis Centres. But at the moment it is up to women to help ourselves and show other women the steps to take; no one else will do it for us.

BATTERED WOMEN: A SAFE PLACE TO GO

Mugging and violence in the streets are considered serious crimes. Normal sentences range up to fifteen years. But the same acts committed in the home by a man upon his wife is relegated to the category of a domestic tiff. And until the emergence of the battered wives hostels the police, the courts, hospitals, doctors, social workers did nothing to help the plight of these women.

> My husband keeps saying I'm mad and keeps on hitting me and whipping me. I've had a broom over -my head and needed medical treatment, a dislocated shoulder, bruises all over me and two black eyes and kicked in the ribs . . . My children scream because he shouts and hits me in front of them. He has thrown me out at night and told me to go but I can't leave the children and it is a job to get a room with children.
>
> (a woman writing in *Scream Quietly, Or the Neighbours Will Hear* by Erin Pizzey)

'Woman-beating' is by no means a new phenomenon, but it has only recently been talked about, studied, and recognized as a genuine problem rather than a joke. For a woman who suffers physical violence from the man she lives with, the most urgent problem is usually finding somewhere safe to go, to get away from the threats and fear and have time to sort out her life.

This may sound simple, but in practice it is far from straightforward. Even if a woman has sympathetic relatives who are willing to take her and her children into their homes, the husband will usually know where they live, and may come round to cause trouble, threaten the woman, or try to snatch the children away. Official bodies tend to be reluctant to classify a woman as homeless until she has actually left her husband . . . and that means having somewhere to go to. In addition, women with children often have no job or money of their own, and thus find it impossible to get rented accommodation. The police and doctors don't want to interfere with what they see as a private, domestic problem, and there is little they can do if a woman has no alternative but to return to the home where she faces another beating.

To cope with this basic need, groups of women all over the country have set up refuges for battered women. They have faced the problems of finding money, getting houses, putting pressure on unco-operative authorities; and many have succeeded. Refuges are often over-crowded, established in short-life or unsatisfactory premises, and constantly worried about getting enough money to keep going. But for thousands of women they have provided the first chance to escape from violence, and the opportunity to work things out with the support of other women.

Two groups which have set up refuges in Manchester are Manchester Shield and Manchester Women's Aid. They worked in very different ways to begin with, and there has been some conflict between them in the past. But although the refuges started off so differently, they now run in much the same way, and encounter similar day-to-day problems.

Manchester Shield

'When we started in 1973 we were a group mainly of social workers who wanted to do something about battered women. We were a mixed group in lots of ways; we had men and women in the group, and although we were all "professional" people we had differing political viewpoints, and different degrees of commitment to the ideas of the women's

liberation movement. I got involved with Shield because I felt the women's movement didn't do anything, and this would be something meaningful to women who needed to know more about things like that.

'We wrote to the Corporation telling them we needed a refuge for battered women in Manchester, asking the Housing Department to rent us a house and Social Services if they'd back us in getting some money. Both Departments agreed, so we applied for Urban Aid through the Social Services Department and the Housing Department said they'd find us a suitable property. They came up with a house in October 1974 and we opened in November with money we'd raised ourselves. It's a small house, four-bedroomed, detached, and on a council estate. We paid no rent for a year, and now the Housing Department gives us a grant to pay them the rent!

'We got the backing of the Social Services Committee for our Urban Aid; they agreed that it was a worthwhile project. Why is perhaps open to question. At the same time as we were starting up, the Manchester Women's Aid group squatted a house, which was very necessary to get something done at that time, but this annoyed the official people. It created a lot of publicity and highlighted the need for refuges. The Corporation saw Shield as a fairly respectable group which it could help, without providing any help for the group which had done things in what they saw as the irresponsible way.

'The Urban Aid grant came through the April after we opened. We'd applied for all this not really knowing what we were doing, and as soon as we opened the refuge and had all the problems of actually trying to run it, a lot of the group members disappeared, and we were left with a nucleus of about five women and two men. When we got the money through we thought it would solve a lot of the problems because we could employ a worker for the refuge and a playleader for the children. We wanted a woman worker because by then we'd realized that it was quite difficult for men to play a part in running the refuge. The first worker started in August 1975.

'At the same time we realized that the refuge wasn't big enough to meet the demand, so we asked for another house and got it in November 1975. We employed two part-time playleaders and one worker, but it was too much for her to manage by herself, so we employed another worker part-time and now we've got two full-time playleaders under the Job Creation scheme — all the workers are women. Urban Aid pays the workers' salaries, all the maintenance costs, gas and electricity bills. We charge rent and the women get reimbursed for this from Social Security, unless they're at work. The rent isn't paid direct to us, the women pay it to the worker out of their SS; they're quite conscientious about that because they realize the money's being used for them.

'We're not financially badly off, compared with a lot of refuges. The money we raise ourselves is for things we didn't realize we'd need when we put in for the Urban Aid grant, especially equipment for the kids (they need toys, playgroup materials, etc.). We want to start building an adventure playground at the second refuge, so we'll have to get the money for that ourselves. A few of the women who've left and been rehoused help us with fund-raising; they're much better at it than we are because they've got more contacts, round the pubs and things. The support group isn't very good at raising money.

'The authorities have never interferred with what we're doing; the Social Services have never even asked to see the places. But we're going to ask them round soon, partly because we want some money for a fire escape. If we create a good impression they might be willing to fork out a bit more for us.

'When we first opened we thought that if we advertised ourselves we'd be inundated and wouldn't know what to do; so we kept it fairly quiet. We informed the police stations, the Samaritans, the Probation Service, Citizens' Advice Bureaux, those who meet people who are in trouble. The Marriage Guidance Council told us they didn't agree with us; they said we were breaking up marriages (which we are in a way; it depends if you think it's the right thing under those sort of circumstances). We soon had a tremendous number of women knowing about the place. But in order to reach women who won't go near anyone official, we're getting together with other homeless

groups in Manchester to put out posters and leaflets with all our different addresses on.

'A lot of women are scared to contact us at first, they think it's going to be every-body sleeping on mattresses on the floor, absolute chaos and dirt; and that puts them off. Our places aren't clean and tidy and institutionalized by any means, they're just homely.

Running the Refuge

'Like most of the refuges, ours is self-managed. The worker is non-residential and in no way supposed to be like a warden or anything like that. Her job is to help the women when they need help. The women are responsible for deciding when they can take people in; in other words, if they feel there's enough people there, they'll say "No, we haven't got any room". This can be a bit of a problem, but you can't allow them to run the place and then tell them they've got to have hundreds of people there when they don't want them.

'In fact, they very rarely turn anyone away. We're supposed to have four families in the small refuge and six in the other one, but we often end up with seven in the smaller one and nine or ten in the big one. They double up on rooms, and make do for a couple of nights.

'The women are responsible for all the housekeeping. If they want to cook together, they do; but it's their place to run how they want. The main need is to organize the housework; sometimes there'll be a rota, or they'll set aside time to do the housework together. Once a week we have a house-meeting for the women, the workers, and members of the support group. That's useful because it means the women are all together and can get things worked out in a group situation. Very often they feel able to say things then (for example, if somebody's not doing any housework) that they can't say individually because then they'd feel they were getting at somebody.

'One of the difficulties is that the women very often want us to tell them what to do, partly so that they've got an "authority" to resent, but also because they're scared of the responsibility.

'The only rule we have is that we don't have any men in the house, ever. That rule gets broken occasionally. Sometimes you get a real outburst of men in the house, and this always leads to dreadful problems. One of the worst times was when we had a party for one of the workers leaving, to which boyfriends could come, and at the end of the party one man assaulted two of the women and smashed the house up. Every time the "no men" rule comes up we tell everybody about that incident.

Children

'Most of the women who come to us have children, since it's easier for women without children to find somewhere else to go. A lot of the children are scared when they first arrive because they've been through bad times, but they soon realize they're onto quite a good thing. Their mum's quite often in a bit of a state, she's got to learn to live with all these other people, she's got big decisions to make about what to do, and she's very often quite depressed, so her control of the children goes down. The children often exploit this like mad; they've got loads of other children to play with at all hours, so a lot of them go a bit wild.

'Having good playleaders helps to direct some of their energy and gives the women a break. We tend to rely on one or two of the women liking to be with kids and wanting to do things with them; that influences the rest and they start getting some enjoyment out of the children as well as just having the problems of feeding them, dressing them, and looking after them. It's difficult sometimes for us to talk about the children because we have such different ideas about how they should be brought up.

'The younger children go to the local school, the older ones quite often stay at the schools they've been at, because it's difficult to break a secondary school education *and they usually don't want to change schools. The schools have always been very help-ful, considering that they have an ever-changing population of children from the refuges. The children get picked on at school occasionally because everyone knows where they come from. Both of the houses are tending to get bad reputations in the neighbourhood, because they stick out, and the trouble we've had with men accentuates that. But the teachers themselves have always done their best.*

Leaving the Refuge

'*The average length of time a woman has to stay if she wants to get rehoused is about three months. We can get most women rehoused who want to be, even if they come from outside Manchester. We're only supposed to take Manchester women, but we've not always kept to that rule, and we've usually been able to work things out somehow with the Housing Department.*

'*Quite a few women go back to their husbands, about 60 per cent. But then a lot of those will come back to us again. A few women have been back three or four times. They have a very real dilemma about whether to return or not. Women often feel guilty about taking the children away from their father, and the men almost inevitably use this as a means of manipulating the woman into going back. But as long as a woman knows that she can come back to the refuge and nobody will say nasty things to her, then if she wants to keep going back to her husband that's up to her. And maybe one day she'll be able not to.*

'*None of the women have moved out to live together yet, because we'd have to get the Housing Department to recognize the need for families to live together, and they're not flexible enough to appreciate that. But they have cottoned on to the idea of second-stage housing, self-contained flats within the same house purely for women who've come from the refuge. I think some of the women would like to move together, because a lot of them make close friends when they're there; they get most of the help from each other. A few of the women who've been rehoused from our refuges have got involved with things like the women's rights group and the National Abortion Campaign.*

The Future

'*The government have put out a White Paper saying that the problem of battered women is a short-lived one; that there's been a pent-up need for refuges which will die down and then the local authorities will be able to make adequate provision. We're very much against local authorities running refuges because they couldn't be flexible enough to let women control their own lives in any way. They think you need all these staff, all these rules, that you have to have institutions. That's the way they run things.*

'*You have to walk a narrow line between getting as much financial aid as possible, without accepting any control. The danger is that they'll say the need is covered by existing homeless provision and try to phase out any help to Women's Aid. Some local authorities have set up what they call refuges, but they have a completely different understanding of what the women need.*'

Manchester Women's Aid

The Manchester Women's Aid refuge is run along the same lines as the Shield refuges, and has had similar experiences and problems, with disturbed children, violent men, and women trying to cope with the decision to leave their husbands. But because Women's Aid got their refuge in a way of which the authorities disapproved, they have also had to cope with far greater financial problems:

'*The women who lived in my house were very involved in the women's movement. At the time, there was a Women's Centre in Manchester (one that doesn't exist any more) and a lot of battered women were coming there. They were housed there overnight, but there was no accommodation to put them up on a long-term basis.*

'*The house next door to where I live was empty, so four women from the women's movement decided to squat it, along with a couple of battered women who were staying at the Women's Centre. We squatted the house in April 1974, and there was a lot of publicity about this, and arguments on the television between us and the Director of Housing, pointing out that there was no provision for battered women at all in Manchester.*

'*After about two months an anonymous donor, a woman, bought the house we'd squatted and gave it to Women's Aid. The house was very chaotic at that time, we were flooded with women, and there was a very strong argument for establishing more refuges in Manchester. We wanted the Housing Department to buy more houses for us. But instead, (and this is where the conflict between us and Shield originated) they supported Shield, because they saw them as more respectable.*

'*We still get no money from the council at all. We put in an Urban Aid application which we had to struggle to get submitted to the Home Office; they approved it in March 1976, but the local authority have never given us a penny of it. Their latest proposal is for us to sell our house and they'll give us another one, but we won't accept that; they just want to control the project, basically.*

'*We've got our money from fund-raising, and last year we got 10 per cent of the Rag money from the University (this came to £1,000). And we get rents from the women, reimbursed by Social Security. With the Rag money we've had a new kitchen built on to the house.*

'*Our three workers are paid under the Job Creation Scheme, we didn't have any trouble getting that. We've got one houseworker, one after-care worker, and a playleader. The playleader and the after-care worker are men, which is a bit difficult sometimes. Martin, the after-care worker, was working there voluntarily because his mum had been in the house. We try to encourage the women to run the place themselves as much as possible; and Martin is who they wanted for the job: they chose him.*

'*With the Job Creation workers there are new problems; it's made the women more dependent really, and we don't seem to be fighting that very effectively at the moment. It's also meant a whole reorganization of roles within the support group. There are about eight people in the support group; we raise money, have monthly committee meetings weekly house-meetings, and at the moment we have a rota where each of us goes in one night a week, we find that's a better way of getting to know the women and what's going on in the house than house meetings, where there's such a lot of business to get through and no time to talk to people individually.*

'*There are usually five women and between ten and fifteen children in the house. It takes four or five months for them to be rehoused. Some people say women from Shield are offered better houses, but I don't know if that's true; women from all the refuges tend to get offered houses in the crummier areas of Manchester.*

'*The local police are useless; we call them when a husband comes, and a policeman stands around outside for ten minutes making silly jokes about women battering husbands, then just disappears. When the new Domestic Violence Bill comes in, the police will have powers of arrest without a warrant when the man's breaking an injunction. It'll be interesting to see whether they'll act on it.*

'*We need a lot of money to do the house up, because it could be closed under the Public Health Acts any time they wanted. So if we don't get the Urban Aid money we'll just have to reapply. Also, we've got the offer of three more houses from the Family Housing Association, so I don't know how we'll manage. It's not getting the houses that's a problem after a while, it's running them. It takes an awful amount of time and energy; you have to be really committed. It isn't something you can do once a week.*'

Both Manchester Shield and Manchester Women's Aid are affiliated to the National Women's Aid Federation and have quite a strong relationship with it. They are aware of the problems that the Federation faces in trying to find new ways of organizing that do not simply reproduce the bureaucratic structure of conventional organizations:

The Federation tries to be as unstructured and unhierarchical as possible, but: the national workers in London were having to take decisions, and then getting sat on for having made them. The only policy-making body was the national conference. Now we're trying to make regional organization stronger so that everyone in the country's involved. It's really important to organize regionally, because things like the DHSS and housing policy are organized regionally, and they vary so much from one region to another.

Groups and Publications

NATIONAL WOMEN'S AID FEDERATION
51 Chalcot Road, London NW1

At the first Women's Aid National Conference in April 1974, Chiswick Women's Aid agreed to appoint a National Co-ordinator, and the DHSS made a grant available for this purpose. In January 1975 there was a second National Conference, at which a resolution was passed calling for a national organization. Local groups wanted to retain their autonomy, but to be linked to each other for information, publicity and negotiations at a national level. The delegates decided to set up a National Federation. They proposed five basic aims:

1. to provide temporary refuge, on request, for women and their children who have suffered mental or physical harrassment;

2. to encourage the women to determine their own futures and to help them achieve them, whether this involves returning home or starting a new life elsewhere;

3. to recognize and care for the emotional and educational needs of the children involved;

4. to offer support and advice and help to any woman who asks for it, whether or not she is a resident, and also to offer support and after-care to any woman and child who has left the refuge;

5. to educate and inform the public, the media, the police, the courts, social services, and other authorities with respect to the battering of women, mindful of the fact that this is a result of the general position of women in our society.

The delegates also suggested that the National Co-ordinator should be accountable to a committee of regional delegates, which should meet at least every three months. There are National Conferences twice a year which make all policy and major decisions. It is open to all Women's Aid groups but only those federated have voting rights. Liz, one of the national co-ordinators, states that 'we are not only providing refuges for women, but are trying to organize a women's organization — finding new ways of battling against others' expectations of how you should *be* an organization'.

CHISWICK WOMEN'S AID
369 Chiswick High Road, London W4

Chiswick Women's Aid was the first battered women's refuge, and through the pioneering work of the group the problem first became established. They have always been in trouble with authority for operating their 'open door' policy allowing anyone who needs to to come in, and as a result they are normally seriously overcrowded. They now provide a central refuge and a network of second-stage houses where women with their children can move to. They run a boys' project providing paid work and accommodation for young delinquents in an attempt to break the cycle of violence where a battered child becomes a battering father. And they run a school for the children of battered women. They have always been vocal in promoting the problem (internationally) and the ways in which the apparatus of the law and the caring professions might help. They have produced a number of films which are available for hire. They remain outside the National Women's Aid Federation.

REPORT OF THE SELECT COMMITTEE ON VIOLENCE IN MARRIAGE
HMSO, 60p

Following an awareness of the problems of baby battering and wife beating, a Parliamentary Select Committee was established to examine the various facets of family violence and to report back. The first year was spent looking at the problems of battered wives and how statutory authorities and voluntary agencies might work to provide a solution, and this is the official report of the committee.

BATTERED WOMEN AND THE NEW LAW

by Anna Coote and Tess Gill, from the National Council for Civil Liberties, 186 Kings Cross Road, London WC1, 60p

The Domestic Violence and Matrimonial Proceedings Act 1976 gave better protection to married and single women assaulted by their husbands or the men they live with. This guide explains the Act and the protection it gives, how to get an injunction, the role of the police and the rights to the home (although the legal position is changing all the time). This is a useful guide to understanding the extent of the protection the law gives, and how to make use of it. There is a short foreword by Jo Richardson, one of the main supporters of the cause of battered women in Parliament.

THAT'S NO LADY

a film made by Sheffield Women's Film Collective, from National Women's Aid Federation

Battered: 'She asked for it'; 'I wouldn't put up with it, she must enjoy it'; 'He must be sick'. Common reactions to the word. This film questions these attitudes, at the same time providing an opportunity for discussion of the legal, housing and welfare problems of battered women.

The film is not a story of one woman and her problems, but a set of scenes illustrating the kind of experiences and relationships that can develop in the life of any woman who is battered. The scenes are linked by a comedian in a working-men's club. His jokes, enjoyed by the men and women in the audience, reflect society's unspoken acceptance of some attitudes towards women and put the rest of the film into context. There are teachers' notes, with suggested discussion questions also available for 2p.

INJUNCTIONS FOR BATTERED WIVES: A Do-It-Yourself Kit

from Paddington Neighbourhood Law Centre, 465 Harrow Road, London W10, 25p

This is a step-by-step, easy to use kit, which includes the information you need to know, as well as the forms you need to fill out. It includes encouragement all throughout the process (don't give up!) and also takes into account the psychological fears a woman may be experiencing. It might be best, though, to use a solicitor, especially if you can obtain emergency legal aid.

OXFORDSHIRE WOMEN'S AID FIRST REPORT (Spring 1976)

from 134 Howard Street, Oxford, 10p

Although this report applies specifically to one refuge and to a particular community, it is useful in seeing how a refuge is run and what is involved. The pamphlet goes through the beginning and the setting up of the refuge, the rule of no men allowed in the house and why, and the role that the support group plays. There is an interesting transcript of an actual conversation that occurred in the kitchen of the refuge that gives a good idea of how important the refuge has been for these women.

BATTERED WOMEN NEED REFUGES

from National Women's Aid Federation, 40p

This is a good introductory pamphlet about the NWAF and the different kinds of refuges that are a part of it. It covers why women come, what it is like living and working in a refuge, the refuge and children, how to start a Women's Aid group, and where the NWAF is going in the future. It is much too short to give an idea of the scope of the problem of battering, but if read in conjunction with Erin Pizzey's book (see below), it should provide a good general background, what is being done, and the hurdles yet to cross.

THE EXISTING RESEARCH INTO BATTERED WOMEN

from National Women's Aid Federation, 15p

This gives an important analysis of how research projects tend to generally stereotype and oversimplify the problem of battered women. The study by Dr Gayford, who spoke before the Select Committee on Violence in the Family, is the most widely publicized research done in this country on battered women, and yet it is full of value judgments, and incomplete. He interviewed 200 women from Chiswick Women's Aid, yet only uses 100 of them in his study without explaining what happened to the others. He also does not use a control group of 100 women who were not in a refuge, something almost always done when research is carried out. This report, written by Elizabeth Wilson, is excellent, not only in her analysis of Gayford's work, but in pointing out how the government uses research and how the political ideas of the researchers can be used to turn 'hard facts' into bent political propaganda.

SCREAM QUIETLY, OR THE NEIGHBOURS WILL HEAR

by Erin Pizzey, Penguin, 45p

In 1971 Erin Pizzey founded Chiswick Women's Aid, the first house where women could come for refuge from continual beatings at home. With the founding of Chiswick Erin unlocked a Pandora's box: in three years 5,000 women and children had sought refuge at Chiswick. This book is an account of what has gone on at Chiswick, the women who come there and the problems they face — not only with their husbands, but with hospitals, social workers, social security, solicitors, police and the neighbours who would just turn up the telly when they heard screams from next door. Most of the book consists of individual cases; the heart-breaking stories of the women who came to Chiswick, the ones who could only write letters, and accounts from the children. Reading this book may take a long time: it's impossible to absorb the dreadful facts in one sitting. Her explanations of the causes of battering are insufficient however (all batterers are not psychopaths). The pressure society puts on men, and the ways they are taught to regard women, are also very much to blame. And the greater stress you're under, financial, about housing or unemployment, the more likely you are to take it out on your nearest and dearest, especially when she's not fulfilling every female stereotype simultaneously.

BROKEN RIB: The Monthly Newsletter of Edinburgh Women's Aid

c/o 44 Albany Street, Edinburgh

Full of jokes, poems and useful information such as articles on retraining schemes and 'How will I meet people on my own', as well as on the work of the refuge. Nearly all the contributions are from women at the refuge, including the following:

How NOT to be a Battered Woman

DON'T dress up when his friends come round. He'll say you're making up to them.

DON'T look a mess when his friends come round. He'll say you're trying to show him up.

DON'T ask *your* friends round. He won't want the house full of chattering females.

DON'T not ask your friends round. Are you ashamed of him or something?

DON'T have supper on the table when he gets in. He'll think you're getting at him for being late.

DON'T let supper be late. The least he deserves when he gets in from a hard day's work is to have his supper ready on the table.

DON'T let the children stay up till he gets home. He'll be too tired to be bothered with a lot of screaming kids.

DON'T send them to bed before he gets there. Do you want them to forget their own father?

DON'T ask him what sort of day he's had, you should be able to see just by looking at him that it's been dreadful.

DON'T forget to ask him how his day was. A wife should show some interest in what her husband's doing.

DON'T tell him about your day. He doesn't want to hear a lot of complaints when he's just got in from work.

DON'T not tell him about your day. Are you sulking or what?

DON'T put on a sexy negligee at bedtime. You look ridiculous, and anyway, whose money do you think you're spending?

DON'T got to bed in your pyjamas. It'd be nice if a man had something attractive to sleep with occasionally.

DON'T put your arms round him in bed. When he wants it, he'll ask for it.

DON'T turn away and go to sleep. Are you frigid or what?

And lastly, when he hits you DON'T fight back. You'll make it worse. And DON'T, whatever you do, cower away. It'll make him feel guilty, so he'll hit you more.

That's it, then. Women's Aid can promise you that if you follow these few little tips, you'll never get battered again. Unless, of course, you ask for it . . .

RAPE

What gratifying concern was shown by Mr Justice Thesiger for a man aged 68 who pleaded guilty to rape at Leeds Crown Court on 28.3.77: 'With your state of health, high blood pressure, you ought not to indulge in conduct of this kind, because you might overtax your own power and die in very unfortunate circumstances.' Unfortunate for whom?

(Women's Report, Vol. 5 No. 5)

Rape is an extreme example of man's aggression towards women. But to understand why it happens and why rape victims are treated as they are, it must be seen as only one end of a spectrum of sexual insult and assault that women are subjected to throughout their lives. The obscene comments from complete strangers in the street, the hand on your bum in a crowded train, are simply less harmful expressions of the attitudes that condone rape — that women's bodies are for men to use, and to use in a violent and degrading way.

In June 1977, Judge Mervyn Griffiths, summing up in a case where a fifteen-year-old girl was dragged from a bus-stop by four boys and raped in the woods under threat of violent attack, stated that parents who let their young daughters roam the streets of South London like 'little harlots' carried most of the blame for what happened to them (*Daily Mail* 16.7.77). He might just as well have put the blame instead on the parents of the boys who let their sons roam the streets.

Implicit in this Judge's attitude is '*a raped woman equals a prostitute equals a rapable woman*' (the slogan used by Italian feminists in their anti-rape campaign). The courts and the media go to great lengths in all rape cases to make the woman appear as a prostitute or 'harlot'. Two quite remarkable assumptions are involved here: firstly, that it is more acceptable to rape a prostitute than any other woman; and secondly that raped women tend to be 'loose women'. In fact the experience of the Rape Crisis Centre is that women of *all* ages, races, and life-styles have been raped, quite independent of their marital status or sexual orientation.

Another insidious assumption commonly invoked in rape cases is that rape is an act of uncontrollable lust, in which the man is completely taken over by his animal urges. Must we suppose that those four boys walking down the street were all simultaneously aroused beyond the point of control by the sight of a girl standing at a bus-stop? Evidence from the Rape Crisis Centre suggests the opposite. In their experience, 63 per cent of rapes are planned in advance. Rape is not an act of lust, it is an act of violence and humiliation that degrades and abuses women through an assertion of male power.

In total contradiction to the above assumption that rape is the result of uncontrollable urges in the normal man, we have the equally unlikely idea that rapists are all sex-maniacs who are in some way psychopathic and hence different from the normal male. On the contrary, psychological studies have shown that rapists in prison are the most 'normal' members of the prison population.

Only 2½ per cent of convicted rapists were sent for psychiatric treatment in 1975 (Rape Crisis Centre pamphlet *Rape and Fighting Back*). Rape is thus *not* generally committed by maniacs. Rape is hardly abnormal in a society which rewards aggressive, dominating sexual behaviour in men and denies women an autonomous sexuality by defining it only in response to men. Man is seen as the initiator and woman as consenter. Rape is the logical extension of male-dominated heterosexuality.

Our definition of rape must therefore be wider than that of the law . . . any *unwanted* forced sexual attention is a form of rape.

Legally rape is defined as 'forcible penetration of the vagina by a penis'. This suggests that sexual assault in the form of genital copulation is the most degrading form of sexual attack possible. Yet, the intent to degrade and humiliate a person sexually by whatever means should be what is significant, not how it is done: forced penetration of the anus and mouth and the use of foreign bodies such as bottles, brooms, hands and fingers are just as degrading and should constitute as grave an offence as the use of a penis.

Also the concept of *consent* is based on a sexist assumption about the nature of female sexuality. The Rape Crisis Centre states very clearly: 'the word consent implies passive agreement, acquiescence to something which is done to us by others . . . something which is allowed and in which the consenter takes no part. Consent carries no positive active idea of female initiatory and participatory sexuality. The idea that sex is a woman's duty, to be endured rather than enjoyed, is perpetrated by the concept of consent.' The need for a woman to prove lack of consent is based on the idea that women are prone to make false allegations of rape: *without consent* should be replaced by *against her will*, reflecting a woman's choice to engage in sexual relations of her own choosing.

Rape within marriage in Britain is not recognized by the law: it is perfectly legal for a man to rape his wife whenever he likes. The law only regards rape as a crime if it is committed by a man who does not 'own' the woman. (The laws of our society therefore make the connection between ordinary sex and rape ambiguous, making it possible for men to both react with anger and even disgust when *their* property is damaged, and yet to deny that rape ever took place in the majority of cases.) To approximate towards even a token amount of equality with a relationship, sexual intercourse must be a mutual decision and not a compulsory legally-sanctioned male right. Feminist campaigning for the recognition of rape within marriage could be as important both in widening the discussion on rape and as a means of raising our consciousness of our right to sexual autonomy by the abolition of the idea that a woman must always be sexually available to her husband.

It is important that rape is recognized as a means by which every man can re-enact and prove the reality of woman as the conquered sex, reminding us and them of their power by belittling our existence with a total humiliation. The reality of rape is that *any* woman can be the victim of a rape attack; she can be absolutely any age, she can be raped by her husband, boyfriend, father, friend, employer, or the local policeman, and often by groups of men. Most rapes are not committed by strangers in dark alleys but by men who are already acquainted with their victims. 'The woman-hunting season is open all years, and 24 hours out of 24.'

Many rapes are not reported because the woman feels ashamed and guilty; she has been taught to believe that she must secretly have wanted to be raped. If she does go to the police another ordeal begins; hours of questioning by police officers (there is no rule that rape victims must be questioned by women), a medical examination by a police doctor, and (possibly months later) she must relive the whole experience in court. None of the people she encounters in this process will necessarily have any training in dealing with this highly emotional situation. The rape victim needs good legal and medical advice, and above all, the opportunity to discuss the experience and the resulting problems with sympathetic people. The system makes no effort to provide this.

(Based on *Women's Report* Vol. 5 No. 5)

Rape Counselling: Someone to talk to

In November 1974 about forty women met at the Women's Liberation Workshop in London to talk about rape. At that time rape was often thought of as an American crime ('*Surely it doesn't happen in England!*') but there was a growing awareness that rape was a significant problem, and that existing organizations were not adequate to deal with it. From this original meeting a group began to plan to set up a Rape Crisis Centre. They spent most of 1975 looking for premises and getting funds, and in November of that year were given a house by the Department of the Environment; at about the same time they found a sponsor to finance the project. They have received no government finance and were refused an Urban Aid grant. We talked to Catherine, a full-time worker at the centre, about how it has developed since then:

'By the beginning of 1976 the house was ready for use, and we began to train ourselves. Obviously there was no training available for rape counsellors, so we invited agencies who we thought could help to come and talk to us about their work, including the Samaritans, the Marriage Guidance Council and doctors with experience of dealing with rape victims. We also learnt through role-playing (acting out the parts of victim and counsellor), and we learnt some co-counselling techniques.

'When we started we had different types of training; some women in the group are counsellors professionally, some have information centre experience, and I worked briefly with a rape crisis group in New York. But basically it's learning about rape that's important, and having a warm sympathetic attitude, not being judgmental.

'On March 15th 1976 the twenty-four-hour phone service opened. The office is open from 10am to 6pm, and outside those hours calls are transferred to one of our home numbers. At first we used the Post Office transfer service, but that was expensive, slow to answer and not always sympathetic to the women phoning in. So now we have an answering machine that redirects callers to our home numbers.

'We sent letters out to all the agencies that might come in contact with rape victims, like the social services, casualty departments of hospitals, VD clinics, law centres and all the police stations, explaining what we were doing and asking for some kind of feedback. We get lots of referrals from social workers, but the police have been less co-operative. Some appreciate our presence in dealing with the emotional side of the woman's experience, but others don't allow us to be with the woman when she's questioned, even if she's asked us to be there. Scotland Yard has refused to recognize us and has directed police stations not to refer women to us unless they specifically ask about us. So we're not hearing from women whose first contact is the police.

'There are now one full-time and several part-time paid workers. Normally there are two women on duty at the Centre each day, and phone duty outside office hours is done on a rota basis, planned a month in advance. We've had two training courses and are working on a third one, so now we have more women on the rota. The collective meets once a week to make decisions about the Centre; these meetings are very important for relaying information and discussing cases. Counselling is very demanding work and it's important to be able to discuss our problems with each other. Because our work is confidential we can never discuss it outside the group, so we're careful to make time to talk things out and learn from other people's experience.

'Our concern is essentially with the rape victim, we are here to help her in any way she thinks we can; if she just wants to talk about her experience that's fine, or we can give her practical information about the legal process, VD, pregnancy prevention, pregnancy testing, or abortion if necessary. If a woman comes to us before she's decided whether to report the rape to the police, then we talk the whole thing over with her. The reporting process is very unpleasant and there's no point going through it unless we both feel she's got a fairly strong chance of being taken seriously by the police.

'We don't try to persuade a woman either way. If she wants to report the rape, we'll support her right through the legal process to the end of the court case, and even afterwards, particularly if the rapist isn't convicted. The legal process then seems to be saying that this woman was not raped, and that can have a shattering impact on a woman in terms of her own feelings about what happened.

'If at any time there's a feeling that we're not the best people for a woman to talk to we can refer her to other bodies, or to individual therapists who have offered to take referrals from us. We make referrals only after full discussion with the woman concerned and only to someone we know personally and feel that she'll benefit from.

'We're willing to see friends and relatives, in fact to do anything to improve things for the victim. For example, if she's married and her husband is having trouble coming to terms with the rape, we have sympathetic men available who can talk to him. We have a room upstairs so that women can stay here in emergencies; we're keen to avoid women developing dependency relationships to us, so the maximum stay is three days, but it *hasn't been used much.*

'Our aim is to allow a woman to work through the experience and come out on top, not feel we should be doing things for her. It's her life and she must come to terms with it in her own way, with our help, and then go out and carry on.

'About half the cases we've dealt with so far have been one-off contacts who just want to talk about it. Women who were raped twenty or thirty years ago ring us up, they've never told anybody; then they hear about us and talk to us for an hour or so and say it makes them feel much better about it. Other women may want specific legal or medical advice, others are on-going contacts — some come here, others we go and see.

'Women in other areas are interested in setting up similar services, and we're trying to put them in touch with each other. We have had calls from women outside London, but it's difficult to maintain a counselling relationship in that situation, and we don't know what resources are available in other towns. We are willing to act as an information point for women all over the country who are trying to set up centres. They can come and talk to us, and we're preparing a leaflet about how we set up the Centre, the problems and so on. We think it's very important that this kind of help is offered on a local basis by women who can meet the victim and who know about local resources. We would like to see a whole network of centres developed. We also go out and talk at schools, colleges, hospitals, housewives' groups, anywhere that asks us; it's important to try to change attitudes to rape as well as to help the victims.

'There's been some criticism of us within the women's movement because we haven't openly declared ourselves to be feminists. We don't really see it as that important; the main thing is that we're a group of women helping other women. If we said in our publicity that we were a feminist group it would put some women off (if their ideas are taken from the popular press they would see us as man-hating women's libbers). We will help any woman who comes to us; we want to help her come to terms with her experience in her own way, we're not going to say to her or imply that the only way to do this is by becoming a feminist. Only if we personally feel that she may benefit from that kind of analysis will we suggest it to her.

'It's impossible to tell if the number of rapes is increasing. We only have figures for the rapes that are reported to the police, but we find that many women who have been raped come to us who would not considered going to the police. Hopefully with the increasing climate of awareness about rape women are more likely to tell someone about it.'

RAPE COUNSELLING AND RESEARCH PROJECT *Rape Crisis Centre, PO Box 42, London N6*

Action against Rape

'Direct feminist action against rape in London during the year 1977 has extended the public debate on the issue of rape within the women's liberation movement, the media and parliament. Slogans saying "What justice for Women" and "Women unite against rape" were painted around the law courts and on military monuments in the Mall — expressing women's anger at the Court of Appeal's decision to free Coldstream Guardsman Holdsworth who had violently attacked seventeen-year-old Carol Maggs.

'This kind of immediate public response exposed the obvious error of the court's decision to reduce Holdsworth's sentence of three years in prison to a six-month suspended sentence. Mr Justice Wein reasoned that Holdsworth's career as an excellent soldier would be completely destroyed if this sentence of three years was allowed to stand. This suggestion that a man's career prospects are more important than a violent sexual assault on a woman is, on its own, an outrageous example of the legal system's denial of rape as a crime.

'Justice Wein further commented that "clearly he was a man who on the night in question allowed his enthusiasm for sex to overcome his normal good behaviour". Yet not only was Carol Maggs not made love to, but the medical evidence shows that she was brutally attacked. Physical injury included three cracked ribs, severe internal injuries caused by repeated insertion of his ringed hand into her vagina, and lacerations of both ear-lobes caused by ear-rings being wrenched out. The doctor stated that the extreme swelling and bruising of her vulva would have caused great pain which he had only seen in cases of prolonged painful childbirth. This was hardly the result of normal enthusiasm for sex.

'The scars of a rape victim are unfortunately not just physical as rape is not just a physical invasion but a violation of a woman's whole being. Rape is seen as something which happens in a flash, but for the raped woman it is the beginning of a long and painful ordeal. Carol Maggs suffered paralysis from the neck down for three weeks due to shock, and had to receive psychiatric treatment for six months. It is a pity that the judge's compassion was not extended to consider the effect the attack had on Carol Maggs' career.

'It is imperative that we as women make clear to ourselves what we mean when we are asking for changes in the law on rape. Legal reforms are obviously important, to alleviate women's treatment by the courts in the short term, but it would be naive to assume that such reforms are enough. We must be fighting for a society in which rape did not exist, and not just for the containment of it by legislation.

'Although social institutions may be reformed, laws may change and the police may even establish special rape squads, reforms alone will not prevent rape whilst women still accept the special burden of caution to avoid being raped, and remain dependent on men to protect them from other men. We can retaliate directly by using our own strengths and resources. Women have taken action such as:

lists of attacks (and if possible attackers) and the car numbers of curb-crawlers have been compiled, and these have been published either in a local newspaper or in leaflets handed out to local women;

public meetings have been organized if there has been a series of attacks, to discuss methods of protecting individual women and formulating actions;

pickets have been organized outside courts and police stations where raped women have not been treated seriously and with respect;

'Wanted' posters with a photo and description of a rapist who has not been arrested have been effective in reaching the public generally.

'Action in America has been taken further: for instance, daubing the houses of known rapists, and following rapists around for days hassling them on tubes and in pubs, announcing to all within earshot that this man is a rapist. Individual women can carry water-pistols filled with dye or ink to squirt at men who accost them in the street and learning self-defence can be an important asset.

'These are some of the ways we can develop our strengths so that we no longer need to rely on our persecutors for protection.'

(Women's Report Vol. 5 No. 5)

For details of the Women Against Rape direct action campaign, see 'WOMEN AT W.A.R.' (see Books about Rape).

Rights of Rape Victims

Each victim of sexual assault should have the right:

to be treated with dignity and respect during questioning;

to be educated about procedures and the law in a rape case and her role as a witness for the state;

to free medical and psychological treatment by sensitive, trained personnel;

to choose what preventive medical measures will be taken;

to the best possible collection of evidence for court;

to have support resources like rape crisis groups, to be accompanied by sympathetic friends, etc.;

to legal representation that supports the victim since the victim cannot have legal counsel of her choice as can the defendant (because it is the *state*, not the woman, who is prosecuting the rapist);

to a preliminary hearing in each case when an arrest is made;

to personal privacy (prior sexual experience should not be admissable as evidence);

to be considered a credible witness equal to one in any other crime;

to consent to sexual relations with the spouse without violence and coercion (at the moment a man is legally unable to rape his own wife);

to be protected from any violent sexual assault regardless of the weapon used, and regardless of which part of the body is violated (penetration by bottles, etc., or forced oral or anal sex are not legally rape);

to submit to rape from fear alone without this being seen as consent, or to ward off the attack without being liable for prosecution herself.

These are the demands of the Rape Crisis Center, PO Box 21005, Washington, DC 20009, which acts as a national clearing-house for Rape Crisis groups around the US.

Rape Prevention Tactics

We would like every woman to be trained in self-defence, but this isn't easy to do, and even so, this in itself won't stop rape. We must, as women, feel stronger about ourselves, and this cannot happen unless we are aware of our situations, and of how we might control some of them. The following rape prevention tactics are only one step in gaining control of our lives, but they are an important step.

WHERE YOU LIVE

Many rapes and attacks happen in the houses and flats where women live. The landlords do not often provide adequate security, and they should be pressured to do so.

1. There should be lights on all entrances where you live.
2. Be aware of places where men might hide; under stairs or between buildings.
3. If you live by yourself or with other women, don't put your full name on your mailbox or in the phonebook; use first initials instead (e.g. S. Smith, instead of Sue Smith).
4. Know your neighbours, and which ones you can trust in an emergency.
5. Always find out who is at your door before you open it.
6. When returning home at night, have your keys ready before you get to the door.
7. If there is a suspicious person in the lift with you, push the emergency button and all the floor buttons. Get off as soon as the lift stops at a floor.

ON THE STREET

How you look is important. An attacker expects a passive victim, so if you walk slowly or in a daze, you will seem untogether to many men. Walking at a steady pace, looking confident, and knowing where you are going makes a difference.

1. Try not to overload yourself with packages, large handbags, or books. Pockets are more practical, keeping your hands free. (Most men on the street have their hands free.)
2. Dress for use: many styles are nice, but they can make it harder to move quickly. Capes, scarves, long necklaces and the like are easy to grab. Tight skirts and trousers make it hard to run.
3. At night, don't walk through dark patches of waste ground, parks, or other places where men might hang about or hide.
4. Don't walk through a group of men. Walk around them, or if possible cross the road.
5. If you are alone, be extra aware of what's around you.
6. Carry a whistle wrapped around your wrist and use it when you think you should.
7. Don't walk alone if you're upset, drunk or high on drugs. Ask a friend to go with you.
8. Don't walk too close to the inside of the pavement, near bushes, alley entrances, driveways, or entrances to private places.
9. Don't walk home the same way every day. (Rapists often follow their victims and plan the attack beforehand.)

'LEGAL WEAPONS' AS PROTECTION

Weapons should not be relied upon because they can be taken away from you and used against you. If you are confronted with an attacker's weapon, yours might not do any good: they are hard to handle correctly, and often they aren't in your hand when you need them. (A hatpin, for example, is useless at the bottom of your bag if someone grabs you.) The following weapons should be used *only to stop an attack with enough time to get away.* Don't worry about winning when your life is being threatened:

worry about saving your life and getting away. Remember, an attacker will usually suspect a weak, unaware victim, and any effort to fight back will surprise him.

1. LIGHTED CIGARETTE: Smash it out on area of his face.
2. PLASTIC LEMON: They will squirt as far as fifteen feet. Fill it with 'caution' liquids such as ammonia. Always aim for the eyes; momentary blindness gives you time to get away. Same idea holds for spray cans (hairspray, perfume).
3. CHEAP, HEAVY RING: If you can afford one, wear it with the heavy part inside and go for a good, strong slap in the face of the attacker.
4. UMBRELLA: Place one hand in the centre of it and the other hand behind it. Use quick jabbing motion to neck or stomach. You can also place one hand on each end and force it down against attacker's face or neck.
5. HATPIN: Carry it in your hand, tightly, or pin it to your clothing. With your hand wrapped around it, scrape it across face or jab at the neck.

SOME BASICS ON YOUR BODY

1. If you just throw your hands out for striking, they can be grabbed by an attacker and used to get you down.
2. If an attacker is close to your body, use your elbows for striking the neck or his sides, or even his stomach to take him by surprise.
3. Any strikes with your hands in fists should go right to the face; eyes, ears, nose, and mouth are weak areas, and if force is used, he might be caught off his guard.
4. If he's really close to you, never forget your voice in the ears, and your teeth.
5. If you want to kick, don't just throw your leg around; aim at his knees, this will knock him off balance. (If you aim too high, you might lose balance.)
6. Don't always think you can knee an attacker in the groin; he will usually protect this first. If you must go to the groin, use your hands to grab, then pull.
7. Pulling hair or clapping your hands over his hair are fairly effective.
8. Your most reliable strong points to think about are forehead, hands, elbows, knees and feet. Know what you can and can't do with them.

IF YOU MUST HITCHHIKE

Hitchhiking isn't a sensible or safe thing to do, but many women find it a necessity. If there is any other way of getting around use it.

1. Try not to hitch by yourself, and especially not at night.
2. Hitch where there is lots of traffic; stay away from deserted places.
3. Never accept a ride with more than one man. Don't be afraid to refuse a group.
4. When entering the car, look to see if someone is hiding in the back seat.
5. Make sure there is an inside door handle that works on your side.
6. Make sure that the man is fully clothed and his trousers are zipped up.
7. Don't take a ride from a man who changes directions to pick you up, like making a turn, or changing blinkers to turn a different way.
8. Always keep your window partly rolled down in case you have to scream or blow a whistle.
9. Ask him what direction he's headed in before you tell him where you're going.
10. If you carry a bag, hold it in your lap with your right hand, and keep the left hand on the door handle. The bag can be used against an attack, and you'll need to get out quickly. Your right elbow can be jabbed into his ribs.

There may come a time when you have to jump out of a moving car. (This also holds true if you are forced into a car.) Make sure that you can roll to a clear spot away from other moving cars. Throw your shoulders first with your left hand near your body. Tuck your head in to your neck and keep your back curved. Let your feet follow. It'll hurt, but if you fear danger, and you aren't near any stop signs or lights, then this may be your only choice. Also, whether you are in or near a car with a threatening man, remember the licence plate number of the car.

We know that it's impossible to follow all of these suggestions. We also know that in some cases, these tactics haven't worked. They can help you, but they are not foolproof.

(from a pamphlet issued by the Rape Crisis Center, Washington)

Books about Rape

AGAINST OUR WILL: Men, Women and Rape
by Susan Bronmiller, Penguin, 95p
'Rape is nothing less than a conscious process of
intimidation by which *all men* keep *all women* in a
state of fear.' This book discusses rape in the past
and today, how it has been used by men, and the
myths that surround it. In some ways a horrify-
ing and depressing account, it is nonetheless essential reading if we are to come to a feminist understanding of rape.

THE FACTS OF RAPE
by Barbara Tomer, Arrow, 90p
A somewhat sensational book which lacks any
analysis of the causes of rape; this book examines
rape in Britain, the facts, and the attitudes of the
police, the courts and the medical profession.

THE RAPE CONTROVERSY
*by Anna Coote and Tess Gill, from National
Council for Civil Liberties, 186 Kings Cross Road,
London WC1, 50p*
This is a clear and interesting examination of the
law on rape and how it should be changed, the
myths and facts about rape, what happens in court,
and a section on what to do if it happens to you;
a good, brief introduction to a difficult subject.

WOMEN, CRIME AND CRIMINOLOGY: A Feminist Critique
*by Carol Smart, Routledge and Kegan Paul,
£4.95*

RAPE CRISIS CENTRE: First Report
*from Rape Counselling and Research Project, PO
Box 42, London N6, 30p*
An account of the first year of Britain's first Rape
Crisis project, how it began, how it operates, their
experience of the police, the media, etc. It would
be particularly useful for groups trying to start a
centre. There is a good resources section.

WOMEN AT W.A.R.
*from Falling Wall Press, 79 Richmond Road,
Montpelier, Bristol 6, 50p*
Women against Rape (W.A.R.) started as a small
group demonstrating and organising direct action
in the courts, parliament, government offices and
the national media to force a recognition that rape
is a serious crime against women and should be
treated as such. In 1978 Women against Rape held
a national conference and set itself up as a national
campaign with local groups, fighting not only to
change attitudes about rape, but also for financial
assistance for rape victims and for recognition
that criminal rape can occur *within* marriage.
Women at W.A.R. gives a brief history of the
Women Against Rape campaign, and it also is the
first collection of personal accounts of rape to
come from Britain including accounts by a married
woman raped by her husband, a black woman, a
woman raped on the streets on her way home
from work as a stripper and a lesbian woman.
Women Against Rape intends to publish a regular
campaign newsletter. For further information
about Women Against Rape contact 01-221 5754
(W.A.R. London) or 0272-422810 (W.A.R.
Bristol).

HOW TO START A RAPE CRISIS CENTER
*from Rape Crisis Center, PO Box 21005, Washing-
ton DC 20009*
This and other information produced by the
Center would be of interest to groups in Britain.

MANIFESTO AGAINST RAPE: Patriarchal Justice and the Threat of Rape
*des Feministes Revolutionnaires, in Cat Call, Issue
No. 6*

FIGHTING BACK: SELF-DEFENCE

'Anger or revolt that does not get into the muscles remains a figment of the imagination.'
(Simone de Beauvoir, *The Second Sex*)

Because women are brought up to be weak and passive, we often find it difficult to defend
ourselves when physically attacked. Little girls are not encouraged to fight, climb trees, play
rough games or do any of the other things that can make you feel confident of your own
strength. Besides being physically weak, we often have a mental attitude that makes it hard for
us to hurt someone deliberately, even if they are hurting us.

The feeling that we are unable to defend ourselves against rape or beatings can limit our
lives in many ways; we may be afraid to go out alone at night, or scared to stand up for ourselves in our relationships with men, in case we get hit.

Many women are no longer prepared to accept this, and instead are learning various forms of self-defence. They often find that this has other benefits besides simply knowing what techniques to use if you're attacked. The physical exercise involved in learning something like karate or judo makes you feel healthier and stronger and enables you to do all sorts of things better. It can increase your mental confidence in yourself as a human being, so that you feel more in control of your whole life. And we cannot ignore the fact that the fight against women's oppression is a *fight*. Oppression maintained by force may have to be fought by force.

At the moment there are few self-defence or 'martial arts' courses taught by and for women. Many local authorities, in large towns at least, run beginners courses in karate, judo and aikido; and you can find out where from your local Adult Education Department or library information service. These will usually be cheaper (and often free if you are on social security or a low income) than private clubs and will give you an idea of what it is all about before you spend a lot of money on training.

If you're going to a mixed class it's a good idea for several women to go together; you'll feel less self-conscious that way, and can practise together at home. Beware of the instructor who lets the women off lightly and doesn't push them as hard as the men. You may not be able to do everything at first, but you should at least be expected to try.

Self-defence classes teach a combination of techniques taken from the other 'martial arts', plus a few extra. Some women's groups have set up their own classes; all you need is someone who can teach you the techniques and a room to practise in (your community centre or a local school may be willing to let you use a room), and if possible it's good to have mats to fall on! If enough women get together and approach the local authority, through the Adult Education Department (in the telephone book) or your Community Education Officer, they may be willing to arrange self-defence classes as part of their adult education programme.

BOOKS

There are any number of books available on karate, judo, etc., and there doesn't seem to be much to choose between them. Most show men demonstrating the techniques. Ask your instructor to recommend one or simply pick the cheapest.

EVERYWOMAN'S GUIDE TO SELF DEFENCE
by Kathleen Hudson, Collins, £2.95
A very well-illustrated book of techniques and ideas you could use to get yourself out of sticky situations. Clear photographs of, for example, what to do if you're attacked by two men at once, or how to deal with the persistent groper in the cinema. A bit expensive, but it would be worthwhile for a group of women to buy it between them, especially if you change from all the machismo men in the kung-fu books.

VOICES FROM WOMEN'S LIBERATION
Signet, 70p
This book includes an interesting article on 'Karate as Self-Defence for Women', which is an account by three women of why they wanted to learn karate, the problems, and how they feel they have benefited from it. Much of what they say echoes our own experience of starting to learn karate.

SPARE RIB: No. 55
This issue contains a six-page special on Self-Defence.

ADDRESSES

ADULT EDUCATION CLASSES
For local classes, contact the Adult Education Department of your Local Education Authority or ask at the library.

BRITISH KARATE CONTROL COMMISSION
4—16 Deptford Bridge, London SE8
The Commission will give you information on karate and kung-fu clubs.

WOMEN'S ARTS ALLIANCE
10 Cambridge Terrace Mews, London NW1
The Alliance holds all-woman karate classes.

10
UP AGAINST THE STATE

GETTING OUR RIGHTS

Woman's status in contemporary society is not only a matter of our position and relationships. Many aspects of our position as 'second-class citizens' are enshrined in the law of the land, making it difficult or impossible for individual women to break out of their subordination. Although our legal status has improved since the days when a married woman couldn't own property, even the Sex Discrimination Act leaves vital areas of our lives untouched. Government functions such as social security and the taxation system have been left out of the legislation, so that we are still defined as dependent on men by bodies that play a large part in our lives. As long as we are legally dependent on men, we will find it hard to think and act as independent people and first-class citizens.

Sex Discrimination

The Sex Discrimination Act came into force on 29 December 1975, and, in the government's own words, the Act 'makes sex discrimination unlawful in employment, training and related matters . . . in education, in the provision of goods, facilities and services, and in the disposal and management of premises'. It does *not* make sex discrimination completely illegal, neither does it repeal all existing laws which discriminate against women (for example, income tax legislation and the laws governing supplementary benefit). It simply makes sex discrimination unlawful in certain specified areas. Nor does the Act allow 'positive discrimination' in favour of women; for instance, an employer can encourage women to take up a particular job previously done only by men, and can provide training for her to do so, but when it comes to actually employing someone to do this job, the employer must not treat the woman applicant more favourably in order to achieve a better balance between the sexes.

The Act does nothing to alter the factors which prevent women from taking up employment opportunities, such as the lack of alternative childcare, the burden of doing two jobs, one in the home and one outside, and an education system that teaches little girls that they won't need a career because they'll be getting married.

WHAT THE ACT SAYS:

Employment: It is now illegal for an employer to discriminate (i.e. treat a person of one sex less favourably than a person of the other sex) when recruiting workers, for instance by refusing to offer someone a job on the grounds of their sex. Certain jobs, where sex is a 'genuine occupational qualification' (for example, in the theatre) do not come under the Act. It is also illegal to dscriminate against people already in employment, for instance by offering them unequal chances of promotion or unequal access to training facilities and so on. Trade unions and employers' associations can no longer refuse to allow women to join.

Goods, Facilities, Services and Premises: It is now unlawful for anyone providing the public with goods, facilities, services or premises to discriminate on the grounds of sex. This applies to places of entertainment, facilities for banking, insurance, credit and the like and the services of any profession or trade. Certain facilities can be restricted to one sex where it is necessary to preserve 'decency and privacy', and religious establishments can discriminate where the religious doctrine demands it. It is also illegal to discriminate when letting houses or other premises (again there are certain exceptions).

Education: Educational establishments cannot discriminate against women by refusing to admit them on the grounds of sex, or by providing facilities to one sex that are not provided to the other. This means, for instance, that medical schools can no longer operate quota systems which let in only a certain number of women, regardless of their qualifications; schools cannot refuse boys the chance to learn cookery, or girls woodwork. However, single-sex schools are still allowed under the Act.

Advertisements: The Act makes it illegal for anyone to publish, or place for publication, an advertisement which indicates that they intend to commit a discriminatory act. Job advertisements cannot use words like postman or salesgirl, which imply that the job is only open to one sex, unless it is made clear that the job is open to both. However, there are ways of putting a woman off applying for a job; for example:

> 'Bath attendant required. Occasional cleaning of men's changing room.'
> 'Factory workers wanted. Occasional night shift.'
> 'Engineer required. Must be apprentice trained, plus five years experience.'

Some of these subterfuges have been declared to be contrary to the Act (must be prepared to wear a skirt', etc.), whilst others have managed to get round the spirit of the Act. One reaction to the Equal Opportunities Commission's attempt to promote equality in employment was shown by the *Yorkshire Evening Post*, which in 1976 published the following comments:

> The deputy chairman of the Equal Opportunities Commission, Lady Howe (or should it be Person Howe?) administered warm praise the other day to a London evening newspaper which, she said, 'was doing a great deal to get the message over'. To win this approval, the newspaper concerned is obliged to perpetrate such follies as advertisements for male or female chambermaids and male or female airport ground hostesses.
> Not to worry! The day must be at hand when the ridiculous Equal Opportunities Commission will be carried away on gales of shrieking laughter.

HOW YOU USE THE ACT

Complaints about employment should be taken to an industrial tribunal. If your income is low you may be able to get legal aid to help you with this. Your union should also be able to help you. Complaints about education, or the provision of housing, goods facilities and services should be brought before a county court in England and Wales, or a sheriff's court in Scotland (but education complaints must first be notified to the Secretary of State for Education). Only the Equal Opportunities Commission (the body set up to oversee the working of the Act) can bring proceedings in the case of discriminatory practices or discriminatory advertisements (discriminatory practices are any requirements or conditions that are so off-putting to women that no woman ever applies, and as a result no woman is refused).

WHERE TO GET HELP

The Sex Discrimination Act is far from perfect, but it won't be any use at all unless we as women make use of it to fight for our rights in as many ways as possible. The thought of going through complicated legal proceedings often makes people give up before they start. But you can get help: your union should be able to give you advice and assistance; your local Citizen's Advice Bureau or Neighbourhood Law Centre should also help. And some women are getting together to help each other use this act and build up experience of dealing with cases.

Women's Rights Action Groups

The Brighton Women's Rights Action Group was set up to keep an eye on how the Sex Discrimination and Equal Pay Acts were working, to inform women of their rights under these Acts, and to help fight individual cases. They spent the first few months making contact with people who could help them or might need their help: solicitors, local government officials, local political parties, women's groups, trade unions, and local newspapers and magazines. The Citizen's Advice Bureau agreed to display their leaflets and to refer relevant cases to them. Although the majority of local solicitors were unsympathetic, one or two women with legal training did become involved in the group.

One evening a week, members of the group were available at the women's centre to offer advice and support to any woman who wanted to fight for her rights, particularly under the two Acts, but they also helped with divorce, maintenance, social security or any other problems. They have an observer at all industrial tribunal cases concerning Equal Pay or Sex Discrimination; a member of the group phones the industrial tribunal (the number of your local tribunal should be in the telephone book) once a week to find out if any cases are coming up, and then arranges for someone to be present. They make notes of what goes on, especially any important points of principle that arise, so that this information can be used in preparing future cases; for this same reason, they keep newspaper accounts of the cases.

Group meetings are used to learn about the Acts themselves. Judy and Gina, two members of the group, felt that solicitors who had been involved in fighting cases had often shown their ignorance: 'A lot of them obviously haven't even read the Acts, and don't know the ins and outs. The Acts are written in very legalistic language, and there are so many "get-out" clauses for employers. Just a word or two can make all the difference; we spent the whole of one meeting discussing a single phrase.' Members of the group have attended lectures and courses in London organized by the National Council for Civil Liberties and the Legal Action Group, and have found these very interesting and helpful.

The group produces a newsletter four times a year, which reports cases and examines different parts of the Acts. It also helps provide funds for their work: women 'join' the group for 50p and receive the newsletter; and any surplus money goes towards expenses for attending courses and fighting cases. The second issue of their newsletter explained why fund-raising was so essential:

> 'We particularly want to help women take their cases to the appeal court. This is important in order to establish proper precedents and case law, especially in view of the obscurity of some parts of these laws and the various interpretations given by different industrial tribunals around the country, which are sometimes contradictory. As so many decisions have gone against women with apparently clear-cut cases in their favour, we think it's important to encourage women to continue their fight by appealing to a higher court and thereby clarifying and testing the meaning of these acts in practice. This is not to say that after recourse to the appeal court every deserving case will be won, as the laws will still contain loopholes.

For both making a claim and appealing, financial support is essential, as employers can more easily afford legal action than the women who are trying to struggle for their rights. Legal aid is not always available and does not meet all the costs. Only £25 worth of free advice can be obtained under the Law Society's Green Form Scheme; this is subject to a fairly stringent means test, and it does not cover professional representation at tribunals at all. This is because tribunals are supposed to be informal places where both sides meet and discuss the case, and solicitors are not strictly necessary. Of course, employers are always represented by solicitors, while the woman may not be able to afford one.

Judy and Gina felt that the Acts were very difficult to use:

> 'It is often one person fighting a whole company, which is always hard; then the complicated procedures and the expense can really put you off. Many cases are settled out of

court, at the pre-trial hearings, so that the principles involved are never put to the test. What seems to be coming out of our work and the work of other groups around the country is that really the Acts are worth very little. Women who do take up cases spend a great deal of time and energy preparing them, and get very little in the end, even if they win. And in the first four months since the Acts came into force, there were only eighteen successful cases out of 1,754 women who started industrial tribunal action.'

Although the original idea of Women's Rights Action Group was to help women who wanted to take up cases with the tribunals, what seems to have happened is that women have dealt with the cases themselves, and Women's Rights Action Group has become a sort of information service. But the members feel that there is still a lot of potential for the group:

'The knowledge that the Women's Rights Action Group exists, that there is a body of people who are concerned and interested and prepared to fight if necessary, does put more pressure on the courts and tribunals. And the women who have been involved have learnt such a lot about how the law works. There are now more women who would know how to fight a case. We think it's really important to go into these Acts, find out how to use them if they can be used, and if they can't be used, show them up for what they are.'

WOMEN'S RIGHTS ACTION GROUP *c/o 9 St Michael's Place, Brighton, Sussex*

Another group recently set up to campaign around women's rights is the Wales Women's Rights Committee. They have produced a detailed statement of their aims and methods, which shows very clearly that fighting for women's rights is not just a matter of trying to change a few outdated laws; the entire state apparatus, including the law, education, and the Health Service, maintains discrimination against women in tiny details as well as in glaring inequalities. The group is concerned with the following areas:

1. *Taxation, Social Security and Pensions:* the extension of the provisions of the Sex Discrimination Act to the fields of taxation, social security and pensions; the guaranteeing to women of the same tax allowances and the same insurance and retirement benefits as men, with the proviso that this shall mean levelling up.

2. *Equal Employment Opportunities:* the rigorous implementation of the Sex Discrimination Act and associated legislation relating to employment opportunities and non-discriminatory practices.

3. *Protective Legislation:* the improvement and updating of legislation relating to hours of work and its extension to men also; the basing of protective legislation on norms relating to both men and women; the securing of adequate compensation for industrial injury; the drafting and implementation of legislation to protect the rights of outworkers; the encouraging of the setting up of outworkers co-operatives.

4. *Educational Opportunities:* the implementation of the provisions of the Sex Discrimination Act relating to education; the elimination of sex discrimination of all levels in education; the provision of loans, scholarships, fellowships, grants and training programmes under government auspices on an equal basis with males, including on-the-job training programmes; the elimination of unnecessary segregation and separation in facilities and curricula for girls and boys; the removal of admission quotas based on sex; the assurance of non-sexist academic and vocational counselling; the elimination of sexist bias in textbooks and course content: 'We seek the appointment of more women at decision-making levels in education. In accordance with the law we support positive discrimination in training and education for both men and women where this is necessary to compensate for inequalities which have resulted from previous discriminatory practices.'

5. *Developmental Childcare:* the provision of a national network of high quality nurseries and childcare centres available to all citizens on the same basis as state schools, parks and libraries; adequate to the needs of all children including those of pre-school age and adolescents, and to the needs of parents and communities, through appropriate services and schedules.

6. *Family Responsibility Leave:* the implementation and improvement of the provisions of the Employment Protection Act, such as the extension of the period of maternity leave, including the period of paid leave, the shortening of the period of employment necessary for this leave to be granted, and improved maternity benefits; also acknowledgment of 'family responsibility leave' for both sexes as a necessary absence to discharge family obligations including, for instance, those to sick children and elderly parents.

7. *Right of Control over our own Reproductive Lives:* the wider availability of birth-control information; education for greater understanding of all aspects of human sexuality; freer laws governing abortion; permission for medical treatment to be the responsibility of the individual and not restricted by a spouse's veto.

8. *Health:* the devoting of adequate resources in the National Health Service to matters affecting the health of women, including the development of preventative medicine such as cancer screening facilities and clinics.

9. *A Chance for Women in Poverty:* the revision of the laws respecting social security to provide a minimum income without prejudice to the parent's right to remain at home to care for children; the revision of the cohabitation rule and other practices which rob women of privacy; recognition of a woman's right to work if she so wishes.

10. *Revision of Marriage, Divorce and Family Law:* the equalization of rights and opportunities of men and women to rent, buy and own property, to establish domicile and retain or adopt nationality, and to maintain individual identity and economic independence; the equalization of their obligations towards each other and towards the care and custody of children, and to support a dependent spouse through a period of economic readjustment upon termination of the marriage; the promotion of marriage as an equal partnership in all aspects; and the extension of such rights and obligations to unmarried couples.

11. *Assault:* the ensuring that laws relating to rape and other assault and the implementation of these laws afford adequate protection to women.

12. *Full Participation:* the full participation of women in public affairs (including politics, commerce, industry, trade unions, professions, voluntary organizations, leisure matters); full representation of women to public bodies, industrial tribunals, commissions, etc., including positive efforts aimed at encouraging the nomination of women to these bodies.

13. *The Image of Women in the Mass Media:* insistence on the portrayal of women in multiple roles as positive, competent and contributing adults, in and out of the home.

14. *Ecumenism, Women and Religion:* the appointment and acknowledgment of women in religious life as spiritual leaders, including their ordination as clergy.

15. *Voluntary Work:* the encouragement of women to have the time and opportunity to do voluntary work to use their energies in policy-making and change-directed activities which are directed at the roots of social problems.

WALES WOMEN'S RIGHTS COMMITTEE *19 Ovington Terrace, Canton, Cardiff*

The Demand for Independence

The fifth demand of the women's movement is for legal and financial independence for all women; this is seen by the women campaigning around it as an attempt to co-ordinate the struggles against all the various ways in which government policy forces women to be dependent on men. It is extremely difficult for a woman to think of herself as a full person in her own right when laws and government regulations continually contradict this idea, and tell her firmly that she is in fact a second-class citizen, dependent on her husband. The Sex Discrimination Act does not cover social security, taxation, matrimonial and family law, and therefore leaves untouched the problems of a woman's situation within her family and home.

Taxation: When she marries, a woman loses her right to keep her tax position private, as all allowances and rebates are handled through her husband's Tax Office (there is a complicated procedure for applying to be assessed separately, but this can take up to two years to come through). She cannot keep her financial affairs private from him, as he can from her. A married woman's tax rebates go to her husband, unless *he* asks for them to be sent to her; tax relief for children automatically goes to the father, unless the couple are legally separated. What is more, if you do leave your husband, any tax rebate due to you for the period before you separated will be sent to him. (See also: Income Tax in Women at Work)

National Insurance: The Social Security Benefits Act and the Social Security Act, due to be implemented in 1978, will remove some of the inequalities faced by women, but still does not recognize that many men and women share in the economic support of the family, and that at least some men want to share in childcare. A married woman who pays full National Insurance contributions will get full sickness and unemployment benefits for herself, but will still not be able to claim extra benefits for her spouse and children, as a man can, unless her husband is actually incapable of employment. The recently introduced invalidity pension and invalid care allowance both discriminate against married and cohabiting women; to get the first, they must not only be ill, but incapable of 'normal household duties'. The second allowance is for a man or woman who gives up paid employment to look after a sick or disabled person; but married or cohabiting women are not eligible, presumably on the grounds that they ought to be at home doing this work anyway.

Supplementary Benefits: A married woman cannot claim supplementary benefit while she is living with her husband. *He* must claim, and *he* receives the benefit. So a married woman whose husband doesn't give her enough to live on cannot turn to Social Security, and no married woman who stays at home to look after children has a right to any independent income of her own. The message is clear: as far as the state is concerned, a married woman is no longer a person. The much-hated cohabitation rule follows from this: a woman living with a man 'as his wife' cannot claim benefit for herself or her children; the man is presumed to be supporting them all, even though neither the state nor the woman can force him to do so.

Family Income Supplement is paid to families with children where the 'head' of the family is in full-time, low-paid work. A single woman with children who works full-time can claim Family Income Supplement. But where a man and woman are included in the family, it must be the *man* who works; couples who have decided, or have been forced by circumstances, to 'swap roles' so that the woman works and the man stays at home, cannot claim. Once again the law reinforces the traditional roles of men and women, and puts financial obstacles in the way of people seeking change.

Campaigning for Legal and Financial Independence

The Women's Liberation Campaign for Legal and Financial Independence was set up at the National Women's Liberation conference in Edinburgh in 1974, and the group called their own conference to get the campaign going in December of that year. At that time there was a great deal of legislation going through Parliament which directly concerned women, and the group hoped to be able to provide a feminist perspective on the changes that were being proposed.

For the first year they acted as a lobbying group, and they put a lot of their energy into producing a pamphlet, *The Demand for Independence*, detailing the ways in which government policy reinforces the position of women. One of the group got on the Jimmy Young show just after the Sex Discrimination Act came into force, and sparked off floods of mail to the group and reports of their activities in the press. They feel that the techniques of publicity are worth knowing, and this enables them to reach women who would not otherwise come in contact with the ideas of the women's movement.

Now that the campaign is well-known to the press, they are often contacted and asked to comment on particular items of news that concern women, and have appeared in the popular women's magazines. They were also asked to give evidence to the Royal Commission on Income and Wealth, and put forward the idea that income should be redistributed between husband and wife, not just between family units.

Many women who do not consider themselves feminists are sympathetic to the issues of 'women's rights', and may think that changes in the law are all that are needed to put things right. But the campaigners themselves see the laws as just part of the forces that form the way women see themselves; laws, social attitudes and emotional expectations all link up as part of a system that oppresses women and makes them see themselves as dependent on men.

The campaign group would like to be able to spend more time on theoretical analysis of the issues involved but often find themselves overwhelmed by the day-to-day demands of practical campaigning. At the moment, however, the group is going through a quieter period after producing their 'Discussion Kit'.

Other women who are interested in the campaign can get the Discussion Kit to take to their own groups and decide if this is an area they'd like to work around; local groups can put pressure on their own Social Security offices and so on as well as campaigning for changes in legislation. At the moment there are about half a dozen Legal and Financial Independence Campaign groups around the country.

The existing groups are keen to get other women involved, and send speakers out to all sorts of groups. Their pamphlet and kit have sold well and have to be constantly updated as legislation changes. At a period when many people seem to think that all women's problems have been solved by the Equal Pay and Sex Discrimination Acts, this group is doing a vital job in keeping women's continuing oppression in the public eye.

WOMEN'S LIBERATION CAMPAIGN FOR LEGAL AND FINANCIAL INDEPENDENCE *214 Stapleton Hall Road, London N4*
The group will also provide the addresses of local groups in the campaign.

Getting our Rights

GROUPS

EQUAL OPPORTUNITIES COMMISSION
Overseas House, Quay Street, Manchester
Many people think that the Equal Opportunities Commission is only concerned with the working of the Equal Pay and Sex Discrimination Acts, but the duties laid down for the Commission by the Sex Discrimination Act are much wider.
These duties are:

a) to work towards the elimination of discrimination;

b) to promote equality of opportunity between men and women generally;

c) to keep under review the workings of the Sex Discrimination Act and Equal Pay Act, and to draw up proposals for amending these Acts when they or the Secretary of State thinks it necessary.

The Commission has power to investigate and make recommendations on anything that may put women at a disadvantage; this could cover educational practices, patterns of discrimination in particular industries, and so on. It also has specific powers: it is the only body that can take action about discriminatory advertisements; it will help individuals wanting to bring cases under the Equal Pay and Sex Discrimination Acts, though it won't actually conduct a case unless it involves an important point of principle; it can bring cases to industrial tribunals and county courts (as individuals can), and can issue non-discrimination notices and obtain county court injunctions.

Individuals or groups can report discriminatory practices and advertisements to the Commission and can write to them suggesting areas they should investigate. The Commission also makes small grants to organizations and projects concerned with getting our rights.

NATIONAL COUNCIL FOR CIVIL LIBERTIES
186 King's Cross Road, London WC1
The NCCL has a full-time women's rights officer who deals with all questions concerning women's rights. They can take up individual cases, help you find sympathetic lawyers, advise you on what your rights are and how to get them. They have also published many very useful pamphlets on subjects of interest to women. The NCCL women's rights work is supported in part by a 'collective fund' which involves the collection of a large number of small donations. The NCCL itself is a membership organization, and relies on its supporters (both affiliated organizations and individuals) to continue its work.

RIGHTS OF WOMEN
2 St Paul's Road, London N1
ROW is a group of women trying to set up a national legal resource centre available to individuals and organizations working to extend and enforce women's rights. They have started a free legal advice service for any woman with a legal problem, but especially dealing with sex discrimination, employment, matrimonial and welfare issues.

CHILD POVERTY ACTION GROUP
1 Macklin Street, London WC2
CPAG campaigns to improve government policy on low-income families, and gives direct help to people trying to claim their welfare rights. Local groups provide information on available benefits and help with appeals. CPAG has campaigned against the cohabitation rule for years, and one of its major concerns is to point out ways in which married women are discriminated against by the Social Security system. They produce a quarterly journal called *Poverty*, as well as pamphlets and a research series; and they also publish a welfare rights bulletin for advisory agencies and Social Services Departments.

RELEASE
1 Elgin Avenue, London W9
Although mainly concerned with advising and campaigning on non-medical drugs, Release also gives help and advice on other legal problems, including matrimonial difficulties, supplementary benefits, and the Equal Pay and Sex Discrimination Acts. They have recently redesigned their newsletter into an attractive and lively magazine, *News Release*.

SIX POINT GROUP
51 Umpfreville Road, London N4
This is a non-party political organization working to establish equality for women on economic, legal, moral, social, occupational and political matters.

LEGAL ACTION GROUP
28a Highgate Road, London NW5
LAG is a group of lawyers and others who are concerned to improve legal services to the community, particularly to people living in 'deprived areas'. LAG does *not* advise members of the public direct. They organize seminars and courses on aspects of social and welfare law and citizens' rights. They produce the informative *LAG Bulletin* which provides information of interest both to the lawyer and the concerned individual. They have a list of addresses of law centres and legal advice centres throughout Britain.

CLAIMANTS UNIONS
As the name suggests, these are groups of people who are claiming state benefits (including the unemployed, single-parent families, pensioners and the disabled) who get together to fight for their rights. Local groups tend to come and go, but you can get the present address of your local claimants union from East London Claimants Union, c/o Dame Colet House, Ben Jonson Road, London E1. A number of useful rights guides are produced by Claimants Publications, 19 Carlyle Road, Birmingham.

BOOKS

WOMEN'S RIGHTS: A Practical Guide
by Anna Coote and Tess Gill, Penguin, £1.25
A completely revised and extended edition of this comprehensive handbook was published in 1977. It covers everything from equal pay to education, contraception to custody, housing to hire purchase. It gives a clear account of the working of often complicated procedures and shows where to go for further advice. The writers point out clearly how the law discriminates against women, but also tells how it can be used to defend our rights. It is a very detailed guide, set out so it is easily read.

RIGHTS FOR WOMEN
by Patricia Hewitt, National Council for Civil Liberties, 65p
This is a guide to the Sex Discrimination Act, Equal Pay Act, paid maternity leave, pension schemes and unfair dismissal. A straightforward and easily understood guide to the legal position of women, what is wrong with the law and how employers try to get round it. The section on 'How to get your rights' sets out the procedures for making complaints and explains each stage thoroughly. It is a very useful guide for individuals or groups who want to take a case to court.

MANCHESTER WOMEN'S HANDBOOKS: Book One, Social Security; Book Two, Getting Your Own Home
from Manchester Law Centre, 595 Stockport Road, Manchester, 20p each
These are two well-done, practical and cheap handbooks, which cover many of the day-to-day problems that people encounter such as lost or late giros, ways to get money if you're desperate, when a woman must leave the marital home at once . . . Book One gives a clear explanation of the things a woman needs to know when she has no means of supporting herself, or is on a low income. Book Two covers divorce, separations, injunctions and basic housing rights.

OFFICIAL LEAFLETS
The Equal Opportunities Commission publishes free leaflets and a guide to the Sex Discrimination Act giving basic information about what the Act means and how to use it. The Department of Employment publishes free leaflets and a guide to the Equal Pay Act (from your local office).

THE UNEQUAL BREADWINNER
by Ruth Lister and Leo Wilson, National Council for Civil Liberties, 30p
An account of the economic obstacles the state puts in the way of couples who decide to 'swap roles', that is, where the woman is the full-time wage-earner while the man stays at home to care for children and run the house. Horrific case stories that make you really angry at the injustice of women's institutionalized dependence on men. Especially worth reading if you are trying to work towards a different sexual division of labour, so you'll at least know what you're getting yourself into!

WOMEN AND HOUSING
by Glasgow Women's Legal and Financial Independence Group, 53 St Vincent Crescent, Glasgow, 30p

A very thorough guide to the housing situation for women in Scotland, particularly Clydeside. Because the law is different in Scotland, guides written for English readers are irrelevant to Scottish women, so this pamphlet is particularly valuable. It covers all the different methods of getting housing, discusses the particular problems of women in finding somewhere to live, and gives an idea of different councils' policies on Clydeside.

CLAIMANTS HANDBOOK
WOMEN AND SOCIAL SECURITY
both from Claimants Publications, 19 Carlyle Road, Birmingham, 30p each

Two practical guides to basic rights and how to get them.

DISCUSSION KIT
from Women's Liberation Campaign for Legal and Financial Independence, 214 Stapleton Hall Road, London N4, 50p

This discussion kit is meant for groups who want to get involved in the Demand for Independence, and is intended as a starting point for discussion and action. It contains general notes, with ideas of how to start a discussion, notes on dependence and independence which talk about women's feelings of dependence and how these are reinforced by legal and social pressures, fact sheets on 'the family' and 'women at work', suggestions for campaigning, book and address lists, and the pamphlet *The Demand for Independence* which discusses in detail the state policies that define women as dependent on men (this pamphlet is also available separately, price 15p).

WOMEN AND SOCIAL SECURITY
from Claimants Publications, 40p

Good background to the rights of working women, supplementary benefit, national insurance, and the position of single parent families showing present rights and what is wrong with the situation.

SEX DISCRIMINATION IN SCHOOLS: How to fight it
National Council for Civil Liberties, 75p

Even before they go to school children have begun to fall into stereotyped sexual roles; and if schools do not begin this typecasting, they certainly reinforce it (woodwork and metalwork reserved for the boys; needlework and cooking for the girls). And all this plays a crucial part in determining attitudes and job opportunities. This guide shows how parents and children can fight this form of discrimination in schools by using the law.

DOING THINGS OURSELVES

Community action

Women have always been particularly active in struggles in their local communities for better housing, better living conditions, and more local facilities. Because women are often responsible for childcare and looking after the sick and elderly, we are directly affected by fluctuations in the provision of public services; if a nursery shuts down it is the women who will be left looking after the children, if home helps are not provided for old people it is women who will take on more of the burden of caring for them. Women are more directly affected by bad housing and our local environment. We usually spend more time in or around the home than our husbands, and have to cope with the results of damp, or heating systems we can't afford, or streets that are unsafe for children. Just as those in waged work fight for better working conditions, so women fight for better conditions where we work, which also happens to be where we live.

Consequently, groups campaigning around local issues, such as tenants associations, campaigns to get pedestrian crossings on dangerous roads, action groups to improve schools or the local environment and so on, often get most of their support from women. Issues like this often bring women together for the first time, and we learn how to work together, how to stand up to the local authority and other officials, and how to get things done. It is through struggles like these that many of us discover our own strength, and begin to recognize the possibility of change.

Because problems are often specific to a particular town or district, and groups work in different ways, it is impossible to describe them all, or to generalize about how they are organized; the campaigns described here are in no way intended to be typical. Nevertheless, the tactics used and lessons learnt in one campaign can often be applied in another. The alternative press, newsletters and other publications are developing as ways of sharing and benefiting from one another's experiences.

One Woman's Struggle

We spoke to Julie about how she first became involved in trying to change things in her own area. She lives in Chapeltown, a multi-racial inner-city area of Leeds with all the usual problems: bad housing, dirty streets, lack of playspace . . . the list is endless. Julie has been active in her community for several years, and has recently joined Big Flame.

In 1973, Julie was involved in a struggle to get a Pelican Crossing on a busy main road near where she lives:

'We used to have zebra crossing on Scott Hall Road, and two little girls got killed when a bus pulled up for them and a car overtook it. Everybody was really shocked; the road was well-known for people being knocked down. Everybody wanted to get together, but nobody knew how to go about it, so the local chemist, whose brother was a councillor, and another bloke called a public meeting. It was a really well-attended meeting; there were about 200 people there from all over the estate, mainly women with kids, who had to cross the road to get to school, and a few old people who had to cross it to get to their Old Age Pensioners' Club.

'The men really didn't want to have any sort of demonstration at all, they wanted to keep it all low-key, but quite a few women were going barmy, they wanted to do something about it there and then. The men were trying to talk them over, I could see the way it was going, even though I'd never done anything like this. So we grabbed the microphone from the men and said, "We're going to demonstrate, and we're going to do it every day until we get a safe road!"

'We formed a committee and decided we'd demonstrate twice a day on two days each .week, in the rush-hour. The first demonstration was really well attended, even though it was raining, because it was fresh in people's minds. We had about 150 people and we managed to block the road completely for an hour. We could see queues all the way up the road and all the way down, and there were traffic jams on another road where they were cutting through to avoid us. We felt really great. At tea-time it went quite well, but there weren't as many people, because many women had to get tea and look after their children.

'We wrote to all the councillors and got a meeting with them. They admitted that zebra crossings were no safer than crossing the road without one; they said what we needed was a pelican light, or an overhead path. We didn't want an overhead path because old people and women with prams wouldn't be able to get up this; and anyway why should we be forced to cross up there when we should be down at ground level? The councillors were scared, I think, because they are scared when ordinary people get together to do anything. And it's mostly women when it's in communities, because the men aren't around.

'The road-blocking carried on but people gradually stopped coming. I think it had a lot to do with their husbands; mornings would have been allright, because the men weren't there, but at tea-time they complained if they had to wait for their teas. The women used to say, "I've got to do the tea" or, "I can't walk across this road, I might get arrested and I've got to go on holiday". That sort of thing shouldn't matter to people when they've got kids that have to use that road. I just thought: "Well, we'll have to eat later; you've got to put yourself out for these things if you want them to work." My husband complained, but I told him his kids had to cross that road, he should be out there doing something about it. He was a driver at the time, and he used to say he'd run us all over.

'In the end there were just four of us keeping up the demonstration; other people weren't willing to carry on that long, but I thought if we stopped we wouldn't get the crossing. We did it four times a week for about three months, on market days. The *police were allright at first, but then they got a bit sick of just four people causing them so much trouble. They threatened to arrest us, but they never did. I think men are more likely to get arrested; women make too good martyrs, especially if you've got kids, so they seem less willing to arrest us. We had the papers on our side, and that's very important. The papers covered the kids getting knocked down; then they came to the public meeting and followed the issue all the way through. We got on Yorkshire Television and got good coverage on their "Calendar" programme. By the end, the papers used to come and wait until people were getting off the bus, so that there was a crowd walking over the zebra crossing, and we had to walk with them with our banners to make it seem that there were a lot of people with us! The papers were really good to us like that. But they never described us as "women", we were always "housewives", "parents", "mothers". It really annoyed me: it can be "men" doing something, but never "women".*

'*Of the four of us, only one had any experience of doing this sort of thing, because she'd been a member of a political organization before. Groups like the International Socialists tried to get in on it, but she told them to go away, only not quite so politely! If she hadn't been there we'd probably have been infiltrated by IS people, because we'd have thought it was great that someone else wanted to support us. But it's not that at all, they wanted to use us.*

'*We all thought it was wonderful that we were meeting councillors, and they were all coming to our meetings, it gave us a feeling of power. And we could tell from the way they were being so nice to us that they were scared. But we should have been more political and not so easily impressed. Instead of thinking it was wonderful we should have been asking more questions.*

'*The council gave in finally because we were persistent; we just didn't give up. We were going to block the road completely if we didn't get anywhere by sitting down. Some people had bright ideas like pouring oil on the road, and setting fire to it; but we didn't feel quite that militant!*

'*We'd have still been demonstrating now, four years later, if they hadn't given us the pelican crossing. But our campaign worked; you see, you don't need a lot of active support.*'

A couple of years later, Julie was involved in another incident where just a few people getting together forced the authorities to act. This time it wasn't as serious as children being killed, but it was typical of the sort of thing that happens when the council neglects an area:

'*There was an enormous pile of rubbish in this garden down a back street. There was a smell coming from it, and everyone in the street complained about it. It was an Asian bloke's house; so, of course, you got all this stuff about Asians being mucky. But it wasn't that. He'd had to do up the whole house when he moved in; so it was plaster, old beds, just what he'd had to throw out, and he couldn't get anyone to come and shift it.*

'*This went on for three or four months. It was summer, a red-hot summer. You'd open your bedroom window of a night, and the smell would come sailing in, and you'd have to shut your window. A couple of us had been talking about it, saying something should be done. So I said maybe we should just take the rubbish and dump it in the middle of the road, then they'll shift it.*

'*I rang up the Cleansing Department at 9 am and told them if they hadn't shifted it by mid-day we were going to do it ourselves. The bloke said, "That's up to you, we can't get round every time someone just rings up." So we got hold of Radio Leeds and the papers, borrowed a wheelbarrow and shovels, and started taking the rubbish into a busy side road. There were just three of us, all women. No-one else in the street would help us, even though they all wanted the rubbish shifted. They thought the way we were going about it was wrong. But you've got to do something like that to make the corporation move.*

'*The smell was that bad that we had to wear masks with disinfectant on them. One* man wouldn't even let us put our bottle of Dettol on his wall, I think he thought he might get arrested for it!

'As we got down the pile of rubbish, we came across loads and loads of dead fish. It stank. It hadn't just rotted, it had collapsed into a sort of brown gunge. There must have been about fourteen pounds of it, enough to fill a big zinc bucket. Someone suggested we take it down to the Cleansing Department to show them what we were dealing with; we got it in a car and drove down town with our heads hanging out of the wndows, the smell was revolting.

'At the Cleansing Department I held up the bucket to show the man behind the desk, and said, "Look what we've been living with for months". As I did it someone tipped the bucket and it emptied all over this man's dinner! He went barmy (I don't blame him), and locked us in. I thought I'd had it this time! The head man came out and said, "Right, you've made your point, now take it back". Where could I take it to? There he was with all these burners and things where he could get rid of it, and he wanted me to take the bloody stuff back!

'Eventually they let us out without the fish, and by the time we got back the street had been blocked with the rest of the rubbish. A nasty policeman came along and arrested us. We were just standing around watching like everyone else, but anyone could tell that we had done it; we were black with all this gunge. So the three of us got arrested. But a nicer policeman came along and let us go, and told us to put all the rubbish back; that seemed to be their big thing. But of course we didn't do that!

'All the time people from the estate were coming up and telling me they'd had rubbish in their gardens for months and hadn't been able to get it shifted, and that they thought we were doing the right thing.

'In the end four dustcarts came and shifted it. Some Hare Krishna people came to sweep it all up, saying, "God's with you, God's with you". I said "Where the bloody hell was he when we were carrying it?" The community constable came, and he thought that was quite funny, but then he's paid to find things funny.

'We made arrangements that any time anyone had a rubbish problem we'd to ring up one particular man at the Cleansing Department and they'd see to it for us. People from all over this area got in touch with us for help. We had another Asian man come to us; it seemed they won't do anything for Asians. I'm not saying the whole council is prejudiced; but it does look a lot like that. They had told him that his rubbish was too big a job. So I rang them up and said, "You know what we do if it's too big a job" and they shifted it straight away.'

Organizing in the community is far from easy. Many people have been putting up with bad conditions for so long that they come to believe that nothing can be done about their situation. They often don't know who to complain to, and are soon discouraged if their first efforts to get something changed do not meet with any success. They are afraid of the police, their husbands, and corporation officials.

Local alternative papers have an important role here; they can let people know what their rights are and how to get them, and publicize people's actions in a way that makes plain that there are genuine grievances to be dealt with, and that people taking action are not just a lot of troublemakers.

One of the dangers, as Julie found, is that people are often content to leave things up to one or two individuals who are particularly active:

'They think I'm a nutter. They'd all say, "We're behind you", and you'd look behind you and there's no one there. People have got this idea that it's never them, always somebody else who does things. They just think there's nothing they can do. And you can't do very much individually; you've got to get together.'

Oh, to have two Dustbins

Oh to have two dustbins
To keep my rubbish in
The way it spreads across the yard
Is really quite a sin

I'd throw some on the fire
That way perhaps I'd win
But the fire's only burning gas
So it all goes in the bin

Each week the cardboard boxes
Pile higher up the wall
And heaps of poly carrier bags
Wait for the dustmen's call

I've chatted up all the dustmen
But they don't care a pin
You'd think that they could give me
One rotten lousy bin

If I was rich I'd buy one
Pay the extra rates as well
Fill both of them with rubbish
Let the dustmen go to hell

How can we hope to manage
In these days of food in tins
And plastic wraps and polythene
When we've only got one bin.

by Cassidy

Stopping the Cuts

As cuts in government expenditure eat away at the welfare state, many women are getting involved in fights to stop facilities at hospitals, nurseries or schools from deteriorating or being closed down. This means that women who work in these services are getting together with women in the community who use the services, to stop this happening. One of the best known campaigns of this sort is the fight to save the Elizabeth Garrett Anderson Hospital in London.

The Elizabeth Garrett Anderson Hospital for Women is one of only two general women's hospitals in the country, run by women for women. It provides an essential service, both locally and for women from all over the country. Three years ago the hospital had 160 beds, a maternity wing, a teaching school and a children's ward. Its outpatient department saw 24,000 patients, all women, in 1976. But over the last few years, the hospital has been steadily run down; it has been allocated insufficient money, and no maintenance has been carried out.

In February 1976, the government announced that the EGA was to become part of a District General Hospital, although it would retain its identity as a unit. No adequate reasons were given for moving the hospital from its present site, and workers and patients at the hospital felt the move would mean a reduction in health facilities in Camden and Islington, as well as job losses. In March, the union branches at the hospital began to have meetings, and several groups in the area, mostly women's groups, tenants and pensioners, and Camden Campaign against the Cuts, took up the campaign against the closure of the EGA. They organized petitions, and lobbied the area health authority, the council, and MPs. There were several local public meetings and demonstrations, but the Department of Health took no notice.

Meanwhile, the main lift at the hospital had broken down, and the health authority would not repair it, so the wards and operating theatre above the first floor could no longer be used. In July 1976, the authority decided to close the maternity wards, and took all the patients away one morning without informing anyone! In September 1976, the Project Team set up by the health authority suddenly said that the two remaining wards would have to be moved to another hospital about four miles away. This was the last straw for the EGA workers; the shop stewards and union officials got together and decided to put the idea of occupying the hospital to the vote at an emergency mass meeting of all the staff. The vote was 100 per cent in favour.

On 15 November 1976, the EGA was officially occupied under workers' control, the first ever occupation of a hospital in this country. At the time of writing, the occupation is still going on. Doctors, nurses and all other staff continue to care for their patients as usual, and new patients are still being admitted. As long as patients remain in the hospital, the authority is obliged to pay the staff. A continuous picket has been set up at the hospital entrance to monitor those entering and leaving the hospital, and to prevent equipment being moved out. The ambulance service is co-operating, and local doctors are continuing to refer women to the hospital for treatment.

There is an Action Committee made up of representatives from the patients, ancillary staff, doctors, nurses and technicians. There is also an Occupation Committee which looks after the day-to-day running of the occupation, and tries to make sure everyone there knows what is going on. They are drawing up contingency plans in case the authority tries to barge in and snatch the patients.

For the campaign to succeed, the occupation needs the full support of all the workers inside, and of local people outside. It will probably be seen as a test case by the unions and the Department of Health; the attempt to close the EGA is part of the government's policy of cuts in social services spending, which threatens 120 hospitals in London alone. If the EGA workers succeed in keeping their hospital open, other groups of hospital workers are bound to follow their tactics.

Hospitals where women can be treated by women in a sympathetic environment are very rare indeed, and we must fight to maintain the few facilities we have. The campaign to save the EGA has shown how women patients and workers, the consumers and the providers of the health service, can get together to do just that.

(information from *Women's Struggle Notes*, No. 1)

SAVE THE EGA CAMPAIGN *30 Camden Road, London NW1*

EGA SHOP STEWARDS COMMITTEE *Elizabeth Garrett Anderson Hospital, Euston Road, London NW1*

EGA STAYS, OK!
a twenty-five minute 16mm colour film by the Newsreel Collective, available from Save the EGA Campaign.

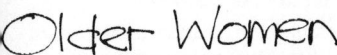 Older Women

Most of the groups working to improve women's conditions tend to be dominated by younger women. Changing social conditions and better educational facilities have given younger women more time and opportunity to think about their lives and come in contact with new ideas, and they have grown up in a time when it is more acceptable to question traditional patterns and try to change them.

This has meant that while there is a lot of activity around questions like abortion, equal career opportunities and childcare, the specific problems of older women have been neglected. Yet the state and society discriminate against them just as much if not more. Provision for older people is scandalously bad. Pensions and other social security legislation discriminates against older women, and it is, of course, women who are expected to care for old or sick relatives.

At last this subject is beginning to be discussed . . . perhaps because the active young women are growing older! At the 1977 National Women's Liberation Conference, a workshop on the problems of older women attracted a great deal of interest. A paper produced for the conference explained why all of us, young and old, should be concerned about the problems of older women:

1. *Finance*   Older women suffer, just like younger women, from the assumptions that society makes about women's position and needs.

Pension Rights now and in the future (with the new Social Security Act) assume the dependence of women upon men. Now, even women who have worked outside the home but have not paid full National Insurance contributions have to rely on their husbands' wage for a pension. In the future, the vast majority of women will have a vested interest in finding and keeping the most highly-paid man possible in order to get a good earnings-related pension. Single women and women who choose not to marry legally will suffer. Only in unusual circumstances will the woman be able to confer her pension on her man. Earnings-related pensions are immoral and sexist; if you can sell your labour at a higher price you can have more to live on when you're old. The government says this is equality. How can women with our commitments *and* with the discrimination that confronts us, possibly hope to earn the same as men?

Many women who have to leave work to care for a dependent relative or because of their own ill-health cannot claim an income in their own right. For instance, married or 'cohabiting' women cannot claim a Non-Contributory Invalidity Pension (unless they can't do the housework!), the new Invalid Care Allowance or a Mobility Allowance if they are over sixty.

Yet watch for the Catch 22: if a married woman is working and her non-working husband is not entitled to the dole or an invalidity benefit, all but the first £4 of *her* pay will be deducted from his social security. So in some circumstances she *is* deemed to be keeping her man!

In short, older women are faced with a morass of discriminatory tax and social security legislation, and they also lose 'fringe' benefits such as concessionary travel which are dependent upon entitlement.

2. *Society is Ageist and ageism/sexism is a lethal combination*   In a society that equates feminity and women's fulfilment with sexual attractiveness, fertility and looking after husbands, older women are deprived of their identity. Society sees them as 'marginal' women. It is seen as 'understandable' for a man to go off his 'ageing' wife and fancy 'dolly birds' (but for her to make the same transition is not acceptable). Both primary sexual characteristics (menstruation, fertility) and secondary ones (often culturally determined, such as slim figure, young unlined face, lack of facial hair) wane as women get older and society's insistence on the importance of them undermines the self-identity of women as they age.

Housework is an essential part of the maintenance of the family unit and its happiness. When children have grown up and the man has retired or died, the rationale of housework becomes meaningless, the stereotyped male/female division of labour redundant, and depression and frustration ensue.

Very old women are a great embarrassment to the state. Women live to ever-greater ages. Their life is prolonged, but the quality of life gets worse and worse. They are either kept in geriatric hospitals or in old people's homes, where staff are overworked and only lip-service is paid to any notion of activity — or they are left to the care of relatives (guess which ones!) with inadequate support.

3. *Community Care means Women!* Especially now, in a period of welfare cuts, many women not only have to spend years looking after their children but they also have to look after those (the mentally ill and handicapped, the physically handicapped, and the ageing or frail) who are, in the words of the government, receiving 'Community Care'. Kathleen Jones, at an Age Concern Conference, said that women are used by society for all these intolerable jobs. Women may be socially isolated for years, with

inadequate Health and Social Services support, unable to claim an income for loss of earning power, and secretly wishing for the death of their beloved relative, after which they often break down. As 'miracle medicine' keeps more and more potentially dependent people alive, society assumes that women's all-embracing loving care will provide endless support on the cheap. Many women beyond the age of retirement are looking after their own parents!

4. *All of us are getting older*   The exploitation of older women is *our* exploitation. In ten years time it could be you, looking after a father who has had a stroke, a mentally-handicapped child, fighting to make ends meet when your husband is retired with industrial injuries ... you feeling that life is not worthwhile.

Mary Wollstonecraft remarks in the Introduction to her *Vindication of the Rights of Women* that 'A lively writer (I cannot recollect his name) asks what business women turned forty have to do in the world'. It's not much different today. Society sees women as disposable. And it trades on their isolation, so that older women have no way of expressing their unhappiness.

5. *What can we do?*
Press for research into the real meaning of 'Community Care' (make sure *we* do the research!).

Organize local groups for women caring for dependent relatives (they may need sitters), to provide mutual support, a common cause and a united voice.

Contradict ageism when it rears its head in public or political life. Write and talk to and about older women, 'middle-aged' women, pensioners; contact them where they are, in their homes, clubs, clinics and surgeries.

Campaign when changes particularly affect older women: for example, public transport cuts and fares increases, or the closure of local shops, surgeries and chemists. Campaign in the Health Service for more 'nuts and bolts' medicine: provision for chiropody, teeth and spectacles, cures for arthritis, rheumatism, cystitis, backache, incontinence, prompt gynaecological treatment (usually these waiting lists are the longest). Remember people can be in a wheelchair and still need a filling!

Resources for Community Action

COMMUNITY ACTION MAGAZINE
PO Box 665, London SW1
This excellent and low-priced magazine is published six times a year and is available on subscription or from most alternative bookshops. It contains news of community activities around the country, including heating campaigns, street committees, tenants associations, fighting the cuts in social services, and so on. It also has articles on issues of national interest, and a series of action notes on particular topics. Packs of back issues which deal with particular themes are available, including: *Fighting the Cuts*, 75p; *Fight the Attack on Council Housing*, 55p; *Direct Action and the Police*, 55p. The magazine is a good way of learning what's going on around the country, and sharing the experiences and lessons of similar campaigns in different areas. There is also an *Investigators' Handbook*, 30p, which is a guide for tenants, workers and action groups on how to investigate companies, organizations and individuals.

THE HOUSEHOLDER'S GUIDE TO COMMUNITY DEFENCE AGAINST BUREAUCRATIC AGGRESSION
by Antony Jay, Jonathan Cape, £1.25
This is a guide to taking on the planners and the bureaucrats, whether 'they' are building an electricity generating station on the village green, running a six-lane motorway past your bedroom window, or simply moving the lamp-post outside your house. It tells you how to set up an action campaign, raise money, manage your PR, present alternative plans, go to public enquiry, etc. The advice is very practical and always useful. It ends on this note ... 'and if you fail, you fail. And the final irony is that when the bulldozers move in and your community is destroyed, the campaign itself will have ensured that it has become a far more healthy, warm, loving, unified community than it ever was before the plan was published.'

COMMUNITY: Directory of Social Change, Volume Two

by Michael Norton, Wildwood House, £3.95
Community is a companion volume to this book. It is a mine of practical information, resources and contacts for anyone who wants to run a pressure group or start a local campaign (or is already doing so). Whether you want to run your own newspaper, get TV or local radio coverage for your point of view, use portable video equipment, turn a building site into a community garden, start a housing co-operative, organize a meeting or a demonstration, or write a press release, you will find ideas, suggestions and advice for these and hundreds of other topics. Around 150,000 words and forty-six separate chapters.

THE ORGANIZER'S MANUAL

by the OM Collective, Bantam Books, 666 5th Avenue, New York 10019, $1.25
This is probably the best book on organizing around. It was written from direct experience of organizing in the peace movement. It is full of useful information on organizing, educating, communicating, taking action and setting up alternative institutions. It is an American book, but most of its information is universally applicable. At 368 pages it is a bargain.

PEOPLE'S NEWS SERVICE

c/o Rising Free Bookshop, 182 Upper Street, London N1
A fortnightly news bulletin of wants and struggles that don't normally make the national press. £1.75 for ten issues.

HOW TO RUN A PRESSURE GROUP

by Christopher Hall, Aldine Paperbacks, £1.25
'One object of this book is to show those who need a pressure group how to run one. They cannot all be equipped with the money to hire public relations consultants, but they can be taught simple publicity techniques which will serve them as well as any PR outfit can. They cannot all command a membership rich in planners, architects, company directors and other practised manipulators of government. But they can be told where to get advice and how to maximise the force of their own arguments.'
This book is a mine of useful information on all aspects of running an action group.

WOMEN'S STRUGGLE NOTES

from Box 339, 182 Upper Street, London N1
Women's Struggle Notes is intended to take up the questions, ideas and actions that women are working around, but which are seldom covered in the press or on TV. It has news about the struggles, small or large, that women are engaged in in different areas, like striking for equal pay, standing up to the Social Security officials, the problems of immigrant women. It's useful and interesting. It costs £1 for a subscription to six issues.

OTHER SOURCES OF INFORMATION

Your local community newspaper, alternative bookshop, Women's Centre or Community Centre, also the Council of Voluntary Service and the information officer at your Town Hall.

CRIME AND PRISON

Besides having to cope with laws that discriminate against us as women, women, like men, may find themselves tangling with the state in a variety of ways. We commit crimes, and are sent to prison; we are the victims of crime, particularly rape and battering; and we often have to fight the state apparatus to get decent housing, heating, schools and nurseries for our children, and a better environment for ourselves to live in. In all these struggles we need the strength we can get from working together.

Far fewer women than men commit 'crimes' and far fewer go to prison. But the pattern of female criminality is changing. The newspapers are full of stories of 'bovver birds' beating people up, and sociologists speculate on the causes of the growing crime rate among women and especially teenage girls. The general opinion seems to be that the changing social position of women causes stress, and that this leads to crime. Women are moving into previously 'masculine' areas in all aspects of their lives, legal and illegal.

The statistics seem to confirm this trend; from 1970 to 1971, crimes of violence by women increased by 16.6 per cent, while similar crimes by men increased by only 11.8 per cent. But the overall numbers of such offences by women remain very low. In 1974, 53 per cent of the women who went to prison had been convicted of some form of stealing. Less than 9 per cent (166) had been found guilty of violence against others. The remainder were imprisoned for offences connected with prostitution, drink or drugs, or other, mainly minor offences. Hardly a bunch of desperate criminals from whom society must be protected!

About two-thirds of the women who enter prison in any year are remanded in custody. Less than one-third of these women eventually receive prison or borstal sentences when they come to trial. At the moment there appear to be only a few small groups in this country who are working specifically around *women* in prison, but there are several general well-established pressure groups campaigning for reform of the prison system in general.

Many women who are sent to prison have to leave their children; others are pregnant when they go inside, and have to keep their babies or very young children in prison with them. In 1976, the *Yorkshire Evening Post* ran a series of articles on women in prison, written by Angela Singer, in which she interviewed several women about their experiences. The women talked about the general conditions in prison, and especially about what it was like to have a baby under those circumstances:

(Jenny) *'The physical conditions are much worse on the remand wing. You are locked in your cell from early evening till morning with a bucket. That's all right if you don't get sick. You have a bell to ring but because the bells are always being rung unnecessarily they can't tell which is genuine and they can leave you to ring for hours.*

'There were 200 girls on the remand wing when I was there. It got to the stage that it was so over-crowded some were having to sleep in the library.

'They put the hardest officers on the remand wing. For an hour every day you have to take exercise and you just walk round and round in circles in the yard and you are not allowed to stop. I stopped one day and leaned against the wall. The officer came up to me and made me go on.

'The next day I stopped again and she said, "Get round", and started screaming at me. I said, "No, I'm four months pregnant and if I want to stop and rest I will." I thought it was going to be nasty but luckily another officer was there and she said tactfully, "It's all right you can leave her, she's pregnant." '

(Ruth) *'I got insomnia and they wouldn't give me anything to help me sleep because the Governor said I was there for punishment and I shouldn't have any help to get through it. I used to wonder how can they think by all this inhumanity they will make me more human.'*

(Jenny) *'Having my first baby in prison, I'd rather have died. I've been out two years now and I've only just stopped having nightmares.*

'The whole thing's like a nightmare. It's so unreal, you spend most of your time trying to get back a bit of reality. You have no privacy, no time for thoughts of your own. You are living a charade of trying to live with other women you would not have chosen to live with, it's like a huge stage play and that causes the most terrible tensions.'

Christine's son, Mel, was ten months old when he came out of prison. Children can stay at Holloway until they are two. Mel had never seen a bus or a dog or a cat. He did not know what grass was, and the first time he saw rain he was terrified. And when the new Holloway Prison is built, it is planned that children will stay there until they are five.

Christine spent fifteen months in Holloway out of an eighteen-month sentence for fraud. She had forged cheques belonging to her employers, a building firm. She stole about £2,000. It was a second offence. Ten years earlier at seventeen, she had taken £3 from the office of the children's home where she worked. Christine says of her life there:

'The child eats not when it's hungry but when it's time to eat, plays when it's time to play, sleeps when it's time to sleep. There are silly things like the highly-polished floors; how do you learn to crawl on a polished floor? Mel never learned to crawl.

'The only time the children go outside at Holloway is into the small, paved back yard with a 16ft wall round it. There are a lot of people about but they're just not living people.

'I asked if Mel's father could take him out of the prison for a while. I was told that in theory he could but they didn't know how it could be done, and in 10 months they never found out. How anybody can think of institutionalizing a child like that until he's five I can't understand.'

Often children are put into care when their mothers are imprisoned. Besides having a terrible effect on both mother and child, this is very expensive. Writing in 1976, the *Yorkshire Evening Post* said:

'It costs £53 a week to keep a woman in prison. The cost of jailing one particular woman (who had four children and had been deserted by her husband) for theft was worked out at £4,141.43.

'. . . A government publication in 1970, "The Treatment of Women and Girls in Custody" stated: "It is well known that this kind of dispersal has a traumatic effect on the children and may be a cause of their future delinquency or other forms of instability."

It added:

"The younger the child the deeper may be the effect. Younger children and babies feel only loss without having the capacity to understand, accept and overcome their grief . . ."

'In spite of that statement more than 1,000 children are estimated to have been separated from their mother last year because of prison sentences and a further 3,000 because of women held in custody before trial, or after trial and before sentence.'

And when you come out, your troubles aren't over — you may have lost your house, your job and your kids, and it can take years to get over the experience:

(Ruth) *'I felt completely alone at first. I couldn't relate to anything or anybody. I remember sitting on the train waiting for someone to say I could go to the loo.*

'I went to bed at eight and waited to be locked in. I woke up in the morning and stripped the bed and waited. I went downstairs and sat at the table and waited for breakfast.

'Then, later, I was excited about being out. Getting on buses fascinated me, and talking to people. I know people who have had difficulty in walking into a shop to buy something but I used to go in just to talk to the shopkeeper. It fascinated me to see people doing normal things unaware of the fact that I'd just come out of prison.'

(Jenny) *'I shall never forget. Your sentence is never over, whatever sentence it is, it's a life sentence. When I came out I just couldn't get involved in the world, all I wanted to do was to sit for 24 hours in my bedroom. I couldn't face any hassles. I couldn't face the hassle of getting on a bus. Girls who had been in before said that it takes two years to get over being in there. For two years I was still in prison, though I was outside. I expect to be half in prison for many years to come.'*

(all quotes from the *Yorkshire Evening Post*)

PROP has produced photostat copies of these *Yorkshire Evening Post* articles, which can be obtained from them.

Prison Reform Groups.

PROP: Preservation of Rights of Prisoners
185 Archway Road, London N6
PROP is the Prisoners' Union, run by ex-prisoners for prisoners. A statement by the London group explains their aims and how they work:

'Prisoners are treated as less than human beings, and this is made easy because they are stigmatized, their rights are taken away, and they are cut off from the world and surrounded by censorship and secrecy.

  'Therefore PROP:

1. tries to explain what crime really is — that it is one of the symptoms of a defective society, and that if it is ever to be ended society must be changed, and people must understand and respect one another;

2. wishes to co-operate with other bodies having a concern for change of this kind, for the problems of the community, and for the furtherance of human freedom;

3. demands recognition and encouragement for the new awareness and drive for reforms now manifest among prisoners themselves;

4. declares that the basic rights taken for granted in the outside world should be the rights of prisoners also, that if the rule of law is to prevail in the outside world then it should really prevail in prison, and that prisoners' lives should not be disposed of by arbitrary decisions;

5. insists that the barrier of secrecy surrounding prisons must be broken, that there must be an end to the misuse of the Official Secrets Act, and that those in prison must be allowed free communication and contact with those outside. In the face of the present secrecy, PROP endeavours to convey to the public a true and full account of prison conditions and of the views and feelings of prisoners.'

PROP supports alternative policies more constructive than imprisonment, but also fights for reforms in the present penal system. They have a Prisoners' Charter of twenty-four rights which they would like to see implemented, including the right to vote, the right to contact legal advisers in confidence, the right to consult independent medical advisers, and so on.

  Full membership of PROP is open to any person who is or has been an inmate of any detention centre, remand centre, approved school, borstal, prison, or other penal establishment. Associate membership is open to anybody else who is in sympathy with the aims of PROP. Only full members can vote.

NACRO: National Association for the Care and Resettlement of Offenders
125 Kennington Park Road, London SE11
NACRO works to improve the range of non-custodial facilities for offenders and ex-offenders, and to prevent crime by remedying the social causes. They run several accommodation schemes and other projects, have an Information Bank, and produce information sheets on different aspects of the judicial system.

PORTIA TRUST
c/o Kenneth Norman, 38 Fisher Street, Working-ton, Cumbria
This charity is setting up hostels for emotionally disturbed women whose problems put them at risk of breaking the law, and is trying to provide supportive care and psychiatric help. They also accommodate and help battered and other homeless women and their children:

  'Our main concern is to keep non-criminals out of prison . . . We want to set up a "retreat", something like a secular convent . . . Women facing the possibility of jail sentences could then plead in court to be allowed to come here instead of being sent to jail.'

(Kenneth Norman, National Organizer)

RADICAL ALTERNATIVES TO PRISON
c/o Christian Action, 15 Blackfriars Lane, London EC4
RAP is a pressure/publicity group working for the abolition of imprisonment. They are not especially directed towards women, but have held a seminar on Women and Crime (the reading list is available from them), and campaigned about the rebuilding of Holloway.

  'We hope, by exposing the realities of the prison system, to bring about a shift in public attitudes and a gradual acceptance of the idea that a new approach to the whole concept of "crime" must be found . . . Only when people begin to question why certain people are called criminals and others whose acts are harmful to the community are not, can real *alternatives evolve.'*

(RAP statement)

RAP provides speakers for groups or meetings, and produces a monthly newsletter, information leaflets and other publications.

HOWARD LEAGUE FOR PENAL REFORM
125 Kennington Park Road, London SE11
The three main aspects of the Howard League's policies are:

1. to watch the operation of the penal system for such things as inappropriate penalties, the conditions inside prison and prisoners' rights, and the allocation of resources to the more desirable features of the system such as education and aftercare;

2. to propose and press for changes in the system, submitting evidence to Royal Commissions and government enquiries, and publishing reports;

3. to spread information about the treatment of offenders by holding public meetings and so on, and to form local groups to investigate prison conditions in their own areas.

Although the Howard League is not particularly directed to women, they are hoping to develop a special information section on women and to involve women's groups of all kinds in campaigning for penal reform in women's prisons. They are willing to provide speakers for meetings, discussion groups, etc., and produce information sheets and booklets.

Prisoners' Wives

Although relatively few women actually go to prison, many more are affected by the prison system as the wives of prisoners. The Howard League estimates that, at any one time, 10,000 families in this country have a parent in prison. A prisoner's wife and children share the social stigma attached to his 'crime', as well as having to face all the usual problems of women bringing up kids on their own. Neighbours may be hostile, or a social scene based on married couples may have no place for a lone woman. In addition she has to cope with living on social security or low wages, and try to maintain a relationship with someone she rarely sees.

Prisoners' Wives and Families Society

Maggie Tuttle, a prisoner's wife, started the Society as a help and information service for other women in the same position as herself. They had found that although there were plenty of voluntary organizations to help offenders and ex-offenders, there was nothing but the statutory organizations for the wives and families of these men. Pauline now works full-time for the Society:

> 'A lot of women I've come across have been to the statutory organizations, the Social Services or the probation service, and these really don't seem to understand the problems. The prisoner's wife is stigmatized, she can lose jobs, friends, and virtually find herself on her own, unless she has a good family behind her.
>
> 'One of the most traumatic experiences occurs when a wife is left in court after the husband has been sent down; you have never relied on the state or the social security, always had a wage coming in, then the wage-earner is sent down. You can imagine the emotional stress, and then on top of that there are financial problems as well. Lots of ordinary people know very little about supplementary benefits: what they're entitled to, what to do when a bill arrives (the bills are the same as before but now there's no wage-earner to pay them; you have to clothe and feed the kids). It's just one big mass of problems. There's no one in court to tell the woman what to do, she just has to use her own initiative unless she has a good barrister, which is rare if you're on legal aid; they're not too concerned with the families unless you are paying.
>
> 'So several women got together and started an advice service. It was difficult to get property. We squatted in a house which had been empty about twelve months, and got a licence to use it. Then we had the problem of getting the word out. We're totally at the mercy of prison governors and welfare officers — we send leaflets out to all the

prisons but it's up to them whether they put them in the waiting rooms. If they don't there's nothing we can do about it. We rely a lot on word of mouth, wives telling other wives. The Citizens' Advice Bureaux know about us, and the press haven't treated us badly.

'The Home Office paid for the renovations needed for a nursery, and the Social Services pay the salaries for the nursery workers. So now we've got a full-time nursery downstairs, a paid worker running the advice service in the office, and a hostel for women who are homeless. We're backed by various charities — we got a grant for a caravan which allows us to give free holidays to twenty-two families a year.

'Women who come in are sometimes quite suspicious at first; they're not always aware that all the women who work here are prisoners' wives or ex-prisoners' wives themselves. As soon as they realize this they can talk about the offence the husband's committed without any embarrassment. Often if a woman is referred to us by the Social Services or a probation officer, we find there's a problem that they are not dealing with because they haven't heard the full story. But if you're talking to someone who knows what it's all about who isn't going to patronize or moralize, then you can talk about it quite freely. As far as we're concerned it's a crime that the man has committed, and nothing to do with his wife.

'Instead of blaming the guy we try to overcome the problems and look to the future. We try to help with the problems within the marriage, but if a woman's at the end of her tether and decides she wants a divorce we can send her to a good solicitor and give her plenty of support.

'Some women come in on a regular basis, others come in for advice on a particular problem, then go away until the next problem crops up. But that's what we're here for: if a woman doesn't want to get actively involved then that's totally up to her. We can tell women about the things they're entitled to: travel warrants, clothing grants, help from the probation service. Even the official bodies sometimes don't know what's available. I had to send a probation officer a copy of a Home Office circular that he didn't know about, and it was to probation officers that the circular was sent to in the first place!

'We have a committee of ex-cons, prisoners' wives and other useful people, but the wives themselves run the place. We want to make sure they have their say, because they know what's best for them, they know about the difficulties of visiting, the lack of communication when letters are censored, the bad housing they're living in. It's no good someone else coming along and saying, "We know in theory what's best for you." We want the wives saying "Look, we know what we want" because no one has ever listened to them before and they are the ones suffering.

'We do have two more groups in other parts of the country, but it's difficult to get new groups going because the wives have so many problems. Before you can help other people, you have to get over your own difficulties; it's not easy to be interested in helping other people when you're loaded down yourself, and you can't always give much time to something like this if you've got kids to look after. People outside London who wanted to get involved could start by having group meetings, getting the press involved, getting on local radio and TV, contacting the probation service and so on.

'Although we recognize the need for long-term changes, and try to put pressure on the government, unfortunately we can't spend much time on campaigning for changes because there are so many women who need help today. I think they should empty the prisons of people inside for silly offences like non-payment of fines, motoring offences, prostitution. Prison doesn't do any good for these people; in fact does great harm. It costs the state money, they're having to support both the man and his family it just doesn't make sense at all. They hide behind the word rehabilitation although there isn't any such thing in prison. All they're doing is locking a man away and taking every ounce of responsibility from him, making him even less able to cope when outside.'

PRISONERS' WIVES AND FAMILIES SOCIETY *14 Richmond Avenue, London N1*

PRISONERS' WIVES SERVICE

378 Lillie Road, London SW6

This is an independent voluntary organization working in the London area. The women volunteers visit the families in their homes, acting as an emergency agency helping the woman with welfare rights and other practical problems and giving her on-going emotional support in her changed circumstances. Women who want to become voluntary visitors can write to them; as well as those who need the service.

PROP PAMPHLETS

from PROP, 185 Archway Road, London N6

The One that Got Away, 25p: a woman's experiences in a children's home and as a prisoner's wife, describing how all her life she has been treated as an object, not as a human being. *On This Side of the Fence* and *A Prisoner's Wife and Poverty*, both 10p: two women describing what it's like to be a prisoner's wife, their struggles with Social Security and other authorities.

Prisoners' Wives Charter

We, the Prisoners' Wives and Families Society, demand:

1. Trade Union rates of pay for work done in prisons by our husbands to enable them to support us, their wives and families, and fully franked insurance cards on their release. ('This would stop us being degraded by the people at Social Security, it would save the government money, and would give the men a sense of responsibility.')

2. 'Family Visiting Centres where a prisoner can meet and stay with his family in private for a period of up to forty-eight hours a month. ('I had a very long way to go and a baby to take with me, which was a strain to start with. I'm quite a shy person, so I was never relaxed on a visit; I'd wait a month for the visit, and get really uptight about it, then when I eventually got there I didn't know what the hell to say. We were strangers, left in limbo. I used to put off the visits because I couldn't face it; all the way home I was terribly depressed.' 'If you could have forty-eight hours in private, not just the prisoner's wife, but kids, friends, relatives as well, it would be so much easier to keep up relationships. I'm sure the security problems could be overcome.')

3. More parole and home leave to enable our husbands to readjust to the outside world.

4. The right to be told the reasons if our husbands are refused parole.

5. Allocation to prisons nearer home. This will save us from long and tiring journeys and will be psychologically better for us and our husbands. It would also save the present enormous drain on the Social Services in providing travel warrants and overnight stay expenses. ('At the moment you may have to travel for hours, and you don't always get overnight expenses. The DHSS has said they might pay if a woman has to be out a particularly long time; but won't say what a "particularly long time" is. So it depends on your local office.')

6. Better visiting facilities (e.g. better sanitary conditions, changing rooms, playspace and facilities to buy or heat food for our children). ('In most prisons there are no facilities for heating food for kids, and if they've travelled a long way and are going to be out late a night, they need something hot. There are no toys or playspace, so you get other people's kids running around — kids don't always want to sit and talk to their dad.')

7. To be able to send and receive unlimited uncensored letters to our husbands. ('I was never able to send a love letter, because of the censorship. I used to spend three hours trying to write a page. Some people get used to it, but lots of us are quite private people. And the men aren't allowed to discuss prison conditions in letters.')

8. Automatic information to be given by the courts to dependents, advising them of rights after conviction.

9. That a prisoner's basic human rights (e.g. marrying, attending funerals, voting) should be allowed to them. ('I've known a man who wasn't allowed to go to his own child's funeral; that was a friend of mine, so I know it happened. They do let you get married if you're pregnant or have already got kids by the man. But it's a pretty rotten experience, I would not advise anyone to do it — they bring the man out in handcuffs.')

10. To be able to send gifts to our husbands, and the right for them to own and sell things they produce during their leisure activities.

11
POWER TO
THE SISTERS

CONSCIOUSNESS RAISING AND WOMEN'S GROUPS

Every group we have talked about in this book reflects a new movement of women working together to change things. Some groups want changes in the law, some want expanded opportunities, some want a total rethinking of attitudes in relation to women and towards society in general. The women's liberation movement (WLM) encompasses all these ideas. It is formed by women who believe that women in our society are oppressed and discriminated against because they are women, and they are committed to changing not only the laws that affect women, but fundamental attitudes about relationships, family, life-styles and roles shared by both men and women. The WLM, since it challenges many of the assumptions upon which our existing social system is based, presents a fundamental threat to that system.

There is no one date that you can point to and say 'the WLM began then'. There have been various movements throughout history in which women have joined together to fight for various issues. This present movement began during the 1960s. During that period there was an upsurge of political protect among groups who saw themselves as oppressed or disadvantaged, such as black people, students, claimants and homosexuals. These groups together with peace groups and left-wing organizations formed the 'New Left'. One important inspiration for the WLM came from women within these left-wing groups, who were beginning to realize that while they were campaigning against the oppression of other groups, they themselves were being put down and exploited by the men they had thought of as their political allies.

Another impetus was a new awareness among women in employment that their pay and their job opportunities were inferior to those of men, and a determination to achieve equality at work. (For example, the Equal Pay Strike at Fords which happened in 1968; and new militancy about pay was seen among nurses at around the same time.)

A sense of frustration was also coming to the surface among housewives, over the isolation, drudgery and boredom which some of them found in the role of full-time wife and mother; a role which they had been brought up to believe was their natural destiny and only possible source of fulfilment.

The rise of the WLM in the United States, together with the publication and wide sale of such books as *The Female Eunuch* (see: Feminist Classics) increased interest in this country, and small women's groups started to appear.

These groups talked about the position of women in society and began to realize that most of the power in society was held by men. With this realization women began to challenge this sex-based power. The WLM has constantly sought to be non-authoritarian, believing that women could work and campaign together co-operatively without the need for arbitrary rules and officials.

The WLM is not an organization that you can join, it doesn't have a head office, a president or a book of rules. Most women's liberation activists are involved in local women's groups or groups campaigning around particular issues which affect women. But you don't have to be in a group to be 'in' the WLM; if you are a woman who supports its aims, you are part of it already.

Conferences are held once or twice a year, at which all sections of the WLM come together, report progress and make policy; there are also numerous smaller conferences on specific topics (ranging from sex discrimination to health care) and there are local and regional conferences. The first Women's Liberation Movement National Conference was held in Oxford in 1970. Here it was agreed that the WLM should press for four minimum demands:

1. equal pay for equal work;
2. equal job and educational opportunities;
3. free contraception and abortion on demand;
4. free twenty-four-hour childcare facilities.

Two more demands were added at Edinburgh in 1974:

5. legal and financial independence for women;
6. an end to discrimination against lesbians and the right of all women to our own self-defined sexuality.

And a further demand was added at Birmingham in 1978:

7. freedom from intimidation, violence and sexual coercion

Groups working within the WLM cover a wide range of ideas. These demands are just a starting point for discussion. Each demand has groups working directly around it: campaigning for its implemtation (legal and financial independence, twenty-four-hour childcare) or for its enforcement (equal pay and job and educational opportunities). The sixth demand not only calls for groups campaigning for an end of harrassment of lesbians (Action for Lesbian Parents) but also extensive self-examination about our feelings and about our own sexuality.

The WLM does not provide easy answers for an end to the oppression of women. Being a 'conscious' woman does not make for an easy life, because at every turn we can see how blatantly women are put down, used, teased and degraded, in every aspect of our lives. But it would have been much harder for women to carry on being trampled on. Women are fighting back, and it's not a fight that will be suppressed.

For more information see: **WOMEN'S LIBERATION: An Introduction** *from Wires, 32a Parliament Street, York, 5p*
This short pamphlet put together by three women's liberation information services gives a brief introduction to the ideas and demands of the WLM and lists useful addresses and reading matter. It is good for individual women seeking information, and for groups to use when giving talks on women's liberation. It would also be handy for teachers, youth workers . . . in fact anyone.

CONSCIOUSNESS-RAISING GROUPS

Combatting the conditioning that women have experienced is not easy. It takes time and we need the support of other women experiencing similar changes. Women have found that meeting in small groups to discuss new feelings and ideas is the most positive way of growing and learning how to live with the new strengths we are discovering within ourselves. These groups are called consciousness-raising (or CR) groups. The term consciousness-raising is an important one. We are in some ways our own worst enemy in our struggle for equality, in and out of the home. As long as we continue to think of ourselves as lesser human beings, we will be treated as such. So we have to re-evaluate totally our relationships with other women, with men, with our backgrounds, and how we relate to people sexually; in other words, we have to raise our consciousness.

The unique quality of the women's liberation movement is the attempt to synthesize the personal and the political, trying to relate our individual experiences to each other's, and from these drawing general conclusions about the position of women in society. The CR group, as a group within the women's movement, is devoted to discussing our personal lives, our feelings, our problems and our backgrounds.

It is important that the group consist only of women. The presence of men often inhibits conversation and honesty. In mixed groups, even well-intentioned men tend to take over the group, set the tone of the meeting and become adversaries who must be convinced. Another reason for women-only groups is that many of us have been taught from a very early age to distrust other women, to be protective of our families and our men, to see marriage as the ultimate form of happiness and fulfilment. The CR group is a place to break down the isolation that this distrust has caused; it is a place where we can be free, where we can be honest, where we can explore our hopes, our successes and our failures. It's a place to find supportive and non-judging friends with whom we can share our frustrations and fears; it is a place for self-examination and for exploration of the alternatives that are available to us.

It is difficult, at first, to begin a CR group, as there is a certain amount of guilt involved in spending one night a week devoted to yourself, to talking about you. For so long we have not given ourselves the chance to discover who we are, and who the women around us are: CR is giving us that chance.

CR groups differ depending on the women involved. Some groups have restrictions, such as being for lesbians wanting to be with other lesbians only. Recently working-class women have started forming working-class CR groups. Groups also differ in their structure: some have none, some have set topics and a rota for who talks when. It would be impossible to show an example here of all the different types of CR groups. Hopefully, the one discussed here will give an idea of what is involved in CR.

Julie lives in Brighton and was involved in a CR group for two years. The group no longer meets, but it made an important impact on the women's lives. Julie talked with us about their group:

'The group started when there was a general meeting in Brighton where we were asked if we wanted to join a CR group. Thirteen of us met in someone's house, with a woman who had been in a CR group before. She told us how they'd organized their group and what they'd done. We decided thirteen was too many, so we split into two groups. Some of the women had been in the women's movement and thought they'd get more out of it through being in CR, others were new to the women's movement and thought it would be a good way of finding out what it was all about. All the women in the group were students. None of us had children, and we were all around the same age. None of us were married.

'At the first meeting we talked about ourselves, our backgrounds, what we were doing, *then we went on to talk about our families, then the family in general. After that we had a different topic every week. Sometimes we would talk about what was going on in the group; how we felt about each other, what we thought the group was doing. That went quite well. By the time we felt able to do that, we all knew there was a basic liking between us. Although we might be critical, it was constructive.*

'*We also set up a system where there was time at the beginning of the evening where people could talk about what had happened to them during the week or indeed about anything they wanted to talk about. If no one had anythng to say we'd go on to the topic we'd arranged, but if anyone had a problem they particularly wanted to discuss we'd talk about it instead. That worked well, it was a good idea.*

'*We tried to have a structure where we went around the circle with each woman speaking in turn and not being interrupted, but we found that wasn't very successful, so we just had free discussion. We were all fairly sensitive about letting people speak, so some women didn't dominate the discussion. Some people didn't. speak at all, others managed to say what they wanted to.*

'*A lot of us were in situations where we were spending a lot of time with people who didn't agree with us, and it was nice to be with people who did. We got a lot of support from it. What I miss about it is that I knew that I could spend one evening a week with people who agreed with me and would support me, with people who liked me. Being so similar, though, was a bad thing, because we found that we all agreed with each other; and because we were all at the University, we tended to talk in rather academic terms instead of getting down to the nitty-gritty.*

'*We didn't see each other socially except that three women in the group lived in the same house. Some people saw this lack of social contact as a problem because it meant we didn't really know much about one another's everyday lives, just the personal and intimate details. The fact of the three women living together didn't make other people feel excluded, everyone in the group had closer relationships with some people than with others. It was quite a good thing for the three of them, because they could talk about problems in their house more easily in the group.*

'*After a year some of the group had left, so we got some new women. This meant discussing again some of the things we'd talked about before, but that was OK. Some of the new women felt those of us who'd been in the group from the start were more together and more experienced, but that soon wore off.*

'*I think the group helped me to sort out my feelings about my opression as a woman. I don't think I could have got the same sort of support that I got from the group from a friendship circle; I think it needs that structure, a definite time once a week when you could get support.*

'*Towards the end we found we talked more about what was happening in our personal lives at the time, because a lot of people were having problems. We found it a bit frustrating, because there was nothing we could do about it; we could all say, "Oh dear, poor you", but that was about it. You can say, "Oh dear, you're in that situation because women are oppressed", but that doesn't really help much either! But it was still worth it to talk about things. It is possible for a group to give a woman the support she needs to change her situation.*

'*By the end of the second year we'd all been involved for such a long time, we'd all done reading and so on, and there didn't seem to be much a CR group could do in the sense of letting us know that other women felt like we did, or giving us support. In the end we decided that we weren't really getting very much out of it any more, it had got to the stage where we were having frequent discussions about "What's gone wrong with the CR group, why isn't it working any more". Two years is a long time for a CR group to keep going, and we'd all got all we could get out of it. We thought of turning it into a study group; we tried to think of things we could do together; but we couldn't think of anything so we decided to give it up. We'd been together for so long, we'd got just about as far as we could.*'

WOMEN AWAKE: THE EXPERIENCE OF CONSCIOUSNESS-RAISING

from Sue Brearley, 38d Clapham Road, London SW8, 25p

This is a detailed examination of one woman's experience of CR within one CR group. She talks about herself, her initial reservations about joining a CR group, and the process she went through to finally join one. She attempts 'to show that CR performs many functions and can be of benefit to any woman, gay or straight, as long as she is interested in her own life'. She looks at the experience step by step: how the group formed, the ground rules they worked out (attendance on regular basis; closed meetings; only personal statements; rotation of houses; etc.), the topics they discussed, along with comments about each topic, and in the order that they were discussed (our bodies; our childhood; work; relationships with men; relationships with women; love; couples; and jealousy). She talks about the ways in which the group changed and the eventual end of the group. She also includes a short history of each of the women involved in the group. If you are unsure about what CR means, and what goes on within a group, this is a necessary pamphlet to look at, also, it can point a group in new directions, which can be useful if you have been meeting for a long time, or are just beginning.

TYRANNY OF STRUCTURELESSNESS

*We haven't manage*d to find a source from which this American pamphlet can be obtained, but if you can find it, it's worth reading! The pamphlet looks at how groups work, and the problems of trying to organize in a non-hierarchical way.

A PRACTICAL GUIDE TO THE WOMEN'S MOVEMENT (in the US)

from Women's Action Alliance, 370 Lexington Avenue, New York, NY 10017, $5

This is an invaluable guide to the Women's Liberation/Radical Feminism in the USA. There is a longish introduction which summarizes the strategies, philosophies and growth of the movement in the US. This is followed by a directory of over 200 women's groups with descriptive listings and categorized by issue areas. There is a reading list annotating over 500 books with a list of women's periodicals and bookstores. And the final section consists of CR guidelines including information on how to structure and run a CR group. There is a comprehensive list of topics for discussion in CR groups (Joining a CR Group/Childhood/Puberty/Sex Roles/Self-Image: Personality/Self-Image: Body/Friendships/Love/ Mothers/Fathers/Siblings/Marriage/Motherhood/ Pregnancy and Childbirth/Abortion/Children/Sex/ Lesbianism/Ageing/Independence-Dependence/ Ambition/Competition/Work/Power/Money/Anger and Violence/Rape/Racism/Religion/Health/ Changing our Lives) and each topic has a list of questions for discussion, for example: on self-image: body . . . 'Do I like my body? What is the nicest thing about my body? What is the worst thing about my body? Do I like my hair, face, figure, legs, breasts, etc.? Am I satisfied with my weight? Do I worry about being over- or under-weight for health reasons or because of my appearance? How do my experiences during adolescence relate to my image of my body? Does my image affect my sex life? Am I modest about my body? Why? Am I unhappy about my body because it does not conform to today's fashion magazine standards?' And there are additional sections on CR for young women and black women.

MEN AND THE WOMEN'S MOVEMENT

Why Women Organise Alone

Groups within the women's liberation movement are usually open to *women only*. Many people find this threatening and think that by doing this, women are being just as exclusive as men have been in the past.

But there are very good reasons why women choose to organize without men. We know that men tend to dominate mixed groups (even left-wing groups); they take the lead, talk more, and so on, because they are used to this role, whereas women are used to being passive and keeping quiet. In an all-woman group, women can talk freely to each other and without the inhibiting influence of husbands, boyfriends and other men. Women get a chance to take responsibility, and to get experience of organizing and working together. This would be infinitely more difficult if we had to fight against the sexism of men in the group *as well* as working to get campaigns and activities going. All men, however sympathetic, have absorbed the values of a society that sees women as inferior; they are in a position of power in relation to women and are unlikely to give it up voluntarily. It is no use expecting men to change things for us; *we have to fight for ourselves.*

However, men representing 49 per cent of the population, cannot be ignored if we are trying to change society as well as ourselves. It would be very difficult if not impossible to live in a world full of 'conscious' women, with men whose ideas are still stuck in the middle ages. Although it's absolutely crucial for women to work together, somewhere along the road we must communicate to men the conclusions we are coming to. Sympathetic men can and do show their active belief in women's liberation by supporting campaigns, providing childcare facilities and food at women's meetings, and as men organizing to fight against sexism.

Men Against Sexism Groups

Just as women need consciousness-raising groups that are for women only, men need to experience a similar process among themselves, developed to fit their particular conditioning.

The women's liberation movement not only challenges women, but at the same time strongly challenges male roles and attitudes. Through the women's movement, many women develop important friendships and find support. Some men who had been in contact with women in the WLM felt the need to get similar feelings and support from men. These desires, along with the feeling that men also had to talk among themselves to fight sexism, helped to foster the growth of Men Against Sexism groups (MAS).

In Brighton, there have been Men Against Sexism groups in existence since 1971. We talked with Tony who has been in several of these groups:

'*When Dorothy and I moved to Lewes from London, she got involved in a CR group. I met some of the men who knew the women in that group; one of them told me they were starting a men's group. When I joined, most of the men in the group were involved with women in the WLM, though there were a few who weren't. Most were associated with the University or the Polytechnic.*

'*I was a bit worried about going. For me it was quite an amazing experience, I was not sure what to expect, but it seemed like an interesting idea to find out what other men felt about themselves. Since then, I feel MAS has been part of a much wider political discussion that I hadn't been aware of before. Basic political questions are being asked and these affect men as well as women (childrearing, work, sexuality . . .).*

'*I've been in a variety of groups. They've all had different problems, but one thing that seems to be common has been the problem of getting over the distance that men seem to put between themselves. It's difficult to get men really to enjoy themselves, to laugh and have a really good time together. They can be very serious and sit round in a very serious way. For our group it's never been a problem getting heavy discussions going.*

'*One group I was in ended up with just four of us, and towards the end we spent most of the time talking about motor-bikes and rock music. We kept going simply because we really enjoyed seeing each other.*'

With the growth of the women's liberation movement, Men Against Sexism started up on a national basis. By 1975, there were about eight groups in Brighton alone; now three different groups still meet. A newsletter group to overcome the problem of lack of communication; a babysitting group, set up because some men didn't particularly want to be involved in a CR group, but wanted to do something practical; a health and sexuality group which is just starting. The three different groups all are very important in keeping men involved with each other:

'*The newsletter is mainly local at the moment, though we do have contacts in other parts of the country and abroad. It's primarily intended to get local men writing so we can distribute it locally. Perhaps eventually we'll get a local conference or something together. But for now it's an important means of communication between the groups.*

'*The babysitting group has a notice up in the women's centre with a number to ring if you want a babysitter. It was originally set up by a group of people, to babysit for women who wanted to do political work but otherwise wouldn't be able to for lack of babysitting facilities. But obviously if a woman rings up wanting a babysitter we can't ask what they are going out to do. A number of the women who use the babysitting group just want to go out and get away from their kids for an evening, which is OK by us.*

'*There are two men who take the phone calls, and they've got everybody else's phone number. The idea was that they'd just ring one of the other men, but that didn't work because it boiled down to three or four men doing all the babysitting; so now we cover six days (we exclude Saturdays) and there are two people who've definitely agreed to be available on each day, plus reserves. There are some regular sits. The service is well used, and we desperately need more people to do it. At the moment there are two women who babysit as part of this group, and since that doesn't really fit in with the "Men Against Sexism" concept, we are thinking of turning it into a mixed group and maybe in this way we will get more people involved. The main people who do the babysitting are people who haven't got kids themselves, which is good.*

'*We feel that having a health and sexuality group is very important. We are working towards compiling a health handbook for men. The idea of the handbook was something that came up at one of the meetings when we were trying to think what we could do. One of the men in the group is writing a sex education pamphlet to be given out in schools, so we're going to try and get our handbook into schools. We decided a while ago that if MAS is going to achieve anything we've got to go out and talk to people.*

'*We also want to get a group together to share our experiences about health and sex, to discuss the sort of things that go wrong with men. For instance, we found out that a lot of men get prostate cramps after they ejaculate, they just don't talk about it. Dorothy tells an excellent story of when she went to tea with some people and one of the men said that he had seen the MAS newsletter with an article on the back about pains men get after sex, and all the men roared with laughter. And then one of them said, "Oh . . . I get a pain . . .", by the time they had all stopped guffawing, they discovered that they all had pains or cramps of one sort or another which they had never talked about before. And they discovered that doctors were unsympathetic too; they'd just say, "Oh everyone gets that . . .". So that made us think there might be a lot of things like that, that men have got, but which they don't talk about. There might be something you can do about it if you knew. We're trying to put together a handbook in the style of* Our Bodies, Ourselves *rather than a workshop manual on the male body.*

'*One of the biggest problems in the MAS group has been defining what exactly the group should do and what purpose it should fulfil. We have had big arguments about what MAS is. The two sides are basically, on the one hand, MAS is a support group for women's liberation and gay liberation, and its purpose is to support the aims thrown up by those two groups: since men aren't confronted with a similar oppression to fight against, their role is to support women and gays. The other side said the job of MAS was to define some new kind of identity for a man, so Men Against Sexism might in fact come into conflict with what the Women's Liberation Movement or the gay movement might want of men.*

'*I believe that MAS is working towards an identity for men that is not oppressive and is actually trying to define men in a new way. Some men are threatened by the idea of consciousness-raising and want to stick to practical things, others see it as a support group because they can't see any obvious political role for MAS. That really hasn't been resolved, we want these arguments to come out in the newsletter.*

'*It's hard to organize any national co-ordination, though there are a few strong groups around the country. In some ways it would be really good if there was something equivalent to* Spare Rib *for men. MAS hasn't really defined itself and doesn't seem able to do so adequately. But defining MAS in terms of the Women's Liberation or the gay movement means that it doesn't have any real independent existence.*'

Trying to work together: A mixed C-R group

Once men and women have gone through CR in single-sex groups, it can be important and productive for them to talk things out together. This may not happen in large numbers for some time, as the centuries of women's oppression by men are not easily forgotten; many women feel this is not worth doing at all and some feel that now is too soon. But some people are beginning to take the chance and try to work together to form a new relationship between the sexes.

Ruth and Fred are students at Sussex University and members of a mixed consciousness-raising group. There are three women and three men in their group, all of whom are at the University. Their group grew out of a meeting which was trying to set up a 'People Against Sexism' group. The six of them came together because of the frustration they felt in this group:

'There were too many people for a start, but also, even though the men were trying not to be dominating, they were. The men there didn't even touch on how sexism personally affected them. Consequently there was a lot of intellectual bullshit going on.

'Our group wanted to break down the bullshit. We began by defining sexism, wondering how much was sexism and how much was natural and why. We went on to jealousy, touching, sex, homosexuality, relationships, personal history, our concepts of love and flirting.

'We spent a lot of time defining terms because to men and women they mean different things. At one point in the group we were talking about how we felt about each other. When a woman would say she was attracted to a man, the man would interpret it in a sexual way, whereas the woman only meant it in a friendly way. It was the epitome of what we were trying to get away from!'

The women in the group tended to stick together and support each other on most issues. Consequently the men felt threatened. Fred says that he felt dubious about joining at first:

'Men have a long way to go to understand their role before we can work with women who have sorted themselves out. Our levels of awareness are behind those of women. I think we have to do a lot of reading and listening to women. The hard part about the group for all the men, I think, is that we find it hard to talk about our role as men without being, or feeling we are being, oppressive. We also don't feel we can challenge a woman regarding her concept of her own liberation. We all feel this group is a natural evolution from a women's CR group, that this is the only way eventually to form good non-sexist relationships.'

LOCAL WOMEN'S GROUPS

Almost all the groups talked about in this book are 'women's groups', groups of women working together. Some groups came together to work on a specific issue (Abortion, Legal and Financial Independence for Women, Equal Pay). Other groups are formed because we want to be with other women and talk to each other about ourselves (Consciousness-Raising). Still another type of women's group is the local one formed to campaign around issues affecting women in the community. The importance of having local women's groups around the country cannot be stressed enough. In many towns and cities it is possible to provide services for women such as pregnancy testing, or to involve women in local politics (Community Health Councils, day nurseries), in ways that before were not seen as viable. Having a women's group that is aware of how local issues affect women can help improve our lives temporarily on a local basis while we are all struggling for change on a national basis. Local groups are also a necessary contact when events of national importance occur: groups have the potential to organize many women, showing that support for the particular struggle lies throughout the country and is not confined to the big cities.

There is no set pattern or organizational style that local groups follow. Each group's emphasis will depend entirely upon what the women in the group deem to be of importance to them within their community.

The *North Staffordshire Women's Action Group* has been active for many years and is a good example of the variety of things a local women's group can do:

The North Staffs. Women's Action Group was started in 1974 and began by discussing the Working Women's Charter. We felt there were some shortcomings in the Charter, so we wrote our own, and this document has formed a background to many of our activities.

'As a group we are affiliated to the National Abortion Campaign and we have been active locally on this issue.

'Some of the women from the group have been campaigning for a Day Nursery on a large council estate in Stoke-on-Trent. After a lot of hard work, a nursery has been set up in a local church hall. They employ a qualified nursery nurse, but the rest of the help comes from mums and other interested people on the estate. This means that the fees charged are comparatively low.

'As a group we are very concerned with the health facilities available for women. We have become involved with the local Community Health Council and are at present pressing for an improvement in local Family Planning Clinics. We have recently begun operating a free pregnancy testing service. Unless a woman pays for a test it is difficult to get a pregnancy test done without having to wait several days for the result. As well as providing our area with a needed service we can show that it is possible for women to get together and do something that would normally be left to the "experts" or those in authority.

'As the group has become more and more active we have felt a desperate need for a local women's centre. We need a place which could act as a focal point for all kinds of local community activities and from which we could run our campaigns. We have been campaigning locally for a women's centre and have recently been in contact with other community groups to see if they will join with us in an attempt to get the council to let us have a large building in the centre of Newcastle-under-Lyme which has been standing empty for two years.

'A women's theatre group has grown out of our original group. We have written two plays: one about the need for a local women's centre, and the other, based on Punch and Judy, is about abortion. Both plays include songs and are very lively and entertaining.

*We have taken the plays to local women's organizations and colleges and performed them
at local street festivals. The theatre group has been very successful. Everyone involved
has learnt a lot and gained a great deal of confidence.*

*'The women's group meets once a week; because of our many and varied activities,
business takes up quite a lot of time although we do try to have some discussions about
issues that affect women.'*

NORTH STAFFORDSHIRE WOMEN'S ACTION GROUP *c/o 15 Heath Street, Newcastle-under-Lyme,
Staffs.*

Women's Centres

As local women's groups become more active within the community they begin to find, as the
North Staffs. Women's Action group did, that having a base to work from is crucial to their
work. A women's centre in every town can be a meeting place, an information centre, a
women's rights centre, a refuge, a nursery — anything that women feel they need. A centre can
be an old house or shop converted to fit the activities that local women want to run.

Besides providing a centre for information, services and groups, a women's centre can be a
place where women come together to learn and to talk to gain support and share or learn new
skills with other women.

Finding a centre and keeping it open is no easy task. Women who have previously worked in
centres recall endless hassles about money, about finding women to do the work, and about
having the centre in a place accessible to all women. Many centres are organized open
collectives of women who run them, all working at the centre on a rota basis, trying to have
someone there as often as possible. Many centres run on donations or money raised from
jumble sales and disco's. Here we look at one centre, the Lancaster Women's Centre:

The Lancaster Women's Centre is unusual in that it received money for six workers under
the Job Creation Programme. They now provide a much-needed service for the local community. The Plough is a former pub which a group of women in Lancaster persuaded the local
council to lease to them for use as a women's centre and as a refuge for battered women and
their children. The refuge is on the two upstairs floors and comprises six bedrooms and a
shared living room, a kitchen and a bathroom. The ground floor consists of the information
centre and a large space which is used for the children's playgroup in the day, and for meetings,
parties and talks at other times.

The refuge has been officially open since July 1976, and in its first six months shelter was
given to over thirty women. Some women stay overnight only, while others stay several
weeks or months. The refuge is affiliated to the National Women's Aid Federation.

During the day there is a playgroup for the children living in the refuge, and outings are
arranged in the evenings and at the weekends with the help of the male support group.

The information centre opens for six hours daily (from 10am to 4pm) and for two hours
on Saturday (11am to 1pm). The group has collected information on all sorts of questions of
concern to women: social services, contraception, abortion, divorce, sexual assault and so on.
They are building up a set of books for reference as well as newsletters and magazines from the
women's movement. There is a small library of women's books which can be borrowed. The
Plough produces its own newsletter every three weeks giving information about what's going
on there and contains articles written by women in the refuge, helpers and others.

Since September 1976 the Manpower Services Commission has been providing money for
six full-time workers through the Job Creation Scheme. They manage the day-to-day running
of the Plough, run the playgroup, cope with 101 crises, and run the information centre. This
money has provided a temporary security until September 1977, but after that they will have
to once more depend on donations.

LANCASTER WOMEN'S CENTRE *The Plough Hotel, Bryer Street, Lancaster*

Women's Information, Referral and Enquiry Service

'I'm doing a school project on the Women's Liberation Movement. Please send me full details of its history, aims, achievements and publications.'

'I've just moved to Portsmouth. Is there a women's liberation and/or lesbian group near here I could join?'

'Please tell me how my legal status regarding tax, National Insurance, etc. will change when I get married next month.'

'Are there any good women solicitors in the York area?'

'I want to claim equal pay. How do I go about it?'

'Our group is putting on a women's festival in the Community Centre. Can you recommend any suitable films, art or photo exhibitions, literature, speakers, etc. for the day, and a band for the evening?'

'I'm fifty; my children have left home; I don't get on with my husband but I'm trapped; I've no job qualifications and there's very little work round here anyway. What shall I do?'

'This is just a sample of the mail and phone calls received by WIRES, the Women's Information, Referral and Enquiry Service, every day. And we can and do deal with it, by answering queries direct or referring enquirers to local and specialist groups and organizations as appropriate. We aim to be friendly, feminist and efficient; and on the whole we seem to succeed.

'Every two-and-a-half weeks the office suffers a major upheaval when the duplicated Newsletter comes out. This is WIRES' other main function. By 1975 most women in the women's liberation movement were convinced of the need for greater communication between groups and co-ordination of campaigns. A newsletter would serve as information exchange between women's groups and individuals so that every little group no matter how isolated could have a sense of national goings-on, could know what the main debates and differences in the movement were, and could contribute to those debates. Feminism has always emphasized de-centralization of power, and information is power. Unless we're all equally in the know, women who live in London and the other large cities, or are part of the national feminist friendship network are bound to dominate in determining the direction of the movement.

'Thus WIRES was set up by a volunteering group in Leeds on the instruction of the 1975 National Women's Liberation Conference. Each subsequent conference has ratified our continuing existence, and major decisions about WIRES' direction cannot be made without reference to the movement as represented by readers of and contributors to the WIRES newsletter. As far as possible, WIRES is totally accountable to the movement.

'WIRES has always been collectively run by between four and ten women. We pay ourselves a small wage out of Newsletter subscriptions and donations, which we've always felt to be important in increasing our commitment and making us feel we're doing a proper job (also some of the work can be really dull, like typing addresses!). It's vital when working for feminism to do things in a feminist way, emphasizing skill-sharing, making it easy for women with children to work, taking decisions and having fun together, giving mutual personal and political support. Well, at WIRES we don't always make it, but these are always our aims!

'As spin-off activities we've organized a benefit with the music group Jam Today, to raise funds; we've acted as "campaign centre" for several women's actions round Leeds; we've offered our office facilities and skills to Leeds women's groups; we've gone to conferences and demonstrations as WIRES; we've co-written and produced the pamphlet Womens Liberation: An Introduction with two feminist information services in London . . . and more. The files are building up well and are useful to women researching addresses and information for talks, projects, campaigns . . . and for books such as this one.

'WIRES invites your queries, and material for the newsletter, whether news of coming events, reports of past ones, your opinions, poems, in fact anything you think would be interesting or useful to women. Send large s.a.e for a sample back-copy of the News-letter, 15p for a current copy. The annual subscription is £6 (£4 if poor) for individual women, or £12 (£8 if poor) for women's groups.'

WIRES 32a Parliament Street, York

A Woman's Residential Centre

The Oaklands Women's Centre is a centre where women and children can stay for retreats, holidays, study groups and small conferences. It is in a small village in the Wye Valley, four miles inside Wales. The valley is surrounded by the Brecon Beacons and Black Mountains, so there are beautiful walks, as well as pony trekking, canoeing and swimming in the river Wye. The house is large, with space for ten at a time, the food is vegetarian (there's even a very friendly goat to provide the milk), and bedrooms are equipped with mattresses and blankets.

The Centre costs £1.50 a day for women (including food); 50p a day for children under eleven and babies are free. Always book and give two alternative dates if possible.

OAKLANDS WOMEN'S CENTRE Glasbury-on-Wye, via Hereford, Powys

WORKING COLLECTIVELY

The Women's movement is about women struggling to take control of our own lives. In a hierarchical society, the power to make our own decisions is severely limited from the start: there is always someone to tell us what to do or what not to do; first parents, then teachers, then bosses, and then husbands. Of course, men suffer from this as well as women, but women get a double dose: even as adults in our own homes our boss-husbands have legal, financial and often emotional power over us.

The power structure in the workplace means that the people with the least power get the worst work. Not only will this be badly paid, it will also be boring and unsatisfying, and although the work may be essential, it will have very little status. What makes things far worse is that the people at the bottom of the heap have no control over their own work, and work is after all an important component of everyone's life. No one asks you what is the best way of performing a task; you are not allowed to be involved in any decision-making; you have no responsibility. This structure operates in factories, offices, shops, schools . . . everywhere.

Because we all grow up within this structure and see all the organizations around us working in the same way, it would be easy to fall into these same patterns when we come to set up our own organizations and campaigns to fight for the issues that concern us as women. But right from the start, individuals and groups within the women's liberation movement have realized that *working for change means also changing the way we work.* If we are trying to break down power structures that oppress women (and men), it is no use organizing ourselves in a way that mirrors those power structures, as this will only per-petuate them. If we are fighting for control and responsibility in our lives, we must find ways of ensuring that control and responsibility are shared when we work within the Movement to change our lives.

It is for this reason that many groups are trying to work collectively. Some are involved in work that also provides them with a living, others are campaigning or working vuluntarily producing newsletters, setting up battered women's refuges, pressing for daycare facilities in the community, and so on. Working collectively means that you become much more involved with your work, and since you're there anyway because it's something you believe in and are committed to, the work takes on a completely different meaning, even if it's typing address labels or sweeping the floor. You are valued as a person as well as for the work you are doing, your opinions carry as much weight as anyone else's, and your skills are valued whether it's being good at filing or propounding brilliant political theory.

In a collective there is no boss whose job it is to tell everyone else what to do. Although collectives are organized in many different ways, they usually have certain things in common:

Important decisions are made by *the whole group* in meetings and not by an individual, so that everyone has a say in what happens.

Everyone has access to information that affects the collective, so everyone is in a position to take part in decision-making.

Tasks are shared in some way, so that one person doesn't get left doing the boring work all the time. There is usually a strong emphasis on sharing skills and knowledge so that everyone does at least some of the more interesting work and as a result those with more experience don't end up taking all the responsibility.

Of course, it's not all a bed of roses. Women have been taught to compete for status just as men have; we may be reluctant to share our skills, our knowledge and our experience with others because they're our only claim to power. It can be difficult to teach people things in a way that doesn't make them feel inferior, or to leave them to learn for themselves when their mistakes could damage the collective work.

There is also the problem of power and responsibility. People who are able to or who want to devote more time or energy to the collective than others, inevitably take more responsibility, and know more about what's going on, and often they will end up in an unacknowledged leadership position. This is why frequent collective meetings are necessary.

Dealing with the world outside can be very difficult. If you are trying to make a living from what you're doing (producing a magazine, working as a printer) you have to compete with conventionally-run organizations, and this can put a collectively-run organization under a lot of pressure. It may be hard to make the time for learning each others' skills when the rent has to be paid. The collective structure clashes with the rest of society; outside bodies are usually unwilling to accept that collective decision-making takes time because everyone must be involved. They persist in looking for à leader and often force someone into that role by demanding instant decisions or comments.

Collectives are criticized as being an inefficient way of working; but because you feel involved in what you are doing, you often work harder and more thoroughly than when you are working for someone else's profit.

Working collectively is not easy but it can be extremely worthwhile. Your relationships with the other people in the collective have to be thought about and worked on, but a collective can provide its members with a great deal of support, it can be an unoppressive way of learning and a chance to see your work as an integral part of your life and beliefs.

Though it demands more of your time and energy than a job where your duties and responsibilities are strictly defined, you are more in control of what you do, of how you spend your time, and of what you are working for. Having to think and question and make your own decisions and choices can be frightening. But once you've started you can't go back, and most of us wouldn't want to anyway.

(*Catcall* magazine has reprinted a long article from an Australian magazine on working collectively. This is available from *57 Lucas Avenue, London E13; 15p plus postage.*)

FEMINIST CLASSICS

Well, readers, here you are, a list of the books that have, over the last ten or so years, changed the lives of millions of women in Britain and in America. Most have been translated to French, German, Spanish, Italian and Hebrew, causing dramatic changes in women's lives throughout the world. Some of these books are theoretical, giving arguments for a feminist revolution, others are personal accounts of the oppression that must have touched each and every one of us at some time in our lives. Some books blatantly impress you with the universal nature of women's oppression; others creep into your consciousness at the most unsuspecting moments.

This list was compiled by a sample of about ten women who are active in the women's liberation movement who were asked what books acted as an impetus for their further involvement in women's politics. It is not a comprehensive list of all books which have been important to the women's liberation movement, which we felt would be overpowering in its sheer size, but a short selective list of just a few. All the books are by women, and most of them are relevant in some way to us all. We give here only a very short review of each. They are all worth reading.

THE WOMEN'S LIBERATION MOVEMENT

THE SECOND SEX
by Simone de Beauvoir, Penguin, £1.60
The first feminist classic ever written, *The Second Sex* observed the 'Second' sex from biological, historical, sociological, mythological and psycho-analytical standpoints. Amazingly well researched and in advance of its time (it was written in the 1950s), this book has influenced the feminist movement tremendously, at least in its early years.

SEXUAL POLITICS
by Kate Millett, Virago, £1.95
This is not an easy read, but it is worth ploughing through, especially for the sections on sexism in literature. It teaches how to read even supposedly 'fictional' works critically, and to appreciate how male domination and sexist values have permeated the works of many 'classic' writers.

THE FEMALE EUNUCH
by Germaine Greer, Paladin, 75p
For many women, this book was their first intro-duction to the ideas of women's liberation. It is easy to read, covers most areas of women's oppression and could make a good starting point if you are unfamiliar with the subject.

THE BODY POLITIC: Women's Liberation
compiled by Michelene Wandor, Stage, 60p
This is a collection of specifically British women's liberation writings from 1969 to 1972. This book does not follow any single line but attempts to show how the movement developed during those years.

DIALECTIC OF SEX: The case for a Feminist Revolution
by Shulamith Firestone, Cape, £2.50
The sex struggle comes before the class struggle, it is the first oppression and there will be no revolution without its suppression. This book has been to important starting point for radical feminism.

LESBIAN NATION: The Feminist Solution
by Jill Johnston, Simon and Schuster, £2.50
This book offers the most in-depth presentation of lesbian separatist theory now available.

WOMEN'S ESTATE
by Juliet Mitchell, Penguin, 60p
The author analyses the women's liberation move-ment and its emergence in the 1960s. She then analyses the position of women in England from three key standpoints: production — reproduction — socialization.

WOMAN'S CONSCIOUSNESS — MAN'S WORLD
by Sheila Rowbotham, Penguin, 60p
In the first part of this book, the author examines the development of the new feminist consciousness and describes the social changes that have triggered off its growth. In the second part she focusses her attention on women within the capitalist state.

OUR BODIES

OUR BODIES, OURSELVES
by the Boston Women's Health Book Collective, Simon and Schuster, New York, £3.95
First published in 1973, this book has now sold over a million copies. It is one of the milestones of the women's movement both in America and England; it was written by a collective of women in Boston to help women share their experiences and help themselves.

> 'Our Bodies Ourselves *is written by and for women in response to an imperative need for women everywhere to learn about our bodies in order to have control over them and over our lives. We seek to communi-cate our excitement about the power of , shared information to assert that, in an age of professionals, we are the best experts on ourselves and our feelings, and to continue the collective struggle for adequate health care.'*

Learning about our bodies means not only healthi-er bodies but healthier minds and happier lives too. By controlling our bodies, our minds, we will control our lives and won't allow anybody else (doctors, husbands, fathers, relatives . . .) to do it for us. We have to discover (or rather rediscover) who we are and not expect anybody to shape us and bring us to life. That is why chapters include a wide range of topics which may appear not to fit in with health (for example, 'Our Sexual Relation-ships', 'In America They Call Us Dykes').

Our Bodies, Ourselves is very practical and full of information on a whole range of topics from childbirth to rape, venereal disease and a sensible diet. It provides information that will be of use to any woman whatever life she leads and whoever she chooses as her sexual partner. It includes a glossary of selected common medical terms and examinations which help to demystify the whole mystery surrounding our bodies when we go to the doctor.

All through the book, women's own accounts of their experiences are included to illustrate the point being made which makes it far more inter-esting and helps us to realize that our feelings about our bodies are shared by other women. There are plenty of photos and diagrams.

NOVELS AND AUTOBIOGRAPHY

DAUGHTER OF EARTH
by Agnes Smedley, Virago, £1.95
This is an autobiography of a working-class American woman at the beginning of this century, whose childhood was spent travelling around with her family chasing jobs. Once grown up and after a long struggle to educate herself and her brothers and sisters, she goes to New York and gets involved with the Indian struggle against their oppression.

THE GOLDEN NOTEBOOK
by Doris Lessing, Panther, £1
All Doris Lessing's novels are worth reading but *The Golden Notebook* has had particular influence on the women's movement. With this account of the daily lives and relationships of two women, the author has managed to convey what it can feel like to be a woman.

FLYING
by Kate Millett, Paladin, £1.50
This is a detailed stream-of-consciousness account of the year in Kate Millett's life following the publication of *Sexual Politics*. The book deals with problems of being a women's movement superstar, bisexuality and getting over a breakdown.

RIVERFINGER WOMAN
by Eleana Nachmann, Daughters Press, £2
The trials and joys of growing up gay in late 1960s America.

RUBY FRUIT JUNGLE
by Rita Mae Brown, Daughters Press, £2
This is the first really funny novel about growing up as a lesbian in America. Honest, political and strong, you'll read it in one night.

WOMEN'S LIBERATION CENTRES

Here is a list of Women's Liberation Centres and of community centres where local Women's Liberation Groups can be contacted. Where there is no local contact for your area, contact either *Spare Rib* or WIRES.

LONDON
Brent: *138 Minet Avenue, NW10*
Camden: *Rosslyn Lodge, Lyndhurst Road, NW3*
Kentish Town: *158 Grafton Road, NW5*
Lewisham: *74 Deptford High Street, SE8*
Paddington: *510 Centre, Harrow Road, W9*
South London: *45 North Street, SW4*
Stoke Newington: *1 Cazenove Road, N16*
Walthamstow: *161 Mark House Road, E17*
Whitechapel: *3 Adelina Grove, E1*
Women's Arts Alliance: *10 Cambridge Terrace Mews, NW1*
A Woman's Place: *see Stop Press*
Women's Research and Resources Centre: *27 Clerkenwell Close, EC1*

SCOTLAND
Aberdeen: *St Chaterine's Community Centre*
Caithness: *2 Bank Place, Thurso*
Edinburgh: *160 Fountainbridge*
Glasgow: *57 Miller Street, Glasgow 1*

WALES
Cardiff: *108 Salisbury Road, Cathays*

EIRE
Dublin: *45 Arslbury Grove, Dundrin*

REST OF ENGLAND
Birmingham: *76 Brighton Road, Balsall Heath*
Brighton: *Old Presbyterian Church, North Road*
Bradford: *Fourth Idea Bookshop, 14 Southgate*
Bristol: *44 The Grove, Bristol 1*
Cambridge: *48 Eden Street*
Cheltenham: *30 St George's Place*
Coventry: *24 Regent Street*
Lancaster: *86 King Street*
Leicester: *79 Laurel Road*
Liverpool: *Lark Lane Community Centre, Liverpool 17*
Manchester: *62 Nelson Street*
Norwich: *Community Centre, St Benedict's Street*
Nottingham: *26 Newcastle Chambers, Angel Row*
Oxford: *88 Bullingdon Road*
Sheffield: *52 Langsett Road, Sheffield 6*
York: *32a Parliament Street*

INDEX

INDEX OF SUBJECTS

INDEX OF GROUPS

STOP PRESS

A WOMAN'S PLACE, formerly 42 Earlham Street, London W1 has been forced to move and at the time of going to press the new address is not known. Write to WIRES, 32a Parliament Street, York, or ring Directory Inquiries for the new phone number.

As this book was going to press the Inland Revenue announced that it was taking steps to remove many of the discriminating practices that were highlighted in the Equal (opportunity Commission's report *Income Tax and Sex Discrimination* (see pages 25–6).

ACKNOWLEDGEMENTS

The bulk of this book is written from the words of other women. We'd like to thank all the women who poured their voices into our trusty tape-recorder for their time, energy and support. Also to those women who have sent us many letters about their work.

And thanks to WIRES for letting us use the information in the office and messing up the filing system. Thanks to Barbara Dinham whose suggestions and advice kept us going, to Al Garthwaite for reading the manuscript and to Shirley Bennett for typing the final manuscript. And thanks to Al, Maria, Crissy, Pennina, Bob, James and Martin for their personal support.

Various parts of the text have been reprinted or adapted from other sources; these have been credited in the text and we acknowledge the copyright of their original publishers.

ABOUT THE AUTHORS

Agnes Pivot — French, living in England 5 years. She has done some journalism, she is a would be academic, a teacher, a past WIRES worker. Now, a freelance worker, she is bringing up her daughter, Macha.

Ellen Friedman — American with English roots, is a sometime university student, musician, gardener and writer. A former WIRES worker, she now works at a refuge for battered women and their children in Los Angeles.

Wendy Collins — Born in London, still living in Leeds. Ex WIRES worker now doing research connected with women's health and trying not to let full-time work take over her life.